MW00782119

Santa Claus
Worldwide

Santa Claus Worldwide

A History of St. Nicholas and Other Holiday Gift-Bringers

Tom A. Jerman

McFarland & Company, Inc., Publishers

Jefferson, North Carolina

LIBRARY OF CONGRESS CATALOGUING-IN-PUBLICATION DATA

Names: Jerman, Tom A., 1955– author.
Title: Santa Claus worldwide : a history of St. Nicholas and other holiday gift-bringers / Tom A. Jerman.
Description: Jefferson, North Carolina : McFarland & Company, Inc., Publishers, 2020. | Includes bibliographical references and index.
Identifiers: LCCN 2020016152 | ISBN 9781476680934 (paperback) ∞
ISBN 9781476638942 (ebook)
Subjects: LCSH: Santa Claus—History. | Gifts—Social aspects. | Winter solstice—Social aspects.
Classification: LCC GT4992 .J47 2020 | DDC 394.2663—dc23
LC record available at https://lccn.loc.gov/2020016152

BRITISH LIBRARY CATALOGUING DATA ARE AVAILABLE

ISBN (print) 978-1-4766-8093-4
ISBN (ebook) 978-1-4766-3894-2

Front cover images © 2020 Shutterstock

Printed in the United States of America

*McFarland & Company, Inc., Publishers
Box 611, Jefferson, North Carolina 28640
www.mcfarlandpub.com*

To Evelyn,
Kat and Lily

Acknowledgments

To steal a line from songwriter Kris Kristofferson, I started out writing this book about Santa Claus but ended up writing about Saturn, Odin, St. Nicholas, Sinterklaas, Father Christmas, Knecht Ruprecht, Der Weihnachtsmann, Belsnickle, Kriss Kringle, Père Noël, Ded Moroz and a lot of other holiday gift-givers I can't remember right now. I want to acknowledge the organization that stimulated my interest in the history of Santa and his European counterparts, the Golden Glow of Christmas Past, an organization of Christmas collectors; two fellow Christmas collectors who read early drafts of the book: the late Steve Fulk, who before his untimely death was proprietor of An Olde Time Christmas Auction and Sales, and Jerry Arnold, who with his wife, Darla, are among America's foremost Christmas collectors; and the numerous librarians employed by the Library of Congress, the New-York Historical Society and the American Antiquarian Society, all of whom responded graciously to my requests. I also thank Daniel Rocha, who assisted me in finalizing the illustrations for the book.

For editorial work on the book, I owe much to my editor, Robin Smith of robinsmithink, who worked with me for almost three years. While she and I will never see eye to eye on the utility of the word "that," she supported my efforts, and suggested many changes, major and minor, that improved the final outcome. I also want to thank Jana Marlene Mader, who until 2018 was a professor of German at University of North Carolina–Asheville while working on her Ph.D. with Ludwig Maximilian University in Munich, for her translation of *Knecht Ruprecht and His Companions* as well as several other German texts, and David Alff, the editor at McFarland who guided me through the editorial process.

Table of Contents

Preface

This book arose out of a hobby, collecting Santa Claus figures, that I took up more than thirty years ago. Today, this collection includes thousands of figurines, ornaments, and Victorian-era Christmas cards depicting an old man with white hair and beard who, depending on the sender's nationality, would have been called Santa Claus (America), Father Christmas (England), Père Noël (France), Weihnachtsmann (Germany), Ded Moroz (Russia), Sinterklaas (Netherlands), Joulupukki, Julemanden, Julenisse or Jultomten (Scandinavia) or St. Nicholas (some twenty different European nations in which the name translates as Sankt Nikolaus, Saint Nicolas, Mikulás, San Nioclás, Sint-Niklaas, San Niklaw, Swiety Mikolaj, Moş Nicolae, Sveti Miklavž, Sveti Nikolaj, Sveti Nikola, Samichlaus, Svyaty Mykolay, Nikolaos, Nicolo, Niklaus, San Nicolás or Svatý Mikuláš).

The primary characteristic of my collection, and what sustained my interest in purchasing portrayals of Santa for three decades at a pace that most would consider neurotic, is the enormous diversity of ways in which Santa and his European counterparts can be depicted. This diversity reflects the universal appeal of the character, celebrated by the wealthy and humble alike. Santa can be found in primitive wood carvings or rag dolls handmade in remote regions of the Appalachians or depicted in elaborately detailed china or crystal figurines from England and France, exquisite blown-glass ornaments from Germany, or elaborate fabric, fur and porcelain dolls by American artists that sell for thousands of dollars. Santa can be depicted in realistic, impressionistic, or abstract styles, and he can be short, tall, fat, thin, elfish, troll-like, solemn, serious, scary, happy, fun, and frivolous.

Santa has been described as the "eternal light with which childhood fills the world,"[1] a "delightful personification of parental kindness,"[2] and someone whose "understanding of the moral world is clear and accurate, and whose generosity is balanced with a perfect sense of justice."[3] He has also been called "the opium of childhood,"[4] accused of holding his elves in indentured servitude,[5] and outlawed by groups as diverse as the Puritans in seventeenth-century New England, the Communist Party of the Soviet Union, and the Nazi government of Germany. My favorite, as recounted by historian Gerry Bowler in *Santa Claus: A Biography*, is a young Canadian couple who spent $1,200, presumably Canadian, urging fellow citizens to "actively reject the capitalist ideology of Christmas" as "white, middle-class, heterosexual, patriarchal [and] Christian," asserting that Santa himself was "the mall's puppet.... Children are taught to worship this white, heterosexual man who overeats. I mean, it's wrong."[6] If I accomplish nothing else with this book, it will be to explain that Santa is not necessarily male, white, middle-class, heterosexual, patriarchal, Christian, or capitalist. The diversity of Santa is limited only by your imagination, and despite what the Canadian couple may have assumed there are historical examples of midwinter gift-givers who were female, black, rich, gay, atheist, and communist.

This book arose out of my efforts to understand the history and diversity of the Santas I have been collecting for thirty-plus years. Whether the figures were new creations or images that were thousands of years old, and whether they were created in America, Europe, Asia, Africa or Australia, all of the figures in my collection were clearly "Santa," a term I will use to describe the midwinter gift-givers around the world, reserving "Santa Claus" for the American version who developed largely in Pennsylvania and New York during the nineteenth century. When I began my research, I wanted to learn is how Santa, and especially our visual perceptions of the midwinter gift-giver, had evolved from prehistoric times to the present day. As I attempted to satisfy my own interests, I realized that the existing sources were few in number, incomplete in scope, and often incorrect in substance.

Some historians have suggested that Santa Claus was created by a handful of wealthy white men who were members of the New-York Historical Society in the early 1800s. In fact, as I will demonstrate, he evolved, like a living organism, from the Winter Solstice festivals and pagan gods of Roman and Germanic mythology, to Christian notables like St. Martin and St. Nicholas, to a variety of secular figures who emerged throughout Europe following the Protestant Reformation and, eventually, immigrated to America. This book will start with prehistoric celebrations of the Winter Solstice and the pagan midwinter festivals, such as the Roman Saturnalia, and explain how those celebrations were Christianized, to greater or lesser extents, between the fourth century in Rome and the twelfth century in Scandinavia. I will explain why the saintly figures often showed up with a Satanic evil helper at their side and examine how the Protestant Reformation altered, and in some cases eliminated, the celebration of Christmas during the sixteenth century. Some two centuries later, the gift-givers traveled to America with the children of European immigrants, virtual stowaways on the trans-Atlantic voyages of the eighteenth and nineteenth centuries.

During the nineteenth century, the European gift-givers and their descendants coalesced into a single, American gift-giver with the elements of his European predecessors: the stateliness and holiness of St. Nicholas and his Dutch doppelganger, Sinterklaas; the rough, back-woods features of the secular gift-givers like Knecht Ruprecht and Pelznickle, who replaced St. Nicholas in Protestant regions of Germany following the Reformation; the stern disciplinarian look of Der Weihnachtsmann; the alcohol-induced jolliness of Father Christmas; the sparky elfin attitudes of the Scandinavian Julenisse and Jultomten; and a name, Santa Claus, which appears to have emerged spontaneously among immigrant children on the streets of New York, an underground movement that succeeded without the assistance of prominent authors, poets, journalists or college professors.

Contrary to common belief, neither the name Santa Claus nor the gift-giver himself were simply an Americanization of the fourth-century Bishop of Myra. St. Nicholas was drafted by Catholic missionaries in the High Middle Ages to replace the pagan god Odin and give a Christian purpose to the midwinter celebration of Yule. Following the Reformation, however, he was replaced in northern Germany by the "faux Nicholases," an assortment of ragged, fur-covered, dirty, unshaven, switch-bearing men who acted as both gift-giver and disciplinarian. It was Pennsylvania's Belsnickle (from the German Pelznickel) and Kriss Kringle (from the German Christkindl) who were the immediate forebears of Santa Claus. St. Nicholas had an important influence, particularly on the red and white color scheme, but he was neither the original European gift-giver nor the immediate predecessor of Santa Claus in America.

Indeed, St. Nicholas has never had much of a presence in America, either on his feast day, December 6, or on Christmas. Rather, the credit given to St. Nicholas arises largely from an 1822 poem by a wealthy New Yorker named Clement C. Moore that became commonly known as "The Night Before Christmas." The version of St. Nick immortalized in that poem was not the historic Bishop of Myra, but an overweight elf dressed entirely in fur; the use of the name St. Nicholas and the eventual popularity of the poem created the widespread misconception, however, that Santa Claus and St. Nicholas were the same person. Indeed, while the poem was hugely important in creating the American practice in which the give-giver arrives while the children are sleeping, pushing the family celebration to Christmas morning, Moore cannot be given credit for creating the story. Rather, Moore's poem was lifted largely from a children's book, *The Children's Friend: Part III, A New-Year's Present to the Little Ones from Five to Twelve,*[7] published in 1821 by a book dealer whose shop was only a short walk from Moore's home in southern Manhattan. If anyone deserves the credit for "inventing" the American gift-giver, it is the nineteenth-century publisher, William B. Gilley, and illustrator, Arthur J. Stansbury, of *The Children's Friend*.

In telling the history of Santa Claus, I must also tell the story of what Christmas historian Bowler calls the "shaggy bogeymen, witches with iron teeth, ghostly figures in white [and] devils with chains"—figures that include Krampus, Klaubauf, Cert, Père Fouettard, and Hans Trapp.[8] Explaining the often misunderstood role of these figures requires making a distinction between the "evil helpers" of St. Nicholas, creatures like Krampus whose animal parts and long, red tongues identified them as colleagues of the devil, and the scary-looking but clearly human "terror men" who assumed the gift-giving role after the Reformation made a Catholic saint unwelcome at Protestant homes. The evil helpers *traveled with* St. Nicholas in Catholic regions, and probably had done so since the saint replaced the pagan god Odin and his broom-riding side-kick Berchta as Yule gift-givers, because a Catholic saint could not implement the gruesome punishments that Berchta had in store for poorly-behaved children. The "terror men," on the other hand, *replaced* St. Nicholas as secular gift-givers when Catholic saints became unwelcome in northern Germany following the Protestant Reformation. These characters, who looked and dressed as if they had lived alone in the woods for many years, worked alone, typically carrying a handful of switches to threaten boys and girls who had misbehaved but providing fruit, nuts, sweets, and toys to good boys and girls, generally tossing them on the floor as he left the home. It is that duality—Santa Claus' ability to know who was good and bad and leave a lump of coal for those who deserve it—that marks Santa as one of the post–Reformation German gift-givers and distinguishes him from the holy St. Nicholas of Myra.

I will also correct a demonstrable error that has appeared in almost every history of Santa Claus since the mid–1950s and which underlies the mistaken belief that Santa Claus was created by a half-dozen members of the New-York Historical Society known as the Knickerbockers during the early 1800s. The perpetrator of this story, however, did not arrive at the historical society until more than a hundred years later. Charles W. Jones, a Berkeley history professor widely viewed as the country's leading expert on St. Nicholas, gave a 1953 speech to the New-York Historical Society, published a 1954 paper, "Knickerbocker Santa Claus,"[9] and published a 1978 book, *Saint Nicholas of Myra, Bari, and Manhattan: Biography of a Legend,*[10] in which Jones argued that author Washington Irving "made" Santa Claus in a mock history, *A History of New York*, Irving published in 1809.[11] The basis for Jones' claim was that Irving's history, although entirely fictional, described the gift-giving practices of St. Nicholas and Dutch New Yorkers in a way that sparked a sudden interest in St. Nicholas among members of the historical society in 1810.

There was a sudden interest in St. Nicholas in December 1810, although the extent of that interest must be considered in the light that it can be attributed entirely to one person, John Pintard, one of the historical society's officers. On December 6, 1810, Pintard distributed a broadside about St. Nicholas at the society's annual meeting, and an historic poem about St. Nicholas was published in three New York papers between December 10, 1810, and December 15, 1810. The unusual spelling of what was identified as the Dutch version St. Nicholas, "Santce Claus," in all four documents implies a single actor, presumably but not provably John Pintard. At any rate, Jones, without any evidence except his own word, argues that the legend of Santa Claus "spread like the plaugue" after these publications, and confidently asserts that the references to St. Nicholas in the 1809 edition of Irving's *History* caused publication of the four St. Nicholas poems in 1810, and that Irving, therefore, deserved the credit for the subsequent popularity of Santa Claus in America.

Since 1954, more than two dozen historians have relied on Jones' work but few of them appear to have noticed two flaws in Jones' effort to write the history. One was that there were no publications about St. Nicholas in America between 1813, the year after Irving actually published references upon which Jones relies, and 1821, making Jones' statement that the legend of Santa Claus spread like the plague after 1810 sound foolish. The other flaw, one which reflects adversely on both Jones and the large contingent of historians who relied on his work without independent research, is that Jones was relying on the wrong edition of Irving's book. As a quick comparison of the 1809 and 1812 editions of Irving's *History* will demonstrate, the passages about St. Nicholas upon which Jones relied were added when Irving revised the book in 1812 to correct some errors in the 1809 edition. Thus, the references could *not* have prompted publication of the St. Nicholas poems in 1810. Nonetheless, more than two dozen publications, including Stephen Nissenbaum's *The Battle for Christmas: A Cultural History of America's Most Cherished Holiday*,[12] have relied on Jones' work without noticing that Jones was working on the wrong book.

1

The Remarkable Diversity, and Simultaneous Commonality, of the World's Midwinter Gift-Givers

This book is intended to showcase the remarkable diversity of the characters around the world who personify the midwinter celebration Americans and the English call Christmas. Santa, who is commonly portrayed as an old man with a long white beard, has been known in earlier times or other nations as St. Nicholas, Father Christmas, Kriss Kringle, Sinterklaas, Babbo Natale, Kerstman, Grandfather Frost, Père Noël, Papai Noel, Papá Noel, Pai Natal, Baba Noel, Pelznickel, Belsnickle, Aschenklas, Ru-Klaus, Weihnachtsmann, Ded Moroz, Knecht Ruprecht, Svaty Mikalas, Veijo Pasuero, Dun Lao Che Ren, Old Man Christmas, Uncle Chimney, Mos Nicolae, Mos Cracium, Daidi na Nollag, Mikulás, Mikolaj, Olentzero, Samichlaus, and Hoteiosho, among many other names.[1]

The Winter Solstice gift-giver, however, can also be a woman (Christkindl, Berchta, Babushka, La Befana, Kolyada, Snegurochka, Tante Arie, Vieja Belen or St. Lucia), a child (Christkindl, El Nino, Gesu Bambino or Le Petit Noel), an elf (St. Nick of "Night Before Christmas" fame and the Scandinavian Julenisse and Jultomten), an animal (Julbock, the Yule goat, in Scandinavia or the Gentle Camel of Jesus in Syria) or a group of gift-givers: Las Tres Reyes Magos, the Three Wise Men or the Three Kings, holiday gift-givers in Spain and much of Latin America, and the Jolasveinar, the Icelandic "Yule Lads," thirteen children of a couple of child-eating Icelandic ogres with such wonderful names in English as Spoon-Licker, Pot-Scraper, Sausage-Swiper, Window-Peeper, Door-Slammer, Doorway-Sniffer, and Meat Hook.

Since the Middle Ages, most of Santa's European counterparts have delivered gifts for children during the Christmas season. The precise dates vary, however, from November 11 (a Catholic feast day on which St. Martin filled the same role as St. Nicholas); November 30 (St. Andrew's Day, a Catholic feast day on which St. Andrew played the same role as St. Nicholas); December 5 (the date on which the Dutch Sinterklaas brought gifts after the celebration of St. Nicholas' Day on December 6 was outlawed by the Dutch government); December 6 (the Catholic feast day in honor of St. Nicholas); December 13 (St. Lucia's Day, a holiday popular in Sweden in which St. Lucia is represented by a young woman dressed in white with a wreath of lighted candles on her head); December 25 (Christmas, of course); January 1 (both New Year's Day, which remains the most popular day for exchanging gifts in many nations, and St. Basil's Day, when Aghios Vassilis, the Greek version of Santa Claus, brings gifts to Greek children); January 5 (known as Twelfth Night, Berchta's Night, or the night before Epiphany in different cultures, the evening when the Germanic goddess

Berchta, Italy's Le Befana and, in many Spanish-speaking nations, the Three Kings bring gifts); and January 6 (the Christian Feast of Epiphany).

As English historians J.M. Golby and A.W. Purdue explain in *The Making of the Modern Christmas*, "[e]very European society had … some legend of a spirit or personification of Christmas, legends that were almost certainly part of the southern European Saturnalia or the Yuletide of the Teutonic north before they took on a Christmas guise."[2] These characters are not limited to bringing gifts. Figures like Knecht Ruprecht and Belsnickle, for example, may also visit homes on any day between St. Martin's Day and Three Kings' Day to question children on their catechism or behavior, a practice not too different from Santa Claus appearing in a Christmas parade or at the local department store before Christmas. The Santa figures also act as grand marshals or figurehead of whatever Winter Solstice festival the particular society celebrated. During Advent, the four weeks before Christmas, the Christmas characters in Europe can be found in Christmas plays, formal parades, Christmas markets, and local Christmas celebrations.

The grand marshals have included Dionysus and his tutor, Silenus, the Greek gods of wine and drink, who presided over a group of Greek midwinter festivals called Rural Dionysia; Saturn, the Roman god of agriculture who presided over the Roman Saturnalia; Odin, the chief of the Germanic panoply of pagan gods, who led the ghostly Wild Hunt during Yule season in northern Europe; Thor, known in Germany as Donar, the pagan god who leads the Scandinavian equivalent of the Wild Hunt on a chariot pulled by two goats; Father Christmas, also known as Sir Christmas or Old Christmas, the Englishman who has personified Christmas since the fifteenth century; and Morozko, the Slavic god who became the Grandfather Frost of Russia and eastern Europe. Santa Claus is the American name for the same figure, having bested St. Nicholas and Kriss Kringle for the title during the nineteenth century.

Although the names, history, habits, and traditions of these characters are remarkably diverse, they are all "Santa," meaning versions of the same midwinter gift-giving character that modern Americans, and increasingly residents of other nations, call Santa Claus. One of Santa's most interesting characteristics is that we can almost always agree that a particular figure is, or is not, Santa, but there is no single feature that defines him (or, in a few cases, her).[3] The important point is that no matter what perspective the artist brings, most of the depictions are instantly recognizable as Santa and no one else. Santa is a spiritual concept and, as a result, each of us is free to decide what Santa looks like in the flesh. Nonetheless, all of us seem to have an innate sense of what Santa looks like, and that appearance dates back thousands of years, before the birth of Christ. While the attributes of commonality and diversity may sound contradictory, that is one of the magical qualities of Santa.

In telling the history of Santa, it is critical at the outset that we define "Santa." The answer most might give—defining Santa as the Christmas gift-giver—does not work because some figures who clearly have to be included, such as England's Father Christmas, did not originally give gifts, and other figures, such as St. Nicholas or Russia's Grandfather Frost, give gifts on days other than Christmas (December 6 and January 1, respectively). If the definition is too broad, one risks including the Easter Bunny. Defining Santa as the spirit of Christmas seems closer to the mark but Santa is a person, not a spirit, and defining him as the personification of Christmas seems to be the right answer. Indeed, in the preeminent sociological study of the holiday in America, *The American Christmas,* sociologist James Barnett opines that "Santa Claus personified the popular spirit of Christmas."[4] Thus, Santa can be viewed as the anthropomorphic symbol of the Winter Solstice festivals as they evolved from prehistoric celebrations of the death and rebirth of the sun god to our modern Christmas season.

This definition does not mean we should view Santa as simply the Christmas version of the Phillie Phanatic or Mr. Met, two professional sports mascots who are the anthropomorphic symbols of their respective teams, because doing so would trivialize Santa in a way that ignores his importance to virtually every society in the northern hemisphere. In an essay titled "The Mind of Santa Claus and the Metaphors He Lives By," authors William E. Deal, a professor of religious history and cognitive studies at Case Western Reserve University, and S. Waller, an associate professor of philosophy at Montana State University, offer a more comprehensive definition of how Santa personifies the Christmas season.

> Santa Claus is our figurehead for a season in which we (ideally) emphasize charity, good will toward others, forgiveness, peace, understanding, and love. He seems to have superhuman powers of knowledge and moral judgment. Santa is the icon for our season of giving, peace, and justice because he has cognitive abilities that are seemingly divine rather than human. The mind of Santa intuits our intentions, knows the consequences of our actions, and makes immediate and accurate assessments of our annual moral performance.[5]

In "Christmas Mythologies Sacred and Secular," another essay from the same book of philosophical reflections on the season, *Christmas—Philosophy for Everyone: Better Than a Lump of Coal*,[6] Guy Bennett-Hunter, an English philosopher and writer, explains how Santa not only embodies "the spirit of Christmas" but how this symbolic figure actually produces the altruism and generosity for which he stands.[7] When parents tell children about Santa, Bennett-Hunter says, the story "isn't a just a way of explaining who put the presents under the tree."[8] Rather, it is "a way of bringing out the significance or meaning that Christmas has in family life. It's about altruism, selflessness, love, and so on. The mythological figure of Santa embodies the selfless kindness that Christmas is supposed to be all about."[9]

If we define Santa as the personification of Christmas, it should become obvious that the well-trod argument over whether it is ethical to "lie" to children about Santa Claus misses the point entirely.[10] When asked by my daughters whether Santa Claus existed, I always answered: "Of course. I have hundreds of Santas in the attic." My daughters, in turn, responded with that well-known my-father-is-an-idiot look but what I sought to convey with this dose of fatherly humor was that Santa indisputably exists as the symbol of Christmas, and Christmas represents our most noble virtues. Symbols are real, and they can be very powerful. Uncle Sam and the star-spangled banner are "merely" symbols of the United States, but they are symbols that have inspired millions of men and women to sacrifice, and often to die, for their country.

While the symbolism of Santa is not nearly as consequential as the many sacrifices in the name of our flag, it is just as real. In "Scrooge Learns It All in One Night: Happiness and the Virtues of Christmas," Dane Scott, Director of the Center for Ethics at the University of Montana, explains how Charles Dickens' novella *A Christmas Carol* demonstrates "the importance of developing the virtues of generosity and gratitude and the consequences of a life of greed and ungratefulness" and shows us "how the Christmas tradition can promote human flourishing by helping people to develop the virtues of generosity and gratitude."[11]

> For humans to flourish and be happy we must know how to give others what they are owed (justice), and we must be able to give without expecting something in return (generosity).... Children must be taught to have the habit of "affectionate regard for others." Directed practice and education are required to develop the disposition of uncalculated giving and graceful receiving. Every Christmas

season there is an opportunity for such training, for it is at these times that children can learn the satisfaction of generosity, while steering clear of the deficiency of greed and the excess of prodigality.[12]

In extolling Santa's virtues, we cannot lose sight of the fact that since pagan times, the Yule gift-givers, like the parents who pull the strings behind them, have always had a disciplinary function as well. When Christianity arrived in northern Europe during the High Middle Ages, and St. Nicholas was selected to replace the pagan god Odin and his witchy sidekick Berchta as Yule gift-giver, the disciplinary function was deemed inappropriate for such a saintly figure. To perform that function, therefore, St. Nicholas acquired a number of evil servants and sidekicks, including Krampus, Klaubauf, Cert, Houseker, Hans Trapp, Le Père Fouettard, and Schmutzl, typically monstrous beings of the underworld who threaten to beat or kidnap naughty children.[13]

The disappearance of St. Nicholas in Protestant regions following the Reformation led to a new regime of gift-givers who could perform both the gift-giving function of St. Nicholas and the disciplinary function of the evil helpers, and to a gradual shift from St. Nicholas' Day to Christmas as the highlight of the Christmas season. These characters, which include Germany's Knecht Ruprecht and Pelznickel and Pennsylvania's Belsnickle, among dozens of other local names, will be called "faux Nicholases" in this book to reflect that they play the role St. Nicholas had before the Reformation but are not the Catholic saint. The post–Reformation gift-givers, who operate under more than two dozen names in Germany and central Europe, typically look like distinctly unjolly versions of St. Nicholas, unshaven and ungroomed men wearing dirty brown cloaks or animal skins and carrying bundles of switches. As secular figures, they assume both the gift-giving and disciplinary roles of St. Nicholas and his evil helpers, and during the nineteenth century these secular figures morphed into Weihnachtsmann ("Christmas man") in Germany and Santa Claus in the United States. There were also two faux Nicholases, the Dutch Sinterklaas and Swiss Samichlaus, who were portrayed as bishops and looked almost exactly like St. Nicholas but were, "in fact," different characters. As saintly figures, both of them had their own evil helpers to impose discipline, Zwarte Piet ("Black Peter") in Holland and Schmutzli ("Dirt") in Switzerland, although Black Peter changed from a terrifying enforcer into a black-faced minstrel performer during the nineteenth century.

Recognizing the extraordinary diversity of the subject, historians, archeologists, anthropologists, sociologists, theologians, folklorists, and art historians who are interested in such matters—and the study of Santa involves all of these disciplines—must decide how to treat historical and regional differences in the Winter Solstice gift-givers observed over many thousands of years. Most modern Americans have no problem treating St. Nick as a nickname for Santa Claus because the first popular story in America, "The Night Before Christmas," calls him St. Nicholas and St. Nick.

There is great irony here. For five centuries, the Protestant regions in Europe objected to the celebration of St. Nicholas' Day, December 6, because one of the basic premises of the Reformation was to eliminate the "idolization" of Catholic saints. Therefore, Protestants in northern Europe either substituted Christmas for St. Nicholas' Day as the date for holiday gift-giving and identified the gift-giver as the Christ child ("Christkindl") or chose one of the faux Nicholases to continue the tradition without directly invoking a Catholic saint. The Dutch people, however, were more diabolical, creating an entirely new character, Sinterklaas, to avoid the legal ban on celebration of St. Nicholas' Day during the Reformation. Sinterklaas was not the Catholic St. Nicholas of Myra, but a resident of Spain who came by steamboat to the Netherlands once a year and dispensed gifts on December 5, the day before the Catholic Feast of St. Nicholas. Today, the citizens of the Netherlands no longer seem to mind the use of St. Nicholas as a synonym for Sinterklaas. They vigorously insist, however, that St. Nicholas and Sinterklaas should not be conflated with Santa Claus.[14]

Equally important, many of the holiday gift-givers whose characteristics became part of the American Santa Claus developed independently from St. Nicholas. England's Father Christmas came to life as "Old Christmas" or "Sir Christmas" in the seventeenth century as an anthropomorphic symbol for Christmas who appeared in plays that belittled the Puritan attempts to outlaw the holiday. Russia's Ded Moroz ("Grandfather Frost") likely owes a debt to the pagan gods of Slavic mythology, who were central to the celebration of the Winter Solstice, but was revived by the Communist Party in the mid–1930s to serve as a secular gift-giver for a New Year's celebration established by the Soviet Union as an atheistic Christmas substitute. Like Ded Moroz, Herr Winter in Germany and Jack Frost in England were also secular figureheads of midwinter but were superseded when Santa adopted the winter sleigh, heavy boots and warm fur coat and hat of Old Man Winter. Scandinavia's Yule gift-givers arose out of folklore in which house elves and gnomes known as nisse or tomten demanded bowls of porridge during Yule. Over the years, each of these figures adopted aspects of the others, creating similar but distinct midwinter gift-givers.

The identification of all of these figures as Santa does not mean they should all be called "Santa Claus," a term we have reserved for the figure created during the nineteenth century in North America, or that they should wear the standard uniform of the American Santa Claus. Quite the contrary, the subtitle *A History of St. Nicholas and Other Holiday Gift-Bringers* is intended to convey that Santa describes a large and diverse collection of gift-giving figures who are integral parts of the midwinter and Christmas celebrations that have existed around the world for thousands of years. No nation or religion owns the rights to these figures; they are part of a universal heritage shared by humanity. We should retain and value the diversity in names, appearance, and gift-giving practices, however, because Santa should reflect the diversity that exists among the people of the world.[15] Too many of these figures have already become clones of the American Santa Claus, and that is a shame.

Defining Santa as the personification of Christmas is also inextricably intertwined with how we define Christmas itself. If the term Christmas were limited to the celebration of Christ's birth on December 25, that definition would exclude not only St. Nicholas, because his gift-giving occurred on St. Nicholas' Day, and the Three Kings, who arrive with gifts on the night before Epiphany (January 6), but Santa Claus himself, who brings presents to the millions of children around the world whose families celebrate Christmas solely as a secular holiday. The late Dr. Seuss would surely shed a tear to learn the holiday so beloved by the Whos down in Whoville was not really Christmas at all.

For the Whos, Christmas was not a day but a season, and, as you may recall, "the Grinch hated Christmas, the whole Christmas season."[16] The Christmas season, which Europeans would call Yuletide or Christmastide, is our version of the Roman midwinter festivals—that is, a celebration of the fall harvest, the Winter Solstice, the New Year, and, for many, the birth of Christ, all within a period of several weeks between late November and early January. The holiday season also includes, by coincidence or design, other midwinter holidays such as Hanukkah, the Jewish Festival of Lights, which starts on twenty-fifth day of the Hebrew month of Kislev, and Kwanzaa, a celebration of African American culture on December 26.[17] If you recognize that Christmas is a *season* lasting for a month or more, rather than simply December 25, it should become apparent that our assumptions about what the word "Christmas" means need to be considered in that context.

English author Michael Harrison, in his 1959 study *The Story of Christmas*, eloquently outlined the elements of the Christmas season.[18] If we define Santa as the personification of the Christmas season, Harrison's description of that season as "the feast of humankind" is as good a description as any of what that really means:

> Christmas is the feast, not only of man's redemption, but of man himself. It is because it releases—if only for a few days in every year—tendencies that a savage self-interest causes mankind in the ordinary to repress. At Christmas-tide tyrants grow benevolent—even merciful; misers spend, not only freely, but willingly; the fierce flames of religious and political prejudice die for a short while to a cold cinder; selfish memories are stirred by the recollection—tardy but intense—of the neglected and the outcast. For a few days, once a year, the atrophied souls of the grown-ups are filled again with that spirit which inspires the wisdom of fools and children.[19]

Even readers who believe Christmas must be defined solely as the celebration of the birth of Christ will recognize that most parts of the Christmas *season* are, and always have been, purely secular elements that formed part of the Roman midwinter celebrations before Christ was even born. The *season* includes a fall harvest festival (which the Romans called Saturnalia but Americans call Thanksgiving), St. Nicholas' Day (celebrated in Catholic but not Protestant cultures), a winter festival (sleigh rides, bonfires, winter sports, and, in some places, fake snow), the Winter Solstice (symbolizing the death and rebirth of the sun, Sol Invictus, and the most of the pagan sun gods), the Nativity itself (the birth of Christ, whose date was chosen to coincide with the astronomical Winter Solstice and the religious celebration of Sol Invictus), New Year's Eve and New Year's Day (which are universally celebrated by all societies according to each culture's calendar), and Epiphany (celebrated as Berchta's Night, the last night of Yule, in pre–Christian Europe but as Twelfth Night in modern times and Three Kings Day in southern Europe and Latin America). Recognizing that Christmas is a season rather than one day is also important because it is our collective ability to turn the darkest, coldest, scariest part of the year into a festival of good cheer for several weeks that makes the Christmas season so wonderful for our spirits and so important to our psyches.

The multi-week celebration of the fall harvest, the Winter Solstice and the new year was the most important observance of the year even before the birth of Christ, and, as explained above, the Christmas season is primarily a series of secular holidays named for one important Christian holiday—a holiday, ironically, that many Christian denominations once refused to acknowledge, and that some still do.[20] As a matter of fact, while few seem to recognize it, the word "Christmas" does not refer to the birth of Christ at all. The Biblical term for the birth of Christ is the Nativity and the celebration of Christ's birth is the Feast of the Nativity. The word Christmas means "Christ's Mass," and refers to the midnight masses that were conducted by Catholic churches throughout Europe on Christmas Eve.[21] Accordingly, the same logic that underlies the slogan "Keep Christ in Christmas" would require that we "Keep Mass in Christmas," a slogan that presumably would encourage everyone to attend midnight mass at their local Catholic church.[22] While no one would seriously urge this interpretation, it illustrates that we must all be careful not to let our own theological blinders impinge on what should be a celebration for all. Understanding this fact should help Christians understand why philosopher David Kyle Johnson asserts that "Christmas should be for everyone, and everyone should feel free to celebrate as they wish."[23]

The failure to understand that Christmas means a season which encompasses important secular holidays, and the misunderstanding the etymology of phrases like Happy Holidays, has resulted in an unfortunate and inaccurate attack on two of the season's long-standing greetings, "Happy Holidays" and "Season's Greetings." The first Christmas card in 1843 contained the common but unwieldy greeting "We wish you a Merry Christmas and a Happy New Year." During the nineteenth century, Happy Holidays and Season's Greetings emerged on Christmas cards as shorthand ways to deliver the same sentiment, and the cards were sent and received on the assumption that everyone involved was Christian. In fact, the term "holiday" comes from the Old English word hāligdæg, meaning "holy day," a term designating those days which either the Bible or the Catholic Church named as special days of worship. Thus, "Happy Holidays" literally means "Happy Holy Days," a term that could hardly be characterized as anti–Christian.

When used during Christmastide, however, the term takes on an even more specific meaning. In an 1866 article, "The Holidays," journalist George C. McWhorter explains that "the holidays" was a long-standing name for the period between Christmas and Epiphany, commonly known as the Twelve Days of Christmas.[24] During the ninth century, according to McWhorter, English King Alfred the Great "established a decree that thenceforth the holidays should begin with Christmas and end with Twelfth-Night, or the Epiphany," a period that encompasses almost a dozen Catholic feast days as well as New-Year's Eve and New-Year's Day.[25] Thus, the most precise interpretation of "Happy Holidays" would probably be "Happy Twelve Days of Christmas."

Santa Claus embodies many qualities we would describe as Christian, including unconditional love, kindness, generosity, equality, faith, responsibility, charity, friendship, celebration, and joy.[26] He is not the creation of any religion at all, however, but a secular figure created to avoid religious restrictions on the celebration of Christmas. Except for Christkindl and, arguably, the Three Kings, the only holiday gift-giver with a religious origin is St. Nicholas of Myra, a Catholic saint who had nothing to do with Christmas and may never have existed at all. Moreover, except in the Eastern Orthodox Church St. Nicholas has been widely disavowed as a religious figure, first by the Protestant denominations that formed following the Reformation of 1517 and later by Pope Paul VI and the Roman Catholic Church during an ecumenical conference known as Vatican II in 1969.

The best-known gift-givers other than Santa Claus—the English Father Christmas, the Dutch Sinterklaas, and the German Weihnachtsmann—are also secular figures, and were chosen for the role of Christmas gift-giver precisely because they did not represent a particular religious viewpoint. One of the reasons the Calvinists, Puritans, and like-minded Protestant denominations sought to outlaw Christmas during the seventeenth and eighteenth centuries was that Christmas, in their view, was a pagan holiday improperly converted into a Christian festival during the fourth century by the Catholic Church. The secular gift-givers were, in effect, a compromise during a period when some religions supported the celebration of Christmas and others sought to outlaw it as unsupported by the Bible or a "popist" creation.

The assertion that what we call Christmas was originally a pagan holiday is accurate but that does not necessarily mean there was anything wrong with converting it to a Christian holiday. For example, pagans also knelt to pray and thanked the gods for the meal before eating, but no one considers kneeling to pray or saying grace before dinner to be "pagan practices." The early Catholic Church's decision to designate December 25 as the birth of Christ, most experts believe, was a strategic move to facilitate conversion of the pagan population to Christianity. After the Roman Emperor Constantine adopted Christianity as the official religion of the empire, the church could not allow the pagan rites to continue but eliminating the beloved celebration in the name of Christianity would have made conversion of the Roman people close to impossible. Thus, the church declared December 25, which was then celebrated as Sol Invictus, the birthday of the Roman sun god Sol, and the birthday of the Persian sun god Mithra, as the birthday of Christ. In other words, the church simply substituted the Son of God for the Sun God.

Some Christians seem to believe that acknowledging a strategic motive by the Christian church in designating December 25 as the birth of Christ undermines the legitimacy of the Nativity celebration. This decision, however, can be interpreted in a more positive light. As discussed at greater length below, Bruce David Forbes, a Methodist minister and professor of religious studies at Morningside College, explains persuasively in *Christmas: A Candid History* that the origin of Christmas as a pagan celebration of the Winter Solstice does not undermine its importance to Christians.[27] Similarly, Francis X. Weiser, a Jesuit priest who published a history of Christmas in 1952, wrote that "all Christians during this period were keenly aware of the differences between the two celebrations—one pagan and one Christian—on the same day. In fact, the popes seem to have chosen December twenty-fifth precisely for the purpose of inspiring the people to turn from the worship of a material sun to the adoration of Christ the Lord."[28]

In *Christmas in America: A History*, historian Penne Restad argues that the modern, secular celebration of Christmas in America was a necessary compromise for a religiously tolerant nation.[29] On one side, the Puritans and Calvinists who settled New England during the 1600s viewed the celebration of Christmas as a pagan celebration which had no basis in the Bible. On the other side, many residents of New York, Pennsylvania, the mid–Atlantic and the southern colonies viewed Christmas as one of the holiest days of the year and loved the traditional celebration of the holiday. However, Restad says, there were also concerns that "urban rowdies—young, male and usually poor—built on the general license of the season and began to cross the line from ritualized mayhem to anarchic melee."[30] In the end, Restad writes, "the Puritans had performed the great duty of stripping the old Christmas of its excess, thereby allowing an emergence of a better holiday."[31]

> Christmas could not be the most beautiful of festivals if it were doctrinal, or dogmatic, or theological, or local. It is a universal holiday because it is the jubilee of a universal sentiment, molded only by a new epoch, and subtly adapted to the new forms of the old faith.[32]

In trying to adjust conflicts between the religious and secular celebrations of Christmas, this principle cannot be overemphasized. It is understandable that many Americans and Europeans, Christians and non–Christians alike, conflate the Christian celebration of the birth of Christ on December 25 with the secular holiday season simply because it is more convenient to call it all "Christmas," but we must be careful not to allow convenience to become an excuse for creating division where none should exist.[33] The bottom line, as the reader will learn in subsequent chapters, is that mixing politics, religion, and Christmas has produced many illogical and unfortunate outcomes over thousands of years. Injecting political controversy has the effect of making a universal celebration of peace, brotherhood, and goodwill into something less joyous and less sacred for everyone involved. For example, in explaining why agnostics or atheists often celebrate Christmas in a big way, Ruth Tallman, Associate Professor of Philosophy at Barry University, emphasizes the importance of universal rituals and values.

> Rituals are an important part of human life. They are a way to honor, remember, mark milestones, rejoice, and grieve. They instill in us a sense of place, belonging, heritage, and purpose. All cultures, regardless of the metaphysical belief structure they embrace, place a high value on rituals. Although

some rituals have special theistic significance, such as the partaking of the Eucharist in the Catholic church, many of the rituals which we embrace are entirely secular.[34]

In other words, the celebration of Christmas is not dependent on holding a particular religious belief, or any religious belief at all. To say Santa personifies the spirit of Christmas is not a statement about theology but a statement about the Christmas season. An annual feast of universal appeal, the Christmas season incorporates trappings such as decorations of evergreens, fires, and lights designed to ward off the cold and darkness of winter; acts of charity, major and minor; visiting with family and friends; giving and receiving gifts; music, singing, and dancing to traditional tunes; eating and drinking over and over again; and engaging in traditions appropriate to any winter celebration without regard to one's religion. The traditions we will remember as we grow older are things like picking out the perfect Christmas tree, baking cookies from grandmother's secret recipe, watching the annual showings of *How the Grinch Stole Christmas* and *A Charlie Brown Christmas*, wearing a beautiful velvet dress to the Saturday matinee of *The Nutcracker*, cutting up carrots and celery to leave in a bowl for Santa's reindeer, and Dad explaining, for the tenth year in a row, why Santa gets too much milk and would probably prefer a glass of ruby port.

In present-day America, the Christmas season begins with Thanksgiving, which we celebrate with food, family, football games, and parades, and, for the majority of us, ends on New Year's Day, which we celebrate with food, family, more football games, and more parades.[35] Aside from the American obsession with football, however, this is not a modern perspective. As explained by sociologist James H. Barnett, in his 1954 study *The American Christmas: A Study in National Culture*, it is the essence of what Charles Dickens brought to the celebration of Christmas in 1843 when Dickens' novella *A Christmas Carol* "gave new life to the secular celebration of Christmas and did it without desecrating the religious festival."[36]

> For Dickens, this was a time when many of the conventional restraints of social life should give way to an expression of a deeper sense of brotherhood and solidarity. Dickens preached that at Christmas men should forget self and think of others, especially the poor and the unfortunate. All should participate in the great festival of brotherhood.[37]

Dickens himself, speaking through the voice of Ebenezer Scrooge's nephew Fred in *A Christmas Carol*, tells us Christmas is "a good time, a kind, forgiving, charitable, pleasant time; the only I know of, in the long calendar of the year, when men and women seem by one consent to open their shut-up hearts freely and to think of people below them as if they really were fellow passengers to the grave … though it has never put a scrap of gold or silver in my pocket, I believe that it has done me good, and will do me good, and I say God bless it."[38] As this passage illustrates, although *A Christmas Carol* is a not a religious work, and does not even mention the Nativity as the reason for the season, it is a deeply moral work with an unmistakable ethical message.

In Germany, Great Britain, and the United States, three of the nations with the strongest Christmas traditions, historians emphasize that Christmas has become, in effect, a national holiday rather than a religious holiday. In *Christmas in Germany: A Cultural History*, Joe Perry writes that "[t]he Germans have quite a religious feeling for their Weihnachtsbaum, coming down, one may fancy, from some dim ancestral worship of the trees of the wood."[39] In *Christmas, A History*, Mark Connell writes that Christmas in England was not about Christianity but, rather, "was a national expression of English culture, habits and aesthetics."[40] In *The American Christmas*, sociologist Barnett tells us that Christmas is "a national festival" and "a vital and unique symbol of our national life and culture."[41] Barnett also explains the holiday in a way that would apply to all of the nations celebrating it as an important national holiday: "One may be sure that if Christmas did not make possible the realization of individual satisfactions and collective values, some other holiday would be used to achieve these ends."[42] Put more personally, how would you feel when the leaves had all fallen, the sun set before the day ended and the temperature dropped below freezing if you did not have the preparations for, and anticipation of, Thanksgiving and Christmas to occupy your mind?

Although the statement that Santa personifies the spirit of Christmas is not about religion, it is fully consistent with the religious aspects of the holiday season. Christmas transcends religion in the sense that one need not be a Christian or a member of any particular denomination to celebrate and respect these ideals. Indeed, the question of whether a belief in God is necessary to celebrate Christmas was explored by English archaeologist Paul Frodsham in *From Stonehenge to Santa: The Evolution of Christmas*.[43] Frodsham, who says he was raised as a Christian but no longer considers himself a theist, grappled with the question of whether one can celebrate a holiday defined as the birth of Christ without being Christian. In concluding that you can have Christmas without religion, Frodsham observes that many Protestant religions following the Reformation outlawed Christmas as a pagan celebration, not a Christian one, but that the Soviet Union under Communist control and Germany during the Nazi regime outlawed Christmas as a Christian holiday, permitting it to be celebrated only as an explicitly pagan national holiday. Poor Father Christmas comes off like Charlie Brown, the Charles Schultz cartoon character who could not win for losing.

Even today, Frodsham writes, the intensity with which Christmas is celebrated in many European nations seems inversely proportional to the percentage of the nation's population that identifies itself as theists. For example, two-thirds of the residents of the Netherlands, and a third of the residents of Germany and the Czech Republic, do not identify with any religion, but these nations celebrate Christmas in grand style. In the conclusion of his book, Frodsham explains this seeming contradiction by distinguishing between religion and spirituality:

> What exactly is it that gives Christmas its peculiar power, making it for many people a spiritually uplifting highlight of every year? The answer, we must conclude, transcends Christianity and relates to the very nature of human existence. The desire to gather round a warm fire with loved ones to reaffirm or debate ancient creation myths and celebrate the mysterious but glorious nature of life, while eating, drinking, singing and generally making merry, is a natural response of human beings to the darkest point of the year.... Christmas remains one of humanity's greatest inventions; it will be with us until the ends of time and its celebration should be open to all, regardless of religious belief.[44]

One can also add a more practical benefit to those listed by Frodsham, one that is inherent in the universal celebration of the Winter Solstice. As Forbes explains, without Christmas we would face three months of darkness and cold without respite each winter, a surefire recipe for depression and despair. By celebrating the midwinter holiday, we effectively cut the period of depressing darkness by 60 percent or more.[45] This is because we spend most of our free time before the Winter Solstice preparing for the holiday, and with Christmas, like vacations, preparing is half the fun. When we finally get to the winter solstice, the celebrations of Christmas and the New Year cut another two weeks of the depressing darkness. By the time we return to our usual schedule in January, we are more than halfway to spring. January is still cold and dark, but every day it gets just a little bit better.

As the rotation of the earth changes, the slightly longer, slightly warmer days lift our spirits until, before we know it, the groundhog is telling us that spring is only a few weeks away.

The role of Santa, then, is that he captures the spirit of this celebration for young and old alike. Santa surely exists as the personification of the spirit of the Christmas, and those who do not appreciate the reality and symbolic importance of Santa miss the personal and spiritual nature of the Christmas season. Few have explained this point as well as veteran newsman Francis P. Church, an editor of New York's *Sun*, who, on September 21, 1897, famously responded to eight-year-old Virginia O'Hanlon's question of whether Santa Claus existed:

> Virginia, your little friends are wrong. They have been affected by the skepticism of a skeptical age. They do not believe except they see. They think that nothing can be which is not comprehensible by their little minds. All minds, Virginia, whether they be men's or children's, are little. In this great universe of ours man is a mere insect, an ant, in his intellect, as compared with the boundless world about him, as measured by the intelligence capable of grasping the whole truth and knowledge.
>
> Yes, Virginia, there is a Santa Claus. He exists as certainly as love and generosity and devotion exist, and you know that they abound and give to your life its highest beauty and joy.… Nobody sees Santa Claus, but that is no sign that there is no Santa Claus. The most real things in the world are those that neither children nor men can see. Did you ever see fairies dancing on the lawn? Of course not, but that's no proof that they are not there. Nobody can conceive or imagine all the wonders there are unseen and unseeable in the world.
>
> You tear apart the baby's rattle and see what makes the noise inside, but there is a veil covering the unseen world which not the strongest man, nor even the united strength of all the strongest men that ever lived, could tear apart. Only faith, fancy, poetry, love, romance can push aside that curtain and view and picture the supernal beauty and glory beyond. Is it all real? Ah, Virginia, in all this world there is nothing else real and abiding. No Santa Claus! Thank God, he lives and he lives forever.[46]

The most hard-minded scientist would have to agree that the qualities of love, charity, generosity, friendship, celebration, and joy—indeed, the look in a child's eyes on Christmas morning—are all quite real. Whether or not Santa actually slides down the chimney or places a child's presents under a tree, Francis Church would tell us Santa exists "as certainly as love and generosity and devotion" because he personifies the spirit of Christmas.

While Church's letter to Virginia is the most famous journalistic defense of Santa's existence, an equally moving but more surprising explanation was provided by Orville L. Holley, editor of *The Troy (N.Y.) Sentinel* on December 23, 1823, when it published "A Visit from St. Nicholas," the poem read aloud by Clement Moore to his family a year earlier and provided anonymously to the newspaper. That poem, which became commonly known as "The Night Before Christmas" as the fame of Santa exceeded that of St. Nicholas, is still read aloud by millions of parents every Christmas Eve almost two hundred years later.

> We know not to whom we are indebted for the following description of that unwearied patron of children—that homely, but delightful personification of parental kindness—SANTE CLAUS, his costume and his equipage, as he goes about visiting the fire-sides of this happy land, laden with Christmas bounties; but, from whomsoever it may have come, we give thanks for it. We hope our little patrons, both lads and lasses, will accept it as proof of our unfeigned good will toward them—as a token of our warmest wish that they may have many a merry Christmas; that they may long retain their beautiful relish for those unbought, homebred joys, which derive their flavor from filial piety and fraternal love, and which they may be assured are the least-alloyed that time can furnish them; and that they may never part with that simplicity of character, which is their own fairest ornament, and for the sake of which they have been pronounced, by authority which none can gain-say, the types of such as shall inherit the kingdom of heaven.[47]

What is fascinating about this introduction is that it was written the first time the small-town newspaper editor read the poem, which he did with the understanding that no one but a handful of Moore's family members had ever heard it. No distinguished professor of literature had labeled it a great work, no focus group had pronounced the poem likeable, and few of the traditions we associate with Santa Claus yet existed. Nevertheless, the editor of *The Troy Sentinel* in 1823 understood, intuitively, what the tradition of Santa Claus would mean. What is equally fascinating for someone trying to document the development of Santa Claus is that the name Holley uses, "Sante Claus," was not in Moore's poem. Sante Claus, Santeclaus, Santaclaw and Santa Claus had been used in print before 1823 but probably fewer than ten times. Nonetheless, Holley knew the character Moore called St. Nick as "Sante Claus," and had no doubt his readers would as well. The only reasonable explanation is that Santa Claus had arrived in America much earlier with European immigrants and was spread by word of mouth, not through the newspapers and books that historians study for clues to his origin.

While Francis Church's response to Virginia's letter and *The Troy Sentinel*'s introduction to "The Night Before Christmas" remain as good as any descriptions illuminating the nature of Santa Claus, they do not tell us what Santa looks like. As Church emphasized to eight-year-old Virginia, we cannot see Santa. Because we cannot see him, we are allowed to—indeed, we must—use our own experiences and imaginations in deciding what he looks like. We have both freedom of expression and freedom of introspection in deciding how to imagine the figure who represents the spirit of our holiday season. Those who celebrate Christmas, whether as a religious holiday, a secular holiday, or both, are a diverse people, and the depictions of the holiday gift-givers encompassed by this book are equally diverse.

2

Setting the Record Straight on the Nicholas-to-Irving-to-Moore-to-Nast History of Santa Claus

If you have read anything about the history of Santa, you have probably been exposed to the Nicholas-to-Irving-to-Moore-to-Nast ("NIMN") legend of Santa. The premise of the NIMN history is that Santa Claus is an American version of St. Nicholas, the fourth-century Bishop of Myra, who, legend says, was known for his generosity to children and performed a number of miracles during his lifetime that presaged his role of leaving gifts in stockings hung by the chimney. The NIMN history postulates that there was no Christmas gift-giver in America prior to 1809 when 26-year-old author Washington Irving published a book, *A History of New York*, about the early Dutch settlers of New Amsterdam who supposedly brought to America a Dutch tradition in which St. Nicholas would leave presents in stockings hung by the fireplace on the night before December 6, the Feast Day honoring St. Nicholas.[1]

St. Nicholas, the legend says, was further popularized by the poem "A Visit from St. Nicholas," commonly known as "The Night Before Christmas," written by a wealthy New Yorker, Clement C. Moore, in 1822 and published anonymously by a Troy, New York, newspaper in 1823.[2] In that poem, Moore moved the visit of St. Nicholas from December 6 to Christmas Eve, portrayed him as a "jolly old elf" dressed entirely in fur rather than the robes of a bishop, and gave him a miniature sleigh and eight tiny reindeer to fly from house to house, where he entered through the chimney to fill children's stockings with gifts. Between 1863 and 1886, according to the NIMN story, *Harper's Weekly* political cartoonist Thomas Nast completed the figurative triple play—Tinkers to Evers to Chance—by depicting the figure described by Moore in pen and ink, creating the American Santa Claus out of a fourth-century Turkish bishop.[3]

The NIMN story appears to have become generally accepted since it was first articulated in full form by Charles W. Jones, a widely admired University of California at Berkeley history professor, in a speech to the New-York Historical Society in 1953. Jones followed the speech with a paper, "Knickerbocker Santa Claus," published in the *New-York Historical Society Quarterly* in 1954,[4] and a book published in 1978, *Saint Nicholas of Myra, Bari, and Manhattan: Biography of a Legend*.[5] The theory—in essence, that Santa Claus is an Americanization of a fourth-century bishop, St. Nicholas of Myra, who had become a popular gift-giver in the Netherlands and that author Washington Irving brought the Dutch tradition to America in the 1809 edition of *A History of New York*—has been repeated in more than two dozen scholarly books and papers about Santa Claus since 1953.[6] Since arrival of the internet as the primary means of communicating information for many, the role of Washington Irving has been given an even more prominent role. If you google the phrase "history of Santa Claus," you will find that the vast majority of amateur histories credit Irving with the "invention" of Santa Claus or something similar.

One of the earlier examples of the false narrative created by Jones is Christ-

mas collector Phillip Snyder's 1985 history, *December 25: The Joys of Christmas Past*, in which he writes that "six nineteenth-century New Yorkers of varied national backgrounds were primarily responsible for transforming the old-world St. Nicholas into the American Santa Claus. The first was Washington Irving."[7] Better known, however, is University of Massachusetts historian Stephen Nissenbaum's 1997 book, *The Battle for Christmas: A Cultural History of America's Most Cherished Holiday*.[8] In that book, which was one of three finalists for the Pulitzer Prize in history that year and deftly covers a number of developments that helped produce a more family-friendly Christmas in the nineteenth century, Nissenbaum extends Jones' theory by arguing Irving had conspired with Moore and John Pintard, both wealthy New Yorkers and members of the New-York Historical Society, to popularize St. Nick in an effort to tamp down the drunken, rowdy street celebrations that then characterized Christmas in New York City.[9]

Despite its long and seemingly distinguished history, the NIMN story is provably inaccurate. Santa was not created by three or four white men from the New-York Historical Society but evolved, like any living thing, from thousands of myths, stories, practices, and illustrations in many nations over thousands of years, and surfaced in America through oral tradition without any involvement by famed Knickerbockers. Moore and Nast had important roles in shaping the evolution of Santa Claus after he arrived in America, as did dozens of other poets and artists throughout the world, and Irving may have had a small role, but the story articulated by Jones in 1954, and adopted without any independent evaluation by historians over the last six decades, was based on two indisputable errors. First, while books too numerous to count have told American children Santa was a real person, the fourth-century St. Nicholas of Myra, the saint was only one of the European predecessors to Santa Claus. The more important predecessors were the German faux Nicholases. We know that one of them, named Pelznickel in Germany, immigrated to Pennsylvania, where he was known successively as Belsnickle and Kriss Kringle and flourished during the nineteenth century without any help from Irving. We can infer, however, that other German figures whose names were close variations of Santa Claus traveled to America with German immigrants because we know from *False Stories Corrected* that "Santaclaw" was well known among American children, presumably in New York, by 1813.

Second, and more remarkable, Berkeley historian Charles W. Jones, who was the godfather of this story and arranged a speech before the New-York Historical Society in 1953 to tout his discovery of the important role played by members of the society in the "making of Santa Claus," relied on the wrong version of Irving's book in forming his conclusions. The 1809 edition of *A History of New York*, which Jones cites as the source for his conclusions, did not include the descriptions of St. Nicholas as gift-giver upon which Jones' analysis relies so heavily. Rather, those elements were added in the 1812 edition of the book, published

Opposite, top left: The religious version of St. Nicholas, before becoming the Christian gift-giver in northern Europe, is shown here in a 1294 painting from an Eastern Orthodox Church. This image is very typical of the depictions from 1200 through 1600. *Top, right:* American author Washington Irving, who some historians say had an important role in the creation of Santa Claus, is shown here in a painting by Matthew Brady between 1862 and 1876 based on an earlier painting by Edward Anthony. *Bottom, left:* Portrait of Clement Clark Moore. Special Collections, Christoph Keller, Jr., Library, General Theological Seminary. *Bottom, right:* Thomas Nast, one of the nation's most prominent political cartoonists, illustrated Santa Claus for *Harper's Weekly* between 1863 and the mid–1880s. Courtesy Miriam and Ira D. Wallach Division of Art, Prints and Photographs: Photography Collection, The New York Public Library.

primarily to fix errors Irving had discovered in the 1809 edition, some two years *after* John Pintard distributed a broadside at a meeting of the New-York Historical Society on December 6, 1810, which described the gift-giving activities of St. Nicholas, and the *New York Spectator,* which on December 15, 1810, printed an anonymous poem about St. Nicholas that told the same story as Pintard's broadside.

In "Knickerbocker Santa Claus," Jones relies on the 1810 broadside and *Spectator* poem as the evidence of a sudden interest in St. Nicholas created by Irving's 1809 book. The fact that the critical references to St. Nicholas were added two years after the 1810 broadside and *Spectator* poem completely undermines Jones' conclusion that "Santa Claus was made by Washington Irving."[10] More recently, Scott Norsworthy, an independent scholar who focuses on Herman Melville, eighteenth-century literature and authorship attribution, found that Jones also failed to discover that two other newspapers printed the same poem, one on December 12, 1810, and one on December 14, 1810.[11] The latter mistake does not really change the analysis but shows that the St. Nicholas poem was distributed more widely in 1810 than Jones thought, making it more likely publication was coordinated by one person, presumably Pintard, and less likely that the minor additions to Irving's *History* in 1812 about St. Nicholas had a significant effect on public opinion.

Contrary to the conventional wisdom that St. Nicholas of Myra was the original Santa Claus, Santa's roots not only predate St. Nicholas, they predate the birth of Christ by thousands of years. Historians, archeologists, anthropologists, theologians, and folklorists all agree the vast majority of our Christmas traditions actually began with springtime New Year's ceremonies in the Mediterranean and Middle East four thousand years ago. There were also feasts held during the Winter Solstice at monuments like England's Stonehenge and Ireland's Newgrange at least twenty-five hundred years before the birth of Christ, and some experts say there were prehistoric celebrations of the Winter Solstice conducted by tribal priests in Europe even earlier. The most significant festival in establishing our Christmas traditions was Rome's Saturnalia, which began more than two thousand years ago.[12] Like our modern Christmas season, the Winter Solstice festivals typically lasted several weeks, featuring decorations of evergreens and lights, warm fires, parties with feasting and drinking, singing of seasonal songs, dancing, acts of charity toward the needy, exchanging of gifts, and visiting friends and family.

As historian William S. Walsh explains in one of the earliest histories of Santa, *The Story of Santa Klaus,* "in every one of these festivals the leading figure was an old man, with a lot of white beard and white hair rimming his face."[13] These "old men" were actually pagan gods from Greek, Roman, Germanic, or Slavic mythology who looked much more like our modern Santa Claus than the medieval portraits of St. Nicholas of Myra.[14] The Roman god Saturn presided over the Roman Saturnalia while the Germanic gods Odin and Thor presided over the northern European celebrations of Yule, still known as Jul in Scandinavia.[15] Odin, and Berchta, the Germanic goddess of home and hearth, were believed to lead the Wild Hunt in Germany, a heavenly procession of gods, ghosts, evil spirits, horses, and hounds that early Europeans believed occurred during Yule, while Thor was believed to lead the Wild Hunt in Scandinavia. There were similar celebrations of the Winter Solstice in Russia and eastern Europe, featuring the pagan gods of Slavic mythology.

Silenus, Saturn, Odin, Thor, and Perun, the chief god of Slavic mythology, all bear an unmistakable physical resemblance to our modern Santa, and most of them share his preference for airborne transportation. Saturn, Thor, and Silenus rode through the skies on sleighs or chariots pulled by serpents, goats and leopards, respectively, while Odin rode a white, eight-legged flying horse. Berchta, who rode a broomstick, was known for entering homes through the chimney on the last night of the Wild Hunt to determine if the children were behaving and the housekeeping was up to snuff.

The extent to which the midwinter ceremonies were documented, allowing historians to describe the observances with accuracy, varied greatly. However, the most important of the midwinter celebrations, Saturnalia, was also the best documented by contemporaneous writers. Saturnalia, which began in Rome about five hundred years before the birth of Christ, ran for about three weeks and was wildly popular. In or about AD 320, Emperor Constantine the Great established Christianity as the official religion of Rome, and as part of what historians agree was an effort to persuade Romans to convert from paganism to Christianity, the empire declared December 25 as the date of Christ's birth, pitting the worship of Christ against worship of the Roman sun god Sol and the Persian sun god Mithra by giving all of them a common birthday. Using this technique, the Christmas season became—and continues to be—a combination of pagan and Christian practices, part harvest festival, part observance of the birth of Christ, part observance of the Winter Solstice and part New Year's celebration.

The strategy of replacing the pagan gods with a Christian figure but otherwise retaining the pagan observances was so successful in converting the Romans to Christianity that it was adopted by Pope Gregory in instructions to Catholic missionaries in AD 601. As the Catholic missionaries worked their way north into the rest of Europe and Scandinavia over the next thousand years, they consistently sought to Christianize the existing pagan holidays rather than eliminate them. For example, they turned the Swedish Winter Solstice celebration, a Festival of Light that occurred on December 13, into a Christian festival simply by renaming it in honor of St. Lucia, a fourth-century martyr with no connection to Sweden, and assigning the oldest girl in each family to wear a wreath of candles and long white dress to represent St. Lucia.

So how did St. Nicholas, an unknown bishop from a small town in western Turkey, who died on December 6, AD 343 without any record of achievement, manage to ascend to such an important role in the Christian celebration of Christmas? A large number of stories about his life have been told over the last thousand years but most historians view these tales, first attributed to St. Nicholas many centuries after his death, as legends rather than historically accurate accounts of his life. Indeed, there is so little historical evidence about the life of St. Nicholas that some historians express doubt about his existence. At a minimum, we can say the life of the actual St. Nicholas was a blank canvas, allowing anyone to paint the picture that best suited their purposes.

While there are no written records documenting how St. Nicholas became a Christmas gift-giver, there is much we can infer. We know from Pope Gregory's instructions to Augustine, Archbishop of Canterbury, in AD 601, that Christian missionaries were encouraged to use the Catholic feast days to "Christianize" the existing pagan celebrations rather than seeking to eliminate them. We also know that as Catholic missionaries moved north during the Middle Ages, the earlier onset of winter in northern climates combined with a glitch in the Julian calendar to push the climatic conditions conducive to the celebration of Yule into early December under the church calendar.[16] Because St. Nicholas' Day occurred on December 6, it is reasonable to assume the Catholic missionaries sought to characterize the pagan Yule festivities in some parts of northern Europe as the celebration of St. Nicholas' Day, transforming the pagan god Odin into St. Nicholas by dressing the tall, white-bearded god with a bishop's vestments, miter, and crosier—and that is precisely what most historians, anthropologists, and folklorists have concluded.[17] The new Christian gift-giver simply adopted the practice of Odin and Berchta entering homes through the chimney, and leaving gifts for well-behaved children and punishments for poorly-behaved ones, and everyone was happy.[18]

The transition from St. Nicholas to Santa Claus, which Jones attributed to Irving's publication of *A History of New York* in 1809, actually began three centuries earlier with the Protestant Reformation. In 1517, a German monk named Martin Luther drafted his famous Ninety-Five Theses, criticisms of the Catholic Church which he purportedly nailed on the door of All Saints' Church in Wittenberg, Germany, precipitating a religious revolution that resulted in most of northern Europe and portions of Great Britain converting to one Protestant faction or another over the next century.[19] Some of the resulting Protestant denominations—in particular, the Calvinist denominations that dominated in Switzerland, Scotland, and the Netherlands, and the Puritans in England and the New England colonies in America—sought to outlaw Christmas entirely on the grounds that it was really a pagan celebration without any basis in the Bible. Others, including the Lutherans who dominated northern Germany, were comfortable with keeping Christmas in what they considered an appropriate manner. Thus, the Lutherans discouraged gift-giving on St. Nicholas' Day, but suggested that the Christ child, known in Germany as Christkindl, could bring gifts to children on Christmas instead.

In central and southern Europe, which remained predominately Catholic, the legend of St. Nicholas had never developed like it did in northern Europe, presumably because the Nativity itself became the Christian meaning for the celebration of the Winter Solstice in the fourth century, and there was never any need to characterize pagan celebrations as the Christian Feast of St. Nicholas. The practice of having the Christ child deliver gifts for children on Christmas Eve, however, proved so popular among Catholics that it remains the practice today in many nations.[20] On the other hand, in the Protestant regions of northern Europe—the very regions where the St. Nicholas tradition had been strongest because that was where the Catholic missionaries encouraged the celebration of St. Nicholas' Day in place of the pagan Yule—the populace seems to have concluded that the gift-giving practices could continue as long as the gift-giver was not actually a Catholic saint. In Germany, the solution was to replace St. Nicholas with one of the faux Nicholases, all of them generally depicted as bearded old men with soot-covered faces who dressed in long cloaks, dirty rags or furs and carried a bundle of switches with them. The popular names included Knecht Ruprecht and several dozen variations of Nicholas without the title saint.

By contrast, the populace of Holland reacted to the prohibition of St. Nicholas by developing a new character, Sinterklaas, a faux Nicholas who dressed like the saint but who the Dutch claimed was not St. Nicholas of Myra, the Catholic saint. Rather, Sinterklaas was a resident of Spain who sailed to Holland for a few weeks every year with his Moorish servant, Zwarte Piet ("Black Peter"). Sinterklaas also left gifts for children on the evening of December 5, not on December 6, effectively evading the Dutch law against the celebration of St. Nicholas' Day.[21]

Historian Jones claimed in his 1954 paper, "Knickerbocker Santa Claus," that he could not find any evidence of St. Nicholas giving gifts for children in New York prior to Irving's book in 1809. The factual premises for Jones' conclusion that Irving "made" Santa Claus were the alleged absence of St. Nicholas before 1809, the sudden interest in St. Nicholas in 1810, and the assumption that Santa Claus was nothing more than the European St. Nicholas with an American name. Each of these premises, however, is incorrect. On the first, most historians who have examined the celebration of Christmas in colonial America have concluded the European immigrants brought their existing gift-giving customs with them, and as those gift-givers evolved they eventually merged into Santa. American sociologist James Barnett, who published the first scholarly study of Christmas in America in 1954, specifically says that the Dutch who settled the island they called New Amsterdam in 1625 "brought the folk cult of St. Nicholas [who] remained the dominant figure of the midwinter celebration until the close of the next century."[22]

For English immigrants, Christmas had been personified by Father Christmas since the fifteenth century. German immigrants, the single largest group after the English and enslaved Africans, brought with them two prominent German gift-givers, Pelznickel and Christkindl, who became known as Belsnickle and Kriss Kringle on the way to Pennsylvania, and contributed much to the development of Santa Claus. Immigrants from Scandinavia, who settled in the mid–Atlantic colonies and the upper Midwest, brought with them the Yule goats, elves, and gnomes of Scandinavian folklore while Maryland, known for its Religious Tolerance Act of 1649, welcomed Christmas-loving Catholic immigrants from England, Germany, France, and Ireland. As Barnett explains in *The American Christmas*, the diverse European customs mingled in the proverbial American melting pot during the nineteenth century and the European gift-givers morphed into the figure known as Santa Claus in the United States.[23]

The final N in the NIMN history of Santa is Thomas Nast, the famed political cartoonist whose newspaper illustrations for *Harper's Weekly* between 1863 and 1886 undoubtedly helped to define and popularize the American Santa Claus. Without diminishing the contributions of Nast in creating the legend and look of Santa, however, those who credit Nast with "inventing" Santa Claus miss the fact Nast did not create his drawings of Santa out of whole cloth. Nast said in later life that his drawings of Santa were based on his boyhood memories of Pelznickel in his native Germany, but by 1863, when Nast was hired by *Harper's Weekly*, there were many depictions of Santa and his European brethren already in existence.[24]

The first depiction of Santa Claus in America was actually published almost twenty years before Nast was even born. In an 1821 children's book, *The Children's Friend: Part III, A New-Year's Present to Little Ones from Five to Twelve* (hereinafter "*The Children's Friend*"), a character named "Santeclaus" wore a tall hat and beard, rode in a sleigh pulled by a flying reindeer, and descended down the chimney to leave gifts in stockings hung by the fireplace mantel.[25] That depiction by artist Arthur J. Stansbury, original and unique to the American Santa in many ways, appears to have been borrowed by Clement Moore in his 1822 poem "A Visit from St. Nicholas," better known as "The Night Before Christmas."[26] If the writing in *The Children's Friend* had been more joyful, it could easily have been publisher William B. Gilley and artist Stansbury who were acclaimed as the fathers of the American Santa Claus.[27]

Between 1821 and 1863, when Nast began drawing Santa for *Harper's Weekly*, artists and illustrators in England, Germany, the Netherlands, and the United States began producing illustrations of a Christmas gift-giver with a long white beard known as Father Christmas, Herr Winter, Weihnachtsmann, St. Nicholas, Sinterklaas, and Santa Claus, and each of these figures contributed something to the ultimate image of Santa. In England, the look of Father Christmas as the jolly, drunken leader of English Christmas parties with wild hair and a long, white, stringy beard was well established by 1850. In Germany, the Weihnachtsmann ("Christmas man"), a stooped, bearded old man with a dirty hooded cloak, often carrying a Christmas tree or a bundle of switches, was fixed in drawings published in 1847. In the Netherlands, artists had been depicting Sinterklaas or Sint Niklaas riding a horse while throwing gifts to children since 1750, and in 1850 a Dutch teacher named Jan Schenkman published a children's book, *Sint Nikolaas en zijn Knecht* ("St. Nicholas and his Servant"), which told the story of Sinterklaas, depicted with a long white beard and bishop's robes and miter, and his servant, a dark skinned young man that served as the model for Black Peter.[28] In 1871, Swedish artist Jenny Nystrom began to publish drawings of the Scandinavian Yule elves and gnomes, Julenisse and Jultomten, who wore red pointed hats, long white beards, and warm winter coats—in effect, pint-sized versions of the American Santa. Finally, as detailed in Chapter 20, a number of artists in the United States took a crack at illustrating St. Nicholas, Kriss Kringle, and Santa Claus in the 1840s and '50s, ultimately producing several images in the late 1850s and early 1860s that were quite arguably as close to the final product as Nast's Santa Claus.

What Thomas Nast had which other artists did not have was a lucrative stage for his work, *Harper's Weekly*, which had a circulation of two hundred thousand and published his drawings of Santa or other Christmas scenes every December from 1863 through 1886. Nast made important contributions to the story and look of the Christmas gift-giver, but Nast's Santa was hardly the finished product. Indeed, the Lilliputian Santas he drew during the 1860s were quite arguably a step backward from the Santas produced by other artists between 1857 and 1863. Nast abandoned the "get small" approach in the 1870s but the iconic Nast Santa did not emerge until 1881. By the 1890s, depictions of Santa became so numerous they created a "family resemblance" in which no individual attribute or artist stood out, thus creating "a collection of Santas."

The contributing sources to this collective concept of Santa included the "real life" Santas who began to appear in costume at department stores in the last decade of the nineteenth century, as well as the German, English, and American artists who created numerous depictions of Santa during the Victorian era for Christmas "scraps," candy containers, Christmas cards, and ornaments. During the first three decades of the twentieth century, commercial illustrators Norman Rockwell, J.S. Leyendecker and Haddon Sundblom—who, like Nast, found a large audience in the widely-circulated weekly *The Saturday Evening Post*, or, for Sundblom, thirty years of soft-drink advertisements—polished the look of the American Santa.

3

The Celebration
of Christmas Before Christ

The Original Reason for the Season: Early Man's Celebration of the Winter Solstice

To tell the history of Santa Claus, we must go back thousands of years before the birth of Christ. While there are no written records of events that occurred five thousand years ago, we can infer how ancient man reacted to the Winter Solstice from what we know about the physical world he inhabited. Today, most of us understand the basic scientific principles that control the seasons on earth. Because of the angle at which the earth rotates around the sun, the amount of sunlight in the northern hemisphere decreases every day between June 21 and December 21 (using the Gregorian calendar adopted in 1582) and increases every day between December 21 and June 21. Thus, December 21, the Winter Solstice, is the shortest day of the year while June 21, the Summer Solstice, is the longest.

We now understand the change of seasons is both normal and necessary for much of the natural environment around us. We also have modern conveniences with which we can light the darkness and heat the cold, and we no longer need give any special thought to stocking up on food for the winter. Despite these advantages, the depth of winter is still associated with conditions like depression and seasonal affective disorder that reveal the importance of sunlight to our psyches. For people living in the northernmost regions of our planet, where the Winter Solstice is not a short day but the middle of a month-long night, life is even more challenging. In *Christmas: A Candid History*, Forbes, seeking to understand the psychological pressures facing early man, explains that if you go to northern Alaska in midwinter you will find that even with the modern advantages of indoor lighting, heating, and multiple sources of entertainment, this is "when depression settles in, when alcoholism and other forms of chemical dependency are at their worst, and when incidents of domestic violence soar."[1]

Now, consider the circumstances facing early man. Without any understanding of the astronomical explanations underlying the change of seasons, and no assurance the sun would return, the period preceding the Winter Solstice was fraught with terror. The sun appeared to be slowly disappearing, temperatures plunged, snow fell, most plant life died, or appeared to do so, wild animals became scarce, and there was not enough feed to keep domesticated animals alive over the winter. These conditions threatened man's very existence unless he was somehow able to establish adequate shelter and a sufficient store of food to carry him through to spring.

Moreover, even if early man could otherwise survive physically, he had to deal with what he believed to be an assortment of unseen gods, goblins, gnomes, elves, and assorted evil spirits. Anyone who has spent a night in the total darkness of wilderness understands that silence magnifies sound, and every howl of a predator, shriek of the wind, or crack of a branch brings fears of unseen evil things. The freezing temperatures of midwinter made things that much worse because of the difficulty in reaching deep sleep in bitter cold. Thus, as explained by folklore expert Tristram P. Coffin in *The Book of Christmas Folklore*, "[t]his was the time when sympathetic magic and ritual were called upon to guarantee the return of 'light' and growth, when scapegoats were slain or expelled to purge barrenness and evil from the land, when the boar, symbol of regeneration, was sacrificed and consumed."[2]

Early man surely knew that as far back as the most elderly among them could remember, the sun began to return each year following what we call the Winter Solstice. The solstice could be identified by placing a stick upright in the ground and observing that the shadow of the stick did not get longer or shorter. Once the shadow began to move again, the point where there was no movement could be identified as the Winter Solstice. By counting the days between the Winter Solstices from one year to another, early man could determine, and could pass on the knowledge, that the sun would reverse course every 365 days, and following the Winter Solstice the amount of sunlight would begin to increase. Without any understanding of the astronomical events that created the seasons, early man generally attributed the changes to one or more gods, and hoped each year he could curry sufficient favor to convince the sun to return once again. As John Matthews explains in *The Winter Solstice: The Sacred Traditions of Christmas*, "[s]ometimes it was enough to celebrate the rebirth of the sun, at others it was necessary to make sacrifices to the god (or goddess) who was the source of its light, to ensure that he (or she) returned…. Virtually every festival that was celebrated, or which still takes place today, owes something to these ancient celebrations of the year's turning."[3]

While one could roughly determine the date of the Winter Solstice by monitoring the length of the shadow cast by a stick in the ground, ancient ruins show that early man was exceptionally focused on the ability to predict precisely the date of the Winter Solstice because the arrival of the Winter Solstice was a life or death matter. It determined the life or death of the sun god, a figure who was born on the Winter Solstice, died on the Winter Solstice, and returned to life each year on the Winter Solstice, but it also determined the life or death of man himself if the sun did not return.

Most historians, archeologists, anthropologists, and folklorists believe there were prehistoric celebrations of the Winter Solstice, led by tribal priests, thousands of years before the well-documented midwinter celebrations in Rome.[4] There are no written descriptions but the celebrants left behind archeological artifacts, such as the ruins of Stonehenge, which are impossible to miss. In *From Stonehenge to Santa*, English archeologist Frodsham describes how the ruins at Stonehenge, Newgrange, and similar prehistoric sites were constructed almost five thousand years ago, based on a detailed understanding of the Winter Solstice.[5] The physical remains of Stonehenge in Britain and Newgrange in Ireland show that the primary axes of each of these monuments were aligned on a sight-line pointing to the sunrise on the Winter Solstice (Newgrange) or the sunset (Stonehenge). For example, at Newgrange in Ireland "for a week before and after the solstice the rising sun sends a beam of light through a narrow slot and down an 80-foot passageway, illuminating the inner chamber for about 17 minutes."[6] Given the massive size of the stones assembled at Stonehenge, the distance they were moved to create the structure, and the precision with which they were aligned by primitive tools, the importance of midwinter to these societies cannot be doubted. Frodsham also cites archeological evidence of large feasts at these sites that likely occurred during midwinter festivals. Because the Winter Solstice was just as important in other parts of northern Europe as it was in England and Ireland, it is reasonable to assume the native peoples held similar midwinter ceremonies in other regions of Europe.

In explaining why early man celebrated the Winter Solstice, Forbes observes that "[e]ven before studying the history and anthropology of early cultures, we could guess what human beings might do to cope with these realities of winter."[7] With mock naiveté, Forbes writes that "[a] great idea would be to organize a big, blowout, midwinter party."[8]

> First of all, it would have to be a festival of lights, pushing back the oppressive darkness, featuring candles and torches and burning logs. It would also make sense to highlight evergreens as symbols or decorations, because the greenery could serve as signs of life in the midst of apparent death. We might look for other plants that stay green and, against the norm, even bear fruit in the middle of winter, like holly, or mistletoe. Of course, there would be feasting and drinking, probably to excess, as there is at almost any party.[9]

This passage, of course, was intended to describe the midwinter ceremonies Forbes knew actually occurred throughout Europe.

Much of our understanding of the early midwinter celebrations comes from British folklore expert Clement A. Miles, who in 1912 published the groundbreaking study *Christmas in Ritual and Tradition, Christian and Pagan*.[10] In that treatise, whose very title emphasizes that Christmas was a combination of Christian and pagan practices, Miles describes the importance of holidays like the Winter Solstice without regard to the society's particular religious beliefs.

> It has been an instinct in nearly all peoples, savage or civilized, to set aside certain days for special ceremonial observances, attended by outward rejoicing. This tendency … answers to man's need to lift himself above the commonplace and the everyday, to escape from the leaden weight of monotony that oppresses him.… It is difficult to be religious, impossible to be merry, at every moment of life, and festivals are as sunlit peaks, testifying, above dark valleys, to the eternal radiance.[11]

In discussing whether the pagan origins of these traditions undermine the religious importance of the Nativity for Christians, Methodist minister Forbes, seeking to protect the joyful celebration of Christmas from allegations of paganism, asserts that "many persons today are surprised to realize much of what they love about the Christmas season is not really Christmas at all."[12]

> We love the lights, the evergreen decorations, the music and the food, the chance to get together with family and friends, and the special feeling of warmth that comes with the festivities. Yet all of these features have no necessary connection with a story of a baby Jesus in a manger. Instead they are the predictable characteristics of midwinter festivities.
>
> This is what it means when some people say that Christmas has pagan roots. In essence, "pagan" is a word that means non–Christian, or in this case, pre–Christian. And yes, it is true that midwinter celebrations existed throughout Europe before Jesus was born and before the Christian religion developed. Seeing a contest between "pagan" religions and Christianity, some Christians try to protect themselves from any association with rival religions. Another way to view it is that a midwinter celebration is simply an understandable human impulse: to help people survive winter. If a culture did not already have such a celebration, people would make one up. Participating in a midwinter festival is an indication of our common humanity, across many cultures and many religions. It just makes sense as a human coping mechanism.[13]

A better way to phrase Forbes' explanation that "the lights, the evergreen decorations, the music and the food" are not really Christmas is to explain that Christmas is only one day of the Christmas season, a series of secular celebrations of the Winter Solstice over the course of a month. Even this explanation, however, does not capture how truly universal the celebration of the Winter Solstice really is. In his 1884 history, *Christmastide: Its History, Festivities and Carols*, historian William Sandys tells us that the Winter Solstice celebrations occurred not only in Europe, where the Roman Saturnalia, the Germanic Yule, and the Slavic Korochun left large footprints on our modern Christmas celebrations, but in the Americas, the Mediterranean, Africa, and Asia.[14] The global nature of these celebrations confirms that the European midwinter celebrations, and, thus, the Christmas season itself, is a universal festival of humankind and not the province of any particular nation or religion.

The Prehistorical Observances of the Winter Solstice Throughout Europe

When he suggested early man might consider a big, blow-out party on the Winter Solstice, Forbes knew such celebrations had occurred throughout Europe well before the birth of Christ. The centerpiece of these ceremonies was typically the death and rebirth

of whatever deity the culture identified as the sun god or, in some cases, the death and rebirth of the monarch. Although isolated by geography and time, these festivals have so many traits in common that when viewed collectively one must conclude that the festivals were, as Forbes suggests, natural human reactions to the gradual disappearance of the sun before the Winter Solstice.

Most anthropologists and archeologists believe that prehistoric man in Europe conducted Winter Solstice rituals even earlier than the construction of Stonehenge almost five thousand years ago.[15] In these rituals, some authors have theorized, tribal priests known as shamans wore animal skins, masks, and horns to reenact the death and rebirth of the "Wild Man," a "beast god who reminded people of the cyclical nature of the world," playing out the themes of death and rebirth.[16] The story of the Wild Man cannot be elevated to the level of "fact," as compared to "theory," but has potential significance for understanding both the celebration of the Winter Solstice and the "prehistory" of the European predecessors to Santa.

Some authors assert that Santa is actually a distant descendant of the prehis-

In *Santa Claus: Last of the Wild Men*, Phyllis Siefker argues that Santa Claus was a descendent of prehistorical tribal priests who dressed as a character Siefker calls the Wild Man.

toric priests who led observances of the Winter Solstice. Archaeologist Frodsham says that "Stonehenge and Santa may appear to have little in common" but "both owe their existence largely to the Winter Solstice, and today's Santa may well embody several characteristics of the priests who officiated at Stonehenge more than 4,000 years ago."[17] In *The Winter Solstice: The Sacred Traditions of Christmas*, folklorist John Matthews writes that "Santa really derives from an even earlier set of figures—the shamans who were the first priests and magicians of the human race."[18] In "The Many Faces of Santa Claus," Melicent D'Amore asserts that "Father Christmas' roots predate Christianity to Norse mythology. Pagan British customs called for the elder man of a community to dress in fur and visit each home as the Old Man Winter. Fashioned by the Druids, Father Christmas was portrayed wearing a fur-lined hood and cloak."[19] Even without written records establishing that tribal leaders played the role of the Wild Man, we can safely assume that the themes of death and rebirth so obviously suggested by the Winter Solstice dominated the midwinter rituals of early man.

Establishing a direct connection between the Wild Man and Santa is more difficult. In *Santa Claus: Last of the Wild Men*, author Phyllis Siefker provides an extended explanation of this theory, concluding that our modern Santa Claus is a descendent of a prehistoric "beast god," presumably meaning a costumed tribal leader playing the role of the beast-god she calls the Wild Man. Addressing the conventional wisdom that Santa Claus was merely an Americanization of St. Nicholas of Myra, she asserts that in Clement C. Moore's "A Visit from St. Nicholas," St. Nick is described as "a sooty, bearded man, mounting to the sky like a hurricane, being pulled by exotic arctic stags with names that spoke of the elemental powers of the earth and sky, not the benign, structured world of sainthood."[20] Accordingly, Siefker concludes, "Santa is an Americanization, all right, but not of a Catholic saint. Instead, Santa's forefather was the very unsaintlike Furry Nicholas, a major player in winter festivals that have been transplanted from Europe to the rugged backwoods of Pennsylvania."[21]

Siefker's explanation is at least partially correct but it is incomplete. "Furry Nicholas" can only mean Belsnickle, the American name for Pelznickel, one of the secular gift-givers who replaced the Catholic St. Nicholas as Yule gift-giver following the Protestant Reformation. St. Nicholas, in turn, was a Christian replacement for Odin, the Germanic god who served as Yule gift-giver before the arrival of Christianity. Thus, identifying Santa as a descendant of Pelznickel makes him a descendant of Odin as well. In explaining that Santa's roots lie in pagan mythology, however, it is not uncommon for scholars to skip a step or two. For example, in "The Evolution of Santa Claus," a 1907 article by Thomas Purcell in the *San Francisco Daily Times*, Purcell tells us Santa Claus actually began life in the pagan festivals of the Romans, Greeks, and Saxons.[22]

> Gallant old Father Christmas or Santa Claus, as he is more familiarly known, presiding genius of the Yuletide, has quite an interesting life's history from which we learn that even in his case there is much to bear out the theory of evolution. He began life as the god of plenty in the dim, mystical past bringing cheer to the old Romans. He was then known as Saturn…. About the same period the Greeks honored him as Kronos in the dreary December days in hopeful anticipation of a rejuvenated earth.
>
> He was known also to the Pagan Briton, by whom he was celebrated under the oak tree, while the hardy Saxons knew him as a double personality—Woden and Thor—and they feasted in honor of those gods at the Winter Solstice.[23]

While there is little doubt that Santa's ancestors include the pagan gods in Greek, Roman, and Teutonic mythology, constructing a defensible history of Santa requires a good deal more detail on the path taken from Saturn to Santa. The path Siefker suggests from the Wild Man to Santa Claus runs through Germany's Knecht Ruprecht. We know "knecht" means "servant," but Ruprecht is otherwise a mysterious figure from German mythology whose history, name, physical appearance, and function are all subject to disputed explanations, and whose connection to Yule has never been clear. Indeed, in *Santa Claus: Last of the Wild Men* Siefker herself provides two different descriptions of him. In the first, Siefker describes him as one of the "evil helpers" of St. Nicholas, "a black, hairy, horned, cannibalistic stick-carrying nightmare. His role and character are of unmitigated evil, the ultimate horror that could befall children who had been remiss in learning their prayers and doing their lessons. He was hell on earth. When a holy figure was present, this was the old Wild Man's role, servant and Satanic foil."[24]

In the second version, Siefker describes a figure who looks much more like Pelznickel and the other faux Nicholases.[25]

> In most German communities, Ruprecht appeared as a slightly frightening but not totally hellish figure. In goatskins, this bag-carrying bearded figure went about examining Teutonic children. If they could not say … prayers perfectly, he punished them with his whip or bundle of sticks; if they performed well, he gave them apples, nuts, and gingerbreads. He was both the rewarder and punisher and contained within himself both the blessedness of forgiveness and the terror of the unknown. He was sometimes comical, rough, and crude but not entirely Satanic. He was generally a strange, bearded figure who carried forgiveness and condemnation in his little sack of goodies and sticks.[26]

In other words, according to Siefker, Ruprecht could play two roles—that of the Satanic evil helper who accompanied St. Nicholas to perform the unsaintly duties Nicholas could not, and that of the "faux Nicholas," a frightening but still human figure who visited in lieu of St. Nicholas. In the "slightly frightening" role, Siefker says, Knecht Ruprecht "was known" as Pelznickel, Aschenklas, RuClas, Joseph Claus, Claws, and Bullerklas—all names of faux Nicholases who appeared when St. Nicholas lost his job in the Protestant regions of Germany following the Reformation. The physical appearance of these figures, Siefker says, "followed a basic pattern. All were dressed in fur or tatters to simulate hair; all had blackened faces or grotesque masks; and all carried bells and whips, sticks and sacks,"[27] a description consistent with other literature on the subject. In short, the faux Nicholases assumed the role of a secular gift-giver *and* disciplinarian whereas the virtuous saint performed only good works and required a satanic assistant to do his dirty work.

Unfortunately, Siefker's explanation that the prehistoric Wild Man became Knecht Ruprecht does not really help us understand anything more than we already know. More specifically, she never adequately explains how the Wild Man, a character played by the tribal priest thousands of years ago, became Knecht Ruprecht in any of his incarnations, nor, for that matter, does she explain Knecht Ruprecht's real identity. She also fails to address the connection, if any, between the Wild Man, Knecht Ruprecht, and the pagan gods such as Odin, who served as midwinter gift-givers before the appearance of St. Nicholas.

There are no clear answers to many of these questions, which raise issues of cultural anthropology, mythology and folklore. Although the next four chapters will attempt to shed as much light as possible on these subjects, the reader should expect a resolution similar to that of paleoanthropologists studying human evolution. Following the discovery of *homo erectus*, an early hominid originally known as Java Man, in 1891, scientists discovered more than a dozen different species that might have represented the development of primates into modern man, *homo sapiens*, and debate raged over which were species that developed parallel to *homo sapiens* but died out; which were species that evolved into *homo sapiens*; which were species that may have "merged" into *homo sapiens*; and which were simply mistaken identification of fossils that had no role in the development of man. With the arrival of DNA testing, paleoanthropologists concluded that one of the presumptively independent species, Neanderthal Man, bred with *homo sapiens*, and that 1 to 4 percent of *homo sapiens* DNA comes from Neanderthal Man.

With Santa, there are no fossil records to guide us, much less any "Santa DNA" to analyze. As with the development of modern man, however, we should assume there is no consistent pattern of development. Some of the prehistoric celebrants of the Winter Solstice, such as the Wild Man, may have disappeared without influencing later celebrants. Some, like Sinterklaas and the original European St. Nicholas, effectively merged into a single character with the look of one and the name of the other. Some, like England's Father Christmas and Russia's Ded Moroz, developed simultaneously but largely independently of other gift-givers. And some, such as Germany's Pelznickel, evolved quite directly into other characters (Belsnickle, Kriss Kringle and, ultimately, the American Santa Claus). What we can say for sure, however, is that Santa Claus was not invented by a half-dozen wealthy white men in the comfy confines of the New-York Historical Society during the early nineteenth century.

The Midwinter Celebration of Saturnalia in Rome

The Roman Saturnalia is critical in understanding how the pagan celebrations of midwinter became the Christian celebration of Christ's birth because the Roman midwinter festival was converted directly into the holiday we call Christmas during the middle of the fourth century after Roman Emperor Constantine adopted Christianity as the official religion of the Roman Empire. Thus, hundreds of years before it was declared the Feast of the Nativity by a Roman emperor in the fourth century AD Christmas entered the world as a pagan harvest festival, a pagan New Year's celebration, and a birthday party for several different pagan sun gods, all of whom were believed to have been born on December 25, Other than replacing the Sun God with the Son of God, the nature of the celebration did not really change much.

Saturnalia was established as a public holiday by the Roman Empire about five centuries before the birth of Christ. The festival began on December 17 under the Julian calendar, and, depending on the emperor in power, lasted between three and seven days. "No one worked during this period, except those whose help was needed to provide food for the lavish feasts," Forbes writes.[28] "Friends visited each other from home to home and also joined in boisterous street processions. Houses, great halls, and streets were decorated with laurel, green trees, and shrubs, illuminated by candles and lamps. Major bonfires were lit at high ground where many citizens could see them. People exchanged small gifts, such as wax candles, wax fruit, and clay dolls."[29] Overeating and drunkenness were the rule, and a sober person the exception, while gambling and dice-playing, normally prohibited, were permitted for all, even slaves. Cross-dressing was common, as was wearing masks and parading in animal skins or other costumes. Entertainment included the performance of plays illustrating the death and rebirth of a god or king who represented the sun, as well as "fertility rites," the nature of which is generally not described in much detail. If this sounds like Las Vegas on New Year's Eve, it probably was.

During Saturnalia, the Romans dispensed with many of the normal rules of propriety. Lucian of Samosota, an early Greek writer commenting on Roman culture and society, wrote a dialogue in which the Roman god Saturn explained that a mock king would be chosen by lot to preside over the Saturnalia, and, by becoming king, "you not only escape silly orders but can give them yourself, telling one man to shout out something disgraceful about himself, another to dance naked, pick up the flute-girl, and carry her three times around the house."[30] The duties of the Saturnalian king seem to be a transition of sorts from the Mediterranean and Middle East festivals, where the job of the mock king was literally to die in place of the real king, to the Medieval customs involving the Lord of Misrule or the Abbott of Unreason, where the job of the mock king was more like that of fool or court jester.

While some of the descriptions of Saturnalia describe behavior that, on its face, might offend certain sensibilities, the celebration takes on a different light when the "laws" of Saturnalia set by the Priest of Chronus are taken into account:

> All business, be it public or private, is forbidden during the feast days, save such as tends to sport and solace and delight. Let none follow their avocations saving cooks and bakers.
> All men shall be equal, slave and free, rich and poor, one with another.
> Anger, resentment, threats are contrary to law.
> No discourse shall be either composed or delivered, except that it be witty and lusty, conducing to mirth and jollity.[31]

Some have described a practice of social inversion in which the slaves assumed the roles of the owners, and vice versa, but Lucian's description depicts more of a rule of equality:

> Each man shall take the couch where he happens to be.
> Rank, family, or wealth shall have little influence on privilege.
> All shall drink the same wine, and neither stomach trouble nor headache shall give the rich man an excuse for being the only one to drink the better quality.
> All shall have their meat on equal terms. The waiters shall not show favor to anyone.
> Neither are large portions to be placed before one and tiny ones before another, nor a ham for one and a pig's jaw for another—all must be treated equally.
> When a rich man gives a banquet to his servants, his friends shall aid him in waiting on them.[32]

Shortly after the end of Saturnalia, on December 25—the date of the astronomical Winter Solstice under the Julian calendar when it was adopted in 45 BC—Romans would celebrate the birth of the Roman sun god, Sol Invictus, and, by the third century, the Persian sun god, Mithras. The third holiday, Kalends, was essentially a New Year's party lasting up to five days and involving many of the same activities—or, some would say, excesses—as Saturnalia (or, in fairness, Las Vegas on New Year's Eve). In a passage that seems designed to rebut the claim that our modern Christmas season has become too expensive and too commercial, fourth-century pagan Libanius of Antioch described Kalends as follows:

> The festival of the Kalends is celebrated everywhere as far as the limits of the Roman Empire extend.... Everywhere may be seen carousals and well-laden tables; luxurious abundance is found in the houses of the rich, but also in the houses of the poor better food than usual is put upon the table. The impulse to spend seizes everyone. He who the whole year through has taken pleasure in saving and piling up his pence, becomes suddenly extravagant. He who erstwhile was accustomed and preferred to live poorly, now at this feast enjoys himself as much as his means will allow....
> People are not only generous towards themselves, but also towards their fellow-men. A stream of presents pours itself out on all sides.... It may justly be said that it is the fairest time of the year.... The Kalends festival banishes all that is connected with toil, and allows men to give themselves up to undisturbed enjoyment. From the minds of young people, it removes two kinds of dread: the dread of the schoolmaster and the dread of the stern pedagogue. It also allows [slaves], so far as possible, to breathe the air of freedom.... Another great quality of the festival is that it teaches men not to hold too fast to their money, but to part with it and let it pass into other hands.[33]

One aspect of Saturnalia worth further evaluation is the practice of masters serving the servants, providing at least a temporary elimination of distinctions based on class and wealth. These practices were repeated in different forms in the developing celebrations of Christmas throughout Europe. For example, the practice of nobles in England holding "open house" during the Christmas season is often viewed as the precedent for Christmas charity as espoused by Charles Dickens in *A Christmas Carol.* Similar examples of the wealthy, or at least the wealthier, providing token benefits for the poor appear in the practices of mumming or wassailing, in which the young or poor went door-to-door, offering carols in exchange for food and drink—practices found in the Christmas traditions of Europe, Russia, and America two thousand years later.

In *The Battle for Christmas*, historian Nissenbaum astutely observes that the "charitable" aspects of such celebrations were not the one-way streets they may appear to be, and the practices were likely more beneficial to the upper classes than admitted.[34] By temporarily demonstrating their willingness to socialize as equals, or actually to reverse roles, and by allowing the underclasses to "blow off steam," the upper classes realized the long-term benefit of reducing the class-based resentment that inevitably occurred when people have unequal roles in society. These temporary exceptions to the normal practices, however, while acting as a steam valve for the lower classes, simultaneously re-enforced the class distinctions, emphasizing their existence because they were being suspended only temporarily.

While the similarities between Saturnalia and Christmas are obvious, what may not be so obvious is the resemblance between Santa and Saturn, the Roman god honored during

The most significant pagan Winter Solstice celebration, Saturnalia, honored the Roman God Saturn. His flying sleigh, pulled by two serpents, and his beard and hat created a strong resemblance to Santa.

Saturnalia. Saturn was depicted as an old man with long white hair and a beard who rode through the air on a chariot pulled by two winged serpents. The combination of Saturn's appearance, clothing, and chariot highlights the similarity between the two. Moreover, as students of mythology may recall, most of the Roman gods were borrowed from the Greek pantheon. The Greek god of wine making was Silenus, a god who also bears a clear resemblance to Santa and rode a chariot pulled by exotic beasts. In "The Evolution of Christmas," William S. Walsh observes that "all the genial traits of Silenus, save only that of drunkenness, are reproduced in Santa Klaus, the jolly pagan who is to-day the personification of Christmas."[35]

The fact that two mythical figures look alike could be coincidence and does not necessarily mean one was the historical descendant of the other. The question is whether one can establish a link between the early European gods and the Germanic gods—in particular, Odin, who most historians believe served as the model for St. Nicholas. In his 1953 study, *4000 Years of Christmas*, anthropologist Earl Count tells us the original New Year's celebration occurred in Mesopotamia where the Tigris and the Euphrates met, at the proverbial cradle of civilization, some four thousand years ago.[36] Part of modern-day Iraq, Mesopotamia was known successively as Babylonia and Persia, both of which had similar New Year's festivals. The celebrations in Mesopotamia, like those in Egypt and Greece, were springtime New Year's ceremonies. The survival of crops each year was dependent on sufficient rain to cause the overflow of the Tigris–Euphrates river system in Persia and the Nile in Egypt, and the ceremonies appealed to the gods for water rather than sunlight. Nonetheless, they

Most of the pre–Christian New Year's or Midwinter celebrations honored a pagan sun god. In the earliest recorded ceremonies, the Mesopotamian sun gods, An and Enka, bore a distinct resemblance to Santa.

all included a number of practices and themes seen in the Roman, Germanic, and Slavic Winter Solstice ceremonies.[37]

The Mesopotamian festival, according to Count, reenacted the creation of the world by the god-king known as Marduk. Because the king died in the creation of the earth, the participants would select a mock king to play that role during the reenactment. "He was given all the homage and indulgence which is the king's right," Count writes, but as soon as the mock reign was over "he was stripped of his kingly trappings and slain in the place of the real king."[38] The themes of death and rebirth, and the selection of a mock king to preside during the ceremonies, were repeated in the Roman, Germanic, and Slavic midwinter festivals and, ultimately, became part of the Christmas traditions in England, where mummers would present Christmas plays in which the plot revolved around the death and rebirth of St. George. Other features of the Mesopotamian New Year's festival that became standard parts of the European midwinter festivals were feasting, drinking, dancing, costumes, giving presents, lights, singing, and a general spirit of merry making.

Anthropologist Count suggests that the similarities in midwinter ceremonies may have been attributable to geographic factors. From Mesopotamia, he says, the festival traveled west to Egypt, northwest to Greece and Rome, and north along the Danube River to what is now Germany. The travel to Germany is important, in Count's opinion, because it means the Germanic Yule festival may have developed simultaneously with the Rome Saturnalia rather than afterwards, as is usually assumed.[39] The chief Mesopotamian gods, An and his son Enki, look much like Saturn and Silenus, with long beards, robes and headdresses that in ancient stone relics looks much like Santa's hat. If one accepts Count's premise, the festival and gods of Mesopotamia could have traveled directly from Mesopotamia to both Rome and northern Germany.

Another explanation—one that does not directly conflict with Count's geographic analysis—is the universal nature of folk traditions. In *Slavic Folklore: A Handbook*, Professor Natalie Kononenko of the University of Alberta explains why the "universality of folklore" makes it difficult to assign a specific national origin to one folktale or another:

> Folklore deals with basic human issues: the longing of family members for each other—and the conflicts between them, the fear of the unknown—and the desire to explore new realms and new possibilities, to mention such a few basic drives. Because certain experiences are characteristic of the human condition, no matter what language people speak, there are commonalities to all folk traditions. Jacob and Wilhelm Grimm, the collectors of … the so-called *Grimm's' Fairytales*, noticed this when they expanded their work to folktales beyond Germany. As they encountered materials from other traditions, they found that story lines … existed not only in Germany but also in French, English, Russian and even Sanskrit.[40]

Whether or not one can directly connect the earlier gods of Mesopotamia or Rome to Odin, there is a great similarity between them. What they all have in common is that they are older men with white hair and a long white beard, seated on a throne or sleigh, dressed in a long cloak or gown, wearing a tall, floppy hat, and carrying a staff. While these details might not be enough to produce an FBI Most Wanted poster, most people will be struck by the similarity between the Mesopotamian, Roman, Germanic, and Slavic gods, the European gift-givers such as St. Nicholas, Father Christmas, Weihnachtsmann, Ded Moroz and Sinterklaas, and the American Santa Claus.

This appearance is virtually identical to that of many other fictional characters with magical powers. For example, the long robes, flowing white hair and beards, long staffs, and floppy hats are shared by five well-known wizards in literature of the twentieth century:

Merlin in *The Sword in the Stone,* Walt Disney's animation of the King Arthur legend (as well as several versions of *Camelot*); Gandalf the Grey and Saruman the White in J.R.R. Tolkien's *Hobbit* and *Lord of the Rings*; Albus Dumbledore in J.K. Rowling's *Harry Potter* series; and Belgarath the Sorcerer of David Eddings' *Belgariad* series. Psychologists and folklorists could probably explain it better, but one can surmise that the common features used to depict the various gods, wizards, and permutations of Santa might be hard-wired into our collective consciousness, where these features impart age, wisdom, kindness, and magical powers. Santa is a wizard with all of these characteristics, and it is not surprising he should look like one.

4

The Establishment of the Nativity
of Jesus as a Christian Holiday

For the first 350 years following the birth of Christ, the number of Christians grew geo-metrically, from a half million people at the end of the first century to roughly ten million during the fourth century—but there was no celebration, public or private, of Christ's birth. This may have been because no one knew exactly when his birth occurred. The primary re-cord of the life of Jesus, the Bible, says very little about his birth, and nothing about the date or time in which it occurred except that shepherds were tending their flocks in the field, a fact most experts believe indicates the birth must have occurred in the spring, when sheep were released to graze, and not in the dead of winter.

Even if the date were known, however, early Christian practices would have precluded a "birthday party." Some early Christians questioned whether Christ was actually human, and, thus, whether he could even have had a birthday in the traditional sense. Others ob-jected in principle to honoring the birth of Jesus. According to Bowler, "[e]arly Christians thought that marking the birthday of their Lord was not unlike the way pagans honored their rulers."[1] The consistent practice of early Christians, on the other hand, was to celebrate a saint on the date of his or her death, and the most holy days in Christianity were the cru-cifixion and resurrection of Jesus. For example, Origen, a prominent Christian theologian who lived from AD 185 to 254, wrote "not one from all the saints is found to have celebrated a festive day or a great feast on the day of his birth. No one is found to have had joy on the day of the birth of his son or daughter. Only sinners rejoice over this kind of birthday."[2]

In AD 313, Roman Emperor Constantine issued the Edict of Milan, legalizing the prac-tice of Christianity, and in AD 325, he called the First Council of Nicaea, a meeting of Chris-tian bishops throughout the empire designed to resolve differences in Christian practice and theology.[3] Historical records show that a Nicholas of Myra attended some, but not all, of these meetings but do not reflect that he did or said anything, and there is no other contemporaneous documentation of his existence.[4] The first mention of the Feast of the Nativity appeared in a Roman Catholic Church document called the Philocalian calendar in AD 353, which listed December 25 as the day of Christ's birth. Parts of the calendar dated from AD 336, however, leaving open the possibility that Constantine decided the church would celebrate the birth of Christ on December 25 shortly before he publicly announced his baptism as a Christian.

During this period, Christians were divided into a Western Church, which was head-quartered in Rome and became the Roman Catholic Church, and an Eastern Church, which was headquartered in Greece and became the Eastern Orthodox Church. Both churches traced their lineage to one or more of the original Twelve Apostles. During the early fourth century, the Eastern Church began to celebrate a holy day called Epiphany on January 6. Epiphany comes from a Greek word meaning "manifestation" or "showing forth," and in this context Epiphany referred to how Jesus was revealed or made manifest to the world as the son of God—an event that some believed was the baptism of Christ and others believed was the visit of the Magi.

The most widely accepted theory is that eastern Christians developed the Epiphany celebration on January 6 to compete with an Egyptian religious festival celebrating the birthday of Osiris, an Egyptian sun god, on the same date. When the Western Church recognized December 25 as the birth date of Christ, it initially met resistance from the Eastern Church, which complained it already had a commemoration of the birth of Christ on January 6. To resolve the dispute, the autonomous, regional divisions of the Eastern Church agreed to celebrate the birth of Christ on December 25 if the Western Church would celebrate the Feast of the Epiphany on January 6.[5] Among Roman Catholics, Epiphany is often called the Feast of the Magi or the Three Kings. Although there is no discussion in the Bible of the wise men except for the three gifts they brought, gold, frankincense and myrrh, Catholic tradition says there were three of them, Melchior, Caspar and Balthazar, and since AD 500 has given them the status of kings in light of Old Testament prophecies that the messiah would be worshiped by kings.[6] In Spain and most Latin American nations, the Three Kings play the role of Santa, arriving during the night before Three Kings Day and providing gifts to children while they are sleeping in honor of the gifts the Magi brought to the newborn Christ child.

There is no direct evidence proving the intent of the church in adopting December 25 as the date of Christ's birth, or even who made the decision, but most scholars share the same theory. In the essay "Putting Claus Back into Christmas," Steven D. Hales, a professor of philosophy at Bloomsburg University, emphasizes that "[i]t's not hard to see why Christians decided to overcome their initial reluctance and start coopting Roman holidays. The Roman gods were a hit with the masses and Sol Invictus was particularly popular at that time. The difficulty was that since Christianity had taken so much from other religious traditions that people kept getting Jesus confused with Sol."[7] Methodist minister Forbes writes that "[w]e have no document in which Constantine or a bishop of Rome tells us exactly why the birthday celebration of Jesus got started on December 25 but it obviously had something to do with the winter festivities already in place."[8]

Whatever the reasons, it requires no speculation to see this as a smart, probably inevitable, political decision for the Roman Empire. Indeed, failure to do it could have spelled the end of Christianity. It would have been impossible for Rome to maintain Saturnalia, Dies Natalis Solis Invictus, and Kalends as pagan festivals while promoting Christianity as the faith of the empire. The elimination of the holidays in the name of Christianity would have caused the populace to blame Christianity for the disappearance of three very popular holidays, which would have been both a political disaster and a serious impediment to converting the pagans to Christianity. "Some way or another, Christmas was started to compete with rival Roman religions, or to co-opt the winter celebrations as a way to spread Christianity, or to baptize the winter festivals with Christian meaning in an effort to limit their excesses. Most likely, it was all three."[9] In short, the Church decided to celebrate the birth of Jesus on December 25 to displace the pagan celebrations of Sol and Mithra.

By the fifth century, Christianity was firmly established in the Roman Empire, although the empire itself was not on such firm footing. Bowler writes that the establishment of Christianity "brought an end to many of the old pagan holidays, but inhabitants of the

Roman world were still able to enjoy the trappings of these midwinter festivals; observances that had accompanied Saturnalia and the Kalends were now transferred to the newer Christian holidays, Christmas and Epiphany."[10] As explained by Todd Preston, an assistant professor of Medieval Studies at Lycoming College, "Christmas, in actual practice, was never strictly about Christ. It was the grafting of a Christian holiday onto an existing non–Christian season of festivity. From the earliest incarnation of the holiday, the celebration was a balance of the Christian and non–Christian."[11] The medieval church, Preston says, would incorporate pagan elements "so long as they were not in direct opposition to the faith."[12] Thus, according to Bowler, the Roman authorities attempted to suppress "some of the more egregious behavior" such as "cross-dressing or parading about in animal skins."[13] Whether the church was actually successful in suppressing this behavior is questionable, however, because cross-dressing and wearing animal skins were still being practiced some fifteen hundred years later as part of Christmas traditions like mumming, guising, and Belsnickling.

During the sixth century, the Western and Eastern churches agreed twice to expand the duration of the Christmas celebration. In AD 567, the Council of Tours proclaimed the entire period between Christmas and Epiphany part of the Christian celebration, creating what became known as the Twelve Days of Christmas. Despite the uniform use of the phrase, there is disagreement on how to count the twelve days. "If Christmas Day is the first of the twelve days, then Twelfth Night would be on January 5, the eve of Epiphany. If December 26, the day after Christmas, is the first day, then Twelfth Night falls on January 6, the evening of Epiphany itself."[14] In western Europe and the Americas, the twelve days traditionally begin on Christmas Day, meaning January 5 is the Twelfth Night and Epiphany is not part of the Twelve Days. In eastern Europe, the twelve days traditionally start on December 26, so Epiphany is the Twelfth Day of Christmas but, oddly, the evening of January 5 is still considered the Twelfth Night.

At the Council of Tours, the Western and Eastern Churches also agreed to add a period called Advent as a time of spiritual preparation leading up to Christmas. In the Western Church, Advent begins on the Sunday closest to November 30, meaning Advent may last from twenty-two to twenty-eight days, making the entire season thirty-four to forty days. In the Eastern Church, Advent begins on November 15, creating an even longer period. Because November 11 was the feast of St. Martin of Tours, also known as Martinmas, this period became known as the "forty days of St. Martin." Thus, what began as recognition of a single day as the Feast of the Nativity in roughly AD 350 had become, by the sixth century, an Advent-Christmas-Epiphany celebration that equaled or exceeded in duration the Roman Saturnalia and the Germanic Yule.

The Catholic Church's rationale for expanding the duration of the Christmas season, and allowing the continuation of most of the pre–Christian elements of Saturnalia and Kalends, appears to have been simple pragmatism. This conclusion is reflected in a letter sent by Pope Gregory the Great in AD 601, giving instructions to Augustine, the Archbishop of Canterbury, allowing pagan celebrations by the Anglo-Saxons to continue while the church was attempting to convert the participants to Christianity. After explaining that the pagan temples should be converted into Christian churches, Pope Gregory addressed how to deal with the existing practices of sacrificing animals to the pagan gods, figures the Catholic Church treated as synonymous with Satan:

> Because they are wont to slay many oxen in sacrifices to demons, some solemnity should be put in the place of this, so that on the day of the dedication of the churches, or the nativities of the holy martyrs whose relics are placed there, they may make for themselves tabernacles of branches of trees around

those churches which have been changed from heathen temples, and may celebrate the solemnity with religious feasting. Nor let them now sacrifice animals to the Devil, but to the praise of God kill animals for their own eating, and render thanks to the Giver of all for their abundance; so that while some outward joys are retained for them, they may more readily respond to inward joys. For from obdurate minds it is undoubtedly impossible to cut off everything at once, because he who strives to ascend to the highest place rises by degrees or steps and not by leaps.[15]

Pope Gregory's letter broadened the apparent reasoning of adopting Saturnalia and its related holidays as part of the celebration of Christ's birth, including the efforts of Catholic missionaries to convert the pagans in northern Europe. As with the conversion of the Roman people, it would have been more difficult, if not impossible, to convert the diverse, polytheistic population of Europe to Christianity if doing so meant the loss of the pagan festivals and celebrations the people valued. As folklore expert Miles concluded, "[w]e see here very plainly the mind of the ecclesiastical compromiser."[16] The church could not permit sacrifice to the pagan gods, but was willing to tolerate the festivity and merrymaking that had been permitted at the pagan festivals if it was able to say the festivals had a Christian focus.

The Church's actions reflect that, as Miles explained, "ritual practices are far more enduring than the explanations given to them."[17] It is also important to recognize the pagan religions preceding Christianity were polytheistic, meaning they included multiple gods. The concept of believing in one particular god to the exclusion of others was foreign but changing or adding a god for whom a particular celebration was dedicated was not unusual. In less than a century, the Winter Solstice had been changed from the birthday of the sun god Sol to the birthday of the sun god Mithra to the birthday of the son of God, Jesus.

The average Roman citizen or potential European convert appeared not to care whether the stated purpose of the winter festivals was to honor Saturn, Sol, Mithra, Christ, or, eventually, St. Martin or St. Nicholas, so long as the festivals continued to remain "the best of times." This practice on behalf of the Catholic Church, however, meant it was much easier to Christianize Europe than it was to eliminate the pagan beliefs and rituals that existed when the Church arrived, a process made even more difficult because most of the priests were taken from a populace that had practiced the same pagan beliefs.

5

The Midwinter Celebrations of Yule in Northern Europe

The other pagan midwinter celebration whose traditions are critical to understanding the modern celebration of Christmas is Yule, known in Scandinavia as Jul, the midwinter celebration of the Germanic peoples in northern Europe, the British Isles, and Scandinavia. Unlike the Roman celebrations, for which many contemporaneous documents are available, there are relatively few records showing when and how Yule was celebrated before the arrival of Christian missionaries during the Middle Ages.

Careful historians have cautioned that the absence of records prior to the arrival of Christian missionaries, coupled with the fact that many "pagan" elements of midwinter celebrations in Rome had already been incorporated into the Christian festival of the Nativity in southern Europe and the British Isles, make it impossible to determine which Yule traditions were pagan practices that existed before the arrival of Christianity and which were Christian practices brought by the missionaries. This note of caution is undoubtedly good advice as a general matter but must be applied on an issue-by-issue basis. Given the similarity between Christmas traditions in the Middle Ages and pagan Yule traditions during the same period, it is logical to assume that any northern European traditions different than the existing Christmas traditions were pre–Christian Yule traditions. For example, it seems highly unlikely the Christian missionaries brought to Scandinavia the tradition of leaving hot porridge with a pat of melting butter out on Christmas Eve to ensure the house elves would behave well during the following year.

Yule shared the décor everyone would expect to find at a midwinter festival—bonfires, candles and evergreens as holiday adornment—which we can assume were partly to make the celebration more festive and partly to encourage the return of the sun by drawing its attention to the light and greenery for which the sun was responsible, a not very subtle reminder that everyone wanted the sun to return. The one Christmas tradition generally attributed to the pagan Yule festivities was the Yule log, the practice of lighting an extremely large log that was expected to burn for the entire twelve days.[1] Custom dictated that when Yule ended, the ashes should be spread over the fields to increase the next year's harvest, and any small pieces of the Yule log that did not end up as ashes should be retained until the following year and used to light the next Yule log, making the log into an eternal flame of sorts. Yule also included lots of mead and ale while feasting on the fruits of the fall harvest and cattle that were freshly killed because they could not be fed after snow covered the ground. A thirteenth-century Norse historian, Snorri Sturluson, who was seeking to document the story of Norway's early kings, wrote it was an "ancient custom that when sacrifice was made all farmers were to come to the temple and bring along with them the food they needed while the feast lasted."[2] While accounts of the early celebrations differed, Sturluson wrote, "what most researchers do agree upon is that ritual beer drinking featured prominently."[3] This comment makes the Nordic Yule sound more like one big fraternity party than a solemn Christian occasion—and there is probably some truth to that.

The date of Pope Gregory's letter to Augustine, circa AD 601, reflects that the British Isles were one of the earliest regions to be converted to Christianity, and, thus, its inhabitants were some of the earliest peoples outside of the Roman Empire to celebrate Christmas. In fact, some of the Celtic peoples in the British Isles adopted Christianity before Roman missionaries arrived. The use of mistletoe at Christmas almost certainly began with the Celtic Druids, who believed it had mystical powers, but it is unclear whether the Celtic or British Christians developed any other new Christmas traditions before the High Middle Ages, when a distinct British Christmas cuisine, ranging from boar's head to mince pie, began to emerge. While historians are confident the legend of King Arthur celebrating Christmas with the Knights of the Round Table following a victory at York in 581 is only a legend, records from the Early and High Middle Ages show Christmas was celebrated by many of the English monarchs, and served as the coronation date for several of them. Unlike most of northern Europe, England had a climate conducive to the celebration of Christmas on December 25 and a feudal system that facilitated celebration. Folklorist Coffin has written that after the Norman conquest of England in 1066 "Christmas became gayer than ever before; each lord kept open house; and food and drink were given to all who entered his walls during the holy season."[4]

The European continent was a different story for several reasons. First, the loss of daylight occurred earlier in northern Europe and the onslaught of winter weather was earlier and more severe.[5] The key elements for conducting a midwinter celebration were the completion of the fall harvest, the brewing of ale from the recently-harvested grain, the slaughter of cattle that could not be maintained over the winter, and, once the population had completed the harvest and winterizing chores, a month or more of leisure time in which to enjoy the celebration. Once the elements for the celebration of Yule were in place, with the depths of winter fast approaching, it was not feasible to postpone the celebration to meet the Catholic calendar where the Feast of the Nativity fell on December 25.

The earlier onset of winter in northern Europe was exacerbated by a flaw in the Julian calendar adopted by the Roman Empire in 45 BC. Due to a rounding error, the calendar failed properly to compute the number of "leap days" needed to keep the astronomical year consistent with the calendar year. As a result, the astronomical Winter Solstice, which occurred on December 25 under the Julian calendar when Christ was born, occurred about one day earlier every hundred years. For example, by 1050, roughly 1100 years after the adoption of the Julian calendar, the astronomical Winter Solstice would have occurred on December 14. By mid–December, even the southern regions of Scandinavia had only six hours of daylight, much of which resembled dusk, with temperatures well below freezing. As a result, the likely period for the celebration of Yule in Scandinavia would have been November.

The earlier dates for celebration of Yule in Scandinavia required the Christian missionaries to identify an appropriate Christian identity for the Yule celebration. As folklorist Coffin writes, although many of the tribes in northern Europe had pagan midwinter holidays "it wasn't until Christianity came to the tribes that the significant changes were wrought. Then, as had been done with the Saturnalia and the Kalends, the Church Fathers refocused the pagan rites onto the various holy days."[6] In one early study, *St. Nicholas: His Legend and His Role in the Christmas Celebration and Other Popular Customs*, historian George H. McKnight described the situation this way:

> The attitude of the Christian church toward pagan custom is well known. Since it could not hope to extirpate old practice, it endeavored to adapt it to Christian use, giving to it Christian meaning and, as far as possible, Christian character. It aimed to make the birth of Christ, and the associated events, the dominating idea in its celebration at the beginning of winter.[7]

This means the missionaries were required to assess the timing of the pagan celebrations to determine an appropriate Christian identity. According to medieval studies professor Preston, "saints' days were peppered throughout the calendar as a way to manage time among illiterate Christians in early medieval Europe. Lacking free calendars from their banks or insurance agents, medieval agriculturalists had to rely on the progression of saints' days throughout the year to help mark time."[8] In practice, the missionaries appear to have used every major Catholic feast day during November and December to create a Christian identity for one pagan holiday or another, including St. Martin's Day on November 11, St. Andrew's Day on November 30, St. Nicholas' Day on December 6, and St. Lucia's Day on December 13. The second most wide-spread of these, St. Martin's Day, was largely indistinguishable from St. Nicholas' Day, with parents leaving gifts for children and telling them they were brought by St. Martin, except that it was a month earlier.[9] These facts support the conclusion that the celebration of St. Nicholas' Day arose because his feast day was in early December rather than because of any special attribute of St. Nicholas of Myra.

The other major challenge the Catholic Church encountered in trying to convert the people of northern Europe was that Germanic mythology, a term which encompasses Norse, Celtic and German beliefs, created a world filled with pagan gods, spirits, witches, elves, gnomes, and goblins that the church typically viewed as demonic. This world, Miles writes, proved impossible to eliminate.

> [T]he practical religion of the illiterate was in many respects merely a survival of the old paganism thinly disguised. There was a prevalent belief in witchcraft, magic, sortilegy, spells, charms, talismans, which mixed itself up in strange ways with Christian ideas and Christian worship…. The world was haunted by demons, hobgoblins, malignant spirits of diverse kinds, whose baneful influence must be averted by charms or offerings.[10]

The literate portion of the population at this time were largely priests, and they could not feel too superior to the pagans because the Christian churches also believed in many of the same beings. The primary difference was that the Christian churches condemned them as evil and demonic, burning incense to thwart evil spirits, conducting exorcisms to eliminate demons, and executing untold numbers of women for practicing witchcraft. The church was also inclined to label figures of German folklore like Krampus as Satanic because they had body parts that were not human. The pagans seem to have taken a more *laissez faire* attitude, welcoming the pagan goddess Berchta, Knecht Ruprecht, and Satan himself to participate in Christmas plays along with the Christ child, Mary, Joseph, and an assortment of angels and saints during the sixteenth and seventeenth centuries.

To understand how these beliefs developed, imagine life in northern Europe in the depths of midwinter. Nights could be eighteen hours or longer, with the dim light of fires or candles extending only a few feet, and even the few hours of "daylight" were shadowy times, the practical equivalent of dusk. The howling winds, cracks of broken branches, and cries of wild creatures would combine with imagination and pagan folk tales to help the populace visualize demons, ghosts, goblins, and evil spirits rampaging through the night skies.

Odin, a primary figure in the Germanic midwinter celebration called Yule. Missionaries who wanted to give Yule a Christian meaning gave him bishop's robes and renamed him St. Nicholas. Shutterstock.com.

THOR.

The pagan populations of northern Europe believed the "demons, hobgoblins [and] malignant spirits of diverse kinds" were particularly active during the Wild Hunt, an ethereal hunting party with spectral hounds and horses

Thor, a Germanic god who was particularly dominant in Nordic regions, was commonly shown in a flying chariot pulled by two goats. Thor led Wild Hunt during the Winter Solstice celebration of "Jul" in Scandinavia. Library of Congress, Prints and Photographs Division.

mounted by a horde of pagan gods, ghosts, and assorted creatures from Germanic folklore such as Knecht Ruprecht.

In Germany, the Wild Hunt was typically believed to be led by Odin, generally pictured with long white hair and beard, riding an eight-legged flying horse named Sleipnir. The Wild Hunt purportedly took place during the Twelve Days of Yule, and the critical role of Odin is reflected by two of his even greater number of names in old Norse: Jólfaðr, meaning "Yule father," and Jólnir, "the Yule one." Odin, who was also known as the Schimmelreiter ("White Horse Rider"), wore a swirling cape and a floppy-brimmed hat or hood that covered one side of his face, disguising that his eye "was not an eye at all but a dark, empty socket."[11] In Scandinavia, the Wild Hunt was called Oskorei, meaning terror, and Jolorei, "Yule Host."[12] Thor, a bearded god who rode through the sky on a chariot pulled by two goats, led the Yule Host in Scandinavia, and the goats became permanent features of Nordic Yule celebrations.

On the last night of the Wild Hunt in Germany, known as Perchtennacht ("Perchta's night" or "Berchta's night"), Odin and Berchta were believed to visit each home.[13] Berchta, the goddess of home and hearth, was originally viewed as an attractive young woman but eventually evolved into the archetype of a Halloween witch: a haggard old woman with a crooked nose riding a flying broomstick. Berchta's job was to enter through the chimney on her broomstick to determine whether the children were well-behaved and whether the housekeeping was up to her standards. For well-behaved children, she would leave small gifts or coins. If she determined the children were not well-behaved, Berchta was said to cut open their bellies, remove their stomach and intestines, and fill their abdominal cavity with straw and pebbles before sewing it back up.

While the Christian churches sought to minimize pagan influence by either changing the names of pagan gods to Christian figures, such as St. Nicholas or St. Martin, or banning the figures as various versions of Satan, famed philologist Jacob Grimm's discussion of the seventeenth-century Christmas plays shows that this was not completely successful. While Berchta was undoubtedly a pagan figure, Grimm's writings reveal Berchta was active in Christian Christmas plays and parades in the late seventeenth century. The Christian players included Mary, Joseph, the Christ child, the angel Gabriel, and the Saints Peter, Martin, and Nicholas. According to Grimm, however, the plays also included Knecht Ruprecht, a mysterious but terrifying figure from German folklore, and Satan, a Christian figure in the sense he was the adversary of Christ but not a dramatic character of whom the church would approve.

Even when the pagan practices were given a Christian name, the resulting "Christian practices" brought with them a strong dose of Germanic mythology. "Bonfires and candles not only brought light," Forbes writes, "but were also believed to keep evil spirits away, or to warm the spirits of the dead."[14] Likewise, Bowler says, the twelve days between Christmas and Epiphany were called the "rough nights" or "smoke nights" because the Germans believed the house and farm had to be cleansed of evil spirits by burning incense before Berchta's Night. On January 6, Epiphany, three men from the village or neighborhood would dress as the Three Kings and walk from home to home to home with censers—metal containers used in church ceremonies for burning incense—to bless the house. After cleansing the house of evil spirits, the Three Kings would show they had done so by marking their initials in chalk on the front door.[15] The German folklore that the smoke of burning incense would guard against the evil spirits still survives. For example, "Rauchermen," which are popular incense burners in the image of historical or mythical German characters handmade by woodworkers in the Erzgebirge region of Germany, are firmly rooted in the belief that the incense will drive away evil spirits.

6

The Emergence of St. Nicholas
as a Seasonal Gift-Giver

Most history books say St. Nicholas was born in or around AD 270, died on December 6, 343, and served as Bishop of Myra, a city in western Turkey that was part of the Greek Empire in the third century. However, as religious historian Adam C. English explains in *St. Nicholas, The Saint Who Would Be Santa Claus*: "[t]he history of Nicholas presents a tantalizing riddle. There is no early documentation of the man—no writings, disciples, or major acts. Then, curiously, story fragments and rumors begin to surface like driftwood in the water."[1] In the Christmas history *December 25*, author Phillip Snyder notes that "[f]rom [Nicholas'] own period, not one single shred of historical evidence proving that he ever lived can be found."[2] In 1969, as the result of an ecumenical conference known as Vatican II, the Catholic Church placed Nicholas and a number of other putative saints into the category of "revered legendary heroes," a label that could describe Paul Bunyan and Pecos Bill as well as St. Nicholas or Santa Claus.

There is also a scholarly debate about whether St. Nicholas ever existed at all. As English states:

> The historicity of St. Nicholas of Myra has been questioned by various persons in various degrees over the years. In recent times … two of the most important Nicholas scholars of the twentieth century: Gustav Anrich, the early-century German who compiled all the early Greek texts related to the saint, and Charles W. Jones, an esteemed Berkeley professor of antiquity. Anrich believes, given the evidence, that a definitive verdict on the historicity of St. Nicholas is not possible. Jones expresses skepticism about every major "fact" of Nicholas' life, including his name, his deeds, and his death date. Added to these indictments is the silence of Peter Brown, the preeminent authority on early Christian saints, who avoids a single mention of Nicholas of Myra in any of his major texts involving saints.[3]

English reports that Nicholas' name appears in some, but not all, of the lists of those attending the Council of Nicaea in the year 325, but there is no evidence he did or said anything during the proceedings, and some historians, including Jones, have suggested that his name was added centuries later, after Nicholas had become well-known.[4] English says that "no contemporary witness testified to Nicholas' existence or deeds in the historical record. Not one of Nicholas' fellow bishops mentions him by name in any of their letters or writings, and no contemporary chronicler referenced him in the histories."[5] English also lists a number of histories that question Nicholas' existence. "The sprawling nineteen-volume *New Catholic Encyclopedia*," he says, states that "[n]o historically trustworthy evidence of his ancestry or the events of his life exists, except for the fact of his episcopate." The German scholar Walter Nigg, author of a 1946 study of great saints, makes no mention of Nicholas, and the *Oxford Dictionary of Saints* "likewise dismisses the historical existence of the man, saying simply that 'Nicholas' life, although he was one of the most universally venerated saints in both East and West, is virtually unknown.'"[6]

English himself concludes St. Nicholas existed but that virtually all of the acts attributed to him were legend. The former conclusion would flow from evidence that someone named Nicholas attended some meetings of the Council of Nicaea in 325 but if, as scholars like Jones assert, his name was added to the records in the thirteenth century, after he became famous, then there really is no evidence he existed. Indeed, there is no claim, credible or not, of actions by Nicholas until the first biography was written some four hundred years following his death. Absent written records, the only evidence of Nicholas' life would have been oral tradition. There is no way that oral transmission of information over a period of four hundred years could be accurate, and if there were reliable information available about Nicholas during the prior four hundred years it seems like some monk somewhere would have memorialized it in writing. "Unfortunately," English says, "most popular offerings on the subject of Nicholas are frustratingly uninformative. Many books have the appearance of an historical work but offer little substance. They tell wonderful stories, but in the process, repeat errors that are at least a thousand years old."[7]

Much of the "history" of St. Nicholas comes from *Life of St. Nicholas*, a biography written by Michael the Archimandrite in approximately 710. As noted earlier, it would have been impossible for him to have known anything about Nicholas' life because of the absence of any written records. Dutch scholar Aart Blom published an analysis of the historicity of Michael the Archimandrite's biography in 1998, concluding that "Michael composed his biography of St. Nicholas primarily to edify, instruct, and improve the moral conduct of his monks who were lodged in the high hollows of central Turkey."[8]

The only one of the many miracles or acts of generosity often attributed to St. Nicholas that appears in the biography by Michael the Archimandrite is the tale of three dowries, in which St. Nicholas, learning that a father intended to sell his three daughters into prostitution because he did not have money for dowries, tossed three bags of gold through the window of the family's home, where they purportedly landed in stockings hung by the fireplace to dry. Putting aside the inherent incredulity of this tale—all Catholic saints must be credited with miracles before that can be canonized but this sounds much more like an extraordinary performance in a carnival midway game—it would have been impossible for any such story to have survived accurately for four centuries in the absence of any written records. And there is, according to England, a remarkably similar story in pagan literature, *The Life of Apollonius of Tyana*, written in Greek around AD 216 by the Athenian author Philostratus, raising obvious suspicions that the story was lifted from the earlier work. The next major biography of St. Nicholas, written by Symeon Metaphrastes in the tenth century, is even less reliable because it not only repeated the unsupported facts in the earlier biography, it mistakenly conflated the fourth-century Bishop of Myra with St. Nicholas of Sion, a sixth-century monk. Many of the oft-repeated stories about St. Nicholas' precocious childhood were stories about St. Nicholas of Sion, not St. Nicholas of Myra.

Despite the absence of any documentation that he even existed—or, perhaps, because of the absence of any history that would make him controversial or unlovable—St. Nicholas had become by the High Middle Ages one of Christianity's most beloved saints.[9] In his biography of St. Nicholas, McKnight writes that "[t]he very vagueness of the information concerning him serves in great measure to explain the remarkable variety of the roles he has assumed in the world's history."[10] For example, one reason for the popularity of St. Nicholas may be that a large number of Catholic saints were martyrs, and even in the Middle Ages it seems unlikely that many parents would relish telling young children stories of saints who were burned at the stake, stoned to death, or who, as with St. Lucia, plucked out her own eyeballs while imprisoned for being a Christian. Nicholas, on the other hand, was rated "PG."

The more significant factor in establishing St. Nicholas' fame, however, may have been that during the eleventh century his "relics"—an odd word used by the church to mean a saint's bones—became the object of a bizarre raid in which the Italian city of Bari stole what it believed to be the saint's relics from a tomb in a region of Turkey that had come under Islamic control. The raiders planned to display them as, in effect, a tourist attraction in Italy, and did so. A few years later, a group of sailors from Venice claimed to have found in the same church a vessel with the saint's name on it that was filled with smaller pieces of bone and took it to Venice to display as a competing tourist attraction. Just as the fame of Leonardo da Vinci's *Mona Lisa* was greatly enhanced by the theft of the painting from the Louvre in 1911, when front-page stories about a daring theft in the famous Paris museum ensured that many more people knew of the painting than prior to the theft, the fame of St. Nicholas of Myra was greatly increased by the theft of his relics, and particularly the race between Bari and Venice to get there first. As Wheeler and Rosenthal put it, "not until his remains were transferred to Bari did the cult of St. Nicholas really explode in the West. From that point on, St. Nicholas rode the crest, by 1400 becoming the most popular non–Biblical saint in the West."[11]

There have also been three other challenges to the assertion that the Bari remains were actually those of the saint. The earliest challenge, according to the St. Nicholas Center, was that described in the text by representatives of Venice, Italy, in the late eleventh century. "After Myra fell to the Seljuk Turks in 1071," according to the center's account, "Adriatic rivals Bari and Venice were in competition to bring the relics of Saint Nicholas to their cities. The Bari expedition, with three ships, sixty-two sailors and two priests, beat out the Venetians and the relics arrived in Bari on May 9, 1087."[12] Roughly ten years later, however, Venetians heading to the First Crusade in 1099 stopped by the Church of Saint Nicholas in Myra where, after purportedly "following a sweet scent, they broke through the floor, and several more layers, until they came to a copper urn engraved 'Here lies the Great Bishop Nicholas, Glorious on Land and Sea.'"[13] At the end of the First Crusade in 1101, the Venetians took the urn to Venice where it was interred in the abbey of the monastery San Nicoló del Lido. In 1992, according to the St. Nicholas Center, an anatomy professor at the University of Bari, Luigi Martino, examined the bone fragments at San Nicoló del Lido in Venice and concluded they were from the same person as the larger pieces of bone in Bari. The St. Nicholas Center explains these findings on the basis that "[t]he many small pieces found in Venice are consistent with accounts of the Bari sailors, in great haste, gathering up nearly all of the larger pieces, thus leaving the smaller ones, before hurrying back to their ships," and opines the relics in Bari and Venice are equally sacred.[14] These findings were a victory for intra-Italian relations, if nothing else, because visitors coming to see the relics of St. Nicholas will leave dollars in both cities.

The second challenge to the Bari claim was from a French family, the de Frainets, who claimed to have helped to steal relics from Myra and bring them to Bari in 1087.[15] When the French Normans lost control of Bari, according to this claim, the relics were moved to France and ultimately to Ireland. In 1200, according to this claim, they were entombed in a Cistercian Abbey in Newtown Jerpoint, a medieval Irish town where the de Frainet family owned land and promoted them as a tourist attraction. The third challenge came much more recently, in October 2017, from a team of archeologists in Turkey who claimed to have discovered a previously unknown tomb beneath the mosaic-covered floor of a church in the southern Antalya province of Turkey, the area formerly known as Myra. These researchers used advanced imaging technology to locate a tomb below the tomb believed to contain the relics of St. Nicholas and contend that the relics taken to Bari were the actually the remains of a parish priest who was buried in the church over the tomb of St. Nicholas.[16]

The absence of any real history created a blank slate on which anyone could write stories that suited whatever moral the author wanted to illuminate. As a result, according to Wheeler and Rosenthal, St. Nicholas "has always been all things to all people."[17] In one legend, St. Nicholas supposedly restored life to three boys who were cut into pieces and pickled in a large crock of brine. After restoring the pickled pieces of human flesh, recreating three living bodies, St. Nicholas supposedly forgave the butcher who had slaughtered the children. Even stranger, according to the legend, the butcher was the same person known as Père Fouettard ("Father Switch") in the French provinces of Alsace and Lorraine and as Houseker in Luxembourg, both of whom are evil helpers of St. Nicholas. The back story is that after re-assembling the boys, St. Nicholas decided the butcher's penance should be working as an assistant on the saint's gift-giving rounds in Northeast France and Luxembourg. This means that the butcher's punishment for dismembering three boys was requiring him to work as St. Nicholas' disciplinarian, a job for which he was given some child-sized bags and a basket of switches to use on poorly behaved children. As a result of the world's propensity for creating stories like this, St. Nicholas, by the end of the Middle Ages, had become the patron saint of "damn near everything,"[18] including such dubious professions as murderers, thieves, robbers, pirates, prostitutes, and lawyers.[19]

The appearance of St. Nicholas, if he actually existed, is another of the many unknowns. The first depictions of him did not occur until four centuries after his death, and therefore could not possibly have been accurate likenesses.[20] One of the earliest, dated between AD 650 and AD 750, is an indistinct icon from the monastery of St. Catherine on Mount Sinai. It was not until the thirteenth century that large numbers of additional icons begin to appear, most created in the Eastern Orthodox Church. Virtually all of these depict an unremarkable middle-aged man with a receding hairline and a narrow, beak-like nose. In these depictions, none of which could be called jolly, he was either clean-shaven or wore a short, well-trimmed beard. A small number of the icons depict him as a dark-skinned man of either African or Middle Eastern origin, but, except for his skin color, the look is generally the same.

Although there are poems about St. Nicholas as the Yuletide gift-giver which date from the fifteenth century, the earliest surviving depiction of St. Nicholas or the Dutch Sinterklaas, who was identical in appearance, was a 1750 woodcut showing a man with indistinct features riding a horse. Between 1750 and 1850 there were a dozen or so Dutch illustrations showing Sinterklaas or "Sint Niklaas" on a horse distributing toys and treats to groups of children. The most significant illustrations of the Dutch gift-giver, however, were those in *Sint Nikolaas en zijn Knecht* ("St. Nicholas and his Servant") published by Dutch schoolteacher Jan Schenkman in 1850, a children's book that introduced the dark-skinned servant who became known as Black Peter. Unlike the occasional painting or woodcut, Schenkman's book was broadly distributed and repeated in multiple editions with new illustrations in which the servant began to look increasingly like the Black Peters of today, with the clothing in the style of sixteenth-century Spain when the Spanish occupied the Netherlands.

During the period between 1790 and the mid–1800s, there were also a dozen or so illustrations of the "real" St. Nicholas in central Europe. In contrast to the Dutch pictures of Sinterklaas tossing gifts to smiling children from his horse, all of the illustrations outside of Holland show St. Nicholas entering homes with one of the satanic "evil helpers" such as Krampus, Klaubauf, Beelzebub and Hans Trapp. The best of these is probably an 1820 painting by Austrian artist Franz Xaver, commissioned by the Baumann family of Vienna, Austria, showing the saint with miter, crozier and full bishop's garb in front of a Christmas tree with Krampus standing guard at the door.

The historical illustrations depict essentially the same figure one finds today as Sinterklaas in the Netherlands or St. Nicholas in Europe—a tall, fit, imposing man with white hair and a long curly white beard wearing the traditional Catholic bishop's vestments. More significantly, however, if a bishop's robes, miter, and staff are added to well-established depictions of Odin, and Odin's missing eye is restored, the resulting figures look exactly like St. Nicholas the gift-giver. On the other hand, the depiction of St. Nicholas the gift-giver looks virtually nothing like either the super-serious icons of St. Nicholas that proliferated in Catholic or Eastern Orthodox churches between the twelfth and sixteenth centuries or the literary version of St. Nicholas described by Clement Moore in his 1822 poem "A Visit from St. Nicholas," a figure who was short, plump, jolly, and dressed in a fur jumpsuit rather than a bishop's robes.

In *4000 Years of Christmas*, anthropologist Earl Count writes when "we trace the roots that [Odin] has struck into the life of the Germanic peoples, we find him turning up in the most unexpected places … [Odin] has become Santa Claus, or, as he is better called, St. Nicholas."[21] In reaching this conclusion, Count observes that St. Nicholas looks like Odin in a bishop's vestments, and that the gift-giving traditions of Odin and St. Nicholas are virtually identical. Many of the practices attributed to St. Nicholas—in particular, flying through the air on an animal-drawn vehicle of some sort, entering through the chimney, and leaving gifts for good children and punishments for the bad—can be found in the Germanic myths of Odin and Berchta. Conversely, folklorist Miles explains that where St. Nicholas is considered the holiday gift-giver, before going to bed "the children put out their shoes, with hay, straw, or a carrot in them for the saint's white horse or ass. When they wake in the morning, if they have been 'good' the fodder is gone and sweet things or toys are in its place; if they have misbehaved themselves the provender is untouched and no gift but a rod is there."[22] Thus, the only material differences between the St. Nicholas traditions and those involving Odin is the name of the horse for which children leave the hay and carrots.

Most historians, folklorists, and anthropologists who have written on the issue have concluded that the legend of St. Nicholas as seasonal gift-giver was created during the Middle Ages when Christian missionaries encountered Germanic tribes who celebrated Yule, the Germanic celebration of midwinter, in early December. Because those ceremonies were too early in the year to be characterized as celebrations of the Nativity, the missionaries used St. Nicholas' Day on December 6 to Christianize the pagan Yule celebrations.[23] In a 1917 biography of St. Nicholas, historian McKnight explains that similar gift-giving practices developed with St. Nicholas, St. Martin, and St. Andrew where their feast days occurred near the Germanic Yule celebrations for which the missionaries needed to identify a "Christian purpose."[24]

> [T]he customs in question, in their origin, had little, if anything, to do with St. Nicholas, and as they exist to-day show only in certain external features any relation with the life story of the kindly eastern saint. This impression of the earlier independence of the popular customs in question from the story of

St. Nicholas, is confirmed by the fact that many of them are associated with other names. St. Martin, as well as St. Nicholas, figures as a giver of gifts to children, especially in the Netherlands. The celebration of St. Andrew's Day also has features similar to those of St. Nicholas' Day.[25]

The practice of identifying a Christian gift-giver based on which saint's feast day occurred closest in time to the pagan Yule celebrations had two interesting consequences in central and northern Europe. One consequence was that the northern regions were Christianized centuries later than central and southern Europe, and because of a flaw in the Julian Calendar that meant that the astronomical Winter Solstice would occur well before December 25. By the year 1350, a date roughly in the middle of the three-century period in which historians say St. Nicholas assumed gift-giving duties, the Winter Solstice would occur on about December 11, five days after St. Nicholas' Day and fourteen days before Christmas Day. The other consequence was that the earlier onset of winter in the northern regions meant that pagan Yule celebrations would occur earlier than in central or southern Europe because all of the required elements, such as the fall harvest, slaughter of animals, brewing of beer and competition of winterizing chores would be completed earlier than in the south.

Taken together, these factors meant that in the northernmost regions of Europe the traditional Yule festivities would likely occur in early November, making St. Martin, whose feast day was November 11, the most likely candidate for Christian gift-giver. Miles says that St. Martin was, in fact, originally designated as the Christian gift-giver in places but was replaced by St. Nicholas.[26] What changed was not the climate of northern Europe but new methods of agriculture that, according to Miles, extended the growing season and, later, the adoption of the Gregorian Calendar in 1582, requiring that roughly fifteen days be permanently eliminated to align the liturgical calendar with the astronomical calendar.[27]

As a result, St. Nicholas became the predominate gift-giver where the pagan Yule celebrations occurred in early December—a band in the northern half of Europe that includes the modern-day Netherlands, Belgium, northern Germany, northeastern France, Poland, Austria, Czech Republic, and Hungary. In England and the southern half of Europe, the pagan midwinter celebrations had already been converted into the Feast of the Nativity, and the church did not need to characterize St. Nicholas or his feast day as the Christian focus for a pagan midwinter festival. In Scandinavia, on the other hand, St. Lucia, a fourth-century martyr with no connection to Scandinavia, was drafted as headliner for a traditional Swedish festival of lights that occurred on December 13, her feast day.

When St. Nicholas first assumed the role of gift-giver is uncertain, and it was undoubtedly different dates in different regions. Snyder, Wheeler, and Rosenthal assert St. Nicholas began serving as a gift-giver during the twelfth century when French nuns began to leave gifts for orphans on December 6 to celebrate the generosity of St. Nicholas.[28] There is no documentation of this practice, and no way to prove or disprove the contention, but neither nuns nor orphans seem likely to have spread the word about this practice outside of the nunnery or orphanage. The earliest written documentation of the St. Nicholas tradition comes from the fifteenth and sixteenth centuries. In the fifteenth century, Swiss writer Rudolph Hospinian wrote it "was the custom for parents, on the vigil of St. Nicholas, to convey secretly presents of various kinds to their little sons and daughters who were taught to believe that they owed them to the kindness of St. Nicholas and his train, who, going up and down among the towns and villages, came in at the windows, though they were shut, and distributed them."[29] In the mid-sixteenth century, Thomas Naogeorgus, a German dramatist and theologian, wrote this poem:

Saint Nicholas money used to give
To maidens secretly,
Who, that he still may use
His wonted liberalitie
The mothers all their children on the eve
Do cause to fast
And when they every one at night
In senselesse sleepe are cast
Both Apples, Nuttes, and peares they bring,
And other things besides
As caps, and shoes and petticotes,
Which secretly they hide,
And in the morning found, they say
That this Saint Nicholas brought.[30]

One notable aspect of the tradition described by Hospinian and Naogeorgus is that St. Nicholas doesn't appear while the children are awake, but, rather, leaves the gifts while they sleep. This practice is consistent with the most prominent visual depiction of the tradition by Jan Havicksz Steen, a Dutch master, in a 1668 painting, *The Feast of St Nicholas*. The Steen painting depicts children on the morning after St Nicholas' visit, conveying that only good children receive gifts from the saint by depicting a little girl with a bucket full of treats and a crying boy with a switch.[31]

There are also accounts, however, including the illustrations discussed earlier in this chapter, where St. Nicholas appears in person on the evening before St. Nicholas' Day with a satanic-looking evil sidekick in tow. In this tradition, St. Nicholas would visit on the evening before his feast day, December 6, knocking on the front door when he arrived. Some accounts say that when the door was opened, the saint or his evil sidekick would throw a variety of sweets or nuts on to the floor, causing the children to scramble in a manner reminiscent of the breaking of a piñata.[32] Other accounts say St. Nicholas would first question the children to determine whether they could answer a few catechism questions before he or the sidekick tossed out the treats. Other than distributing the treats, the evil helper's only role was to stand silently behind the saint.

When St. Nicholas traveled with an evil helper, and, if so, who, is a more complex question than it might seem. Most accounts say St. Nicholas traveled with an evil helper because he could not perform the disciplinary function himself. As Will Williams, a professor of religion, observes in his essay "You'd Better Watch Out," St. Nicholas "was a Christian bishop. That means he was charged to care for and protect the souls of those in his diocese."[33] Under this premise, the religious reins on the saintly bishop made it impossible for him to threaten the type of discipline that his pagan predecessors did, a conclusion consistent with the historical drawings from the eighteenth and nineteenth century that all show St. Nicholas with Krampus or a similar-looking satanic figure.

How the legend played out in practice, however, is a different issue. This is because the accounts that St. Nicholas traveled with an evil helper tells us nothing about how frequently St. Nicholas was reported to travel with an evil helper. By way of illustration, the general practice in America is that Santa comes while the children are sleeping, a practice established by "The Night Before Christmas," but there are families where an older male dressed as Santa appears and distributes presents on Christmas Eve. In other words, each family was free to design its own method of gift-giving. Even when St. Nicholas did appear in person, however, bringing an evil helper was undoubtedly optional, and staging a credible impersonation of St. Nicholas and a satanic evil helper is much more complex than an appearance by Santa. It seems more likely, therefore, that most parents chose the simpler course of telling children the saint did not appear until the child was sleeping or, as with the Christ child on Christmas Eve, that he came and left while the family was eating dinner.

7

The Identity and Emergence
of the Evil Helpers of St. Nicholas

The reason for a chapter on "evil helpers" in a book about Santa Claus is that the seasonal gift-givers have always served a dual role, rewarding good behavior and punishing bad behavior—or, at least, threatening to do so. In the Middle Ages, the disciplinary function was probably more important to most parents than the gift-giving. The German name for this theory of child-rearing is "zuckbrot und peitsche," meaning sugarbread and whip, or what Americans might call a "carrot and stick." The premise was telling children they will receive a reward for good behavior encourages that behavior whereas threatening punishment for misbehavior discourages that behavior.

Prior to the arrival of Christianity, the Germanic gods Odin and Berchta served as both gift-givers and disciplinarians during the pagan Yule. They were believed to lead the Wild Hunt, and on the Twelfth Night of Yule would visit homes, entering through the chimney to leave small gifts or coins for good children and punishments for those who misbehaved. Berchta's punishments, as we know, could be particularly gruesome, disemboweling children who she thought had misbehaved. After Christianity arrived in northern Germany, Catholic missionaries were compelled by the strategy dictated by Pope Gregory in AD 601 to have St. Nicholas, or an equally holy figure, take over the gift-giving role of Odin and Berchta. The fact that St. Nicholas was a Catholic saint who was supposed to serve as an example of pious behavior meant beating children was outside of his job description. The church, therefore, could not endorse the kindly and virtuous saint implementing the horrific punishments attributed to Odin and Berchta. It is also unlikely German parents would have accepted a gift-giver who only rewarded the good and did not punish the bad. Therefore, the good cop, St. Nicholas, needed a bad cop to fill the disciplinary role.

Accordingly, as a matter of legend if not reality, St. Nicholas began to appear with a variety of grotesque assistants, generally armed with chains, whips, switches, and child-sized bags or baskets to haul the bad kids away to some dark and evil place that was never identified in further detail. The best known of the evil helpers is Austria's Krampus, but there were at least thirty evil helpers who accompanied St. Nicholas in one region or another. The evil helpers acted as silent enforcers—sort of like St. Nicholas' own version of godfather Don Corleone's henchman, Luca Brasi, whose job was to stand behind the godfather and say nothing.[1]

Most of the evil helpers are satanic creatures with animal parts such as horns, fur, hooves, and tails, designed to terrorize children into behaving properly or learning their prayers. The threat created by these characters is that St. Nicholas "not only withholds gifts from the unruly but sees to it that miscreants are punished. This ugly duty, however, is

This painting by Austrian artist Franz Xaver von Paumgartten, "Am Christ Abend und St. Nicolaus kam der Krampus auch in's Haus," was commissioned by the Baumann family in 1820. Wein Museum.

below his ecclesiastic dignity and falls therefore to the Krampus, who either punishes them on the spot or carts them off in a basket to later be rent limb from limb, tossed into a pit or lake, or eaten."[2] While the Catholic Church has had varying degrees of tolerance over the centuries for depictions of Satan and his comrades, the prevalence of the evil helpers in predominately Catholic regions of Europe implies that so long as St. Nicholas was clearly in charge, bringing along an evil helper was deemed consistent with the long-standing Catholic practices in which saints and angels were depicted as having defeated or vanquished Satan or his servants. Indeed, during the Late Middle Ages, Catholic theology inspired such works as Dante's *Inferno*, a tour of Hell at its most repulsive, as a method to teach lessons in morality. The appearance of Krampus on a chain held by St. Nicholas was a stark reminder of what happened to those who chose the ways of the devil over the ways of the saint.

St. Nicholas' evil helpers should not be confused with the faux Nicholases. As explained earlier, the latter were humans, not satanic beasts, who *replaced* St. Nicholas as a holiday gift-giver, rather than traveling with him, after the Protestant denominations created during the Reformation urged their members to forego the gift-giving traditions involving the Catholic saint.[3] The faux Nicholases adopted a look in which St. Nicholas appeared to have been stripped of his bishop's robes, sent to live alone in the wilderness for several years, and returned with filthy long hair and a beard, wearing a ragged coat, cloak, or animal skin and covered with dirt or ashes. Critically, the faux Nicholases performed both the gift-giving function of St. Nicholas and the disciplinary function of the evil helpers, and generally carried a whip or bundle of switches to convey their ability to punish young offenders. The exception was two faux Nicholases who appeared as St. Nicholas look-alikes in bishop's

garb but were "really" someone else, the Dutch Sinterklaas
and the Swiss Samichlaus. Both
had evil helpers of their own:
the Dutch Zwarte Piet ("Black
Peter"), originally envisioned as
Satan dressed entirely in black,
and the Swiss Schmutzl ("Dirt"),
a human figure who appears entirely in brown and represents
the devil, pairings that seem to
confirm the evil helpers acted as
enforcers for gift-givers who were
too saintly to act for themselves.

The other character whose
practices differed from the norm
was Christkindl, who replaced St.
Nicholas but who was not really
a faux Nicholas either. In theory,
Christkindl was a representative
of the Christ child but he—or is
it she?—was depicted by a girl or
young woman, typically blond,
and wearing a white dress that
gave the overall appearance of
an angel. In some illustrations,
a teenage Christkindl is shown
with an evil helper, often Hans
Trapp, or with St. Nicholas and
Krampus. In others, a younger
Christkindl is shown with a faux
Nicholas who seems as much
chaperone as disciplinarian.

Whether the evil helpers
performed any function for the
faux Nicholases is uncertain but

"St. Nikolaus und Beelzebub bei der Einker in einem Schwarzwalder Haus" is an 1853 illustration by German lithographer J. Nepomuk Heinemann, showing Beelzebub, a common synonym for Satan, with St. Nicholas at the entrance to the Schwarzwalder home.

would probably have been rare if it occurred at all. The evil helpers were servants of St. Nicholas and appeared in the predominately Catholic regions of Europe with the saint him-self holding them tightly on a heavy chain. There is little evidence of the evil helpers in the Protestant regions of Germany following the Reformation, and no apparent need for them because the faux Nicholases generally could perform the disciplinary function themselves. Nonetheless, there were so many different German Christmas characters who were mixed and matched in strange ways it is hard to know for sure.

When the evil helpers first appeared is in dispute. One theory is they arrived at the same time St. Nicholas replaced Odin and Berchta, which was probably somewhere between the thirteenth and fifteenth centuries. This theory reflects the idea that in designating the pagan Yule as the Feast of St. Nicholas, those involved did not think the good St. Nicholas, by himself, presented the harsh choice between good and evil that was necessary to make an impact on the minds of young children. If so, logic dictates the evil helpers would have arrived at the same time as St. Nicholas, perhaps three hundred years or more before the Protestant Reformation.

Some historians, however, say the evil helpers did not arrive until the sixteenth century, during the Reformation, when the Protestants' tinkering with the status quo begat a variety of new Christmas characters.[4] These historians include Gerry Bowler, author of three books about Christmas, including *Santa: A Biography*, and Joe Wheeler and Jim Rosenthal, authors of *Saint Nicholas: A Closer Look at Christmas.*

Mikulás and Krampusz, the Hungarian names for St. Nicholas and Krampus, are shown in an 1865 illustration by an unknown artist. Krampus stands behind the saint so that his presence alone conveys the potential of discipline.

Bowler, for example, writes that although St. Nicholas was no longer welcome in Lutheran Germany following the Reformation, "there was a host of mysterious figures able to take his place," including "shaggy bogeymen, witches with iron teeth, ghostly figures in white [and] devils with chains."[5] Bowler attributes the arrival of St. Nicholas' assistants to the Lutheran efforts following the Reformation to replace St. Nicholas with the Christkindl and move the date of gift-giving from St. Nicholas' Day to Christmas.

[A]ny adult could dress up as Saint Nicholas and stage an appearance at home or school to awe the children and quiz them on their behavior, but genuine human babies were unreliable impersonators of the new divine gift-bringer. Consequently, the Christ child was portrayed by a young adolescent female dressed in white.... This assistant could also serve as a useful intimidator—while few would be frightened into good behavior by a baby, a devil or other ogre wielding chains, rods, or a whip could concentrate the minds of errant children wonderfully. So welcome then Krampus and Cert, demonic figures from central Europe; Père Fouettard ("Father Switch") from France; Hans Trapp in Alsace; or Knecht Ruprecht in Germany. A whole menagerie of shaggy sidekicks emerged from a strange metamorphosis suffered by Saint Nicholas.[6]

In their biography of St. Nicholas, Wheeler and Rosenthal seem to be on the same page as Bowler, writing that Protestant opposition to St. Nicholas "unleashed a host of semi-pagan pseudo-St. Nicholases. Instead of making the observance of Christmas more

THE CHRIST-CHILD AND HANS TRAPP.

This illustration from the January 1873 edition of *Harper's New Monthly Magazine* shows Christkindl with Hans Trapp, a demonic-looking evil helper. Library of Congress.

sacred, the reverse occurred. For out of the woodwork of European and near eastern mythology arose long-slumbering pagan deities that now, by default, were given new life."[7] The phrase "semi-pagan pseudo St. Nicholases" presumably means the faux Nicholases who replaced St. Nicholas in northern Germany, but the reference to "long-slumbering pagan deities" seems like it could only be a reference to the evil helpers like Krampus who accompanied St. Nicholas.

In contrast, Siefker asserts in *Santa Claus: Last of the Wild Men* that the evil helpers were the same figure as the Wild Man—a beast-god of German folklore who, she says, evolved into Knecht Ruprecht, Pelznickel, and, ultimately, Santa Claus. She makes clear that the Wild Man preceded the arrival of St. Nicholas, however, by writing that when St. Nicholas was designated as Christian gift-giver "the Wild Man found his chain held by a saint, and his role relegated to that of a clumsy servant … the scourge that awaits evildoers."[8] Siefker also cites evidence that during the thirteenth century—some three centuries

This 1896 illustration by an unidentified artist shows Nikolaus and Krampus in a Viennese home. Nikolaus is clearly wearing a costume beard. Courtesy Austrian National Library.

before the Reformation—the Catholic Church began to condemn the evil helpers as heathen figures.[9]

The argument that the evil helpers arrived to assist St. Nicholas before the Reformation is both more logical and better supported by the little documentary evidence that exists. The Germans believed the Yule gift-giver's role of punishing bad children was just as important as rewarding the good ones, and the fact the pagan goddess Berchta accompanied Odin in visiting homes on the Twelfth Night of Yule clearly reflects that perspective. The one-eyed Odin, frequently portrayed as a warrior, could not be called warm and cuddly but it was Berchta who held the knife. The entrance of Catholic missionaries in northern Europe, and the designation of St. Nicholas as the Yule gift-giver, fundamentally changed the dynamic of the Winter Solstice celebration. It is impossible to imagine the kindly, child-loving St. Nicholas whipping naughty children, much less disemboweling them, nor would the Catholic Church have permitted him to be portrayed in that manner. It makes perfect sense, therefore, that the populace, having accepted St. Nicholas as gift-giver in lieu of Odin, accepted, and perhaps insisted, the saint be accompanied by someone who could play the disciplinary role as well as Berchta did.

On the other side, notwithstanding Bowler's theory that the Christ child needed a

Das Niklasfest. Originalzeichnung von Karl Jauslin. (S. 207.)

XXXV.

"Das Niklasfest" is an 1876 illustration by Swiss artist Nach Karl Jauslin in *Über Land und Meer: Deutsche illustrierte Zeitun*, a German newspaper. Sint Niklas stands at the door of a home with an unidentified evil helper lurking behind him.

tough bodyguard, there is no obvious reason why the evil helpers would have appeared at the same time the faux Nicholases replaced St. Nicholas in the Protestant regions of northern Europe. The evil helpers virtually always appeared with St. Nicholas, who, in turn, appeared only in regions where Catholicism remained strong despite the Reformation. By comparison, in regions where the Protestant churches had discouraged the St. Nicholas tradition, the faux Nicholases could—and did—play both gift-giver and enforcer. If this analysis is correct, the evil helpers would have begun to appear at the same time as St. Nicholas, several centuries before the Reformation. In Protestant regions, the evil helpers would have disappeared at the same time as St. Nicholas but in those Catholic regions, where St. Nicholas was still active, the evil helpers would have continued to accompany St. Nicholas. In fact, Krampus remains extremely popular in Austria and southern Germany, both Catholic strong-holds.

One other subject is worth discussion. While the depictions of satanic creatures such as Krampus are often shocking to modern sensibilities, these practices cannot be fairly viewed through modern American lenses. Berchta, the Germanic goddess who visited homes with Odin on the last night of the Wild Hunt, was quite arguably the original evil helper, and research by Jacob Grimm established that Berchta continued to participate in Christmas plays and parades until at least the seventeenth century. By comparison to Berchta's practice of disemboweling young children, the satanic-looking creatures attached firmly to the end of a chain held by St. Nicholas were not as shocking as they might appear today.

The most complete list of evil helpers is contained in a German book, *Worterbuch der Deutschen Volkskunde* ("Handbook of German Folklore"),[10] which includes a map identifying more than forty Nicholastag gift-givers throughout Europe, thirty of whom are designated as "Schreckgestalten," a German term that translates literally as "frightening figures" but means essentially the same thing as evil helpers.[11] Organized by region, the evil helpers are Pelzmarte, Butz, and Rumpleklas in the German state of Baden-Württemberg (southwestern Germany); Klaubauf, Butz, Pelzebock, Zember, Thama, Luzia, and Bercht in Bavaria (southeastern Germany); Pulterklas, Booklaus, and Schnabuck in the state of Lower Saxony (northwestern Germany); Klas Bur, Duvel, and Hans Muff in the state of Rhineland-Palantine (southwestern Germany); Bullerklas, Rubbi, and Robber in Schleswig-Holstein (north-central Germany); Krampus, Bartle, and Wubartle in Austria; Leutfresser in the Eastern Alps; Old/Ale Josef, Schimmelreiter, and Klapperbock in Poland; Schmutzli and Dusselli in Switzerland; Zwarte Piet in the Netherlands; Houseker in Luxembourg; and Beelzebub, Rubbels, Hans Trapp, and Père Fouettard in the Alsace-Lorraine region on the border of Germany and France.[12] A number of these names, like Krampus, are very familiar; some appear in most lists of evil helpers but are seldom discussed in any detail and a number do not appear even in a search of google.de, the German version of the popular search engine.

The most famous of the evil helpers, Krampus, operates in the Catholic strongholds of Austria, southern Germany, Croatia, Slovenia, and Hungary. Krampus is depicted as an upright creature with a human torso, arms, and hands, but the legs of an animal with cloven hooves, black fur or lizard-like skin, the pointed ears of a Great Dane, swirling horns like a goat, and a long, thin tail with a tuft on the end. The real reason for Krampus' fame, however, is his tongue—a very long, red, disgusting tongue that makes Gene Simmons of the rock group KISS look like a three-year-old girl who is upset with her older brother.[13] Krampus is generally depicted attached to a heavy chain held by St. Nicholas if he is present, with a basket on his back used to cart away misbehaving children. Other evil helpers who look very similar to Krampus are Klaubauf, Bartel, Butz (also known as Butzemann, Bus-chemann, Butze, Butzenmann, and several other similar names), Kramperl, Tuifl, Ganggerl, Beelzebub, and Rubbels.

Krampus, who seems at times to have his own public relations firm, has developed a remarkably large following for someone whose job is to abduct and beat or kill young children.[14] During the late nineteenth century, Krampus was the subject of numerous Victorian Christmas cards called Krampuskarten that depicted Krampus in all of his Satanic, red-tongued, child-abducting glory.[15] He also has his own holiday in Austria and southern Germany, Krampusnacht ("Krampus Night") on December 5; his own "fun runs" called Krampuslauf ("Krampus run") that occur annually in some Alpine towns[16]; several horror movies, none of which seem to have any real connection to Christmas[17]; and several picture books and biographies released in the past few years.[18] As with most of the evil helpers identified below, St. Nicholas would often appear in pre–Christmas festivals and parades with a group of characters portraying Krampus. For this reason, Krampus biographer Ridenour created "the Krampus" as a plural term, making Krampus the name of a species rather than an individual.

Cert, whose name means the devil in Czech, is the evil helper of St. Nicholas in the Czech Republic. Cert looks much like Krampus, including the long, red tongue, but has developed a more stylish entrance, descending from heaven with St. Nicholas and an angel on a golden rope.[19] Unlike Krampus, however, Cert is sometimes depicted as a cute cartoon character with small red horns, perhaps because his appearance with St. Nicholas and an angel on a golden rope gives him an aura of respectability Krampus does not have.

Schmutzl, whose name derives from the German word for dirt, is the evil helper of Samichlaus in Switzerland. He is generally dressed in brown, but he occasionally appears all in black, with brown hair, a beard, and a face darkened with lard and soot. Schmutzl is arguably an exception to the rule that the evil helpers are not human but "some guy dressed in brown" doesn't really strike fear into the hearts of children. In all other ways, Schmutzl is clearly an evil helper, not a faux Nicholas, because he has no independent role and he is seldom, if ever, seen without Samichlaus. It is most sensible, therefore, to view Schmutzl as a symbolic representative of Satan who simply doesn't don the elaborate costume of Krampus.

The oddest grouping of evil helpers are four fellows who accompany St. Nicholas in a slim slice of land on the border between France and Germany, a region better known for Gewurztraminer wines and Quiche Lorraine. This region, which includes the provinces of Alsace and Lorraine in northeast France and extends north through Luxembourg, has four evil helpers of its own, three of whom often appear to be human but have names that denote the devil. Père Fouettard, which is French for "Father Switch," is an evil helper of St. Nicholas who roams the same regions of northern and eastern France as Rubbels and Hans Trapp. Père Fouettard looks much like the faux Nicholases, dressed in dirty, dark robes with a darkened face, dirty unkempt hair and a long beard. He carries either a whip, a large stick or, most true to his name, a basket with bundles of switches. As mentioned earlier, he also has the strangest backstories of the evil helpers, which is that he was the butcher who cut up and pickled the three boys St. Nicholas miraculously reassembled. In an action that surely deserves the award "Worst Sentencing Decision by a Saint," St. Nicholas forced the butcher, as penance for his sins, to serve as the saint's deputy in charge of punishing poorly behaved children. Houseker is the name given Père Fouettard in Luxembourg, which abuts the northeast border of France where Père Fouettard is active, but Houseker dresses entirely in black, presumably making him a symbol of Satan.

Hans Trapp, who wears a white beard and pointed hat and carries a long rod, is St. Nicholas' evil helper in Alsace, a province on the eastern border of France just south of Lorraine. He is the only evil helper with a real-life predecessor although he has morphed into something that looks less human. Hans von Trotha (c. 1450–1503) was a German aristocrat and knight known for his adversarial nature and unscrupulous conduct, including damming a river to deprive a town of water and then releasing the dam, flooding the town. After his death, he became known under the name of Hans Trapp, a black knight whose spirit terrorized children. Why he was selected to accompany St. Nicholas is unclear except, perhaps, because he was the most horrible character known to the children of Alsace.

Some German Schreckgestalten characters look like evil helpers but do not actually participate in the gift-giving process. For example, Klausen is a Schreckgestalten in the Oberallgau region of Bavaria, Germany, and bears a surface resemblance to Krampus. The Klausen—whose name, like Krampus, is both singular and plural—generally appear in parades or other public celebrations with other Klausen. He has the antlers of a deer or elk rather than the horns of a goat, however, and wears lighter-colored animal skins than the black-skinned Krampus. Another such figure is Buttenmandl, a Schreckgestalten in Berchtesgaden, Bavaria, whose distinguishing feature is being wrapped entirely in straw except for a fur mask and horns, making him look like a bale of hay that exploded. The Buttenmandl travel with St. Nicholas in a group that sometimes includes a woman who plays St. Nicholas' wife, an interesting touch given that St. Nicholas, a Catholic bishop, presumably never had a wife. It appears, although we cannot be certain, that the role of the Buttenmandl is limited to parades or festivals, and they do not accompany St. Nicholas on St. Nicholas' Day.

8

The Protestant Reformation
and the Suppression of St. Nicholas

By the High Middle Ages—the period between 1000 and AD 1300—virtually all of Europe had become Christianized, and all of those Christians were part of either the Roman Catholic Church, centered in Rome, or the Eastern Orthodox Church, which was officially headquartered in Greece but operated autonomously in each Eastern Orthodox nation. The two branches of the Christian church formally split in 1054 but seemed content to let each other preside over their respective territories both before and after the Great Schism, perhaps because both groups were too busy fighting Muslims for control of land around the eastern Mediterranean. The live-and-let-live attitude of Christians toward other Christians would soon change, however, when the Protestant Reformation swept through Western civilization in the sixteenth century after a monk named Martin Luther published a list of criticisms of the Catholic Church that became known as his Ninety-Five Theses.

Luther did not initially seek a break with the Catholic Church, but his criticism set in motion a religious upheaval that unfolded over a period of 150 years and altered, or in some cases eliminated, the celebration of Christmas for two hundred years or more. In much of central and northern Europe, the Reformation resulted in wholesale displacement of the Catholic Church by one of several Protestant denominations: the Lutheran Church in northern Germany and Scandinavia; the Dutch Reformed Church in Holland; the Presbyterian in Scotland; and Calvinist denominations in Switzerland and Hungary. England also split with the Catholic Church in 1534, but not over issues of theology. Rather, King Henry VIII left the church over the Pope's refusal to grant him a divorce from Catherine of Aragon, the first of his six wives. In response, Henry VIII established the Church of England, naming himself as the head of the church and annulling his marriage to Catherine, but largely adopting the Roman Catholic theology to which Henry had adhered all of his life. Some Englishmen, known as the Puritans, found the Church of England was still too Catholic for their liking, resulting in the English Civil Wars during the seventeenth century.

The premise of the Reformation was that people should have a direct relationship with God, unencumbered by the meddling of saints and popes, and that the Bible, not the pronouncements of those saints and popes, was the only valid source of religious authority. The Protestant reformers objected to the Catholic Church's use of religious authority outside of the Bible; the treatment of saints in a manner that the reformers believed implied some Christian souls had more influence in heaven than others; and what they believed was rampant corruption in the Catholic hierarchy in which priests purported to sell access to heaven for the right price. Roughly twenty years after the Reformation, there was a counter-reformation, generally known as the Catholic Restoration, which returned Austria,

Poland, and Hungary to Catholicism. As the example of England demonstrates, the sudden change of religion was not typically the product of individuals deciding to convert en masse, but one monarch deciding to change the national religion by fiat.

The most radical Protestant groups—or, arguably, the most conservative, depending on where you stand—were the Calvinists and the Puritans. They objected to any celebration of Christmas because the Bible directed Christians to keep the Sabbath holy and did not sanction any other holy days or say anything about keeping the birth of Christ as a religious holiday. Many also questioned the very premise of Christmas, finding no support in the Bible for the assertion that Christ was born on December 25 and believing the entire holiday was a pagan, or "popist," creation. For the millions of Catholics in the world, an accusation that you were aligned with the Pope might seem like a compliment, but for the Calvinists and Puritans of the seventeenth century "popist" was the most derogatory insult you could fling at someone. The Lutherans took a more moderate approach, supporting the celebration of Christmas in a religious manner, but objecting to the drunken, boisterous, and sometimes lewd excesses that marked the Roman Saturnalia and never really disappeared.

Many histories say the Lutheran Church also objected to any observance of the feast days of Catholic saints and prohibited the existing practice in northern Germany under which St. Nicholas would leave gifts for well-behaved children on St. Nicholas' Day. While this conclusion is understandable given the anti–Catholic and hagiophobic rhetoric that accompanied the Reformation, as an explanation of the Lutheran Church's position it is probably an overstatement. The facts typically cited for this conclusion are the church's "deliberate substitution of the Christ Child for St. Nicholas as the bringer of gifts."[1] In *Christmas in Ritual and Tradition*, Miles explains what happened as follows:

> In the early seventeenth century a Protestant pastor is found complaining that parents put presents in their children's beds and tell them that St. Nicholas has brought them. "This," he says, "is a bad custom, because it points children to the saint, while yet we know that not St. Nicholas but the holy Christ Child gives us all good things for body and soul, and He alone it is whom we ought to call upon."[2]

Although this statement has been interpreted as a ban on any involvement with Catholic saints, Lutheran doctrine does not really support that conclusion. In 1530, the Diet of Augsburg, a meeting of the states that constituted "the Holy Roman Empire of the German Nation," the forerunner of modern Germany, produced a document titled the Augsburg Confession, setting forth twenty-eight principles which became the official statement of Lutheran church beliefs, and remains in force for most Lutheran denominations today. Article XXI, "On the Worship of Saints," says Lutherans "keep the saints, not as saviors or intercessors to God, but rather as examples and inspirations to our own faith and life."[3] This means Lutherans did not have any objection to recognition of the lives of saints as examples of behavior to be emulated, but objected to the idolization of saints and the Catholic practice of prayer to saints, which set up the saints as intermediaries between man and God. Recognition of St. Nicholas as someone to whom children would address requests for gifts, and St. Nicholas' decision to grant or deny that request depending on the child's behavior, placed him on the wrong side of that line.

The Reformation produced a great deal of hagiophobic rhetoric, some of it quite vicious. Given the combination of rational and irrational arguments against continuation of the St. Nicholas tradition, it is not surprising that German Lutherans would have ceased customs involving the saint even without a directive to do so. Accordingly, it is correct to say the Reformation disrupted the traditional celebration of St. Nicholas' Day in northern Germany, but the assumption that Lutherans actually prohibited the recognition of St.

Nicholas' Day is not really accurate. It is even more difficult to generalize about Lutheran beliefs today. The Lutheran Church, like many other Protestant faiths, has splintered and consolidated many times in the five centuries since 1530, resulting in a number of different Lutheran denominations representing a range of theological views, and some Lutheran denominations have lists of saint days that include St. Nicholas' Day on December 6. In sum, one cannot generalize about "Lutheran doctrine," much less assume that northern Germany had a common religious perspective.[4]

Nonetheless, no factor has been more important in the development of the Winter Solstice and Christmas gift-givers in Germany and central Europe than religion, broadly defined. The worship by early man of pagan gods like Odin and Thor, the arrival of Christianity in the Middle Ages, the Protestant Reformation of the sixteenth century, the affirmation of Christmas celebrations by the Anglican Church during the seventeenth century, and the official policies of atheism imposed by the Nazi and Communist governments during the twentieth century, each left an important mark on the observation of the Winter Solstice and Christmas. It was the Protestant Reformation, however, that had the most significant impact because it added new gift-givers and splintered the existing ones into dozens of pieces.

The effect of the Reformation depended, of course, on the religion ultimately adopted by the nation or state in question. In southern Germany—the modern states of Rhineland-Palatinate, Baden-Wurttemberg, and Bavaria—and the regions constituting the current Czech and Slovak Republics, the population remained Catholic despite the Reformation. In Austria, Poland, and Hungary, the populations initially converted to Protestantism, but returned to Catholicism roughly two decades later during a period known as the Catholic Restoration. Thus, putting aside the two periods in which the Nazi government of Germany and the Communist governments under the control of the Soviet Union implemented official policies of atheism, southern Germany and all of the nations in central Europe except Switzerland have been predominately Catholic since the sixteenth century. Switzerland is split between Catholics and Protestants. The states that now constitute northern Germany, on the other hand, converted to Lutheranism at the time of the Reformation. As noted above, the Lutheran Church took a middle-of-the road position on the celebration of Christmas, supporting the holiday but seeking to eliminate the excesses and discouraging the involvement of St. Nicholas. The Lutheran Church did not want to eliminate the Yuletide gift-giving altogether, however, and therefore encouraged members to change the date of holiday gift-giving from St. Nicholas' Day to Christmas and to use the Christ child ("Christkindl") if a Christmas gift-giver was desired.

The Lutheran approach was partially successful. That success, however, was primarily among Catholics, not Lutherans. As a consequence of geography more than religious doctrine, southern Germany did not have the St. Nicholas traditions that existed in northern Europe because there was never any need to introduce St. Nicholas as gift-giver to replace Odin in southern Germany. Rather, those states had already adopted Christmas as a Christian holiday. That meant, however, that the Catholics in southern Germany did not have any children's gift-giver, religious or secular, on either St. Nicholas' Day or Christmas. The Lutheran solution had appeal because it combined an overtly Christian custom, a new Christmas ritual, and an enjoyable but morally instructive experience for children. As a result, virtually all of the Catholic regions of Europe quickly adopted the Christ child as the Christmas gift-giver, giving him the names Christkindl in southern Germany and Austria, El Nino in Spain, Gesu Bambino in Italy and Le Petit Noel in France.[5] Catholics were free to celebrate St. Nicholas' Day, but with the Christkindl serving as Christmas gift-giver the celebration of St. Nicholas' Day never caught fire in the south like it had in northern Europe.

The newly-converted Lutherans in northern Germany, on the other hand, did not want to lose their beloved St. Nicholas tradition, and seem to have concluded that tradition could continue so long as the gift-giver was not a saint. This was probably a misinterpretation of the Lutheran admonition that children should be told all good things come from Christ, but, as Snyder writes in *December 25*, St. Nicholas was removed from the churches but "lived on in the street and homes."[6] On an *ad hoc* basis, the Protestant residents of northern Europe developed sev-

This German depiction of "Sanct Nicolaus" by Alexander Strahuber in 1849 looks nothing like the tall, stately St. Nicholas, and therefore is better categorized as one of the faux Nicholases than the Catholic saint.

eral dozen different versions of a secular Nicholas, who, at least initially, delivered gifts on St. Nicholas' Day. These characters, who we have defined as the faux Nicholases because they played the *role* of St. Nicholas, typically had long, unkempt hair and beards, soiled, torn coats or cloaks, often made of animal skins, heavy boots, and a bundle of switches. In Holland and Switzerland, which adopted Calvinist religions rather than Lutheranism, the post–Reformation gift-givers Sinterklaas and Samichlaus were also faux Nicholases because although they looked like St. Nicholas, and even had their own evil helpers, they were not the Catholic saint.

The vast majority of names used by the faux Nicholases are nicknames for Saint Nicholas or versions of the name Nicholas in different German dialects or other European nations: Aschenklas, Boozenickel, Busseklas, Bussklas, Class, Claws, Hel Niklos, Helijemann, Herrsche-klas, Joseph Claus, Hutscheklas, Klaôs, Klas, Klâs, Klasbur, Klaus, Klawes, Klôs, Klose, Nekels, Nêtklas, Nickel, Niglo, Nikelos, Niklas, Niklaus, Niklo, Niklobes, Niklosa, Nikola, Nikolo, Nikolai, Pelznickel, RuClas, Ruhclas, Rugclas, Samichlaus, Sante, Santiklaus, Santi Klaus, Schandeklôs, Seneklos, Sente Kloas, Sunner Klaus, Sunnerklas, Zedelsklasse and Zinterklas. According to the Handbook of German Folklore, some of these names, like Weihnachtsmann, Klaus, Nickel and Niglo, were used very widely while others are more localized and some do not appear at all in the handbook although they are mentioned elsewhere.[7] The real St. Nicholas could be called Sankt Nikolaus, der heilige Nikolaus ("Holy Nikolaus"), or simply Nikolaus in Germany, and almost two dozen of the regional names—the variations of Nick or Klaus—could mean the saint himself or one of the faux Nicholases, depending on local practice. Counterintuitively, "Nick" was also used as another name for Satan.

One name deserving special mention is Pelznickel ("Nicholas in furs"). Although one of many names used by the faux Nicholases throughout Germany, he was the direct predecessor of Belsnickle, the gift-giving character who arrived in Pennsylvania and contiguous states with the waves of German immigrants during the eighteenth and nineteenth centuries. In *December 25*, however, Snyder expresses the view that "[n]o scholar has ever solved totally the mystery of the origins of another major German Christmas figure known as Pelznickel."[8]

> Seemingly the servant without the master, Pelznickel traveled alone.... Evidently, as a result of the Reformation St. Nicholas underwent a lot of irreverent changes in Protestant homes to make him appear ridiculous and frightening to children. Dirty and disheveled furs, stout stick and a sack were the emblems of his office.[9]

With the exception of historian Charles W. Jones, however, historians have expressed no doubt about the origin of Pelznickel as a secular, fur-covered replacement for St. Nicholas in post–Reformation Germany.[10]

Der Pelzmärte.

This depiction of Pelzmärte from a German book, *Silhouetten aus Schwaben* by Theodor Griesinger (1863), incorporates the hooded cloak, long beard and bundle of switches common to Knecht Ruprecht and Pelznickel.

While calling it a "mystery," even Snyder seems to understand Pelznickel is simply another regional name for post–Reformation gift-givers who replaced St. Nicholas. The real mystery for Snyder seems to lie in the statement that Pelznickel appears as "the servant without the master." The answer, and a point that is critical in understanding the history of Santa Claus, is that Pelznickel was not a "servant" to anyone, and that when Pezlnickel arrived on the scene the putative "master," meaning St. Nicholas, had departed. He and the other faux Nicholases *replaced* St. Nicholas as Protestant gift-givers following the Reformation, and they did not need a servant, like St. Nicholas did, because they could perform both the gift-giving role of St. Nicholas and the disciplinary role of the evil helpers themselves. It is precisely this duality which distinguishes Pelznickel, Belsnickle and, ultimately, Santa Claus from St. Nicholas who traveled with an evil helper.

The precise roles of the faux Nicholases, like their names, varied by geography and time period. Different nations, different regions, and different villages could have different practices, and the nature and appearance of the gift-givers evolved over time. We can say with some certainty, however, that their original *raison d'être* was to allow the cherished St. Nicholas tradition to continue without an actual saint, but these practices plainly evolved over the next four hundred years. Over time, they expanded their role as substitutes for St.

Nicholas on December 6 and began appearing on any day between December 6 and Christmas, sometimes as the Christmas gift-giver's advance man and sometimes as the gift-giver himself.

By analogy to Pennsylvania's Belsnickle, the most direct descendant of Germany's Pelznickel, the faux Nicholases may have (1) visited the child's home to bring gifts on the evening before St. Nicholas' Day (December 6), which could be done in person or while the child was asleep; (2) visited the child's home any time during the month before Christmas to determine if the child was deserving of gifts by asking some basic catechism questions or listening to a song or poem, which required the child be awake and seems to have been a great source of fun for young men who blackened their face with soot and donned a fake beard, an old hat and long, dirty coat for the event; (3) accompanied the Christkindl on her Christmas Eve visit where that tradition was observed, which could be done while the child was having dinner or sleeping; or (4) came alone to deliver gifts on Christmas Eve, which could be done in person or while the child was sleeping.

In describing the development of Santa Claus, however, the most important aspect of the faux Nicholases is not their names or when they would appear because we know they eventually merged into a single character known as Der Weihnachtsmann who brought gifts on Christmas, making the details of their past lives mostly an historical curiosity. The important fact that distinguished them from St. Nicholas is they simultaneously embodied both the gift-giving function of St. Nicholas and the disciplinary role of the evil helpers, and the American Santa inherited this attribute through the German gift-givers who immigrated to Pennsylvania in the late eighteenth and nineteenth centuries. While the disciplinary responsibility of Santa Claus has never been quite as overt or as frightening as the German gift-givers, it is one of the critical attributes that distinguishes Santa Claus from the historical St. Nicholas.

Some will argue that the modern Santa Claus, in concert with modern, namby-pamby parents, no longer plays a disciplinary role at all. While American versions of the "whip" are decidedly less extreme than those of Berchta, Krampus, or even the switch-bearing faux Nicholases of nineteenth-century Germany, the same duality is an inherent part of Santa Claus. Rather than corporeal punishment, however, the modern American Santa relies on withholding benefits, leaving a lump of coal or a switch in place of a present, a disciplinary scheme reinforced by the admonition that Santa is all knowing when it comes to determining whether children are naughty or nice. Indeed, there are probably few parents alive today who have not given the warning, "Santa's elves were watching!" And there is probably not a child alive today who has not heard "You better watch out" because "Santa Claus is coming to town." Santa's "secret surveillance systems" is a *de facto* disciplinary practice that quite arguably is more effective than the threat of a switch.[11]

What many may find more interesting is that there are at least a half-dozen of the German faux Nicholases whose names could have become Santa Claus on the trip from Germany to New York: Sante Claus, Santiklaus, Santi Klaus, Schandeklôs, Seneklos, Sente Kloas and Sunner Klaus. While academics such as Berkeley historian Charles W. Jones have sought to determine who "made" Santa Claus by studying books or newspapers that the vast majority of the population did not, and many could not, read. We know from *False Stories Corrected*, however, that a phonetic version of Santa Claus was being used in conversation in America long before it was ever seen in print, and the most logical explanation is that German immigrants brought these names to America when they immigrated in the late eighteenth and early nineteenth centuries.

We also know from *False Stories Corrected* that the phonetic name must have been in use long enough before 1813 to justify calling it a common practice for "Santaclaw" to fill stockings hung by the children on Christmas Eve, and Washington Irving's reference to "Santeclaus" in an 1807 edition of *Salamagundi* makes it likely the name had been around at least that long. By 1823, when "Account of a Visit from St. Nicholas" was first published in *The Troy (N.Y.) Sentinel,* the editor was comfortable that his readers would construe the character St. Nicholas in Moore's poem as simply an alternative name for "Sante Claus," and over the next few decades many other editors who published the poem made the same decision.

9

Knecht Ruprecht

Pagan God,
Evil Helper or Faux Nicholas?

Many people will be surprised to learn that a figure named Knecht Ruprecht, a name most of us have never heard, is the most popular gift-giving figure in Germany after St. Nicholas, Christkindl, and Der Weihnachtsmann. That Ruprecht is virtually unknown outside of Germany is not so surprising; however, when one realizes he's also the most mysterious Christmas figure within Germany. There is no definitive account of his name, his origin, his function, or even his appearance despite early research by five highly distinguished scholars: Jacob Grimm, author of *Teutonic Mythology*, the definitive work on German mythology, in 1835[1]; Franz Weineck, a German anthropologist who created *Knecht Ruprecht und Seine Genossen* (*"Knecht Ruprecht and His Comrades"*) in 1898[2]; Alexander Tille, the German philosopher who authored the 1899 study *Yule and Christmas, Their Place in the Germanic Year*[3]; Clement Miles, an English folklorist whose 1912 study *Christmas in Ritual and Tradition* is still acknowledged by many as the leading English-language work on the history of Christmas[4]; and American George H. McKnight, whose 1917 biography *St. Nicholas: His Legend and His Role in the Christmas Celebration and Other Popular Customs* was one of the first modern biographies of St. Nicholas in his role as gift-giver.[5] Nonetheless, like Weihnacht versions of the title characters in the movies *Zelig* and *Forrest Gump*, Ruprecht always seems to show up in odd places or inexplicable roles.

Other than the fact "knecht" means "servant," rendering his name as Servant Rupert in English, virtually everything about him is subject to inconsistent, and often directly conflicting, explanations. Even the meaning of "knecht" is disputed by some who say it means "knight." It was this fact that prompted folklore expert Clement Miles to write in 1912 "[i]t can hardly be said that any satisfactory account has as yet been given of the origins of this personage, or of his relation to St. Nicholas."[6] In the century-plus since this statement was written, it remains true. Based on historical illustrations and literature one can view Ruprecht as a minor pagan god who worked for Thor, a companion or servant of Berchta, an "evil helper" adopted as a companion to St. Nicholas, a faux Nicholas who emerged after St. Nicholas left northern Germany, or something *sui generis*. In telling the history of Santa Claus, this is significant because more than one scholar has described Santa Claus as a descendent of Knecht Ruprecht though no one ever really explains those statements.

There are at least three theories that have been advanced about the origin of Knecht Ruprecht's name. One, suggested as a possibility by Grimm almost two centuries ago, is that Ruprecht means "the Devil." Grimm's explanation that the name Ruprecht is similar to the names Rubel and Rupel, which in some regions were names used as terms for the devil, is not particularly persuasive. While it is perilous to challenge history's best-known philologist in his area of expertise, the supposed similarity in the names Ruprecht and Rubel seems like too thin a reed upon which to form a conclusion. Tille's explanation that the "term Rupert became identical with [the] spirit from below" is more persuasive, but it is really only an assertion that Ruprecht *came to mean* the devil because that was the part Ruprecht played, just as Scrooge came to mean a miserly old man because the character Ebenezer Scrooge in *A Christmas Carol* was a miserly old man. That is different from saying, for example, that the surname Miller means someone who mills grain. Berryman's assertion that "Ruprecht was an ancient German name for the devil" does not really add anything to the analysis because it assumes the fact in question, which is *whether* Ruprecht was an ancient term for the devil.

The second theory, summarized by Raedisch in *The Old Magic of Christmas*, is that "Knecht Ruprecht's name, from the Old High German Hruodperaht, suggests that he was once the servant of the goddess 'Peraht,' or Perchta," another spelling for Berchta.[7] Grimm's treatise also supports this argument, stating that Ruprecht "makes his appearance around frau [Berchta], as her servant and companion, sometimes her substitute, and like her a terror to children."[8] Grimm places Ruprecht and Berchta into a category of mythical beings called the Perchten, mountain spirits whose most notable trait was they could either be good (*e.g.,* giving gifts to well-mannered children) or bad (*e.g.,* inflicting punishment on ill-mannered children).[9] Weineck's position acknowledges the name Ruprecht comes from the Old High German name Hruodperaht but goes further, asserting the name Hruodperaht means "the one that shines of victory or honor" and denotes Donar, the German name for Thor.[10] Thus, Weineck argues, Ruprecht is the servant of Donar: "everything fits (the dark look, the black face, the big beard, the noise, the chains, the bells, the harsh voice, the angry appearance and the intense grumbling when leaving) with the god of thunder [Donar]."[11] Weineck also says that Berchta "in my point of view" is Donar's wife. The importance of this mythological pairing, though never explained by Weineck, is presumably that it makes Ruprecht the servant of both Donar and Berchta, a conclusion consistent with Grimm's assertion that Ruprecht is Berchta's "servant and companion, sometimes her substitute."

The third theory about Ruprecht's name, which Tille adopts in *Yule and Christmas*, is that Ruprecht was a common name for servants and does not have any special meaning at all. Tille, a philosopher rather than a philologist, does not dispute Grimm's assertion that Ruprecht's name was from the Old High German Hruodperaht, meaning "glorious Percht," which ties him to Berchta as her servant or substitute, nor does he dispute that Ruprecht's name became synonymous with the devil in the late 1600s. Indeed, Tille writes that Ruprecht "became popular so quickly, that as early as 1680 his appearance could be interdicted by law, and the term Rupert became identical with [the] spirit from below."[12] The basis for Tille's opinion is simply that a character named Knecht Ruprecht began to appear in local plays in 1530, more than a century before his first appearance in a Christmas procession. It is hard to see how that fact undermines the evidence that Ruprecht was a figure in Germanic mythology who served as servant to Berchta and, in Weineck's view, Donar.

Grimm says Ruprecht first appeared in public at a Christmas parade in Nuremberg in 1668, whereas Tille asserts Ruprecht's initial appearance was as a fictional character in a parade in 1530, "and had originally nothing whatever to do with Christmas."[13] The timing of his appearance is important mostly because if Ruprecht appeared before the Reformation, he cannot be defined solely as a figure who took over St. Nicholas' gift-giving functions in Protestant regions following the Reformation. An appearance in 1530, only thirteen years after

Martin Luther initiated the Reformation, is such a short time that it would be surprising to learn Ruprecht was a product of the Reformation rather than pre-existing German folklore.

Both Grimm and Tille agree, however, that in the 1680s he began to appear regularly in Christmas processions and plays. His typical role was that of switch-bearing assistant to Christkindl, St. Nicholas or "dame Berhta."[14] Berhta, whose name comes from the same Old High German word as Ruprecht, is an early name for our old friend Berchta.[15] How Berchta, the pagan goddess who helped lead the Wild Hunt and whose specialty was disemboweling naughty children, came to appear in these plays—not to mention why she needed a switch-bearer to scare young children—is not explained, but it confirms the many assertions that Christianity did not eliminate pagan practices entirely, and that Christian and pagan figures continued to mingle for hundreds of years.

What Knecht Ruprecht looked like is another question to which one finds completely inconsistent answers. In his 1917 history of St. Nicholas, historian McKnight unmistakably describes Ruprecht as looking like one of the faux Nicholases, the human figures dressed in rags or hides that undertook the role of St. Nicholas in northern Germany following the Reformation.

> In all north Germany, too, on Christmas Eve, there goes about a bearded man covered with a great hide or with straw, who questions children and rewards their good conduct. His name varies with the locality. In many places, he is called "Knecht Ruprecht," a name probably going back to a pre–Christian time before St. Nicholas became associated with the children's festival.[16]

In other places, McKnight says, the man is called "De Hele Christ," Holy Christ, or one of many "juvenile derivative[s] from the name Nicholas"—the same group of names adopted by the faux Nicholases.[17] Thus, McKnight contends that "a bearded man covered with a great hide" who "questions children and rewards their good conduct" and was known in the region by one of the nicknames for Nicholas—a description that fits perfectly the post–Reformation gift-givers we have defined as the faux Nicholases—was "really" Knecht Ruprecht under a different name. This statement illustrates the problems inherent in historians or folklorists trying to tell the histories of St. Nicholas, Ruprecht and the faux Nicholases identifies the gift-givers based on who they "really are" rather than who they appear to be. For example, what Bowler calls the "strange metamorphosis" of St. Nicholas could only mean he has adopted the appearance of the raggedy, bearded, switch-bearing terror men.

One of the earliest depictions of Knecht Ruprecht, shown trying to grab an unruly child, was a woodcut by Joseph Franz von Gotz in 1784. Ruprecht's horns, which mark him as non-human, later disappeared.

This illustration by artist Oskar Plesch Holzstich from a German paper, *Illustrierte Zeitung*, on December 18, 1875, shows Knecht Ruprecht, wearing a long dark coat and hat which conceals his identity.

This illustration of Knecht Ruprecht is from the 1852 Deutscher Jugendkalender ("German Youth Calendar") but based on his appearance he could be any of the faux Nicholases who traveled alone as a combination of gift-giver and disciplinarian.

These characters could not be St. Nicholas, however, regardless of attire, because he was a Catholic saint unwanted in northern Germany. The defining features of St. Nicholas are not only that he dresses as the bishop he is but that the good saint would never carry the bundle of switches used to punish misbehaving children. The failure properly to identify the characters makes it impossible to make definitive statements about them. For example, the assertion that St. Nicholas did not appear in the Protestant regions of Germany following the Reformation makes no sense if one conflates the faux Nicholases with St. Nicholas. The same problem arises when historians or folklorists use the name Knecht Ruprecht to describe the terror men—that is, the faux Nicholases—who go by another name. You can say they look alike (if they do) or act alike (if they do) or that Knecht Ruprecht was the visual inspiration for the faux Nicholaes (which might be true) but to say they are all Knecht Ruprecht without explaining the basis for that conclusion makes it impossible to tease out the real Knecht Ruprecht, and explain how he differs from the other post–Reformation gift-givers. By way of illustration, the map of Gabenbringers in der Nikolauszeit (German gift-givers) in the Handbook of German Folklore shows Ruprecht as the gift-giver only in a small section of central Germany, a fact that cannot be reconciled with assertion that all of the terror men are "really" Ruprecht.

In fact, McKnight's description is quite consistent with that of the "terror man" in Weineck's *Knecht Ruprecht and His Companions*. In *The Krampus*, Ridenour provides a

Opposite: In this 1848 illustration, Weihnachtsaufzug ("Christmas Lift"), from a German paper, Christkindl is accompanied by Knecht Ruprecht in a long, hooded cloak.

similar portrayal, saying Ruprecht "is typically dressed in a dark hooded robe accented with fur, wears a dark, bushy beard, carries switches, and totes a large sack (once used to carry off naughty children, but now used to carry gifts)."[18] In *The Old Magic of Christmas*, Raedisch describes Ruprecht in the same manner with fewer words, saying he looks like a bearded monk covered with soot, wearing a black or brown robe with a pointed hood.[19] Read together, these sources give us a fairly consistent description of the appearance and behavior of Ruprecht in his role as solitary Christmas gift-giver, one that is virtually identical to post–Reformation faux Nicholases who replaced St. Nicholas in Protestant regions. There are also a number of historical drawings of Knecht

This illustration of Knecht Ruprecht by Otto von Reinsberg-Düringsfeld from an 1863 German book, *Das Festliche Jahr* (*The Festive Year*), demonstrates how Ruprecht delivered treats by tossing them on the floor.

Ruprecht from the nineteenth century that depict him in a similar manner.[20] In 1847, German artist Adrian Ludwig Richter drew him as a stooped man in a long cloak who looks more like Moritz von Schwind's Herr Winter than anything else, and in 1881, German artist Berthold Woltze depicted an even more ordinary-looking man, wearing an overcoat and fur hat, and carrying a bundle of switches and a bag.

There are other descriptions of Ruprecht, however, that are completely at odds with these descriptions and drawings. The oldest depiction of Knecht Ruprecht is a 1784 engraving by J.F. Gotz of a man wearing a basket of switches. Gotz' engraving, which is expressly labeled as Knecht Ruprecht, looks like a respectable man of the era except for three details: the basket of switches he carries, the fact he is grabbing one of the young children with an apparent intent to place him in a bag: and two small horns that emerge from his hat. The same engraving, however, appears in other books where it is labeled as Krampus. Similarly, in "Christmas Throughout Christendom," Spencer says Ruprecht is "dressed in fur, and covered with chains, with blackened face and fiery eyes, and a long red tongue protruding out of his mouth."[21] In *Christmas Folklore*, Coffin describes Ruprecht as "a refugee from [a] heathen ritual" who "has been closely associated with Nicholas in many areas, sometimes accompanying the saint as 'Black Pete,' a terrible assistant with a dingy face, horns, a long red tongue, fiery eyes, and chains that clank."[22] In *Christmas in Ritual and Tradition*, Miles describes a play in which St. Nicholas and Ruprecht appear on Christmas Eve, and St. Nicholas "makes each child repeat a prayer and show his lesson-books. Meanwhile, Ruprecht in a hide, with glowing eyes and a long red tongue, stands at the door to overawe the young people."[23]

The only logical explanation for the inconsistencies among otherwise credible sources

By 1890, Knecht Ruprecht in Berfegenbeit, by artist K. Rubne in 1890, displays the look of a reasonably respectable citizen with long fur coat, fur hat and dark beard.

is that Knecht Ruprecht evolved, ridding himself of the devil-like features over time (or, perhaps, in one episode of "Extreme Makeover—Satanic Edition"). This conclusion is supported by some of the authors who described Ruprecht in Satanic terms in the first place. For example, Berryman writes Ruprecht "experienced a transformation in the 1900s and became a kinder, gentler soul nearly indistinguishable from Santa Claus. Although Ruprecht's name remained the same, his behavior was less devilish. He still made his rounds before Christmas, knocking at the door and questioning the children about their lessons."[24] In *Santa Claus: Last of the Wild Men*, Siefker observes that when Ruprecht was working alone, rather than as an assistant to St. Nicholas, he "appeared as a slightly frightening but not totally hellish figure."[25] In the *Encyclopedia of Christmas*, Gulevich goes even further, asserting "somewhere along the line his identity merged with St. Nicholas."[26] The evolution described in these books continued into the twenty-first century, and the most recent versions depict the bearded monk identified by Raedisch without the soot, a warm and cuddly Knecht Ruprecht who, like Snow White, comes out of the woods surrounded by birds and forest creatures to accompany St. Nicholas.

The third unanswered question about Ruprecht, and ultimately the most interesting and difficult, is his origin and his role in the German Christmas celebrations. Virtually all of the German Christmas characters were created to perform a specific job, and, with a little research, one can generally determine the origin of the character. St. Nicholas and the evil helpers, for example, were created to fulfill the gift-giving role of Odin and Berchta after the Catholic church forbade the involvement of pagan gods, and the faux Nicholases were created after the Lutheran church discouraged the involvement of a Catholic saint in holiday gift-giving. For Knecht Ruprecht, however, as Clement Miles complained in 1912, "[i]t can hardly be said that any satisfactory account has as yet been given of the origins of this personage."[27] The most likely explanation for this quandary is that Ruprecht appeared in 1530, if not earlier, when he had no role, as gift-giver or otherwise, in the German Christmas celebration.

To be clear, we know a lot about what Ruprecht actually did during the German Christmas celebrations. For example, in the seventeenth-century Christmas plays described by Grimm in *Teutonic Mythology*, Ruprecht would "come on with rod and sack, threatening to thrash disobedient children, to throw them into the water [or] to puff their eyes out."[28] Similarly, in his position as "terror man," we know Ruprecht shows up at the front door sometime during the Christmas season to ask the child to pray, and, if they do, to toss nuts and apples onto the floor.[29] We also know, however, that he occasionally appears with a wide variety of seemingly unconnected Christmas characters, including Nikolaus and Christkindl, and that, as explained in more detail below, he supposedly sends various evil helpers to appear on his behalf. Unfortunately, the fact Ruprecht performs a large variety of tasks with a variety of other characters in a variety of circumstances does not tell us much about the origin or function of Ruprecht himself. Indeed, this chameleon-like quality only deepens the mystery of his origin and function in German folklore.

In trying to determine Ruprecht's role, one of the most puzzling facts is the number of statements that Ruprecht "was known as" a variety of figures who anyone familiar with the German Christmas characters would immediately recognize to be someone else. By way of example, one will find statements in the literature that Ruprecht was "known" as, "disguised" as, or "represented by" Krampus, Hans Trapp, Buttenmandl and Pelznickel, among many other characters. As the reader should recognize, these are completely different characters who look nothing like each other. Hans Trapp looks a bit like a 1970s rock singer—think Ian Anderson of Jethro Tull playing the flute while standing on one leg—with tights, long, stringy hair and beard but no obvious animal parts, Krampus looks like the devil, Buttenmandl looks like a bale of hay with a face hidden inside and Pelznickel looks like a dirty, backwoods version of St. Nicholas (and, coincidentally, the character named Aqualung on one of Jethro Tull's early albums). The statement that Ruprecht was known as or represented by these characters, without further explanation, simply makes no sense.

In "Christmas Through Christendom," an 1873 article in *Harper's New Monthly Magazine*, O.N. Spencer arguably sheds more light on the subject than most of the scholarly treatises. Spencer writes that "the bugbear Ruprecht, under different names and disguises, plays a conspicuous part among German-speaking populations in the Christmas festivities."[30] The "different names and disguises" cited in this article include Klaubauf and Krampus as assistants of St. Nicholas; Rumpanz, Hans Trapp and Pelzmarte as assistants to the Christ-child; and Clas and Joseph as "a black-bearded peasant, wrapped in straw," who went house to house in northern Germany "asking the children if they know how to pray, rewarding those who can with gingerbread, apples, and nuts, and punishing unmercifully those who cannot"; and a "Christmas bugbear" named "Ashy Claws" who "carries a rod, at the end of which is fastened a sack full of ashes, with which he beats the children."[31] In these passages, Spencer effectively defines the category of characters that Ruprecht represents as a "bugbear," an archaic term synonymous with bugaboo, bogeyman and hobgoblin, all of which mean an imaginary being invoked to frighten children.[32] The faux Nicholases, except for the two who assume the look of bishops, and "terror men" are unmistakably bogeymen.

One of the most thorough discussions of this character is titled, in English, *Knecht Ruprecht and His Comrades*. The short book is actually the transcript of a speech published in 1898 by Franz Weineck, a German professor who co-founded the Niederlausitz Society for Anthropology and Antiquity and was a member of the Berlin Society for Anthropology, Ethnology and Prehistory.[33] At the outset of that speech, Weineck describes a visit from Ruprecht:

> When Christmas, the most beautiful of holidays, approaches, the children wait every evening with sorrow and yet excited desire of the "terror man" who announces it to them. Finally, outside in the dark hallway it rings or rumbles or pitter-patters, horror hits the children's hearts and then already he comes in in an inside out dark fur, the face darkened, and covered in a giant beard, on the head a fur cap, an old hat, a grey pointed hat or something similar, in the one hand the big rod and on his back the bag in which he threatens to put the children and from which he gets the presents for the good ones later. With a rough voice he asks if the children are behaving and can pray and when they, shaking and shivering, recited a song verse, the Our Father or another prayer, he gives to them, now friendlier, nuts and apples, also dried fruits or he throws those with noise into the chamber and hits now with his rod the bigger boys and girls, while the little ones, greedy yet still in fright, pick them up; or he also leaves, after he let the children pray, with strong muttering and throws now finally to the little ones who are freed from their fright through the half open door the nuts and apples.[34]

Based on German mythology defining the three major Germanic gods and their associated animals, Weineck divides the German Christmas characters into three groups: (1) "Woden [Odin] with his white horse, Schimmelreiter, the male holy Christ, Niklaus, Niklas, Niklo, Niklosa, Niklobes, Nekels, Klôs, Klaôs, Klaus, Klâs, Bullerklâs, Ruklas, Aschenklas [and] Nêtklas," all of which appear to be versions of St. Nicholas[35]; (2) "Frigg (Frija, Hulda, Perachta) with the Storch [stork], Heilger Christ (female), Christkind, Engel, Frau Holle, Percht, Perret, Berchta, Berchte, Berchtel, Budelfrau and Pudelmutter," all of which are female gift-givers; and (3) "the Ruprecht or Pelzmärtel, Märte, Bartel, Krampus, Klaubauf, Putenmandl, Schmutzi, Hans Trapp, Rüpelz, Schandeklôs, Sunnerklaus and the Erbsbär, and Donar [Thor] with the 'Bock' [goat] as Klabberbock, Schnabbuk, Ziege, Habersack, Habergeiß," all of which are much darker figures than Nicholas.[36] In this approach, Ruprecht becomes a servant to Thor, as well as Berchta, and perhaps a demigod in his own right.

One could define the first group, the Odin and Nicholas characters as the "light" group, the second group as the female characters, and the third group, with the Donor and Ruprecht, as the dark group. This approach gives the character known as Ruprecht a commonality the characters otherwise lack. Weineck also describes, in some detail, where, when and with whom Ruprecht and his representatives appear, noting that in some areas he "only appears for the Protestants while the Catholics have their 'Niklas' who terrifies and makes the children happy."[37] In the western and northern parts of Germany, he says, "Nikolaus," meaning the saint, "appears for the Catholics while for the Protestants he appears with Ruprecht or Pelzmärtel."[38] Weineck also writes, somewhat inconsistently, that "in the areas where Donar is honored the most and as the highest of all gods, Ruprecht and his representatives also appear; however, wherever Woden is celebrated and admired, it is exclusively the territory of the Niklas."[39]

In Chapter 10, "Gift-Givers in Germany and Central Europe," you will see that in the age of mass media, where information can be conveyed more widely and consistently, another Christmas character, Der Weihnachtsmann, has risen to the top of the pyramid and Knecht Ruprecht, although he still has a role, has evolved into a friendly helper of St. Nicholas in the Protestant regions of Germany. St. Nicholas probably should not appear in Protestant regions or with figures, like Ruprecht, who are supposed to appear "where Donar is honored the most and as the highest of all gods," but Ruprecht, like Forrest Gump and Zelig, always seems to show up when and where he is least expected.

10

Gift-Givers in Germany and Central Europe

St. Nicholas, the Christ Child, Der Weihnachtsmann and Knecht Ruprecht

In the celebration of Christmas, Germany and central Europe are the ultimate survivors. No region has undergone as much change in its Christmas gift-givers, or faced the celebratory headwinds imposed by Martin Luther, Adolf Hitler and Joseph Stalin, but no region has retained as much Christmas spirit. Unfortunately, as explained by folklore expert Tristram P. Coffin in *The Book of Christmas Folklore*, trying to track the various gift-givers and helpers, or to explain their arrival in unexpected places at unorthodox times, is an exercise in futility: "There is little point in trying to summarize centuries of adjustments in custom and calendar as they affect thousands of persons in dozens of lands," Coffin writes. "Just about any conceivable combination of pagan and Christian ritual developed somewhere about Christmas during these years."[1]

To the same effect, the late Val R. Berryman, former curator of history at the Michigan State University Museum and a widely-respected expert on Christmas, wrote a series of articles on Christmas in Germany for *The Glow,* a bimonthly magazine published by The Golden Glow of Christmas Past, an organization of Christmas collectors.[2] Berryman wrote that "[t]he one thing one learns when trying to find the *one true story* of German Christmas characters is that it doesn't exist. Many holiday figures have a variety of names depending on the region or village in which the story is told. The origin of each character is lost in the past and then added to and distorted over the centuries by a variety of story-tellers and artists. Explanations are numerous and contradictory."[3]

Even for natives, unwinding the names and history of the German gift-givers complicated by numerous changes in national boundaries and some thirty-five languages and dialects is head-spinning. Indeed, the use of the name Germany to describe the entire region of Europe is really a misnomer because there were a number of ever-changing states rather than one nation, and there are independent but closely related nations, such as Austria, that have contributed as much to German Christmas as the Germans. With regard to language, the phrases High German, Middle German, and Low German describe German spoken in different geographic regions while phrases like "Old High German" describe earlier versions of the languages. There are also a large number of different dialects within each language, with some thirty-five different dialects in Germany alone, and a large number of Germanic languages spoken in nations contiguous to Germany.

The number of German languages and dialects is particularly burdensome when dealing with folklore and oral tradition. The complex combination of different dialects and divergent folk practices means the same figure can have many names. What seems like the same name can identify more than one figure, and some names, such as Klaus, have a large number of variations that may, or may not, reflect substantive differences. To further the confusion, the same historical drawings are often identified in the literature as different characters, the characters can change their function or appearance over time, and, in many cases, the existing resources are simply wrong, sending the researcher down a rat hole like a terrier in pursuit of its prey.

The gift-giving characters would be easier to distinguish if all they did was show up on St. Nicholas' Day or Christmas, which would at least create a bright line between St. Nicholas and his secular replacements and the Christmas gift-givers. In practice, however, the German Christmas characters did not always stick to one holiday. They would often show up in advance of Christmas, monitoring the behavior of German children, appearing in Christmas markets, plays, and pageants, or simply carousing about town in the month before Christmas. Over time, many of the faux Nicholases, originally intended as substitutes for St. Nicholas on Nicholastag (December 6) became Christmas gift-givers and were eventually absorbed into the character Der Weihnachtsmann. In plays and pageants, figures from German folklore, including Berchta and Knecht Ruprecht, interact with figures from the Bible, including the Angel Gabriel, Mary, Joseph, the Christ child, the shepherds, the Magi, aka the Three Kings, Catholic saints such as Peter, Martin, and Nicholas, and, finally, Satan, who seemed always to show up when there was a party. These characters, in turn, could be mixed and matched with some combination of the faux Nicholases and the evil helpers in numerous odd and unpredictable ways. The outcome, more often than not, was a gigantic German jumble of gift-givers, helpers, heathens, and holidays, and trying to understand them makes one wonder how the Germans could produce such fine automobiles.[4]

Accordingly, in describing the German gift-givers it makes more sense to explain what we know with reasonable certainty rather than to spin our wheels explaining what we don't know, something we have already done to a great extent done in the prior chapters. In the five centuries since the Reformation, four major Christmas gift-givers emerged from the dozens who preceded or arose out of the Reformation: (1) St. Nicholas, the Catholic bishop known in Germany as Sankt Nikolaus, Nikolaus, or Der Heilige Nikolaus; (2) Christkindl, a Protestant invention who nevertheless became the gift-giver of choice on Christmas in Catholic regions as well following the Reformation; (3) Der Weihnachtsmann, the secular gift-giver who resembles the American Santa Claus more than any other gift-giver and who eclipsed the faux Nicholases during the nineteenth century by, figuratively, creating a monopoly through smart use of mass media and buying up or forcing out of business all of its smaller competitors; and (4) Knecht Ruprecht, the mysterious figure of German folklore who was, in succession, an evil helpers, a terror man and a friendly companion of St. Nicholas in Protestant regions. The following is a more detailed discussion of each focusing on the gift-giving practices that developed around them.

St. Nicholas. Several hundred years prior to the Reformation, St. Nicholas replaced Odin and Berchta as the Yule gift-giver in northern Europe, creating a Christian holiday, St. Nicholas' Day, in place of the pagan Yule. In some regions, St. Nicholas would appear in public events such as plays or parades before St. Nicholas' Day. On the evening of December 5, the day before St. Nicholas' Day, one of the evil helpers would often join him to leave gifts or treats at the homes of good children or visit some punishment on children who were not well behaved. For most families, the long-standing tradition was for the children to leave their shoes or stockings by the fireplace or front door, often filled with hay or carrots for St. Nicholas' horse, a practice that folklorists say began with German children leaving food for Odin's eight-legged horse Sleipnir. St. Nicholas would arrive while the children were sleeping, leaving small gifts such as fruit or candy in their shoes after feeding the snacks to his horse. In other cases, however, St. Nicholas would arrive in person with one of the evil helpers by his side.

Following the Reformation, most of northern Germany converted to Lutheranism, and the visits of St. Nicholas in those regions waned. At the same time, one website on German customs suggests, the in-person visits of St. Nicholas became more common in Catholic regions because Catholics "did not quietly accept the diminishment of their saint" and responded "by making Nicholas a figure who visited families' homes on his appointed day and stood in judgment over children. If the young ones could answer religious questions and said their bedtime prayers faithfully, they received a gift from the sack that Nicholas' companion, Knecht Ruprecht, had slung over his shoulder. Those that slacked in their religious commitments got the switch or were threatened with being hauled off in Ruprecht's sack."[5]

Unfortunately, there is no way to verify whether the Reformation created a newfound interest by Catholic families in visits by St. Nicholas and Knecht Ruprecht. Ruprecht is generally identified as a Protestant figure, making it unlikely he would accompany the Catholic saint, and most of the illustrations of Ruprecht show him visiting alone whereas St. Nicholas is accompanied by one of the devilish evil helpers. Moreover, Krampus or other dark assistants to St. Nicholas are often identified as "representatives" of Knecht Ruprecht, which could mean that the author used the name Ruprecht when we would have called the character Krampus. One must be reminded of Berryman's admonition that the "one true story" of German Christmas characters does not exist, that many figures "have a variety of names depending on the region or village in which the story is told," and that "explanations are often contradictory."[6]

One obvious question about St. Nicholas rarely acknowledged in the existing histories is how long the German Protestants stuck to the position articulated in the sixteenth century that Catholic saints should have no role in the Protestant Christmas observances. It is not uncommon, of course, for people to revert to long-standing traditions and practices as efforts to change those practices lose their steam. As Miles puts it, "ritual practices are far more enduring than the explanations given to them."[7] If Protestants could resume the St. Nicholas tradition, that begs the question of why Germans would continue having the faux Nicholases appear on St. Nicholas' Day. As it turns out, according to Linda Raedisch in *The Old Magic of Christmas: Yuletide Traditions for the Darkest Days*, that by the eighteenth century the faux Nicholases "had already disentangled themselves from the date of December 6, which is, after all, a saint's feast day and therefore not in the spirit of Protestantism. Those who were engaged to make house calls now did so on Christmas Eve."[8]

Miles, likewise, says that "Nicholas [was] not confined to his own festival; he often appears on Christmas Eve. We have already seen how he is attended by various companions, including Christ Himself, and how he comes now vested as a bishop, now as a masked and shaggy figure. The names and attributes of the Christmas and Advent visitors are rather confused, but on the whole it may be said that in Protestant north Germany the episcopal St. Nicholas and his Eve have been replaced by Christmas Eve and the Christ Child, while the name Klas has become attached to various unsaintly forms appearing at or shortly before Christmas."[9]

Despite Miles' reputation as one of the most prominent experts on Christmas folklore, there is a critical ambiguity in his analysis. Use of the name St. Nicholas to describe "a masked and shaggy figure" makes no sense if taken literally because we know that St. Nicholas was not masked and shaggy. Miles must mean, therefore, a masked and shaggy figure playing the role usually played by the saint, which under our nomenclature would be a faux Nicholas. Moreover, although Klas was a name used by the faux Nicholases, so were Klaus, Klos, Klose, Klawes, Kloas, Klaws, Nickel, Niglo, Niklo, Nikolo, Nikola, Nikolai, Nikelos, Niklosa, Niklobes and Niklas—all nicknames, of course, for Nikolaus, the formal German version of the English Nicholas. This may seem like quibbling, but clarity of exposition requires that such statements be exact, or at least explained, because a good deal of the confusion among German gift-givers is attributable to sloppy use of existing names.

For example, we know that St. Nicholas largely disappeared in northern Germany following the Reformation but that a number of faux Nicholases—"masked and shaggy figures" who bore nicknames for Nicholas—quickly appeared. We can also surmise that the appearance of the faux Nicholases was often patterned after Ruprecht because the descriptions and illustrations of the characters look so much alike. By calling these figures St. Nicholas, however, Miles leaves us to wonder whether he intended to contradict the premise that St. Nicholas disappeared in the Protestant regions of Germany following the Reformation. Miles is almost certainly using the phrase "masked and shaggy figures" to mean the faux Nicholases because, as Raedisch says, many of these figures moved their appearances to Christmas during the seventeenth or eighteenth century (and, as explained below, largely merged into a single secular gift-giver, Der Weihnachtsmann, by the nineteenth century). Moreover, although Miles may be correct that St. Nicholas and his feast day were seldom observed in northern Germany when Miles' study was written in 1912, the failure to make a distinction between the saint and secular gift-givers makes it impossible to know exactly what he means.

In any event, St. Nicholas seems to have made somewhat of a comeback as a gift-giver in northern Germany in the last century, and reports say he now appears more frequently, often with Knecht Ruprecht, on the evening of December 5. Unlike Americans, who studiously ignore St. Nicholas' Day on the premise that St. Nicholas and Santa Claus are like travelers in a time machine who cannot co-exist in the same space without damaging the space-time continuum, Germans still mark St. Nicholas' Day on December 6. The Christmas gift-givers, however, have become a much more important part of the holiday season while St. Nicholas has become, in effect, an *amuse-bouche* to the full Christmas dinner.

Although St. Nicholas is best known as a gift-giver, he also had an important role in German Christmas plays and parades popular from the Reformation to the nineteenth century. These were public appearances by roving bands of actors that resembled in many ways the traveling mummer plays that were common in England during the same time period. According to Jacob Grimm's 1835 treatise, *Teutonic Mythology*, the basic plot of the plays common in the seventeenth century involved the journey of Joseph and Mary to Bethlehem, the birth of the baby Jesus, the persecution by King Herod and the flight of the Holy Family into Egypt. The job of Knecht Ruprecht and Satan, who were reportedly most popular with the audiences, was to provide comic relief by chasing the children in the audience in a mock effort to punish them for whatever offense the players could find.

O.N. Spencer's "Christmas Throughout Christendom," a lengthy and well-researched article about European Christmas customs, explains that "[b]efore the presentation begins [Satan] capers about through the village—a sort of peripatetic playbill—furiously blowing his horn, and frightening or bantering both old and young. During the performance, though figuring in the rather humble role of a messenger, he does not cease to joke with the players or rail at the public."[10] In describing the respective roles of St. Nicholas and Knecht Ruprecht, the article states:

> The saint, who rather plumes himself on his high office of heavenly janitor, carries matters with a high hand. He examines the children's copy-books, it may be, bids them kneel down and pray, and then, by virtue of his high prerogative, pronounces sentence upon the unfortunate delinquents, and calls upon the black Ruprecht, who stands waiting outside the door, to execute his orders. "Ruperus, Rupert's, enter! The children will not be obedient." The frightful bugbear [Ruprecht] … roars out to the children, "Can you pray?" Whereupon they fall upon their knees and repeat their prayers at the top of their voices.[11]

After the children prayed, the players representing heavenly figures would finish with a song or two while St. Nicholas or Knecht Ruprecht would scatter fruit, nuts, and candy on the floor for the children. When the play ended, the parents would offer the players a few coins for the entertainment.[12]

The Christkindl. The Christkindl ("Christ child") is purely a product of the Reformation, resulting from a Lutheran minister's assertion that St. Nicholas should not be given credit for Christmas gifts because all good things come from Christ. The Christkindl is not depicted as an actual infant, presumably because newborns aren't really suitable for dramatic roles, much less carrying heavy bags of gifts, but often appears as a girl, typically with blonde hair dressed in white and gold. Christkindl is sometimes portrayed by a young girl, creating the look of an angel or cherub, but more commonly is played by a teenager or young woman similar in age to Sweden's St. Lucia and Russia's Snegurochka. The older girls will often wear a wreath of candles, creating an even greater similarity to St. Lucia.

While use of Christkindl as the Christmas gift-giver was supposedly a Lutheran idea, it was embraced wholeheartedly by Catholics throughout Europe, and the tradition, therefore, spans the Protestant-Catholic religious divide. In Christmas cards, scraps, or other illustrations, the Christkindl is sometimes shown sitting on a horse ridden by a bearded, cloaked male—he could be Knecht Ruprecht, Pelznickel, or one of the other faux Nicholases—whose job was to act as chaperone and valet. Like Weihnachtsmann, Christkindl is often pictured carrying a small Christmas tree, presumably because in the German tradition the tree and presents were often displayed together for the first time on Christmas Eve.

In practice, however, Christkindl seldom delivers gifts in person, which would be a huge logistical challenge even if the tree were not included. The most common tradition for those families who treat the Christkindl as the Christmas gift-giver is that the Christkindl arrives and departs while the family is eating dinner on Christmas Eve, traditionally a meal of roast goose, duck or rabbit, potato dumplings, and red cabbage, a spiced wine known as glühwein and Dresdner stollen, gingerbread and cookies for dessert. The parents would erect and decorate the Christmas tree in advance in a separate room, placing the gifts on or under the tree before Christmas Eve arrives and locking the door until Christmas dinner. When the dinner was over, one of the parents would ring a bell, signifying that the Christkindl had arrived. The parents would then take the children into the parlor, revealing the decorated tree and gifts at the same time. Based on the various descriptions, these gift-giving practices are common in other European nations as well and have changed little over time.

The Christkindl may also appear in person at Christkindl markets, the modern successor to the Christmas markets of the seventeenth century, or Christmas parades, pageants and other public displays. For a young woman, impersonating the new-born son of God may seem like a dead-end job, but it wasn't. As Berryman emphasizes, "Christkindl does not represent the actual Baby Jesus."[13] Rather, the girl is viewed as the mature Jesus Christ's symbolic representative on earth.[14] While Christkindl is the most common name, she is also known as Engel ("Angel") and Heilger Christ ("Holy Christ"). Although Christkindl originated in Germany, she rapidly became the primary Christmas gift-giver in France (where she is known as Le Petit Jesus), in Italy (where she is known as Gesu Bambino), and in Austria, Hungary, and Switzerland (all of which use the name Christkindl). She has also inspired gift-givers in the Czech Republic, where she appears as an angel who descends from heaven with St. Nicholas and Cert on a golden rope; in Russia, where she was likely part of the inspiration for Snegurochka ("Snow Maiden"), the young woman with long blonde braids who accompanies Ded Moroz; and in America, where Pennsylvanians interpreted the name "Christkindl" to be "Kriss Kringle," and assumed that was the name for the adult gift-giver known as Belsnickle.

The Christkindl has also given her name to one of the most common Christmas celebrations in Europe: the Christkindl market. One of the earliest markets was reportedly held in Munich in 1310, and there are now more than fifty large Christmas markets in Germany and well over a hundred throughout Europe. Virtually every large city in Europe has a market, and the larger cities in Germany often have several markets catering to different interests. While Christkindl is the historic name for these markets, the majority these days are called Christmas markets in the language of the nation in which they are held. For those interested in attending, one can visit a new market each day with only a short train ride to another European city. The markets typically start on the first day of Advent, marking the start of the Christmas season, and run until a day or two before Christmas itself, and there are a number of guide books or group tours that can be located easily through an internet search.

In the Middle Ages, European villages typically had central squares serving as markets for the community, and the original purpose of the Christkindl markets was to sell gifts and food for the holidays. Over the centuries, they have evolved into something that might remind many readers of a state fair held during the winter, but without the livestock, tractor pulls, racing pigs, and slice-it/dice-it demonstrations. Held outdoors, the markets feature wooden booths selling traditional Christmas foods of the region, such as grilled sausages and gingerbread in Germany, beer, wine, and traditional Christmas beverages like Glühwein, eggnog, and wassail, gifts for friends and family, locally-made Christmas decorations, and similar products. The markets are beautifully decorated and lighted, with recorded Christmas music or performers, and often include rides such as Ferris wheels and merry-go-rounds. Many of the markets will also feature, in person, Christkindl and the local equivalent of Santa.

Der Weihnachtsmann. The history of Der Weihnachtsmann appears almost as simple as the histories of St. Nicholas and Knecht Ruprecht are complicated. To explain the history of Der Weihnachtsmann, however, it will be helpful briefly to remind the reader of the roles of Knecht Ruprecht and the faux Nicholases, groups who performed both the gift-giving and disciplinary roles performed by St. Nicholas and his evil helpers. Unlike the saint, Knecht Ruprecht and the faux Nicholases did not have or need an evil helper because their appearance and demeanor, buttressed by a handful of birch switches, were sufficiently scary to convey that the Christmas visitor could provide gifts or punishment and, unlike St. Nicholas or the Christkindl, there was no religious impediment to use of their switches. Moreover, despite the distinct explanations of the history and development of Knecht Ruprecht and the faux Nicholases, all of them, in practice, were the roughly bearded, fur-wearing, switch-bearing, face-blackened, angry-looking "terror men" who appeared as seasonal gift-givers in northern Germany following the Reformation.

In the last half of the nineteenth century, these figures, with the possible exception of Knecht Ruprecht, merged into a single, secular gift-giver called Der Weihnachtsmann. It is not a coincidence that Der Weihnachtsmann developed at roughly the same time as Father Christmas began to appear on the *Illustrated London News* and American publishers began marketing children's books about St. Nicholas, Kriss Kringle and Santa Claus. The critical factor in creating a common Christmas gift-giver in all three nations was the rise of mass media. In 1800, books were so expensive that Thomas Jefferson was supposed to have nearly bankrupt himself by purchasing two thousand books while assigned as envoy to France (books he later donated to rebuild the Library of Congress after it was burned in the War of 1812). By 1850, books, newspapers, and magazines were widely available and affordable to those of even moderate means, with England, Germany and the United States all having illustrated newspapers and magazines that displayed pictures of Christmas figures during the holidays. The very nature of mass media is to standardize and spread information, thereby consolidating or eliminating the local practices that had dominated in earlier centuries.

There were two "media events" that helped catalyze the amalgamation of the faux Nicholases into a single character named Weihnachtsmann. The first was a song written in 1835 by German composer August Heinrich Hoffmann, a university professor who wrote hundreds of children's songs as well as the German national anthem during the nineteenth century. His song "Morgen Kommt Der Weihnachtsmann" ("Tomorrow Comes the Christmas Man") does not describe Der Weihnachtsmann other than as a man who distributes gifts to children on Christmas, and Hoffman apparently did not have a particular figure in mind when he wrote the song. The song became quite popular, however, presumably creating anticipation among German children for such a character in "real life."

The second event occurred in 1847, when Moritz von Schwind's created the character Herr Winter to create a page of illustrations with written captions for a German magazine, *Münchner Bilderbogen*.[15] In these drawings, the stooped look and hooded cloak of Herr Winter is reminiscent of the faux Nicholases but Herr Winter is shown carrying a lighted Christmas tree, a detail that clearly marked him as a Christmas gift-giver. In 1849, another artist, August Krelling, created a more elaborate version of Herr Winter, copying von Schwind's character but adding elements such as toys that make him look even more like Santa Claus.[16]

By 1850, therefore, Der Weihnachtsmann had all of the elements necessary to produce a popular Christmas character. Like Rudolph the Red-Nosed Reindeer in the 1950s, he had a name, a picture of what he looked like, and a popular song named for him. Although Der Weihnachtsmann did not have cowboy singer Gene Autry to extol his virtues, as Rudolph did, he had one thing Rudolph did not have: a group of gift-givers who could assume the name Weihnachtsmann and begin bringing gifts in his name without so much as buying a new hat—or an old one. Although it is an overstatement to say he was an overnight success, within a couple of decades the Weihnachtsmann had developed into a standardized image and name for the secular Christmas gift-giver in northern Germany.

In 1859, German publisher Gustav W. Seitz sought to expand the popularity of Herr Winter by publishing a short children's book, *King Winter*, in English.[17] In this pamphlet,

Die Chriſtnacht iſt gekommen. Aus allen Fenſtern erglänzt heller feſtlicher Schein und das Jubeln der fröh=
lichen Kinder ſchallt hinaus bis auf die ſchneebedeckten einſamen Straßen. Da trippelt ein Männlein gar eifrig
einher und ſpäht von Thür zu Thür, ob nicht Jemand ihm öffne und den geſchmückten Weihnachtsbaum annehme
als willkommene Spende. — Vergeblich! — keine Pforte geht auf, den einzulaſſen, der ja das Chriſtfeſt unter
ſeiner Herrſchaft begehen läßt von Groß und Klein.

The most important contribution to the look of the Weihnachtsmann in Germany was Moritz von Schwind's illustration of Herr Winter which appeared in the German magazine *Munchner Bilderbogen* in 1847. Library of Congress, Prints and Photographs Division.

which is cut into the shape of Herr Winter, about three inches wide, and bears an illustration of Herr Winter, now called King Winter, on the cover, Herr Winter has been given an assistant, Jack Frost. Whether the publisher was aware of the names Santa Claus and Father Christmas being used in America and England, the story is undoubtedly about a Christmas gift-giver.

> The King trims Christmas trees,
> to give to good girls and boys,
> With tapers and trinkets of silver and gold,
> And all sorts of dainties and toys.
> The Queen cuts twigs of birch,
> of birch so supple and keen,
> And daintily ties them up into rods
> The finest that ever were seen.
> By and by with this word to the King
> Back comes Jack Frost at a trot:
> "Most of the children have been good,
> but some of them have not."
> The King gives him all the trees,
> the Queen gives the rods so smart,
> And away goes Jack again with his load,
> Till every house has its part.

"Herr Winter und die Kinder," an illustration from Georg Scherer, *Alte und neue Kinderlieder: Fabeln, Sprüche und Räthsel* (1849), was a more elaborate version of Herr Winter by German artist August Kreeling.

> Cakes too, and nuts and apples,
> Good children get from the King.
> You can guess what the naughty get, I suppose;
> Yes, the rods are the only thing.[18]

Left: "King Winter," an English version of the name Herr Winter, was the title of a booklet published in English by a German company, Gustav W. Seitz, in 1859. *Middle and right:* These photographs show what became known in America as "Belsnickle" candy containers. They reflect the look of Herr Winter and Der Weinachtsmann, made in Germany during the late nineteenth century.

While the book *King Winter* was apparently not a great success—copies are very rare, and none of the existing English-language histories of Santa mention it—the popularity of the underlying character, Herr Winter, was an important milestone in the creation of a single German gift-giver. We can see the appearance of von Schwind's Herr Winter, a stooped, bearded man with a hooded cape, arms folded so his hands were not visible, and switches or evergreen branches in the crook of his elbow, on Christmas ornaments in the 1860s,[19] metal chocolate molds in 1870,[20] and papier-mâché candy containers in the 1880s.[21] By the 1890s, many of the Santa figurines treasured by American collectors—in particular, the candy containers known as Belsnickles that were manufactured in Germany and imported to America between 1890 and 1910—plainly reflect the appearance of the 1847 Herr Winter.

By the end of the nineteenth century, Weihnachtsmann became the accepted, if not universal, name for the secular gift-giver who visited the homes of those children in northern Germany.[22] As a result, during the first decade of the twentieth century, Germany's Weihnachtsmann joined England's Father Christmas and America's Santa Claus on the award stand as the gold, silver and bronze medal winners in the international sport of Christmas gift-giving.

Knecht Ruprecht. The five texts about Knecht Ruprecht discussed in Chapter 9 were written in 1835, 1898, 1899, 1912 and 1917, and none of them, therefore, deal with the emergence of Weihnachtsmann in the late nineteenth century. However, just as Kriss Kringle largely disappeared when the American gift-giver became uniformly known as Santa Claus, many of the German gift-givers disappeared after Der Weihnachtsmann became the acknowledged secular gift-giver.[23] Ruprecht, on the other hand, did not disappear but changed his role and appearance from the terror man of the nineteenth century to a relatively innocuous bearded man in a brown monk's robes whose primary function seems to be assistant to St. Nicholas.

The reason Knecht Ruprecht survived was probably publication of a popular poem about him in 1862. Just like Der Weihnachtsmann and Rudolph benefited from a popular song, "Knecht Ruprecht reached the pinnacle of fame by way of a poem by north German poet and novelist Theodor Storm," an 1862 work that presents Ruprecht as the loyal servant of the Christ child.[24] Here it is:

Knecht Ruprecht

From out the forest I now appear,
To proclaim that Christmastide is here!
For at the top of every tree
are golden lights for all to see;
and there from Heaven's gate on high
I saw our Christ-child in the sky.

And in among the darkened trees,
a loud voice it was that called to me:
"Knecht Ruprecht, old fellow," it cried,
"hurry now, make haste, don't hide!
All the candles have now been lit—
Heaven's gate has opened wide!

Both young and old should now have rest
away from cares and daily stress;
and when tomorrow to earth I fly
'it's Christmas again!' will be the cry."

And then I said: "O Lord so dear.
My journey's end is now quite near;
but to this town I've still to go,
Where the children are good, I know."

"But have you then that great sack?"
I have, I said, it's on my back.
For apples, almonds, fruit and nuts
For God-fearing children are a must.

"And is that cane there by your side?"
The cane's there too, I did reply;
but only for those naughty ones,
who have it applied to their backsides.
The Christ-child spoke: "Then that's all right!
My loyal servant, go with God this night!"

From out the forest I now appear;
To proclaim that Christmastide is here!

Now speak, what is there here to be had?
Are there good children, are there bad?[25]

This poem, Raedisch says, "has been recited before many a German Tannenbaum on Christmas Eve. Recite the opening line … to any north German native, and he or she will be unable to resist rattling off the remainder of the poem. Rather than a devil who must be restrained, Storm's Knecht Ruprecht is the dedicated helper of the Christ child."[26]

A number of modern German websites describe Ruprecht as an assistant to St. Nicholas in Protestant regions of Germany, and there is a 2010 children's book, *Sankt Nikolaus und Knecht Ruprecht*, which depicts Ruprecht as something you might call warm and cuddly, a figure who emerges from the forest looking like Snow White with little birds encircling his head to help St. Nicholas carry his bags before the saint ascends into heaven after all of the gifts have been delivered.[27] Given the long history in which St. Nicholas visited Catholic homes in southern Germany and Ruprecht visited Protestant homes in northern Germany, the transformation of Ruprecht into an assistant to St. Nicholas in northern Germany may be explained by the fact that two-thirds of northern Germany is either Catholic or non-religious.

Other Central European Nations. Most of this section has focused on Germany, but the discussion of southern Germany applies to the other central European nations as well. In Austria, a majority of citizens adopted Protestantism at the time of the Reformation, but the impact was very short-lived. Roughly twenty years later, during the Catholic Restoration, the vast majority rejoined the Catholic Church. As a result, Austrians continued to celebrate the Feast of "Sankt Nikolaus" on December 6, with the evil helper Krampus playing an outsized role in the celebrations. As in the Catholic regions of Germany, the Christkindl, or Christ child, leaves gifts on Christmas Eve.

Poland's experience during the Protestant Reformation was similar to Austria's, with a large proportion of the population initially converting to Protestantism but returning to Catholicism only decades later during the Catholic Restoration. On December 6, Mikolaj, the Polish name for St. Nicholas, leaves small gifts such as apples and honey-spiced cakes for Polish children. On Christmas Eve, the Polish celebrate with a dinner known as Wigilia that begins at the appearance of the first star of the evening, known as Gwiazdka, or "the little star," in honor of the Star of Bethlehem. The dinner, which traditionally has twelve courses, often features carp as the main course. After dinner, the Star Man—a friend or neighbor who is dressed in a manner similar to Father Christmas but carries a large star at the end of a long pole in honor of the Star of Bethlehem—may visit and distribute presents in person. The evening ends with attendance at midnight mass.

Hungary adopted Lutheranism and Calvinism in quick succession during the Reformation. A few decades later, however, during the Catholic Restoration, the nation returned to Catholicism. As a result, Hungarians celebrate both St. Nicholas' Day on December 6, when the saint, known in Hungary as Mikulás, leaves candy in children's shoes, and Christmas, when either angels or the Christ child leave gifts on Christmas Eve.

Switzerland split roughly evenly following the Reformation between those who joined the Swiss Reformed Church and those who remained Catholic, a division that remains today. Like its neighbor Austria, Switzerland celebrates both St. Nicholas' Day and Christmas. On December 6, the Swiss gift-giver, Samichlaus, is generally accompanied by his long-standing evil helper, Schmutzl, who dresses completely in brown or black. Samichlaus falls into the same category as the Dutch Sinterklaas: a faux Nicholas that retained the look and bishop's garb of St. Nicholas, but who, "in reality," was someone else. On Christmas, the most prominent gift-giver for both Protestants and Catholics is the Christkindl.

The Reformation had no direct effect on Christmas in the Czech Republic or the Slovak Republic, the former constituents of Czechoslovakia, because the nations remained predominately Catholic through the Reformation (although neither is now). In both nations, St. Nicholas, known as Svatý Mikuláš, arrives on December 5, St. Nicholas' Eve, to leave presents, and the Christ child leaves gifts on Christmas Eve. The Czechs also have one of the most endearing St. Nicholas traditions in which he descends from heaven on golden cord, along with Cert, the Czech version of the evil helper, and an angel in white.[28]

11

Gift-Givers in the British Isles

Father Christmas Still Reigns

England. England is unique among European nations in the history of Christmas, and, along with Germany and the United States, has contributed more memorable traditions than any other nation. England was Christianized in the fifth century, before most of Continental Europe, and purportedly began the celebration of Christmas in a big way in AD 597 when Augustine, the first Archbishop of Canterbury, allegedly baptized some ten thousand pagans on Christmas Day. Despite the long history of Christianity, England has also been called the most pagan of nations with regard to its celebration of Christmas, a comment which reflects the largely secular nature of Christmas in England. As English historian Mark Connelly explained in *Christmas, A History*, English Christmas is not so much a celebration of Christ's birth as it is "a national expression of English culture, habits and aesthetics."[1]

We know that England's monarchs began to mark Christmas with coronations and marriages during the Early Middle Ages, but few of the details can be confirmed. Nineteenth-century historian William Sandys, in *Christmastide: Its History, Festivities and Carols*, includes a poem that supposedly outlines the Christmas dinner served to King Arthur and the Knights of the Roundtable in the sixth century.[2] Most of the stories involving King Arthur are legend, and the poem about King Arthur's dinner likely is as well, but we can probably assume this poem fairly represents the variety of foods that an English king or queen might have consumed at Christmas during the Middle Ages. It also marks the beginning, in concept if not in detail, of England's development of a distinct Christmas cuisine.

> They served up salmon, venison, and wild boars,
> By hundreds, and by dozens, and by scores,
> Hogsheads of honey, kilderkins of mustard,
> Muttons, and fatted beeves, and bacon swine,
> Herons and bitterns, peacocks, swan, and bustard,
> Teal, mallard, pigeons, widgeons, and, in fine,
> Plum-puddings, pancakes, apple-pies, and custard,
> And therewithal they drank good Gascon wine,
> With mead, and ale, and cider of our own,
> For porter, punch, and negus were not known.[3]

By the High Middle Ages, the English monarchs were known for celebrating the holiday with monumental feasts in which thousands of English men and women consumed hundreds of oxen, pigs, and sheep as well as an unusual assortment of fowl, including "swan and peacock, both of which were highly regarded, and heron and crane, whose reputation was not so good."[4] In *The Englishman's Christmas: A Social History*, J.A.R. Pimlott recounts that for Christmas in 1213, King Richard ordered four hundred head of pork, three thousand chickens, fifteen thousand herrings, ten thousand salt eels, twenty-seven hogsheads of wine, and unspecified numbers of pheasants, partridges and other fowl.[5]

In describing the famous feasts, Pimlott emphasizes "it is important not to fall into the romantic fallacy of glamourising the medieval festivities on the basis of exceptional occasions which may only have been recorded because they were exceptional."[6] At the same time, Pimlott says, "[i]t would be no less mistaken to swing the opposite direction."[7] Not every Christmas dinner during the Middle Ages involved dozens of courses, but "everybody, we are safe in assuming, could expect to eat better than was his normal custom."[8] During the thirteenth and fourteenth centuries, he writes, "a typical Christmas dinner probably consisted of meat, chicken or a wild fowl, with plenty of home-brewed ale or cider accompanied by white bread, which was always a luxury in the Middle Ages."[9]

England's celebration of Christmas was also unique because the nation was neither Catholic nor traditionally Protestant. In 1534, a few years after the Reformation began, King Henry VIII broke with the Catholic Church and established the Church of England. The break with Catholicism occurred before the Reformation's challenges to the church had time to coalesce, however, and it was a dispute over authority rather than theology. As a result, Henry continued the celebration of Christmas in the elaborate style of his predecessors. Following his death in 1547 and the short reigns of his son Edward VI (who died at age sixteen) and oldest daughter Mary I (the infamous "Bloody Mary," a determined Catholic who reigned for only six years), Henry VIII's youngest daughter, Elizabeth I, became queen and head of the Church of England, reigning until 1603.

With her first Christmas as queen in 1558, Elizabeth signaled her intent to maintain Christmas in the lavish styles of her predecessors, and throughout the Elizabethan era, the English—and Elizabeth—celebrated Christmas with vigor.[10] While the practice of social inversion, in which the wealthy landowners would provide Christmas cheer for their tenants, continued, the lords and nobles also lavished gifts or cash on their superiors. Elizabeth, at the top of the social pyramid, was the chief beneficiary of this practice, and maintained careful records about what gifts she received, and from whom, each year. In his 1885 study of Christmas in England, historian Sandys made the following observation:

> Queen Elizabeth, who, to powerful intellect, joined much of the arbitrary temper of her father, possessed also great vanity and fondness of display. In her time, therefore, the festivities were renewed with great pomp and show; and theatrical entertainments were also particularly encouraged, and were frequently performed before the queen, especially at Christmas time…. With Elizabeth's fondness for luxury and dress, and her passion for adulation, it may well be imagined that her New Year's Gifts were rigidly expected, or exacted, from all classes connected with her; from Matthew Parker, Archbishop of Canterbury, down to Smyth the dustman.[11]

Given the number of gifts each year, Sandys says, "it does not appear so very surprising that at her death, Elizabeth left a hoard of 2000 dresses fit for a queen behind her."[12] Elizabeth was also a great fan of gambling—in particular, playing dice—during the Christmas season. She did extremely well at this game, historians say, because she cheated, using loaded dice. It was during the reigns of Elizabeth's successors, James I of England (1603–25), who had been King James VI of Scotland before assuming the English throne, and his son, Charles I (1625–49), that the English Puritans began to condemn more vocally the celebration of Christmas, alleging it was a Catholic invention and its celebration the trappings of popery. In contrast, the Church of England sought to expand the traditional forms of celebration and, in an apparent effort to gain popular support, Charles I directed his noblemen and gentry to return from London to their landed estates in the countryside during December to keep up their old-style Christmas generosity.

Surprisingly, Father Christmas developed independently from the gift-givers in Continental Europe and America, first appearing as the personification of Christmas in the mid–1400s when an English rector, Richard Smart, wrote a musical dialogue between a choir and a figure addressed at various points in the dialogue as Nowell, Sir Christemas and My Lord Christemas.[13] Wheeler and Rosenthal write that the ancient Saxons had their own pagan leaders of the Winter Solstice, "wintry figures such as Father Ice, King Frost, and King Winter, and honored them in their mid-winter festivals," and that "Father Christmas is partly Christian and partly pagan with strong ties to Odin and Saturn (brought to England by the Romans)."[14]

There is, unfortunately, no genetic testing kit through which we can determine whether Father Christmas has German or Italian genes. Whatever his genetic origin, it was during the battle for religious dominance between the Puritans and the Anglicans in the seventeenth century that Father Christmas really gained his identity. In 1616, English playwright Ben Jonson, second in fame only to Shakespeare among playwrights of his era, wrote *Christmas, His Masque*, a play featuring the character Old Christmas, who defended Christmas and criticized the Puritans. In Jonson's masque—a "masque" was an elaborate stage play popular in the seventeenth century with music, dancing, sumptuous costumes, and ornate sets—Old Christmas appears with eight appropriately-named children: Mis-rule, Caroll, Minc'd-pie, Gamboll, Post and Paire, New-Yeares-Gift, Mumming, Wassail, Offering, and Babie-Cake.

When the rise of Puritanism led to increasing condemnation of the existing Christmas traditions, those who supported traditional celebrations turned to Father Christmas for support, portraying him as a venerable old gentleman, someone who was given to good cheer but not to excess. In 1638, the character Christmas appeared in a masque by Thomas Nabbes as "an old reverend gentleman in furred gown and cap" who defended the celebration of Christmas in the face of Puritan critics.[15] In 1646, an anonymous satirist wrote *The Arraignment, Conviction and Imprisoning of Christmas, in which a Royalist lady is frantically searching for Father Christmas.*[16] During the same year, royalist poet John Taylor published *The Complaint of Christmas*, in which Father Christmas mournfully visits Puritan towns but sees "no sign or token of any Holy Day."[17]

The attempted defenses of Father Christmas had no impact on the Puritans, who in 1642 launched a civil war to eliminate the monarchy and the Church of England. In 1649, Puritan forces led by Oliver Cromwell beheaded Charles I, an action that seems less Christian than the Puritans claimed to be but definitively declared the Puritan victory. The same year, Parliament established a Commonwealth government to replace the monarchy. In 1653, however, Cromwell dissolved the existing government and declared himself 1st Lord Protector of the Commonwealth of England, Scotland, and Ireland, a position from which he led a genocidal campaign against Catholics in Ireland and Scotland.

While Cromwell was in power, the Puritan-dominated Parliament outlawed seasonal plays, declared Christmas a day of penance instead of a feast day, and proclaimed that "no observance shall be had of the five and twentieth of December, commonly called Christmas day, nor any solemnity used or exercised in churches upon that day in respect thereof."[18] The Parliament also prohibited businesses, including taverns, from closing on Christmas. The fact that Parliament ordered the churches to close but the taverns to remain open on the anniversary of Christ's birth as an act of religious purity was one of many glaring inconsistencies in the Puritan position. In 1653, this irony was observed in *The Vindication of CHRIST-MAS or, His Twelve Yeares' Observations upon the Times*, a story involving Old Christmas advocating a merry, alcoholic Christmas and casting aspersions on the charitable motives of the ruling Puritans.[19] This pamphlet included a drawing of Father Christmas caught between two men quarreling over whether Christmas was welcome. The drawing, which as far as can be determined is the first depiction of any of the modern Christmas gift-givers, reflects all of the elements we have come to associate with the figures, including a long white beard and hair, a simple hat, and long robes.[20]

This 1652 woodcut by John Taylor of "Old Christmas" was part of an English political dispute in which Old Christmas, also known as Sir Christmas or Father Christmas, is defending the celebration of Christmas.

The Puritan revolution was relatively short-lived. After Cromwell died of natural causes in 1658, his son assumed the position of Lord Protector, but the English royalists regained control of Parliament in 1659 and re-established the monarchy with Charles II, son of Charles I, assuming power in 1660.[21] In 1678, Josiah King published a pamphlet entitled *Examination and Tryal of Old Father Christmas,* describing Father Christmas "of the Town of Superstition, in the County of Idolatry."[22] In the trial, Father Christmas was accused of having "from time to time, abused the people of this Commonwealth, drawing and inticing them to Drunkenness, Gluttony, and unlawful Gaming, Wantonness, Uncleanness, Lasciviousness, Cursing, Swearing, Abuse of the Creatures, some to one Vice, some to another; all to Idleness."[23] The charges were presumably made with tongue in cheek because the jury acquitted him after the defense argued that even if the conduct occurred, "it is none of this old man's fault; neither ought he to suffer for it."[24] The 1686 pamphlet included the second visual depiction of Father Christmas, one in which he is seated, reflecting an even more serious look and tenor than the 1653 drawing.[25]

After surviving the Puritan revolution as the personification of Christmas, Father Christmas became a recurring character in seasonal mummer's plays that were the descendants of early midwinter reenactments of the death and rebirth of the king or sun god. In this tradition, troupes of actors would travel from town to town presenting short dramas in which the principal character, often the English patron St. George, would collapse on stage to be revived by an actor playing the role of a physician. Although the characters were new, the plot repeated the theme of death and rebirth that had dominated prehistoric Winter Solstice celebrations some four thousand years earlier. Father Christmas was a stock character who generally spoke only the following lines:

In comes I, Father Christmas,
welcome or welcome not, I hope
old Father Christmas will never
be forgot.[26]

Father Christmas was
not forgot but the English celebration of Christmas would
not fully recover from the
Puritan Revolution for 150
years. The conventional wisdom is that England experienced a revival of Christmas
in the mid–1800s, attributable almost solely to two individuals, Charles Dickens
and Queen Victoria. In 1843,
Dickens published a novella,
*A Christmas Carol in Prose
Being a Ghost Story of Christmas*, which was undoubtedly
the most influential Christmas story in history save the
Nativity story itself.[27] Queen
Victoria's primary contribution, on the other hand, appears to have been marrying
a German, Prince Albert, who
brought German Christmas

This woodcut of Father Christmas appeared in a satirical
pamphlet, *The Examination and Tryal of Father Christmas*,
published by Josiah King in 1686.

traditions to England. In 1848, the *Illustrated London News* published an iconic drawing of
the royal family standing about an elaborately decorated Christmas tree set on a table and
decorated with some of the first hand-blown figural glass ornaments created in Germany—a drawing that helped popularize both Christmas as a family holiday and the Christmas tree and hand-blown glass ornaments as a necessary part of the celebration. In 1850,
the same drawing was published in America on the cover of a popular monthly magazine
for women, *Godey's Lady's Book*, modified to make the couple appear as a typical American
family rather than English royalty.[28]

There is no question the Protestant government in England, although short-lived, did
long-lasting damage to the celebration of Christmas in England, or that Dickens contributed much, and Queen Victoria contributed some to increase the popularity of the holiday during the Victorian era. What historians like to argue about is whether the Victorian
Christmas that became common by the end of the nineteenth century was an "invented
tradition," meaning a new practice (invented) that had the appearance of age (tradition),
a concept historian Stephen Nissenbaum uses in *The Battle for Christmas* to describe his
theory that a handful of New Yorkers, including Washington Irving and Clement Moore,
"invented" the tradition of Santa Claus in America to change Christmas from a drunken,
boisterous street celebration to a wholesome, family-oriented holiday.[29]

The controversy over whether Victorian Christmas was an invented tradition is largely a semantic dispute of interest to historians who care more about the scholarly concept of what constitutes an "invented tradition" than they care about the history of Christmas itself. The two English historians who popularized this theory regarding the Victorian Christmas, J.M. Golby and A.W. Purdue, authors of *The Making of the Modern Christmas*, explained their thinking as follows:

> It is the central argument of this book that the festival was extensively reworked and reinterpreted during the nineteenth century to meet the needs of modern urban society; yet, like every vital tradition, it built upon foundations which, like rock formations, contain layers from different ages. The Old Christmas, which Victorians so admired even while they changed it so dramatically, was itself the result of Christianity's partial incorporation of and partial coexistence with the old pagan Winter Feast.[30]

If one ponders this statement, it should become clear that the Victorians did not really change "Old Christmas" because by the beginning of Queen Victoria's reign it had already disappeared, the victim of changes in society over a period of two hundred years that made it impossible for Old Christmas to survive. The Christmas celebrations during the reign of Elizabeth I, James I, and Charles I were designed for a rural society when no work was available during the dead of winter and a feudal society where the nobles, who owned huge tracts of land, could provide extravagant, multi-day Christmas celebrations for all connected with their estates. By the 1800s, however, England had become an urban, industrial society where employers might provide one day off at Christmas, and each family was responsible for providing its own Christmas celebration in its own home. No one should consider this surprising. These changes were beyond anyone's control and had nothing to do with Christmas as such.

Although the primary components of the English celebration of Christmas—decorating for the holiday, attending church, exchanging gifts, eating a special dinner, enjoying a drink or two, and visiting with family and friends—were not covered in the newspapers, the best evidence is that they never disappeared. In his 1885 study, *Christmastide: Its Origins and Associations*, Sandys states:

> Even down to the present time—although the spirit has sadly abated, and been modified, and is still abating under the influence of the genius of the age, which requires work and not play—the festivities are yet kept up in many parts in a genial feeling of kindness and hospitality, not only in the dwellings of the humbler classes, who encroach upon their hard-gained earnings for the exigencies of the season, and of those of higher grade, where the luxuries mingle with the comforts of life; but also in the mansions of the opulent, and in the baronial hall, where still remain the better privileges of the feudal state; and especially in the palace of our sovereign, who wisely considers the state of royalty not incompatible with the blessings of domestic enjoyment.[31]

Three points from this paragraph jump out. First, the celebration of Christmas, although diminished, had not disappeared. Second, Sandys believed it was still abating in 1885, an assertion strangely inconsistent with the premise that the Victorians revived Christmas, and illustrating that such judgments are always subjective, particularly when the subject is what people did in the privacy of their homes. Third, Sandys does not place blame on the Puritans or the monarchy, but on "the genius of the age, which requires work and not play." Sandys' use of the word "genius" was undoubtedly sarcastic.

In *Christmas in America*, Restad also observes that the English who immigrated to the American colonies in the seventeenth and eighteenth centuries brought the English traditions with them.[32] To the extent Christmas changed—and there is no question it did—the more defensible position seems to be Mark Connelly's conclusion in *Christmas, A History* that the nature of the celebration changed in response to "conditions of the time."[33] Indeed, in the passage by Golby and Purdue quoted above, that theory is all they really espouse. The economic reality of the Industrial Revolution precluded the average working man from spending days eating and drinking at the manor of his local nobleman and made supporting that practice beyond the means of the nobility. Connelly also observes "[t]he various commentators all seem to agree that the English Christmas was so great because it brought rich and poor together and that it was the tragedy of their age that so little was left of this spirit."[34]

Here, too, the culprit was economic circumstances beyond the control of any given person and attempts to eliminate the economic disparity in modern societies—in particular, Russia's adoption of the philosophy of Karl Marx—did nothing to benefit the celebration of Christmas. The rise of large cities, an inevitable result of the Industrial Revolution when people worked in factories rather than farming the lands of a nobleman, made it impossible to retain the Old Christmas during which rich and poor celebrated together at the noble's manor after the onset of winter made it impossible to work in the fields. To make the new, home-centered forms of celebration more festive, the Victorians in England adopted customs such as Christmas trees in the family parlor, exchanges of gifts, family dinners of roast turkey, Brussels sprouts, and plum pudding, Tom Smith's Christmas Crackers and, by the 1870s, stockings filled by Father Christmas.[35]

To say Christmas was reworked "to meet the needs of modern urban society" is far different than the claim, made by some, that Christmas was essentially on life-support during the eighteenth century, and dead by 1820, before being resurrected by Charles Dickens and Queen Victoria in the 1840s.[36] While Golby and Purdue assert Christmas "was neither a major event on the calendar nor a popular festival" between 1800 and 1840,[37] it is hard to square that conclusion with the many notable publications about Christmas during the period. In 1808, English poet Sir Walter Scott published the masterpiece "Marmion," a substantial portion of which is devoted to a description of what was called Old Christmas.[38] In 1819–20, Irving wrote the short story "Old Christmas," which was about many of the same customs identified by Scott, as part of the serial *The Sketchbook of Geoffrey Crayon, Gent.*, a commercial and critical success in England as well as the United States.[39] In 1822, Clement C. Moore wrote "The Night Before Christmas," which influenced celebrations in England as well as America, albeit not until it had been published more widely as a children's book in the second half of the century. In 1836, English author Thomas K. Hervey wrote *The Book of Christmas*, an extensive history of the holiday which included wonderful drawings by English author Robert Seymour of a wild-haired Father Christmas, one an iconic picture of him riding a goat while balancing a bowl of wassail and another leading mummers at a Christmas party.[40] The same year, Dickens published *The Pickwick Papers*, which included a chapter that might be described as a cross between Irving's "Old Christmas" and *A Christmas Carol*.[41] In 1842, the *Illustrated London News* began to publish the first in a series of covers featuring Father Christmas with a number of different beverages, all alcoholic.[42] The most persuasive evidence, however, is the immediate and widespread popularity of *A Christmas Carol* when it was published in 1843, a fact which belies any conclusion that Christmas had died.[43]

One might describe the dispute as a question of whether the glass—we will call it a glass of wassail for this purpose—was half empty or half full. Connelly and other historians, including J.A.R. Pimlott, take more of a half-full approach, pointing out that even if the newspapers were not filled with pictures and articles about Christmas, the day was consistently treated as a public holiday, marked by religious services and celebrated at home with family. With the exception of cracker-maker Tom Smith, the English Victorians did not really "invent" any of the new traditions—the Christmas tree and ornaments were from Germany, the turkey was native to the Americas, and the Brussel's sprouts were presumably from Belgium—nor does it appear they were trying to give their celebrations the appearance of long-standing tradition. Rather, they merely adopted forms of celebration appropriate for smaller family celebrations. "Thus," as Connelly writes, "if Christmas was artificially devised in the early nineteenth century, it was done so unconsciously."[44]

The focus on Dickens and Queen Victoria also ignores the contributions of others. To a large extent, the perceived popularity of Christmas, or lack thereof, both in England and America, was actually attributable to the journalistic practices of the day. The *Illustrated London News* in England and *Harper's Weekly* in the United States changed the perception of the holiday simply by featuring numerous engravings of Christmas scenes during the Christmas season. Significantly, the *Illustrated London News* did not begin publication until 1842, and *Harper's Weekly* until 1857, but both immediately began publishing Christmas drawings, including iconic images of Father Christmas and Santa Claus, on the cover of their December issues.

Father Christmas was not a Victorian invention, but he contributed much to the revival of Christmas, making his first appearances since the seventeenth century. In 1836, Robert Seymour illustrated Hervey's *Book of Christmas* with an obviously inebriated Father Christmas riding a goat. In 1842, the *Illustrated London News* got into the act, publishing the first of a number of illustrations of Father Christmas. In December 1842, Father Christmas was shown on the cover holding a steaming bowl of wassail overhead,[45] and most of its subsequent drawings of Father Christmas also showed him drinking one alcoholic beverage or another. The source of Santa's jolly demeanor, broad midsection, and "nose like a cherry" is supposed to be a combination of cookies and hot chocolate but for Father Christmas it was undoubtedly some combination of ale, wine, and brandy.

The other factor often overlooked by those trying to characterize Victorian Christmas as an invented tradition is that inventions don't mean much if no one uses them. The best example of this is the 1821 publication of *The Children's Friend* featuring "Santeclaus," a story that

In 1836, Father Christmas returned to England with a distinctly wild, boozy look illustrated by English artist Robert Seymour in Thomas Hervey's *Book of Christmas* (1836).

In this illustration by Robert Seymour for Hervey's *Book of Christmas*, Old Christmas leads a group of mummers in song during the Christmas season.

Left: This illustration of Old Christmas with a steaming bowl of wassail was published on December 24, 1842. It was the first depiction of Old Christmas from the newly launched *Illustrated London News*. Library of Congress. *Right:* The alcohol-drenched illustration of "Jolly Old Christmas" surrounded by a garland of wine bottles by an artist identified only as Smyth is from the December 1844 edition of the *Illustrated London News*. Library of Congress.

apparently was read by virtually no one except, presumably, Clement C. Moore, a friend and customer of publisher William E. Gilley. Moore seems clearly to have lifted much of "The Night Before Christmas" from the booklet but *The Children's Friend* was long forgotten by the time Moore's poem was published as an illustrated children's book in 1848. In other words, William B. Gilley and Arthur J. Stansbury quite arguably "invented" the American Santa with a sleigh pulled by reindeer, but that invention had no effect until the story was rewritten by Moore and gained popularity.

One of the most interesting twists in the dispute over invented traditions is the tradition that England somehow overlooked. Most people assume the gift-giving practices of Father Christmas developed simultaneously with those in Continental Europe and the United States. In fact, according to Pimlott, English children did not hang stockings, and Father Christmas did not fill them, until about 1870, when the practice spread throughout England in just a couple of years.[46] The tradition of filling Christmas shoes or stockings— the precise article of clothing changed from place to place and time to time—appears to have originated in Continental Europe with Odin and Berchta, was picked up by St. Nicholas in the fifteenth century, if not earlier, and traveled to America in the eighteenth or early nineteenth century.

The tradition of hanging stockings should have been known in England by at least the 1850s because an American author, Susan Warner, wrote a Christmas book, *Karl Krinken, His Christmas Stocking*, in 1953 that was widely distributed in England.[47] Remarkably, any memory of the practice seems to have disappeared by 1870, when rumors began to spread of a mysterious figure named "Santiklaus" filling stockings hung by the fireplaces. Within a couple of years, Pimlott writes, virtually all of England had adopted the concept without recognizing it had been embraced in America for many decades and in Continental Europe for centuries.[48] Once the practice was established, Father Christmas took over the duties from "Santiklaus."

Scotland. Unlike England, where the Puritans were held at bay until the mid–1600s, the Calvinists acquired power in Scotland in 1561, forming the Presbyterian Church. Upon acquiring power, the Calvinists not only eliminated Christmas as a holiday, the church excommunicated members who celebrated Christmas and the government prosecuted those who facilitated the celebrations, including bakers who made the traditional Scottish Yule bread and those caught singing carols in public. James I, a Scottish monarch who assumed the throne of England and Scotland following the death of Elizabeth I, sought to counter the religious forces by mandating the celebration of Christmas in the English style, as did his son, Charles I, but they had little success.

In remote parts of northern Scotland, Catholicism survived the Reformation, and those regions continued to celebrate Christmas following the Reformation. In southern Scotland, on the other hand, citizens responded to the prohibition of the celebration of Christmas by moving the traditional Christmas celebration to New Year's Eve, where it was renamed Hogmanay. If one views Christmas as a season instead of a single day, it becomes clear the Scottish response did not eliminate Christmas at all, but merely changed the timing of certain parts of the holiday season—the same thing that the Soviet Union did in 1935 when it established a New Year's holiday with New Year's trees and Ded Moroz ("Grandfather Frost") as the New Year's gift-giver.

Ireland. The monuments at Newgrange establish that the celebration of the Winter Solstice in Ireland dates back thousands of years, and likely involved the same ceremonies by prehistoric tribal leaders that occurred at Stonehenge and other similar sites. In the fourth century, however, Christian missionaries began to convert the Irish, and despite numerous attempts by the English and Scottish to convert the Irish to Protestantism or dilute the Catholic population with Scottish immigrants, Catholicism has been the dominant religion since then.

The potential effect of the Reformation on Catholicism in Ireland was preempted by King Henry VIII of England. In 1536, he deposed the existing Irish dynasty, and in 1541 he declared himself king of the new Kingdom of Ireland. At the same time, Henry VIII sought to impose Anglicanism as the state religion over the objections of the Catholic majority. As a result, the relationship between England and Ireland over the next three centuries was marked by a series of bloody battles between the Catholics and Protestants, many of whom were Presbyterians who emigrated from Scotland into the northern part of Ireland in order to dilute the predominately Catholic population. It wasn't until the United Kingdom was established in 1802 that the Irish enjoyed some measure of peace and self-government, although bloody fighting between Protestants and Catholics continued for almost two hundred more years.

There is surprisingly little written about how the Irish celebrated Christmas, but in the absence of religious objections to the celebration of the Nativity by the Catholic Church, and in light of the propensity of the Irish to enjoy a drink or two, it is logical they adopted many of the customs of England during the period. In Irish Gaelic, the gift-giver is known as Daidi na Nollag, which means Daddy Christmas. In Irish English, he is known as Father Christmas, but he is often called Santy or Santa. The longstanding tradition has been for children to leave him a slice of mince pie and a glass of Guinness on Christmas Eve, although milk has reportedly been displacing the Guinness in recent years.

12

Gift-Givers in the Benelux Nations

Sinterklaas and Black Peter

The Dutch, whose historic home was Holland, are now divided into parts of three nations collectively called the Benelux countries: the Netherlands (which encompasses most of historic Holland), Belgium, and Luxembourg. The Dutch were sailors, with the Dutch East India Company plying the spice trade between Europe, India, and America. Most of the population of the Netherlands is Dutch, while Belgium and Luxembourg have large French- and Dutch-speaking populations. Following the Reformation, the Dutch founded the Dutch Reformed Church, a Calvinist faith, while most of the French population remained Catholic. The adoption of Calvinism by Holland in the 1570s brought a regimen of anti–Christmas legislation similar to other Calvinist nations, making the traditions of "gift-giving, gingerbread cookies, puppet shows, doll sellers' booths, and the Saint Nicholas market" all unlawful as "idolatrous displays plainly transgressing the word of God."[1]

Some historians have asserted the Dutch openly resisted these restrictions, overcoming the governmental attempts to prohibit the existing traditions of St. Nicholas, and leaving gifts for children, thus allowing St. Nicholas to remain part of the Dutch Christmas traditions. In *Santa Claus: A Biography*, Bowler writes:

> While there was evidence of resistance to this sort of action in other countries, and signs of covert Christmas observance in other Calvinist jurisdictions, in the Netherlands the resistance was quite open and remarkably successful. When Amsterdam legislated against the making of cookies and candles in effigy forms, a rebellious group of eleven-year-olds protested and with the help of their parents saw to it that the proclamation was never enforced.… Clearly, Sinterklaas had evaded his attempted extinction in the Netherlands.[2]

The premise that a group of rebellious eleven-year-olds somehow succeeded in preserving the celebration of a Catholic saint the Dutch Reformed Church and the church-controlled government had declared "idolatrous displays plainly transgressing the word of God" is difficult to accept. Remember, the Dutch government banned *gingerbread cookies* as "plainly transgressing the word of God," and this was a period where people could be hanged, burned at the stake, or drowned for appearing to violate the word of God.[3] If the Dutch children were like mine, they couldn't keep their rooms clean, much less launch a governmental rebellion, at age eleven. Rather, it appears the Dutch successfully *evaded* the law without directly violating it. This is because the people declared the character that survived the Reformation, Sinterklaas, was **not** St. Nicholas of Myra, the Catholic saint, any more than the furry German figure Pelznickel. Both were faux Nicholases designed to avoid any allegation of worshiping a Catholic icon while changing the celebration as little as necessary.

The Dutch translation of St. Nicholas would have been Sint Niklas or Sint Nikolaas, not Sinterklaas, and the Dutch created an entirely new biography for Sinterklaas that had nothing to do with the Catholic saint.[4] Sinterklaas, according to this story, was a man who spent most of the year in Spain with his Moorish servant keeping track of the behavior of Dutch children from afar, and preparing for his annual visit to the Netherlands. Sinterklaas would arrive by steamboat in mid–November, riding a white horse and carting oranges, and would parade through town on his horse with an army of Black Peters in early December. He would deliver gifts on December 5, the day before St. Nicholas' Day, following which he would go back to Spain via a secret passage through Germany.[5]

There are a dozen woodcuts or paintings executed between 1750 and 1850 that show Sinterklaas or Sint Niklas in the robes of a bishop, along with the traditional miter and crozier, riding a horse through Amsterdam while tossing toys to a group of children running beside him. The physical appearance of Sinterklaas, however, is virtually identical to that of St. Nicholas in Europe—a tall, erect, serious man with white hair and a long white beard wearing red and white vestments—but the Dutch gift-giver is virtually always shown riding a horse whereas the European version is virtually always shown on foot.

As a man of the cloth, Sinterklaas merited an evil helper, and Zwarte Piet ("Black Peter") fulfilled that role. According to Berryman, "Black Pete's origins are lost in the same

Hier doet ons Sinter Klaas weer aan zyn dag gedenken,
Nu hy de Kind're Koek en Marsepyn wil schenken.
Maar zagt houw en werpt geen suyker meer nog prik,
Een Jonge Juffer die begeert geen houte klik.

This 1766 woodcut, "Sint Nicolaas almanach, voor het jaar 1766," by P. Servaas, is one of the earliest depictions of Sinterklaas. Like many Dutch illustrations, it shows him riding a horse while distributing gifts to Dutch children but Zwarte Piet is not included.

In "De intocht van Sint-Nicolaas," an 1840 woodcut by Dutch artist Theodorus Johannes Wijn-hoven-Hendriksen, Sinterklaas is once again depicted distributing gifts to children while riding a horse. Courtesy Rijksmuseum, Amsterdam.

murky fog as the German Krampus. There are some who say Black Peter, like Krampus, started out as a devil whom St. Nicholas subjugated so he could serve him at Christmas time."[6] While Black Peter would be a perfectly logical name for a satanic helper, and both Schmutzli in Switzerland and Houseker in Luxembourg demonstrate their connection to Satan by wearing all black rather than sprouting the animal parts that characterize Cert and Krampus, there is little information available about Black Peter before 1850.

It was publication of an 1850 children's book, *Sint Nikolaas en zijn Knecht,* by Dutch schoolteacher Jan Schenkman that cemented the relationship between Sinterklaas and Black Peter. Schenkman does not identify the dark-skinned "knecht," meaning servant, but readers assumed he was Black Peter. Since the mid–1800s, Sinterklaas has arrived in the Netherlands each year, purportedly coming from Spain, on a steamboat. Wearing a bishop's attire and miter in red and white, Sinterklaas typically mounts a white horse after setting off the boat (although in some versions he mounts the horse and rides off).

Once on land, the Black Peters, wearing the costumes of Spanish soldiers who occupied

In "Aankomst van Sint Nicolaas" by Barend Cornelius Albek, a painting in the collection of the Rijksmuseum in Amsterdam, Sint Nicolaas is shown on horseback with his assistant Zwarte Piet ("Black Peter"). Courtesy Rijksmuseum, Amsterdam.

the Netherlands during the sixteenth century, black face and dark curly wigs, surround him, following a parade route through town. In the Netherlands, the ceremonies occur on December 5 because Dutch law enacted after the Protestant Reformation prohibited celebration of St. Nicholas' Day or any similar holiday "on December 6." On the evening of December 5, Dutch children will fill their shoes with carrots or other treats for Sinterklaas' horse, and place them outside on the doorstep. If the children have been well-behaved over the prior year, Santa will fill the shoes with gifts when his horse finishes eating. The same ceremony occurs in Belgium and the southern parts of the Netherlands on St. Nicholas' Day, December 6.

In recent years, the Dutch have encountered a good deal of criticism that the Sinterklaas ceremony, and in particular the practice of dressing Black Peter in blackface, is insulting and racist, harkening back to nineteenth-century minstrel shows in which white performers would appear in blackface. Some Dutch residents have protested the practice whereas others have taken a remarkably defensive attitude toward claims Black Peter is racist, with some arguing he is not of African descent and his dark skin actually comes from sliding down chimneys. The "soot" claim has no credible factual basis, however, because the curly wigs, black face and white lips of the Black Peters who trail Sinterklaas come directly from nineteenth-century minstrel shows and are plainly designed to recreate individuals of African descent. The St. Nicholas Society, an organization that promotes the image of St. Nicholas around the world, has come down on the side of those who urge elimination of the practice. "The Dutch Zwarte Piet has become over time a more benign figure, but he, too, presents serious difficulties. It would be wise, in our thinking, to do away with the black-face and simply call them jesters, or just Piets, making it clear all can be St. Nicholas' helpers."[7]

13

Gift-Givers in Scandinavia

The Yule Goats, Gnomes and Elves

Scandinavians, like other Germanic peoples, celebrated Yule to hasten the return of the sun. In much of Scandinavia, however, the Winter Solstice was more than just the longest night of the year.[1] In the northernmost regions, the sun does not appear directly for more than a month, allowing only a few hours of what might be called dusk, temperatures rarely rise above freezing and the lows can plunge to forty below. As a result of the remote location of Scandinavia and the inhospitable winters, Christianity did not arrive until the eleventh century, some two centuries later than Continental Europe, and was not complete until the thirteenth century.

When the Reformation arrived during the sixteenth century, only three centuries after Scandinavia converted to Catholicism, virtually all of Scandinavia converted to Lutheranism. The effect on Christmas traditions, however, appears to have been relatively minor. Most of the Germanic traditions of Yule and the Christian traditions of Christmas had already merged when Christianity arrived, but even then, the holidays in Scandinavia remained greatly influenced by Nordic mythology and folklore. Whether the Christian influences were weaker than other nations, or the pagan influences stronger, most of Scandinavian folklore remained intact, and holiday gift-givers retained the names and histories based on goats, gnomes, or elves.

The most prominent god in Scandinavian mythology was Thor, who Scandinavians believed led a Scandinavian version of the Wild Hunt on a chariot pulled by two goats, Tanngrisnir and Tanngnjóstr. As a result, the goat has enjoyed a remarkably large role in Scandinavian midwinter celebrations. Until the mid–1800s, the Yule buck (male goat) was the principal gift-giver in Scandinavia, known as Julebukk in Denmark and Norway, Julbock in Sweden, and Joulupukki in Finland. At some point, however, the Lutheran Church objected to the prominent role given to the pagan god Thor during the Christmas celebrations—or, at least, to the roles given Tanngrisnir and Tanngnjóstr (although, in fairness, both goats may have been devout Lutherans as far as we known). In the mid–1800s, therefore, most of the Yule goats were replaced as gift-givers by the elves and gnomes known as nisse, tomte, or tomten in Sweden, nisse in Denmark and Norway, and tonttu in Finland. Although the role of the Yule buck as gift-giver faded during the nineteenth century, images of goats, often constructed of straw, remain an important part of Yule décor throughout Scandinavia, and goats are often pictured pulling wagons or being ridden in Yule scenes.

Nisse is generally translated as elf, while tomte, tomten, and tonttu are generally translated as gnome, but there does not seem to be a great difference between them. Adding the prefix "Jul" produces the names of the Scandinavian gift-givers: Julenisse and Jultomten in

In 1871, Swedish artist Jenny Nystrom began painting illustrations, primarily for use in Christmas cards, of the Swedish nisse and tomten as miniature versions of Santa.

Sweden and Norway, Julenisse in Denmark and Joulutonttu in Finland. Every farm in Scandinavia was believed to have a bright-eyed old man, about two- or three-feet tall depending on the country, whose role was to help with the chores at night. These elves and gnomes, known as the "hidden people" or the "unseen," were difficult to find because they slept during the day and worked at night, moving stealthily and silently. Although they generally managed to avoid detection by the humans in whose houses and barns they toiled, they could be mischievous if the residents offended them or did not take proper precautions. On Christmas Eve, tradition required leaving them a warm bowl of porridge with a pat of butter melting on top before going to sleep. Whether one treated the elves and gnomes well or poorly could produce good or bad luck during the following year, so a smart Scandinavian did not neglect the porridge and butter.

Because the elves and gnomes of Scandinavian folklore were, by definition, unseen by humans, there are few early images of what the Scandinavian gift-givers looked like. In 1871, a Swedish artist, Jenny Nystrom, began to illustrate the nisse and tomten with red pointed hats, long white beards, and red clothing—in effect, elf-sized versions of Santa Claus—that were used widely on Christmas cards.[2] A decade later, in 1881, Sweden's Viktor Rydberg and Harald Wiberg wrote and illustrated, respectively, *The Christmas Tomten*, a book about the Jultomten, or Christmas gnomes. Based on the illustrations by Nystrom, Wiberg and the artists who followed, the nisse of Sweden and Norway are about two feet tall. City nisse wear red or blue suits, farm nisse wear smocks and trousers of natural colored wool, and they both wear buckled black shoes, often very scuffed.

In Denmark, the nisse are very similar to those in Sweden and Norway except they don't have tassels at the end of their caps. The tomten look like the nisse except they are taller and wear gray stockings and wooden clogs instead of black buckled shoes. The tomttu of Finland, known as Joultonttuja during Yule, are gnomes who generally live underground, and differ in appearance from the other Scandinavian elves and gnomes primarily because they shave their mustaches, creating an Amish look. At Christmastime, however, the Finns will dress up and parade as the tonttu in red stocking caps with bells. The Christmas gift-giver, however, is not a Joultonttuja but a Joulupukki, or Yule buck, a figure who evolved from a goat into a man with goat features, and then into a man resembling Santa Claus. The Christmas gift-giver in Denmark, however, is called Julemanden, which translates as Christmas Man. He looks much like the other nisse except he is taller.

The Scandinavian gift-givers who are the most fun, at least for those of us with an offbeat sense of humor, are the thirteen Icelandic Jólasveinar ("Yule Lads"), the sons of two child-eating ogres, Grýla and Leppalúði, who live together in a cave. Grýla, the mother, is a hideous-looking woman with horns spends the day looking for children to cook in a large pot. Leppalúði, the father, is known for his laziness and mostly stays at home in their cave but he does prepare the pot for cooking the day's meal. According to some stories, Leppalúði is Grýla's third husband. The other two were trolls, and one was eaten by Leppalúði.

The thirteen lads, with an English translation of their names, are Stekkjarstaur (Gimpy), Giljagaur (Gully Imp), Stúfur (Itty Bitty), Þvörusleikir (Pot Scraper), Pottasleikir (Pot Licker), Askasleikir (Bowl Licker) Hurðaskellir (Door Slammer), Skyrgámur–Skyr (Skyr Gobbler, Skyr being an Icelandic yogurt), Bjúgnakrækir (Sausage Snatcher), Gluggagægir (Window Peeper), Gáttaþefur (Doorway Sniffer), Ketkrókur (Meat Hooker), and Kertasníkir (Candle Beggar). They are mischief-makers, and their names generally indicate their specialty. In the thirteen days before Christmas, one of the lads leaves the cave each day, traveling to town where he will leave a gift in shoes the Icelandic children have set outside on a windowsill. Thus, a well-behaved child could get thirteen gifts. If the children are not well behaved, however, the lads will often leave only a potato.

The only Scandinavian Christmas tradition that reflects a direct Christian influence is Sweden's St. Lucia's Day on December 13.[3] Even this festival, however, is largely pagan in origin. The genesis of St. Lucia's Day was a festival of lights held in Sweden on the Winter Solstice. At the time the festival was converted to a Christian event, according to Christmas historian Val Berryman, the Winter Solstice occurred on or near December 13, the Catholic Feast of St. Lucia. The Swedes marked the festival of lights "with candles dispelling the darkness of December 13, the shortest day of the year on the ancient calendar."[4]

St. Lucia, who died as a Christian martyr on December 13, AD 304, had no connection to either Scandinavia or Christmas but, presumably, had some free time on her hands when the Christian missionaries needed to name a Christian symbol for the festival of lights. According to legend, she was jailed for having spurned the marriage proposal of a wealthy pagan to devote her life to serving Christ and the poor. While in jail, Lucia "plucked her own eyes out to mar her beauty and avoid the unwanted advances" of the jailer.[5] Historically, St. Lucia has been pictured holding two eyeballs on a plate while she gazed into the distance with her own eyes clearly in place, presumably because most folks were somewhat repulsed by the look of a young woman with empty sockets where her eyes should be. Not surprisingly, the Swedish Festival of St. Lucia reflects little of this history. The traditional highlight of the holiday is that the eldest female daughter in the family appears dressed entirely in white with a wreath of candles on her head (and her eyeballs intact) before providing gifts to family members. In this costume, St. Lucia bears a strong resemblance to eighteenth- and nineteenth-century illustrations of the Christkindl wearing similar candle wreaths.

14

Gift-Givers in the
Southern Half of Europe

The Christ Child, Le Befana and the Three Kings

Italy, Spain, and France have been grouped together as southern Europe because they all share the influence of Rome in language, religion and culture. These nations, whose languages evolved out of Latin, were Christianized in the fourth or fifth century and have remained predominately Catholic since then. Greece is also included in this section because, although it does not fit the religious and language profile of the other three nations, its ancient history of advanced civilization, its shared mythology with Rome and its political and social independence from Russia give it more in common with southern Europe than eastern Europe.

The Reformation had no significant effect on these nations because they all remained Catholic, or, in the case of Greece, Eastern Orthodox. Consistent with the strong Catholic tradition in Italy, Spain, and France, the most popular Christmas traditions have always been those with the strongest religious appeal. Most popular is the display of a Nativity scene, known as a manger in English, a crèche in French, a presepio in Italian, and a putz in Moravia, a nation that became part of Czechoslovakia following World War I. The scene typically contains figures representing Mary, Joseph, baby Jesus in a manger, the shepherds who visited the Christ child, the Three Wise Men, and assorted animals and angels in an open-air stable. The concept is often credited to St. Francis of Assisi in 1223, but most historians believe this story to be apocryphal. In Catholic tradition, the Biblical Magi, who came to be known more commonly as the Three Wise Men or the Three Kings, were said to have arrived to visit the Christ child on January 6, the Feast of the Epiphany, bringing with them gifts of gold, frankincense, and myrrh. The explanation for the leaving of gifts for children on the eve of Epiphany, common in many Catholic nations, is that the Three Kings now bring gifts for all children, not just the Christ child.

Italy. Until the twentieth century, there were two gift-givers in Italy. On Christmas Eve, Italian children would receive gifts from the Christ child, known in Italy as Gesu Bambino, generally after the family attended midnight mass and enjoyed a Christmas Eve dinner. The traditional dinner is known as the Feast of the Seven Fishes, a meal that was supposed to include seven different varieties of seafood but no meat because fasting, a term that Catholics interpret to mean fish is allowed but not meat, was required during Advent. On Epiphany, the traditional gift-giver was Le Befana, a witch-like woman on a broomstick who is similar in many ways to the female Russian gift-giver Baboushka. Her name, Befana, is a variation of Epiphany but her looks and actions strongly suggest she evolved from the Germanic goddess Berchta.

113

Le Befana, like Berchta, is now depicted as an old woman with the haggard appearance and crooked nose we associate with a witch. Like Berchta, she also rides a broom, enters homes through the chimneys, and delivers gifts on Epiphany Eve. While unlike Berchta, who left gifts on January 5 because that was the last night of the Wild Hunt, Befana leaves gifts on Epiphany because when Christ was born she was invited by the Magi to accompany them to visit the Christ child. Befana, however, had declined the offer to visit the Christ child in favor of finishing her housework. She quickly realized her mistake and, according to legend, has spent two thousand years bringing gifts to children in order to make up for this disrespectful error in judgment. The differing explanations for the same conduct should remind us of Miles' admonition in *Christmas in Ritual and Tradition* that the rituals and traditions often last much longer than the explanations initially given for them.

St. Nicholas of Myra is recognized primarily in Bari and Venice, the coastal cities that sponsored raids during the eleventh century to steal the bones of St. Nicholas from his tomb in Myra, which had come under Islamic control, and take them to Italy. According to Miles in *Christmas in Ritual and Tradition*, "[t]he festival of St. Nicholas is naturally celebrated with most splendour at the place where his body lies, the seaport of Bari in south-eastern Italy.… The tomb of St. Nicholas is a famous centre for pilgrimages, and on the 6th of December many thousands of the faithful, bearing staves bound with olive and pine, visit it."[1] The feast day, however, is treated as a religious event rather than an excuse for secular partying and gift-giving.

The fact that Italy celebrates Epiphany but not St. Nicholas' Day despite Italy's control over his relics illustrates that, by chance or design, most European nations celebrate one holiday or the other, but not both. Those nations celebrating Epiphany as a day for gift-giving by the Three Kings or Befana are typically in southern Europe, where there was no need for Catholic missionaries to promote celebration of St. Nicholas' Day to give a Christian identity to the pagan Yule celebration. There is no reason why those in northern Europe could not celebrate Epiphany, long treated as an important date in German folklore known as Perchta's Night, but the two holidays were exactly a month apart, and celebration of both, with Christmas and News Year's in between, would probably be more than most could take. Accordingly, even without researching the history of gift-giving in a particular nation, it is a safe bet that nations which celebrate St. Nicholas' Day as more than a religious feast day will have little in the way of festivities on Epiphany, and nations which celebrate Three Kings Day will not celebrate St. Nicholas' Day.

Spain. In Spain, the celebration of Christmas also emphasizes strong Catholic traditions. The traditional date for Christmas gift-giving is Epiphany, and the gift-givers for children are Las Tres Reyes Magos, the Spanish translation of the Three Kings. The explanation for this tradition is that the Biblical Magi, having arrived on Epiphany with gifts for the Christ child, were inspired to repeat that custom every year by bringing gifts to worthy children throughout the world. This tradition, which began in Spain, has been adopted in most of Latin America.

On Christmas Eve, which the Spanish and most Latin Americans call Noche Buena (the "Good Night"), the traditions in Spain are similar to those in Italy and France. The traditional Christmas Eve dinner is Pavo Trufado de Navidad, turkey with truffles, although the cost of truffles these days likely puts the cost of that meal far out of range of the average family. After dinner, most Spaniards will attend midnight mass, known as La Misa Del Gallo ("The Mass of the Rooster"), after which they will crowd the streets, carrying torches or playing musical instruments. While this schedule might be tough for most of us, it is not unusual for Spaniards to eat dinner close to midnight and stay out drinking or partying after that but unlike America the children do not jump out of bed the next morning at 6 a.m. to see what Santa brought.

While some gifts may be given on Christmas Day, most are given on Epiphany. In a tradition that resembles American children writing letters to Santa Claus, Spanish children will write letters to the Three Kings on December 26. The kings are Gaspar, a brown-haired and bearded king, who wears a gold crown with green jewels and carries frankincense; Melchior, a king with long white hair, a white beard, and a gold cloak who brings the gift of gold; and Balthazar, a king with dark skin and beard and a purple cloak, who brings the gift of myrrh. They come and go while the children are asleep, but in the morning some children find a dark smudge on their cheeks, which their parents will say shows they were kissed by Balthazar while sleeping. Later that day, parades are presented in many cities featuring floats, the Kings, and, sometimes, the camels they reportedly rode to visit the Christ child.

Spain also has some unique regional traditions. In the Basque region of Spain, the Olentzero is a pre–Christian feast of the Winter Solstice. The traditions and rituals vary from village to village but in most versions a life-size effigy is created of Olentzero, an overweight Basque peasant smoking a pipe and wearing farmer's attire with traditional abarketa shoes. The effigy arrives late on Christmas Eve with presents for the children and is then carried through the streets on a chair by children seeking "alms," typically candy, and singing songs. At the end of the celebration, the figure is typically burned.

In the Catalonia region of northeastern Spain, residents have what is probably the strangest Christmas tradition in the world, the Tió de Nadal ("Christmas log") or Caga Tió

This photograph shows one of the most unusual Christmas traditions, Tió de Nadal, the "pooping log" of Catalan, Spain. Shutterstock.com.

("shit log"). Tió de Nadal is a log about two feet long and six inches wide, with stick legs, a painted face and a red hat, that parents bring out each year on December 8, the Feast of the Immaculate Conception. The connection, if any, between the feast day and the log is unclear because the tradition is far from immaculate. The children of the family are charged with feeding the log with nuts and dried fruit each night and covering him with a blanket to keep him warm. On Christmas, the adults plant more gifts, fruits, or candies under the blanket while the children are out of the room. When the children return, they beat the still-covered log with sticks while singing the traditional Tió de Nadal song. In English, these are the lyrics:

> Shit log,
> Shit nougats,
> Hazelnuts and mató cheese,
> If you don't shit well,
> I'll hit you with a stick,
> Shit log!

The adults periodically look under the blanket, eventually announcing the log has pooped and removing the blanket so the children can grab the treats. Tradition, if not sanitation, demands the log is then burned as part of the Christmas celebration.

France. Like Spain and Italy, France has been a Catholic stronghold for more than fifteen centuries, and its traditional celebration of Christmas reflects that fact. The primary gift-givers in France are the Christ child, known in French as Le Petit Jesus, and Père Noël. Pere did not appear until the late nineteenth century, when Father Christmas had become well established as a gift-giver in Great Britain, and the French needed only translate the name and provide him a traditional French grape-picking basket to wear on his back.

Some regions also have their own gift-givers. St. Nicholas survived the Reformation intact as a Catholic saint in France, but he was popular primarily in the northeastern part of the nation, where France abuts Germany. The provinces of Alsace and Lorraine did not convert to Protestantism, but their Christmas traditions were influenced by the proximity to Germany, and St. Nicholas delivers gifts on December 6.[2] In Franche-Comte, the gift-giver is known as Tante Arie, the good fairy of the Montbéliard.

In France, the Christmas season begins with the opening of Christmas markets. In French homes, the families will typically set up a "sapin de Noel," the French term for a Christmas tree, and a crèche depicting the traditional nativity scene. On Christmas Eve, the French tradition is to attend Midnight Mass, often preceded by participating in a recreation of the journey of Joseph and Mary, followed by dinner. The dinner, called Le Revellion, might include goose, turkey, foie gras, oysters, and sausages, but dessert is traditionally Buche de Noel, a rolled chocolate sponge cake in the shape of a Yule log, filled with pastry crème, and covered with chocolate ganache to create the appearance of bark. In some families, the parents will inform the children after dinner that the Christ child has come, leading the children into a parlor where they see for the first time the sapin de Noel and the gifts left by Le Petit Jesus (or, perhaps, Père Noël). In other families, children leave their shoes by the fireplace, often filled with carrots or other treats for Gui, the donkey who Père Noël rides from house to house. Père Noël and Gui arrive after the children have fallen asleep, and Père Noël leaves gifts while Gui eats the treats left for him. Whether the children receive gifts on Christmas Eve or Christmas morning, adults usually do not exchange gifts until New Years' Day.

Greece. In 500 BC, prior to the rise of the Roman Empire, ancient Greece was the

The Greeks celebrate the midwinter holidays on January 1, St. Basil's Day, when Aghios Vassilis, the Greek name for St. Basil, plays the role of Santa Claus.

world's most advanced civilization, providing the foundation for modern western culture in the areas of philosophy, government, theatre, music, dance, art, and architecture. Prior to Christianization, the Greek Empire had a panoply of pagan gods that was largely adopted by the Romans, albeit with different names. Ancient Greece celebrated both a New Year's festival, Kronia, similar to the springtime New Year's festivals in Mesopotamia, Babylon, and Egypt, and a midwinter festival, Rural Dionysia, during the month of Poseidon, which straddled the Winter Solstice. The midwinter festival honored Dionysus, the god of wine and a student of Silenus.

The Protestant Reformation had no direct effect on Greece because its citizens were members of the Greek Orthodox Church, one of the autonomous divisions of the Eastern Orthodox Church. The complex relationship between the Roman Catholic and Eastern Orthodox churches—the Western and Eastern churches, respectively, until they parted ways in the Great Schism of 1054—is beyond the scope of this book but a brief summary may be helpful. The Eastern Orthodox Church, officially known as the Orthodox Catholic Church, describes itself as "a communion of self governing Churches, each administratively independent of the other, but united by a common faith and spirituality."[3] The regional churches comprising the Eastern Orthodox Church trace their lineage to one or more of Christ's original apostles, Peter, Paul, John, and James. For almost two thousand years, the predominant religion in Greece has been the Greek Orthodox Church, one of the original four self-governing divisions.

For present purposes, the important distinction between the Roman Catholic and Eastern Orthodox churches is that the Eastern churches are regional and autonomous. It is for this reason, presumably, that during the Middle Ages the Eastern church did not have the same focus as the Western church on converting the pagan population of Europe to Christianity. The more people who converted to Catholicism in western Europe, the more powerful and wealthy the Roman Catholic Church would become. In order to convert the pagan population, therefore, the Catholic Church was willing to tolerate the pagan festivals as long as they were given a "Christian meaning." For the Eastern Orthodox churches, on the other hand, converting the people of another nation would likely result in the creation of an autonomous division of the Eastern Orthodox Church named for the other nation and governed by its own bishop. The Eastern Orthodox churches, therefore, had less incentive to convert the pagan population in other regions or to tolerate the mingling of pagan and Christian traditions. Thus, in those nations where one of the Eastern Orthodox Churches is the predominant religion, there is a more explicit line drawn between religious figures (the Christ child and St. Nicholas) and folk figures (the secular Father Frost and similar characters from Slavic folklore).

St. Nicholas is the patron saint of Greece, but it has no tradition of gift-giving on St. Nicholas' Day or Christmas. Traditionally, the only seasonal gift-giver in Greece was Aghios Vassilis, the Greek name for St. Basil, who leaves presents for children on January 1, the Feast of St. Basil. Thus, Aghios Vassilis is often described as the Greek Santa Claus but he has no connection to Santa. The Greeks celebrate St. Basil's Eve, which coincides with New Year's Eve, and St. Basil's Day with special foods such as vasiló-pita, or St. Basil's bread, songs, religious services and other traditions but on the whole the holiday is more religious and less commercial than Christmas in other Christian nations. More recently, however, the "American Santa Claus" has obtained a foothold in the nation and he may become more of a factor in the future.

15

Gift-Givers in Russia and Eastern Europe

Ded Moroz and Snegurochka

While the primary criterion for grouping the European nations in this book was geographic proximity, that has the side-effect of dividing the nations by religion and ethnic background as well. Northern Europe is predominately Protestant and Germanic while southern Europe is predominately Catholic and Latin. In eastern Europe, including Russia, the predominate religion is Eastern Orthodox, and the predominate ethnic background is Slavic. Thus, Russia and Eastern Europe have both different religions and different ethnic backgrounds than any of the nations previously discussed.

Eastern Europe, as used in this book, includes a diverse group of nations once known as the Balkans. It can be divided into two groups based on twentieth-century history: the former European constituents of the Soviet Union (Russia, Ukraine, Belarus, Lithuania, Latvia, Estonia, and Moldavia) and the former Communist Bloc nations that came under Soviet control following World War II (Bulgaria, Romania, and six nations that were part of the former Yugoslavian: Serbia, Slovenia, Croatia, Bosnia Herzogovenia, Macedonia, and Montenegro). The first group was part of the Soviet Union from 1917 through 1990, when the nations all declared their independence over a short period of time. The second group came under control of the Soviet Union in 1945, when it began formal military occupation of these nations following World War II. Despite the terms of the agreement governing military occupation by the Allied forces, the U.S.S.R. refused to cease occupation, and began an informal military occupation to keep those nations subject to Soviet control until roughly 1990, when the Soviet Union began to break apart and the Communist Bloc nations were successful in eliminating Soviet control. During the same period, Yugoslavia splintered into multiple nations as the result of a bloody civil war prompted by ethnic and religious disagreements.[1]

Most of Europe had converted to Christianity by the ninth century, if not much earlier, but in Russia and eastern Europe Christianity did not arrive until the end of the tenth century and was not firmly in place for several centuries after that. One reason for the relatively late arrival of Christianity, already mentioned, was that the Roman Catholic Church took a more aggressive approach to converting the pagan populace in western and northern Europe than the Eastern Orthodox Church did in eastern Europe. Unlike empires where the monarch—or, in our example, the pope—had an incentive to expand the kingdom to increase his or her power, the regional structure of the Eastern church did not reward such ventures.

There were also practical, geographical, and logistical reasons for the slower Christianization of eastern Europe. The nations of Russia and eastern Europe were sparsely populated and far removed from the seats of power in Eastern Christianity—Constantinople (modern Turkey), Alexandria (modern Egypt), Antioch (modern Turkey), and Jerusalem—creating little incentive for the existing churches to send missionaries to far-flung and geographically inhospitable regions. Between the tenth and fifteenth centuries, the Eastern Orthodox Church was also preoccupied by a number of existential challenges, including a series of disagreements with the Roman church that lead to the Great Schism in 1054 in which the Western and Eastern churches permanently parted ways; the influx of Islam into the regions the Eastern church controlled, culminating in the Crusades, a series of battles between 1095 and 1230 over Muslim control of land that had been occupied by Eastern Christians; and the battle for control of Constantinople in 1453 between the Byzantines (an Eastern Orthodox, Greek-speaking empire that controlled most of the nations on the eastern half of the Mediterranean Sea) and the Ottomans (an Islamic-controlled, Turkish-speaking empire that controlled Turkey and the lands surrounding it, but which actually had a slight Christian majority). In what was the most significant military loss in the history of Christianity, the Ottomans prevailed, gaining control of Constantinople and expanding Islamic control of the region.

The impetus for the Christianization of Russia was not external efforts by Christian missionaries but a political decision by an early monarch of what became Russia, Prince Vladimir the Great. At the time, the regions that became Russia were a loose confederation of states headquartered in Kiev and known as Kievan Rus'. Believing a single religion would help unify the states into a single nation, Vladimir, then a believer in Slavic paganism, conducted what modern businesses might call a beauty contest in which Prince Vladimir or his aides visited the leaders of the world's major nation religions to choose one that would be imposed upon the people of Kievan Rus'. In AD 987, after concluding Eastern Orthodox was the best choice—in part, it appears, because Islam did not permit the consumption of alcohol and in part because Vladimir did not want the heavy hand of the Catholic Church trying to control his nation—Vladimir had himself baptized and announced that all citizens of Kievan Rus' would become members of the Eastern Orthodox religion.

While AD 987 is cited as the year in which Russia adopted Christianity, converting the pagan population of a region almost as large as the rest of Europe was not that simple. Most of the citizens at that time were polytheistic pagans who viewed Christ as simply another member of the panoply of Slavic gods. More significantly, the coalition of states that constituted Kievan Rus' disintegrated early in the eleventh century, and the entire region fell to an invasion by the Mongols in 1240.[2] Over the next few centuries, both the governments of Russia and what officially became the Russian Orthodox Church in 1589 experienced a series of expansions and contractions before stabilizing under control of the Russian Tsars from 1547 to 1721 and the Russian Empire from 1721 to 1917. Thus, as far as can be determined, the Russian Orthodox Church did not obtain meaningful influence over the daily life of Russians until the sixteenth century at the earliest, and it never obtained the influence the Catholic Church had in southern Europe or the Protestant denominations had in northern Europe.

There is very little documentation of Slavic mythology and traditions before Christianity arrived, but in light of what we know about Slavic paganism generally and the pagan practices elsewhere in Europe, one has to conclude there were annual celebrations of the Winter Solstice. We can also assume Slavic mythology shaped the pagan celebration of the

Winter Solstice in Russia and eastern Europe in the same manner Roman and Germanic mythology shaped the midwinter celebrations in western Europe. Unfortunately, according to Linda J. Ivanits, a professor of Russian literature at Pennsylvania State University and author of *Russian Folk Beliefs*, there are few reliable sources on the details of those beliefs.

> Most studies of eastern Slavic paganism have been based on written sources. These sources are scant and consist mainly of brief chronicle entries, sermons and instructions, all dating from the Christian era and hostile to pre–Christian beliefs. Accounts of ancient myths and detailed descriptions of cults such as we have for Greece and the Near East are almost entirely lacking. What East Slavic written sources do is give us a list of probable deities and, occasionally, their attributes and functions.[3]

In *Slavic Folklore*, Natalie Kononenko writes that Prince Vladimir selected the six "official" gods of Slavic mythology before he converted to Christianity.[4] This does not necessarily tell us anything about the Slavic gods, beliefs, or ceremonies before the tenth century, but it seems highly likely, in light of the enduring nature of pagan beliefs generally, that most if not all of the gods identified by Vladimir had long-standing positions in the Slavic pantheon of pagan gods. Those most relevant to the Winter Solstice were Perun, who was both the chief Slavic god and the god of thunder and lightning, Dahzbog, the god of the sky and the sun, and Striborg, the god of the wind.[5] There is another figure, Khors, who some say was another name for the god Dahzbog and others say was the god of the moon.[6] On the Winter Solstice, known as Korochun, Khors, symbolizing the old sun, dies but is reborn the following day as Dažbog, the sun god. There was also a female figure, Kolyada, who is variously described as the goddess or the personification of Korochun.[7] Following the arrival of Christianity, Kolyada and Korochun became the names for Christmas and the Winter Solstice, respectively. The Christmas season, which is the twelve days between Christmas and Epiphany, became known as Svyatki or Svyatuie Vechera ("Holy Evenings").[8]

While there is not much information available about the Slavic gods, there is even less information about what those gods looked like. The only contemporaneous depictions of the Slavic gods are a few stone statues from the High Middle Ages, so weathered as to be almost unrecognizable. Those depictions have been used by modern artists, however, to create more elaborate images. Not surprisingly, the modern depictions of the Slavic gods associated with the Winter Solstice look a good deal like the Egyptian, Greek, Roman, and Germanic gods associated with the Winter Solstice—old men with long white hair and beards, long robes, pointed hats, and a staff of some sort. There is also a clear resemblance between these gods and Ded Moroz ("Grandfather Frost"), and Ded Moroz bears such a close resemblance to Santa Claus that most American collectors assume that Russian or Ukrainian made figurines of Ded Moroz are depictions of Santa Claus.

Because of the absence of historical records, one must be cautious about concluding that nineteenth- or twentieth-century depictions accurately reflect the original Slavic gods, even if they were intended to do so, and anything produced after 1917 is subject to suspicion the Soviet government was attempting to create pagan gods to displace Christian symbols, just as the Nazi government of Germany appealed to Germanic paganism to displace St. Nicholas with Odin as the "real" German gift-giver. In the Soviet Union, which officially banned the practice of Christianity between 1917 and 1990, some sources say that the Communist government recreated a pagan Slavic god named Morozko in the 1930s to serve as Ded Moroz, the gift-giver in the newly-promulgated Festival of Winter, a secular New Year's holiday designed to plug the hole left by the government's ban on the celebration of Christmas.

Other than the association of the Winter Solstice with the pagan gods Perun, Dahzbog, Khors, and Striborg, and use of the names Khors and Kolyada, there is very little information available about the Slavic midwinter festivals. Kolyada refers to both the Slavic celebration of the Winter Solstice before the arrival of Christianity, and the celebration of Christmas thereafter, in the same way the Germanic term Yule refers to both the pagan and Christian celebrations. Given the common features of Winter Solstice festivals throughout Europe, however, and the amount of interaction between Germanic and Slavic peoples in parts of Eastern Europe, it is safe to assume the Slavic traditions were fairly similar to the traditions of the Germanic tribes that celebrated Yule with decorations of evergreens, bonfires, candles, feasts, singing, dancing, and, almost certainly, a good deal of drinking. According to some sources, the Slavic beliefs also included an element very similar to the Germanic Wild Hunt.

This statue is Ded Moroz, the gift-giver in Russia and Eastern Europe. A secular figure whose name means "Grandfather Frost," he brings gifts on New Year's Eve. Photograph by Sergeev Pavel.

Somewhat more is known about the Christmas season in Russia following the arrival of the Eastern Orthodox Church during the reign of Prince Vladimir the Great.[9] The Russian Christmas season, Svyatki, starts on Christmas Eve and ends on Epiphany. In the 1902 history *Christmas: Its Origin and Associations*, Dawson writes that the Christmas Eve festivities begin with Kolyadki, a term that identifies songs related to Kolyada and, thus, is the Russian equivalent of Christmas carols.[10] In a tradition that sounds like a cross between English wassailing and Sweden's St. Lucia Day, a young woman was chosen to play the role of Kolyada, the personification of the Winter Solstice. Dressed in white, she rides on a sleigh "from homestead to homestead" with a group of young people who sing traditional songs in her honor—"Kolyada, Kolyada! Kolyada has come/ We wandered about, we sought holy Kolyada in all the courtyards."[11] Dawson reported that as of 1902 "these songs have in many places fallen into disuse, or are kept up only by the children who go from house to house, to congratulate the inhabitants on the arrival of Christmas and to wish them a prosperous New Year."[12] It is reasonable to speculate, however, that Snegurochka, the Snow Maiden who was drafted to accompany Ded Moroz when the Soviet Union instituted a Christmas-like New Year's celebration in the 1930s, was the Communist combination of Kolyada and Christkindl.

Dawson and Miles also say that even in the nineteenth century, when the Russian Orthodox Church was firmly in place, the Russian Christmas celebration retained many elements of the pagan celebration of the Winter Solstice. Dawson writes that Russian ceremonies "resemble, in many respects, those with which we are familiar, but they are rendered specially interesting and valuable by the relics of the past which they have been the means of preserving—the fragments of ritual song which refer to the ancient paganism of the land, the time-honoured customs which originally belonged to the feasts with which the heathen Slavs greeted each year the return of the sun."[13] Miles echoes the point: "More often than not these are without connection with the Nativity; sometimes they have a Christian form ... but frequently they are of an entirely secular or even pagan character."[14] Many of the songs, Miles says, focused on "the sun, moon, and stars and other natural objects," and even when Christian characters are introduced "they seem to be based on myths to which a Christian appearance has been given by a sprinkling of names of holy persons of the Church."[15]

The histories by Dawson and Miles date from 1902 and 1912, respectively, and thus were written before the Communist Revolution of 1917. This is helpful in that they tell us about Christmas in Russia without using any political lens but creates a puzzle in that neither book says anything about Russian gift-givers. One cannot construe their silence on the subject to mean there were no Christmas gift-givers in Russia in the early twentieth century because we know Vladimir Lenin went out of his way to eliminate "Nikola" in 1919. although it is not clear whether Nikola was the Russian name for St. Nicholas or, as was so common in Germany at the time, a secular gift-giver who had borrowed the name. The best source on Russian gift-givers appears to be Val Berryman's series in *The Glow* on "Christmas in Russia,"[16] and it doesn't answer the question. In these articles, Berryman identifies four Russian gift-givers—two that were active prior to the Communist Revolution (Baboushka and St. Nicholas), one that may or may not have been in existence at the time (Ded Moroz) and one that clearly post-dates the Revolution (Snegurochka, the Snow Maiden).[17]

Baboushka, a name that likely comes from a head scarf worn by Russian women, was the Russian version of Italy's Le Befana, both of whom were likely based on the Germanic goddess Berchta. All three have the appearance we now ascribe to a witch—an old, ugly woman with a crooked nose and tall hat who rides a broomstick. Baboushka, like Befana, delivered gifts on Epiphany, and both have the same backstory that they refused the request of the three Magi to accompany them to see the Christ child because they had too much housework to do. Upon realizing their mistake, they have spent two thousand years leaving gifts for children as they look for the Christ child.[18] The Communist Revolution of 1917, however, appears to have ended Baboushka's days as a Christmas gift-giver. Although she would presumably be free to return in light of the end of the Communist government in 1990, it does not appear she has done so.

The other gift-giver who everyone seems to agree operated in Russia prior to the Revolution was St. Nicholas, but his popularity as a gift-giver, as compared to a saint, is subject to debate. Berryman writes St. Nicholas "never figured as prominently" in the Russian celebrations of Christmas as Santa Claus does in the United States, but that does not tell us much because even at the height of St. Nicholas' fame in northern Europe his presence did not approach the modern day Santa Claus.[19] In Russia, however, St. Nicholas retained his reputation as a religious figure. Prior to the Communist Revolution of 1917, Russian Orthodox Churches gave special recognition to St. Nicholas' Day, providing children with chocolates wrapped in gold foil but did not otherwise mark the date.

One question on which experts disagree is whether Ded Moroz acted as a Christmas gift-giver in Russia prior to the Revolution. In the *World Encyclopedia of Christmas*, Bowler asserts Ded Moroz was a product of the Communist government, and that he, along with his granddaughter Snegurochka, were created by the Soviet government only after it decided in 1935 to sanction a secular New Year's celebration with many elements of Christmas.[20] Berryman, however, says Ded Moroz "dates from the late nineteenth century as a tradition that was borrowed from the West, probably Germany. This borrowed Santa was Russianized by putting him in a traditional Russian troika sleigh pulled by three horses. He doesn't go down the chimney to deliver gifts, and instead knocks on the door. And instead of traveling with a little girl called Christkindl, he was accompanied by his granddaughter, the Snow Maiden."[21] If this timing is accurate, it might explain why the Dawson and Miles histories, written only two and twelve years, respectively, after the turn of the twentieth century, did not address this gift-giver. Unfortunately, Berryman does not cite any external documentation to support his claim, one way or another.

Bowler and Berryman are not the only potential sources. The Russian news agency, Russia Today, maintains an internet encyclopedia, Russipedia, which provides a different explanation, describing the history of Ded Moroz in a manner that resembles the German Weihnachtsmann. Under this explanation, the Slavic counterpart of the Germanic god Odin was Morozko, a dark god who reputedly threw misbehaving children into a large sack and ransomed them back to their parents.[22] In response to the Eastern Orthodox Church's desire for a lighter, more Christian gift-giver, Morozko was rechristened Svyatoy Nikolay ("St. Nicholas") but Nikolay was eliminated as a result of the Russian Revolution of 1917. In explaining the details, Russia Today writes:

> The original Russian gift-giver was Saint Nicholas [but the] image of Saint Nicholas originates from the image of another hero—the ancient Morozko.... In fairy tales Morozko is, at times, kind and, at times, evil. To be precise, he is kind towards the hard-working and the good-hearted, but extremely severe with the mean and the lazy. And it is not only about justice. It is rather about two personalities living in one magical person.[23]

This explanation aligns Slavic folklore with Germanic folklore in which pagan gods led the Winter Solstice observance until replaced by a Christian saint. According to Russipedia, the Russian Orthodox Church objected to the frightening depiction of a pagan god as an integral part of a religious feast. Over time, therefore, Morozko morphed into a character very similar in looks, personality, and function to the other European and American gift-givers, at some point acquiring the name Ded Moroz ("Grandfather Frost"). After St. Nicholas was eliminated during the Russian Revolution, Russipedia says, and the Soviet government sanctioned the Festival of Winter in 1935, Ded Moroz was reinstated as the symbolic head of the Soviet Winter Solstice celebration. If this explanation is accurate, Russia's Ded Moroz and Germany's Odin have more in common than one would assume from western sources, but that is precisely what folklorists would tell us to expect.

In *Christmas and Its Origins and Associations,* Dawson buttresses the contention that the Orthodox Church sought to quash pagan customs it found offensive, albeit without mentioning Ded Moroz as such. "The Russian Church sternly sets its face against the old customs with which the Christmas season was associated, denouncing the 'fiendish songs,' and 'devilish games,' the 'graceless talk,' the 'nocturnal gambols,' and the various kinds of divination in which the faithful persisted in indulging."[24] Although the pagan practices were repressed, Dawson says, "they were not to be destroyed," and at the time of the Winter Solstice the Orthodox pastors "went home and sang songs framed by their ancestors in honour of heathen divinities."[25]

Thus century after century went by, and the fortunes of Russia underwent great changes. But still in the villages were the old customs kept up, and when Christmas Day came round it was greeted by survivals of the ceremonies with which the ancient Slavs hailed the returning sun god, who caused the days to lengthen, and filled the minds of men with hopes of a new year rich in fruits and grain.[26]

Whatever his origin, Ded Moroz's appearance has become more polished than one would expect from a figure from Slavic folklore. Ded Moroz's current outfit, according to Russia Today, is an ankle-length fur coat, generally light blue, embroidered with silvery stars and crosses, and a hat, typically red, embroidered with pearls. Ded Moroz's shirt and trousers are usually made of flax decorated with white geometrical patterns, according to the website, and he wears mittens, a wide white belt, and *valenki*, high, felted boots popular in Russia, with silver ornamentation.[27] It is the ankle-length fur coat that really defines the appearance of Ded Moroz, creating the shape of a pyramid that gives him more grandeur and substance than the other gift-givers. While most official depictions of Ded Moroz show him in a light blue coat, one can find pictures or figurines of him in virtually any color. The second most popular color appears to be white, presumably reflecting his close connection with snow and ice, and he is often depicted in figurines made of cotton.

The fourth Russian gift-giver is Snegurochka, the Snow Maiden, for whom Berryman provides two explanations.[28] In one, a combination of "The Gingerbread Man" and "Frosty the Snowman," Snegurochka "is based on an old Russian folk tale of an elderly couple who regretted never having children. They made a snow figure of a young girl and she came alive for them during the winter months, melting away in the spring and returning the following winter."[29] He also says, however, that the Snow Maiden may have been borrowed from Germany's Christkindl. German Christmas cards imported into Russia during the late nineteenth and early twentieth centuries, he says, "depicted the common German Christmas characters Nikolas and Christkindl," which in America would be considered to be Santa and a young girl.[30] A third explanation, not mentioned by Berryman even though it seems most likely, is that Snegurochka was modeled after Koleyda, the young woman who was the personification of the midwinter festivals and the object of many early folk songs. In all probability, however, Snegurochka was inspired by all three tales.

Snegurochka is generally portrayed as an attractive young woman who wears long blonde braids with a silver-blue costume—sometimes floor length, sometimes scantier— and a furry cap or snowflake-like crown. She and Ded Moroz ride a traditional Russian sled pulled by three horses, called a troika, and sometimes appear with a young man known as the New Year's Boy. Ded Moroz is said to live in a log cabin in Veliky Ustyug in the Vologodsky Region of northern Russia, about 500 miles northeast of Moscow, but it is not clear whether Snegurochka lives with him.

The two Christmas customs to which the Russian Orthodox Church most strongly objected, Dawson says, were divination, in particular the practice of young women using various tests during the Christmas holiday to determine when or whom they would marry, and mumming, the practice of going door to door, offering carols in exchange for drink, food, or money. Precisely why the church found these practices objectionable is unclear. If one views divination in the same manner as a bride tossing her flowers to the single women at a wedding or a young girl pulling the petals off a daisy, it seems completely harmless, but the church may have lumped divination with other, darker forms of fortune-telling that assumed a power beyond that of Christ or connected the practice with the Romani, derisively known as Gypsies, an ethnic group subject to great prejudice throughout Europe.

The church's objections to mumming are also unclear but are less surprising.

Mumming, in its various forms, has a long history in Europe but has often generated controversy as a form of extoration, a disturbance of the peace, or both. One of the most fascinating descriptions of Russian Christmas comes not from historians but from Russian novelist Leo Tolstoy in *War and Peace*.[31] In this masterpiece, Tolstoy describes members of the Russian aristocracy in Tsarist Russia as they celebrate Christmas during the nineteenth century. Those celebrations, by themselves, say little about how Christmas was celebrated among Russia's rural peasants. The wealthy Russians described by Tolstoy were something like the original jet-setters—albeit without the jets—traveling throughout Europe to play with the wealthy, and speaking French, not Russian. On the other hand, the serfs were on the bottom rung of the feudal systems that developed in Europe during the Middle Ages.

In the 1859 novel *War and Peace*, Tolstoy describes one of the few occasions for social interaction between the two groups—one that occurred only during the Christmas season. In this scene, a group of mummers has arrived at the home of Count Nikolai Rostov and his sister, Countess Natasha Rostova.

> The mummers (some of the house serfs) dressed up as bears, Turks, innkeepers, and ladies—frightening and funny—bringing in with them the cold from outside and a feeling of gaiety, crowded, at first timidly, into the anteroom, then hiding behind one another they pushed into the ballroom where, shyly at first and then more and more merrily and heartily, they started singing, dancing, and playing Christmas games. The countess, when she had identified them and laughed at their costumes, went into the drawing room. The count sat in the ballroom, smiling radiantly and applauding the players.[32]

What Tolstoy describes here are the long-standing Yuletide practices of social inversion, mumming and guising—practices that originated with Saturnalia more than two thousand years earlier and became significant parts of the Roman, German, English, and American Christmas traditions. While the details differ, the essence of the practice is the lower classes would dress up in costumes that disguised their identity and go house to house among the wealthier members of society, seeking food, drink or coins in exchange for songs or plays to celebrate the season. The practices, which have been described both as a form of social inversion and as a form of charity, are believed to have grown out of the practice in which wealthy Romans would serve the slaves and lower classes and the practice of dressing in clothing of the opposite sex, animal skins and other costumes to hide one's identity during Saturnalia.

The practice of mumming and guising have been a consistent element of most midwinter celebrations. Other examples we will see in this book include the open house at the fictional Lord Bracebridge's manor in rural England as described by Washington Irving in "Old Christmas"; the rowdy, inebriated Callithumpian bands who sought to enter the homes of wealthy New Yorkers like Clement Moore, as described by Stephen Nissenbaum in *The Battle for Christmas*; and the young men who dressed in clown costumes to go "belsnickling" in rural Pennsylvania as described by Alfred Shoemaker in *Christmas in Pennsylvania*. The fact that all of these were occurring simultaneously during the nineteenth century, from the rural farmlands of central Pennsylvania to the dirty streets of New York City to the luxurious country estates of northern England to the fictional Count Nikolai's mansion in Moscow, illustrates the universal nature of our midwinter traditions.

16

How the Celebration of Christmas Came to the English Colonies in America (or Not)

Many folks with a strong interest in colonial history have visited Colonial Williamsburg, a living history museum in Williamsburg, Virginia, that has preserved or recreated the colonial city that served as the capital of the Colony of Virginia from 1699 until 1780. One of its most popular features is Christmas in Williamsburg, a period of several weeks when the colonial village is decorated in gorgeous wreaths and swags using natural ingredients, and celebrants may spontaneously break into Christmas carols after dinner at a local tavern. Although it is a wonderful and highly recommended Christmas experience, many participants wonder whether it accurately reflects the celebration of Christmas in America during the colonial era.

The answer, according to sociologist James H. Barnett in *The American Christmas* and historian Penne L. Restad in *Christmas in America*, depends largely on the colony in question and, more specifically, the predominant religion of the colonists.[1]

- The three religions that dominated the New England colonies—Puritans, who became known in America as Congregationalists; Presbyterians, who were members of the Calvinist religion of Scotland; and Baptists, a religion established in Rhode Island in 1638—strongly opposed the celebration of Christmas as inconsistent with the Bible.[2]
- Members of the Church of England, who were known in America as Anglicans before the Revolutionary War and Episcopalians thereafter, dominated Virginia and the southern colonies, celebrating Christmas in the style of the English in the same social and economic classes.
- Members of the Lutheran Church, who settled largely in Pennsylvania and central New York, and the Catholic Church, the dominant religion in Maryland, celebrated Christmas from the time of their arrival on American shores, but had their own traditions and gift-givers.

New England. The first settlement in the northern colonies was by a group of English Puritans, commonly known as the Pilgrims, who docked their ship, *The Mayflower*, at Plymouth, Massachusetts, in 1620. Every American school child knows the story, accurate or not, of how the Pilgrims celebrated the first Thanksgiving with Native Americans in the fall of 1621. Less well known is the attitude of the Puritans toward Christmas.

The Massachusetts Bay Colony, as it was originally known, formally prohibited the celebration of Christmas until almost the eighteenth century. The Puritans' objections to the celebration were both theological and social although among the Puritans there was little distinction between the two. The theological basis was that the Bible identified only the Sabbath as a day of rest and said nothing about when Christ was born or keeping that day holy. Many believed, with some justification, that Christmas was a pagan invention or, worse yet, a Catholic one. The social objection was that Christmas was a "wanton Bacchanalian feast," a statement reflecting their distaste for earthly pleasures more generally.[3] This attitude was demonstrated as early as 1621 when Governor William Bradford of Plymouth Colony reprimanded several young men for shirking work and playing ball on Christmas Day.[4]

In 1642, the Puritan factions in England began a civil war over religion in which the celebration of Christmas had significant symbolic importance. In 1647, after overthrowing the monarchy and winning control of the English Parliament, the Puritans abolished the observance of Christmas, Easter, and Whitsuntide, the English term for Pentecost, the seventh Sunday after Easter, which commemorates the descent of the Holy Spirit upon Christ's disciples. In 1659, the Massachusetts legislature followed suit, enacting a law to punish "anybody who is found observing, by abstinence from labor, feasting, or any other way, any such days as Christmas day" with a fine of five shillings.[5]

After restoration of the monarchy in 1660, King Charles II demanded Massachusetts rescind the prohibition. Josiah Winslow, colonial governor until his death in 1681, apparently refused to do so because the colony did not rescind the prohibition until shortly after he died. Even then, New England remained hostile to the celebration until after the Revolutionary War.[6] At that point, the antipathy toward Christmas began to soften, partly because the population had become more diverse through the arrival of immigrants who celebrated Christmas, and partly because the Puritans had less objection to the celebration of Christmas once it was no longer, in their view, being dictated by the Church of England.[7] Another factor explaining the New England attitude towards Christmas was that New England created its own holiday, Thanksgiving, as a day of feasting and relaxation that served some of the secular functions of a midwinter festival without raising religious questions.[8] In the mid–1800s, New Englanders led by Sarah Josepha Hale, editor of *Godey's Ladies' Book*, a popular women's magazine, pushed for recognition of Thanksgiving as a national holiday. In October 1863, at the height of the Civil War, President Abraham Lincoln finally assented to her lobbying, declaring the last Thursday of November a "general day of Thanksgiving."

As the entire nation began to celebrate the "New England holiday" of Thanksgiving, New Englanders began warming to the now-American holiday of Christmas. Restad explains that the diverse regional customs of Christmas in America "underwent yet another transition. Similarities eclipsed differences, and the festival began to acquire a distinct profile as a national holiday."[9] During the Civil War, a number of states on both sides of the Mason-Dixon Line that had not previously declared Christmas as a holiday did so. In 1870, thirteen years after *Harper's Weekly* and *Harper's New Monthly Magazine* began to publish stories and illustrations of Santa Claus, including "The Night Before Christmas" in 1857 and the iconic drawings of Santa by Thomas Nast, Congress formally declared Christmas a federal holiday.

Part of the explanation for national recognition of a Christmas holiday in America, as in England and Germany, was the power of the press in standardizing and popularizing Christmas traditions. One can also view the national recognition of Thanksgiving and Christmas within a few years of each other, however, as a compromise similar to that in which early Eastern Christians agreed to mark the birth of Christ on December 25 if Western Christians agreed to mark January 6 as Epiphany. Ultimately, the period between Christmas and Epiphany became celebrated as the Twelve Days of Christmas, unifying the two days into a single holiday period that ran for twelve days, and which eventually was extended to begin with Advent. In the United States, the recognition of Thanksgiving and Christmas as national holidays less than a decade apart created the modern Christmas *season* we celebrate today. As Barnett explains, Christmas in America became—and remains—as "part of a midwinter cycle of activities which begins with Thanksgiving and ends at New Year or on January 6."[10]

The Middle Colonies. In New York and the mid–Atlantic colonies of New Jersey, Delaware, Pennsylvania, and Maryland, the celebration of Christmas during the colonial period was a patchwork quilt of local practices—Dutch and English traditions in New York; Scandinavian traditions flourishing in New Jersey and Delaware on the East Coast and Minnesota and Wisconsin in the Upper Midwest; Germany's Pelznickel and Christkindl developing into Belsnickle and Kriss Kringle in Pennsylvania, New York, and Maryland; Moravian immigrants with their unique Christmas traditions in Pennsylvania and North Carolina; and English Lord Baltimore welcoming English, Irish, and German Catholics into Maryland. In sociologist Barnett's words, the local practices "diffused" into regional practices between 1800 and 1860, with Christmas becoming a truly national holiday by 1870.[11]

The most contentious historical question in the middle colonies is to what extent the Dutch immigrants brought Sinterklaas with them to New York, and to what extent that influenced the development of the Santa Claus during the nineteenth century. New York was founded as New Amsterdam by Dutch settlers in 1625, following which the Dutch government purchased the island of Manhattan from the Lenape Indians for 60 guilders, and remained under Dutch governance until the English took control under threat of force in 1664. Once New York came under English control, Dutch immigration to America dribbled to virtually nothing whereas New York City became the nation's center of commerce and the primary gateway for European immigrants from other nations. As a result, the Dutch by 1800 constituted less than 2 percent of the total population of the colonies. Moreover, the Dutch who immigrated between 1625 and 1664 were long since dead, and except in a few bastions of Dutch heritage their great-grandchildren and great-great-grandchildren had grown up with English, Scottish, Irish and German immigrants. Nonetheless, with the notable exception of historian Charles W. Jones, all of the historians who have looked at the issue concur that during the seventeenth century the Dutch who settled New Amsterdam brought with them the tradition of visits by the Dutch Sinterklaas on the day before St. Nicholas' Day but the Dutch dwindled to a small portion of population and that the Sinterklaas tradition never caught on with the rest of the nation. Consequently, in searching for the European predecessors of Santa Claus the Dutch Sinterklaas was not the likely candidate some historians seem to believe.

These historians include Berryman, who says the Dutch brought the tradition with them in the early 1660s[12]; Barnett, whose sociological study *An American Christmas* says that during the eighteenth century colonists from England, Holland, and Germany "emphasized eating, drinking, family gatherings, merrymaking, and joyousness during the Christmas season, which usually began well in advance of December 25 and extended often to January 6";[13] and Restad, who says in *Christmas in America* that both Christmas and New Year's Day were being celebrated in New York City as secular and social holidays in the early 1800s, and, by the 1830s, stores were staying open until midnight to accommodate the rush of Christmas and New Year's shoppers.[14] None of this would probably be of much interest except that the lone dissenter, Jones, relies heavily on the absence of any existing gift-giver in the early 1800s for his assertion that Washington Irving created the legend of a gift-giving St. Nicholas in New York.

In fact, the group whose traditions undoubtedly had the most influence on the celebration of Christmas in America were the "Pennsylvania Dutch" and similar populations in New York and contiguous states. These immigrants were German, not Dutch, and the misleading label arose from the immigrants identifying themselves as "Deutsch," the German word for German. By 1800, more than three hundred thousand German immigrants had settled in Pennsylvania, bringing with them two German gift-givers—Pelznickel, one of the faux Nicholases created following the Reformation, and Christkindl, the Christ child. During the nineteenth century, roughly seven million more Germans immigrated to America, with a million settling in Pennsylvania alone and many more in New York, creating a huge, and hugely receptive, audience for the development of Santa Claus.

The celebration of Christmas in Pennsylvania by the German immigrants in the nineteenth and early twentieth centuries was documented by folklorist Alfred L. Shoemaker in his 1959 study, *Christmas in Pennsylvania: A Folk-Cultural Study*, creating a rare and invaluable opportunity to learn how Christmas was actually celebrated.[15] The original German names of the gift-givers Christkindl and Pelznickel were simply lost in translation, Shoemaker reported, as German immigrants began to converse in English. The term Kriss Kringle was an American mispronunciation of Christkindl, often by the American-born spouses or children of German immigrants, which gradually created the belief the German gift-giver was a man named Kriss Kringle. The only figure who fit that description, however, was Belsnickle, and the name Kriss Kringle seems to have stuck to the bearded, tattered figure who came alone, with gifts for good boys and girls, during the Christmas season. Although some native Germans objected to the term, it was used so commonly by Pennsylvanians that, by the 1840s, it was widely considered the Pennsylvanian name for the Christmas gift-giver.[16]

In retrospect, Kriss Kringle was clearly the Cinderella story of the potential aspirants to the title of American gift-giver. While Santa Claus had a strong oral tradition, he was still struggling to get his name in paper during the first half of the nineteenth century. Kriss Kringle, meanwhile, was memorialized in three children's books, *Kriss Kringle's Book*, published in 1842,[17] *Kriss Kringle's Christmas Tree*, published in 1845,[18] and *Kriss Kringle's Raree Show for Good Boys and Girls*, published in 1847.[19] These books were among the first five Christmas books for children published in America. The other two, *The Children's Friend* in 1821 and *A Visit from St. Nicholas* in 1848, apparently found no audience.

In Pennsylvania, the name Kriss Kringle was so popular the J.W. Parkinson's Department Store in Philadelphia began advertising appearances by Kringle in 1841, and by 1846 declared itself "Kriss Kringle Headquarters." Santa Claus, on the other hand, would not obtain a department store gig for five more decades when The Boston Store in Brockton, Massachusetts, began presenting appearances by Santa Claus. St. Nicholas never got one anywhere. The relative importance of Kriss Kringle is also demonstrated by an article in an English newspaper in 1853 that described the persons who filled the stockings of American children on Christmas Eve as Kriss Kringle in Pennsylvania and St. Nicholas or Santa Claus in New York.[20]

The 1845 publication *Kriss Kringle's Christmas Tree* is also notable for its cover illustration of a gnome-like Santa figure crawling up a Christmas tree.[21] This illustration was published three years before the iconic drawing of Queen Victoria and Prince Albert in the *Illustrated London News* that popularized the German tradition of decorating Christmas trees in England, and five years before an Americanized version of the engraving was published in the United States. Without more detail than the cover illustrations on *Kriss Kringle's Christmas Tree*, it is hard to determine what the artists who drew this picture and the art for this book and its sequel, *Kriss Kringle's Raree Show,* had in mind because they both look more like an unshaven version of actor Danny DeVito than Santa.[22] In one of his articles in *The Glow*, however, Berryman depicts Kringle as one of the Belsnickle figurines that began to be produced in Germany before the end of the century.[23]

In *Christmas in Pennsylvania,* Shoemaker explains that the term "Belsnickle" developed a number of different meanings and, thus, became the source for much confusion even today. When applied to a person, Belsnickle could mean (1) someone who went to the child's home in advance of Christmas, often carrying a whip or switch, to determine whether the child was being good by quizzing the child or asking some basic catechism questions; (2) someone who accompanied St. Nicholas or Christkindl on their gift-giving visits, generally carrying a whip, sticks, or a basket designed to hold unruly children, silently emphasizing the disciplinary role of the gift-giver; or (3) someone who went alone to deliver gifts on St. Nicholas' Day or Christmas Eve, essentially assuming the role of St. Nicholas or Santa Claus.[24] The second role seems to have been much less common in Pennsylvania than Germany, and the third seems to have been more common, but no visit was necessary if children were told the gift-giver did not come until after they were asleep. In all three roles, the typical disguise donned by whoever was playing the role was similar to the costume of the faux Nicholases, or terror men, in Germany—a long beard, a dirty, ragged hat, face darkened with soot, an old, dirty coat, preferably fur, heavy boots, a bag or basket suitable for carrying gifts or disobedient children, and a whip or a handful of switches.[25]

In these three roles, Belsnickle is a noun. In Pennsylvania during the nineteenth century, Belsnickle could also be used as a verb, as in "we are going Belsnickling," and a separate noun made from that verb, "Belsnickler," which means a person who is going "Belsnickling." A Belsnickler, however, was much different than a Belsnickle. When used as a verb, Belsnickling was the Pennsylvania version of Christmas mumming or guising—that is, going door to door in disguise, and offering songs or short plays in exchange for food, drink or money, as practiced in Europe for many centuries. The only thing "a Belsnickle" and "Belsnickling" really had in common was they both involved young men in costume and lots of beer. In Pennsylvania, the "Belsnicklers," meaning those engaged in Belsnickling rather than playing the part of Belsnickle, could go door to door as a group any night during the Christmas season.

According to Shoemaker, the troupe would ask the homeowner "[is] Belsnickling allowed?"[26] If the homeowner consented, the troupe would sing a carol or put on a short play involving death and resurrection. At the end of the performance, the Belsnicklers would expect remuneration in the form of food, drink, or coins. If the homeowner did not consent, there was a possibility that their mailbox, fence or outhouse might soon need repair! Understanding the distinction between Belsnickle, the American version of Pelznickel, and Belsnickling, the American version of mumming, and Belsnickler, someone engaged in Belsnickling, is important because otherwise the descriptions, drawings, and photographs in Shoemaker's book and similar sources that refer to unruly gangs of Belsnicklers or depict a group of young men in clown costumes make no sense.

Unlike playing the part of a Belsnickle, where custom dictated a dirty, bearded man in a heavy fur coat, the costumes worn by Belsnicklers could range from clown suits to woman's outfits to antlers, all remnants of the cross-dressing and animal costumes that began in Saturnalia and were still popular costumes two thousand years later. Belsnicklers often wore masks as well because, like European mummers and guisers, the Belsnicklers came uninvited and attempted to keep their identity secret. Some American families appreciated Belsnickling as a long-standing Christmas tradition while others found the boisterous, often drunken Belsnicklers an unwelcome intrusion or worse. In practice, Belsnickling and its European counterparts seem to have been more acceptable in small towns, where the homeowner would probably know who the Belsnicklers were, mask or not, creating pressure for the homeowner to welcome them into the house and for the Belsnicklers to behave themselves. In larger cities, the Belsnicklers were truly anonymous and, therefore, less constrained and more frightening.

During the twentieth century, the noun Belsnickle developed another meaning, identifying the elaborate papier-mâché candy containers imported from Germany between about 1890 and 1910 depicting a stern version of a hooded Santa. The containers, which were handmade in German homes and could range in size from four inches to twenty-four inches high, have become highly collectible and quite expensive if in quality condition. According to advertisements from the period, the containers were marketed in Germany as Weihnachtsmann and in the United States as Santa Claus. Belsnickle is simply the name adopted by American collectors during the twentieth century, and while it was originally used to describe the papier-mâché candy containers made in Germany at the end of the nineteenth century, it is commonly used today to identify any figure of an old man with a stern visage, a long white beard, a long, hooded cloak, folded arms with hands tucked inside the sleeve on the other side, and a switch or small Christmas tree held in the crook of his elbow. The name likely arose from the fact that the stern, almost frightening look on the candy containers reminded folks of the frightening look of the real Belsnickles in Pennsylvania but no one knows for sure.

The final group of immigrants to the middle colonies who made significant contributions to the celebration of Christmas in America were the Moravians, whose homeland was the eastern half of the current Czech Republic. They were one of the earliest Protestant groups to flee what they believed was religious persecution in Europe, settling in Pennsylvania and North Carolina. These immigrants not only celebrated Christmas, they had an outsized influence on American Christmas traditions. Two of the most popular traditions they brought to America were Moravian stars, complex, colored paper stars of different designs made to be hung on Christmas trees, and the putz, an unfortunate name for the elaborate Nativity scenes designed to be placed under the Christmas tree. Moravian putzes were sometimes so large and elaborate they could fill an entire room with miniature buildings, animals, and people. The appearance of the putz in Pennsylvania also created a precedent for elaborate displays under the tree, often enclosed by a small fence, that could did include scale-model buildings, trees, roads, railroads, and the like.

Virginia and the Southern Colonies. The first English settlement in America was established in 1608 by a group of English cavaliers led by Captain John Smith. The cavaliers were royalists in the battles between the monarchs and the Puritans, and "properly observed" Christmas during the first December following their arrival by "feast[ing] on fish, oysters and game they had caught."[27] Smith and the English settlors who followed him also "brought with them such holiday customs as ringing bells, burning a Yule log, dining elaborately, dancing, playing games and singing carols."[28] Most of the other southern colonies were also founded by Anglicans as well, and after the hardships of initial colonization stabilized they "looked to England for models of dress, manner and social behavior." The southern colonies, like most of England in the seventeenth and eighteenth centuries, were rural regions whose economies relied on agriculture. The plantations that began to dot the southern colonies in the eighteenth century fit the model of rural England from which most of the colonists had come. The one significant exception, of course, were the enslaved African Americans, who were typically given between three and seven days free of service.[29]

17

The Purported Role
of Washington Irving
in the Introduction
of St. Nicholas to America

The conventional wisdom described at the outset of this book credits American author Washington Irving with introducing St. Nicholas—and, thus, Santa Claus, according to the proponents of this theory—to America in a book, *A History of New York*, published on December 6, 1809. The book was written under the pseudonym Diedrich Knickerbocker, identified as a Dutch historian, and purports to be a history of Manhattan from the "beginning of time," which means the Dutch settlement of New Amsterdam in 1625, until the English took control of the island in 1664 and renamed it New York. Anyone who keeps an eye out for mentions of Irving's mock history will be astounded by the frequency and consistency with which authors discussing the history of Santa Claus in America since 1954 credit Irving's *A History of New York* with a significant role in creating the American gift-giver.[1] Many of these are short summaries of the history of Santa Claus which were written by individuals without any research or expertise, and could easily be dismissed as misunderstandings, but a number are works by nationally prominent historians who focus in detail on Irving's purported role in the creation of Santa Claus. Why did so many experts conclude Washington Irving had a critical role in the creation of Santa Claus when, as demonstrated in this book, he did not?

The answer lies in two works by the late University of California at Berkeley history professor Charles W. Jones—a scholarly paper, "Knickerbocker Santa Claus," published in 1954,[2] and a book, *Nicholas of Myra, Bari and Manhattan: Biography of a Legend,* published in 1978.[3] In these works, Jones opines that Santa Claus is a "bifurcation" of St. Nicholas, meaning the separation of folk tradition of St. Nicholas, the Christmas gift-giver, and the religious tradition of St. Nicholas of Myra. Jones then opines, without the slightest hesitation, "that the split occurred in New York City is indisputable."[4] Having in his own mind narrowed the bifurcation of St. Nicholas and the origin of Santa Claus to New York, Jones states with equal confidence that "Santa Claus was made by Washington Irving."[5] These assertions were demonstrably inaccurate. As discussed earlier, the split between the historical St. Nicholas of Myra and the secular gift-givers actually occurred during the sixteenth century in northern Germany, following the Protestant Reformation, and dozens of gift-givers emerged from the split in the Protestant regions of Germany. The saintly half of St. Nicholas remained intact but under Lutheran doctrine a Catholic saint could not legitimately serve as a Christmas gift-giver. Washington Irving had nothing to do with any of this.

Nevertheless, based on Jones' reputation as one of the world's preeminent scholars on St. Nicholas, the vast majority of books and scholarly papers on the topic since 1954 adopted Jones' position as gospel without any independent investigation. Jones first presented his contention that Washington Irving "made" Santa Claus in a speech before the New-York Historical Society on St. Nicholas' Day, 1953. That talk was published as a scholarly paper in *The New-York Historical Society Quarterly* in 1954.[6] In explaining his research, Jones made much of the fact that between 1859 and 1954, historians relied on an 1859 history of New York by Mary L. Booth, *History of the City of New York from Its Earliest Settlement to the Present Time*, which cited Irving's mock history without recognizing it was satire.[7] In obvious ridicule of Booth and the historians who relied on her book without reading the source material, Jones borrows a line from Chauncey Depew, a member of the historical society who served as U.S. senator and had an illustrious career as a New York attorney, that "it is often better for fame to have eminent historians than to have enacted history. The judgment of mankind among nations and peoples of the past is never formed from original sources."[8]

Read today, this quotation drips with irony because the dogmatic conclusions of Jones, who was exactly the type of "eminent historian" that could create fame even if the original sources did not merit it, were based on the same type of mistake made by those historians at whom his sarcastic barbs are aimed—that is, the failure to read the original sources. As a result of this mistake, Jones and the historians who rely on his work have created the false narrative that "Washington Irving was instrumental in creating the modern Santa Claus."[9] Unfortunately, Jones' theory was based on the mistaken assumption that he was working with the first edition of Irving's work, or at least that the handful of passages about St. Nicholas in the 1812 edition of *A History of New York* upon which Jones relied were also in the first edition published in 1809. In actuality, the quotes were not in the 1809 edition, but Jones obviously did not read it, perhaps because the 1812 edition was published primarily to correct errors in the 1809 edition and Jones did not realize there were two editions. Jones, however, was "an esteemed Berkeley professor of antiquity" who has been described as one of the two "most important Nicholas scholars of the twentieth century."[10] As America's pre-eminent scholar on St. Nicholas, he was the type of academic emperor that few professional historians would seek to challenge in his area of expertise, clothes or no clothes, and more than two dozen histories did so. This book will set the record straight.[11]

Irving's *A History of New York* was not intended as a serious history, but as a satire in the form of a documentary, a literary form of the cinematic style called a "mockumentary."[12] One would think that anyone reading *A History of New York* would immediately recognize it as a farce, a book of pure fiction intended to amuse the reader about the foibles of mankind. If one did not get it after reading the full title—*A History of New-York from the Beginning of the World to the End of the Dutch Dynasty, Containing, Among Many Surprising and Curious Matters, the Unutterable Ponderings of Walter the Doubter, the Disastrous Projects of William the Testy, and the Chivalric Achievements of Peter the Headstrong the Three Dutch Governors of New Amsterdam Being the Only Authentic History of the Times That Ever Hath Been or Ever Will Be*—it should have been apparent when author Knickerbocker explained the first Dutch governor of New Amsterdam spent six hours each day eating, six hours smoking, and twelve hours sleeping, which unfortunately left no time for thinking.

For those who might not have caught the joke in the thirty-nine years after the book was first published, Irving wrote an "Author's Apology" for the 1848 edition in which he explained the original work was written as a comical satire of an earlier work, *The Picture of*

New York; or, The Traveller's Guide through the Commercial Metropolis of the United States, by Dr. Samuel Mitchell, a socially prominent, but, at least in Irving's view, extraordinarily pompous professor at Columbia University. Mitchell was also a member of the New-York Historical Society, an organization that one can infer the twenty-six-year-old Irving believed to be equally pompous because he included in the introduction to *A History of New York* a mock dedication to the society by the putative author, Diedrich Knickerbocker, and a statement by Knickerbocker's fictitious landlord that Knickerbocker had died and his estate was bequeathed to the New-York Historical Society with the hope it build a "wooden monument" to Knickerbocker on its grounds.

To create the appearance of a serious work, Irving conducted extensive research that was incorporated into the satire, and he brilliantly marketed it through a series of advertisements in New York newspapers about the unexplained disappearance of a Dutch historian, Dietrich Knickerbocker, and the subsequent sale of Knickerbocker's manuscript to satisfy an unpaid debt to the keeper of the hotel where Knickerbocker had lived. As a result, when the book was released on December 6, 1809, New Yorkers lined up (figuratively speaking, at least) to buy it. According to biographies of Irving, it quickly became apparent the book was a satire—one aimed more at the foibles of then-current politicians such as Thomas Jefferson, and other politicians at large rather than the Dutch governors who were ostensibly the subject of the history. Within a few weeks, it became common knowledge in New York literary circles that Irving was the author.

More than two hundred years later, the book is still as readable and funny as when English poet Sir Walter Scott spent an evening in 1810 reading it to his spouse and a friend. One of the running jokes in the book was the Dutch admiration for St. Nicholas and the events and monuments in New Amsterdam honoring the saint, all of which were fictional— and all of which the well-informed reader should have known were fictional because the Dutch Reformed Church, founded in 1570, was a hagiophobic product of the Reformation and the Dutch government had outlawed paying homage to St. Nicholas. Fifty years after Irving's book was published, in 1859, an author named Mary L. Booth wrote another history of New York, *History of the City of New York from its Earliest Settlement to the Present Time*, in which she relied on Irving's book to describe how the Dutch brought the tradition of St. Nicholas to New Amsterdam when they founded the colony in 1625.[13] Booth somehow failed to recognize Irving's account of the Dutch devotion to St. Nicholas in America was a complete fabrication.[14] Nonetheless, according to a 1953 speech by Jones, historians consistently relied on Booth's book for almost a hundred years to repeat, as historical fact, Booth's assertion that Dutch settlers brought the tradition of St. Nicholas to New York.

Why Jones cared in 1953 about whether the Dutch settlers of the 1600s celebrated St. Nicholas' Day in the same manner as their homeland is uncertain; perhaps he was merely pandering to members of the New-York Historical Society by attributing to the society a large role in the "invention" of Santa Claus. Whatever the reason, Jones decided to give a speech on the subject titled "Knickerbocker Santa Claus" to the New-York Historical Society in 1953. In that speech, Jones quite effectively demolishes Booth's reliance on Irving's *History* as the basis for her assertion the Dutch brought the tradition of St. Nicholas to New Amsterdam when they founded the colony in 1625, but this was easy pickings. Jones had only to explain that Booth failed to recognize Irving's history was a farce, following which Jones expressed his concern that none of the other historians who relied on Booth's book questioned Booth's reliance on Irving's mock history. Jones also noted that in 1625 the Dutch Reformed Church was a Calvinist religion that would have prohibited public displays or celebrations involving a Catholic saint, and any historian reading Irving's text should have proceeded skeptically on that basis alone.

To dispel any doubt, however, Jones claims to have conducted a detailed review of newspapers, public records, and other contemporaneous sources to confirm there was no mention of St. Nicholas in the New York papers prior to 1809.[15] It is unclear what Jones was expecting to find in his review of the public records but with the exception of one obscure reference to St. Nicholas' Day in 1773, Jones says he found no references to either St. Nicholas or Santa Claus prior to 1809. It would have been newsworthy, of course, if there were reports that resembled Irving's description in *A History of New York* of a Dutchman flying a wagon over the rooftops of Manhattan, tossing gifts down chimneys, but, presumably, that is not what Jones was not expecting to find in the local papers. If Jones was expecting to find reports that children of Dutch descent woke up on December 6 to find a stocking they had hung by the chimney the night before filled with candies, oranges and nuts, he should have recognized that would not be newsworthy.

Whatever Jones was expecting, we can accept at face value he found nothing in the Manhattan newspapers reporting the Dutch residents were celebrating either St. Nicholas' Day on December 6, which the Dutch did not observe, or the arrival of Sinterklaas on December 5, which the Dutch parents may have observed by filling their children's stockings with goodies and telling the children Sinterklaas had done it. Jones, however, concluded the absence of references to St. Nicholas in the local papers meant the jocular references to St. Nicholas in Irving's satire were entirely fabricated.[16]

Irving's references to St. Nicholas were entirely fabricated but Jones' inferences based on that fact were misguided. Assuming, correctly, that Irving invented the stories he told about the gift-giving practices of St. Nicholas in New York City, Jones concluded, incorrectly, that Irving's *History*, released in 1809, must have prompted John Pintard to distribute a broadside about St. Nicholas to the New-York Historical Society in December 1810, and the *New York Spectator* to publish a poem very similar to the broadside on December 15, 1810, events that Jones believed were the first evidence of any tradition in America involving a holiday gift-giver similar to St. Nicholas. Jones also concluded, incorrectly, that Irving's 1809 edition of *History of New York* prompted the sudden interest by John Pintard in St. Nicholas in 1810, a position from which Jones jumped to the conclusion that "Santa Claus was made by Washington Irving."[17] In explaining this conclusion, Jones states:

> Without Irving, there would be no Santa Claus. The *History* contains no less than twenty-five allusions to him—many of them the most delightful flights of imagination in the volume. Here is the source of the legends about St. Nicholas in New Amsterdam—of the emigrant ship *Goede Vrouw*, like a Dutch matron as broad as she was long, with a figurehead of St. Nicholas at the prow. Here are the descriptions of festivities on St. Nicholas' Day in the colony, and of the church dedicated to him. Here is the description of Santa Claus bringing gifts, parking his horse and wagon on the roof while he slides down the chimney.[18]

The premise that the December 1809 edition of Irving's book prompted a sudden interest in St. Nicholas during December 1810 was the bedrock underlying Jones' analysis. In his 1954 article, Jones explains that "Santa Claus was a parasitic germ until the Knickerbocker History in 1809; after 1809 Santa Claus spread like a plague which has yet to reach its peak."[19] Describing the St. Nicholas poem in the December 1810 edition of the *New York Spectator* as "the first American Santa Claus poem," Jones confidently asserts that "[i]t is obviously derived from both the [1810] Pintard verses and the [1809] Knickerbocker History."[20]

Even if Jones' theory that Irving's 1809 *History* caused the *New York Spectator* to

SANCTE CLAUS good heylig Man!
Trek nwe seste Cabaert aen,
Reis daer me'e na Amsterdam,
Van Amsterdam na 'Spanje,
Daer Appelen van Oranje,
Daer Appelen van granaten,
Die rollen door de Straaten.
SANCTE CLAUS, myn goede Vriend!
Ik heb U allen tyd gedient,
Wille U my nu wat geven,
Ik zal U dienen alle myn Leven.

SAINT NICHOLAS, good holy man!
Put on the Tabard,* best you can,
Go, clad therewith, to Amsterdam,
From Amsterdam to Hispanje,
Where apples *bright* † of Oranje,
And likewise those *granate* ‡ surnam'd,
Roll through the streets, all free unclaim'd.
SAINT NICHOLAS, my dear good friend!
To serve you ever was my end,
If you will, now, me something give,
I'll serve you ever while I live.

* Kind of jacket.   † Oranges.   ‡ Pomegranates.

This is a broadside distributed by John Pintard for a New-York Historical Society meeting on December 6, 1810. Pintard commissioned the woodcut from artist Alexander Anderson and reportedly obtained the Dutch poem from an elderly Dutch woman. Used with permission of the New-York Historical Society. ID 28883 St. Nicholas, first celebration of the Festival of St. Nicholas by the New-York Historical Society, Broadside by Alexander Anderson, Dec. 6. A.D. 343, SY1810 NO. 94, commissioned by John Pintard, 28 × 19 cm.

publish the St. Nicholas poem in 1810 were plausible, there is no evidence to support the conclusion that the *Spectator* poem caused the legend of Santa Claus to "spread like a plague." What conclusively refutes Jones' argument, however, is that he was relying on the wrong edition of Irving's book. A comparison of the 1809 edition of *A History of New York* to the 1812 edition shows that roughly half of the twenty-five references to St. Nicholas—and *all* of the passages about the gift-giving practices that Jones describes as "the most delightful flights of imagination"—were not in the 1809 edition.[21] Jones' failure to recognize that the critical references to St. Nicholas were not added until the second edition of *A History of New York* three years later might not have been significant except that Jones' belief Irving had sparked a sudden interest in the tradition of St. Nicholas was based explicitly on the timing of the St. Nicholas poems published in December 1810, a year *after* the 1809 edition. If the passages first appeared in the 1812 edition, which Irving published primarily to correct various errors made in the rush to release the 1809 edition, Jones cannot claim Irving's book triggered the 1810 publications.

The first of the publications upon which Jones relies was released on December 6, 1810, exactly a year after the publication of Irving's book. John Pintard, one of the officers of the New-York Historical Society, commissioned a broadside (a publication on one side of a single sheet of paper) about St. Nicholas for the group's annual meeting. That broadside featured drawings of St. Nicholas and two children standing by a fireplace with stockings presumably filled by St. Nicholas, one (the girl) with goodies and the other (the boy, naturally) with switches.[22] Under the illustration, which has been identified as the first printed depiction of St. Nicholas in America, the broadside included a poem about St. Nicholas in Dutch and English.

> St. Nicholas, good holy man
> Put on the Tabard, best you can
> Go, clad therewith, to Amsterdam
> From Amsterdam to Hispanje
> Where apples bright of oranje
> And likewise, those granate surnam'd
> Roll through the streets, all free unclaimed
> Saint Nicholas, my dear good friend!
> To serve you ever was my end,
> If you will, now, me something give,
> I'll serve you ever while I live.

One of inexplicable oddities in Pintard's broadsheet is the use of the phrase "Sancte Claus" as the Dutch name for St. Nicholas. In Dutch, saint would be translated as "sint," which is the title used in a number of Dutch books or illustrations of St. Nicholas, and "Nicholas" could be translated as Nikolaas, Niklaas or Nicolaas based on the titles used in the same books and illustrations. St. Nicholas could also credibly be called "Sinterklaas" or "Sinter Klaas," although these are not actually translations of "Saint Nicholas" but the name used in Holland for a character created to evade a legal ban on celebration of St. Nicholas' Day. The phrase "Sancte Claus," on the other hand, is a strange combination of "Sancte," the Latin word for "saint" or "holy," and "Claus," a fairly common diminutive for Nicholas in Germany but not common in Holland.

Jones writes in *St. Nicholas* that Pintard obtained the words, a traditional Dutch poem, from a Judge Benson who, in turn, obtained them from Mrs. John Hardenbrook, an elderly woman of Dutch descent who recalled the poem from her childhood in New York, likely in the 1740s or 1750s.[23] Jones does not seem to notice the inconsistency between this fact and his theory that the Dutch did not bring their St. Nicholas tradition to America. Knowing the source of the poem, however, which Pintard later said was widely known but only Mrs. Hardenbrook remembered all of the words, does not tell us where the name "Sancte Claus" came from because Benson or Pintard did not need an elderly Dutch woman to provide a Latin-German name for St. Nicholas. The name is important because the poems published on December 12, 1810, by the *New York Commercial Advertiser*,[24] on December 14, 1810, by the *New York Evening Post*,[25] and on December 15, 1810, by the *New York Spectator*,[26] all used the same unusual name. The poem, described by the *New York Commercial Advertiser* as "A Paraphrase of the Dutch Hymn to Saint Nicholas," was otherwise in English:

> Oh good holy man! whom we Sancte Claus name,
> The Nursery forever your praise shall proclaim:
> The day of your joyful revisit returns,
> When each little bosom with gratitude burns,
> For the gifts which at night you so kindly impart
> To the girls of your love, and the boys of your heart.
> Oh! come with your panniers and pockets well stow'd
> Our stockings shall help you to lighten your load,
> As close to the fireside gaily they swing,
> While delighted we dream of the presents you bring.
> Oh! bring the bright Orange so juicy and sweet,
> Bring almonds and raisins to heighten the treat;
> Rich waffles and dough-nuts must not be forgot,
> Nor Crullers and Oley-Cooks fresh from the pot.
> But of all these fine presents your Saintship can find,
> Oh! leave not the famous big Cookies behind.
> Or if in your hurry one thing you mislay,
> Let that be the Rod—and oh! keep it away.
> Then holy St. Nicholas! all the year,
> Our books we will love and our parents revere,
> From naughty behavior we'll always refrain,
> In hope that you'll come and reward us again.

The fact that three newspapers all printed the same poem within a three-day period, and that the poems used the highly-unusual name "Sancte Claus," makes it possible, if not highly likely, that Pintard himself promoted reprinting of the poems to give his broadside a public relations boost. Some historians may also have wondered whether the name was part of a bridge from St. Nicholas to Sancte Claus to Sante Claus to Santa Claus. That possibility cannot be disproven but as far as can be determined there are no other American publications in the early 1800s which used that name Sancte Claus whereas Sante Claus, Santeclaus and Santa Claus are unexceptional.

What really matters, however, is this. Knowing now that there was nothing in the 1809 version of Irving's *History* that could have inspired the Pintard broadside or the three newspaper poems, and that the references to St. Nicholas Jones cited in his scholarly paper and book were not included in Irving's *History* until the second edition published in 1812, Jones' assertion that "Santa Claus was made by Washington Irving" disintegrates like a sand castle in heavy surf. Nonetheless, more than two dozen works of history, anthropology, folklore and literature have relied on Jones' conclusions about Irving's *History* over the last sixty-plus years, repeating the tale that "Santa Claus was made by Washington Irving" in the same uncritical manner as historians had previously relied on Booth's book, all because the eminent historian didn't read the original sources.

Remarkably, three of these histories—*The Battle for Christmas* by historian Stephen Nissenbaum, *Nicholas: The Epic Journey from Saint to Santa Claus* by Jeremy Seal, an English author of historical fiction, and *The Original Knickerbocker: The Life of Irving Washington* by Andrew Burstein—not only repeat Jones' conclusion that Washington Irving "made" Santa Claus, they expand upon the conclusion by speculating that Irving may have conspired with other members of the New-York Historical Society to spread the legend of St. Nicholas in New York City.[27] The impact of Jones' error can also be seen in the historical treatment of Washington Irving. Biographies of Irving written between 1925 and 1974 make no mention of any effort by Irving to promote the St. Nicholas tradition in New York, something any biographer would have included if there were evidence to support the conclusion in Irving's publications and private records.[28] In a 2007 biography, however, *The Original Knickerbocker: The Life of Irving Washington,* author Andrew Burstein extends the argument by asserting, as fact, that Clement C. Moore did not write "The Night Before Christmas" and, as speculation, that Irving's *History* may have prompted the person Burstein thinks was the true author, Henry Livingston, Jr., to pen the poem.[29] Burstein states:

> [T]he literary detective Don Foster has credibly disproved Moore's claim of authorship and attributed the popular poem instead to Major Henry Livingston of Dutchess County, New York, a far livelier writer who was of mixed Dutch and Scottish ancestry. Whereas Moore was stern, pedantic, and largely humorless, Livingston was thoroughly infused with the spirit of Christmas from early adulthood; he delivered the lines of "The Night Before Christmas" at a gathering as early as 1807–1808, which means that he had imbibed the Dutch tradition and committed it to paper around the time Washington Irving was preparing his History. Although we can only speculate on the timing of the two writers' inspired attachment to St. Nicholas, we do know that Irving was an intimate of certain members of the extended Livingston clan.
>
> The purpose of extending the story of how Christmas came to America is to give Irving the precise amount of credit he deserves. He did not "invent" the holiday, but he did all he could to make minor customs into major customs, to make them enriching signs of family and social togetherness. With unprompted help from the likes of Henry Livingston, he provoked his countrymen into accepting what soon developed into a treasured holiday.[30]

One can almost hear the breathless tone in Burstein's voice as he announces the discovery of a Literary New World. Unfortunately, Burstein's vessel runs aground on at least four rocky points: (1) he assumes the accuracy of Jones' conclusion Washington Irving "made" Santa Claus, a conclusion we know is untrue because Jones was relying on the wrong edition of *A History of New York*; (2) he accepts, as fact, the claim by Vassar College Professor Don Foster that Livingston wrote "The Night Before Christmas," a claim that upon analysis evaporates into nothing; (3) he ignores that key elements of "The Night Before Christmas"—in particular, the reference to St. Nicholas "laying a finger aside of his nose" and the basic story of a Christmas gift-giver riding in a sleigh pulled by a flying reindeer—come from works not published until 1812 and 1821, respectively, and the poem therefore could not have been written until 1821; and (4) he cites no record of any interaction between Irving and Henry Livingston, Jr., who was thirty-five years older than Irving. or, for that matter, any evidence that either man had "an inspired attachment to St. Nicholas."

One might counter that Jones' real mistake was he should have said it was Pintard—not Irving—who "made" Santa Claus by publishing the broadside about St. Nicholas in 1810 and publishing or inspiring the St. Nicholas poems published in three newspapers in December 1810. In fact, historian Nissenbaum comes close to doing so in *The Battle for Christmas*. This argument, however, begs the questions of whether Jones was correct in insisting there was no evidence of any "Dutcb St. Nicholas" tradition in America prior to December 1810, and most experts dispute this. In *The American Christmas,* a 1954 study by sociologist James H. Barnett that is generally acknowledged as the first scholarly study of the celebration of Christmas in America, Barnett writes "the Dutch who settled New York during the seventeenth century brought the folk cult of St. Nicholas"[31]; that "he remained the dominant figure of their midwinter celebration until the close of the next century"[32]; and "[t]he Dutch celebrated St Nicholas (or Sinterklaas) Day on December 6, but gradual numerical dominance of the English settlers shifted the midwinter festival to December 25."[33] Berryman reaches the same conclusion in "Santa Claus Comes to America, The Dutch-American St. Nicholas."[34]

It is the most recent study of the issue, "From Amsterdam to New Amsterdam: Washington Irving, the Dutch St. Nicholas, and the American Santa Claus," that most persuasively refutes the theory espoused by Jones and Nissenbaum.[35] The author, Elisabeth Paling Funk, an independent scholar who was raised in the Netherlands and now focuses on early American and Dutch-American literature, asserts without doubt that the Sinterklaas tradition was prevalent in America well before Irving's *History,*[36] and that Pintard would have understood this fact because he obtained the poem on the 1810 broadside, a version of one common in the Netherlands in the 1700s, from an eighty-year-old woman of Dutch descent who remembered the poem from her childhood in New York.[37] More directly, Funk asserts:

> Ignorant of St. Nicholas's dual role as venerated saint and secular hero and the fact that as popular hero Nicholas survived the Reformation in Dutch family circles, Jones, professor emeritus at the University of California, Berkeley, and later Stephen Nissenbaum, professor of history at the University of Massachusetts, Amherst, deny Nicholas's seventeenth-century arrival in New Netherland and wholly credit his early-nineteenth-century [appearance in] New York to the need for a patriotic rallying point.[38]

As noted earlier, even if Jones had his dates correct, it is not at all clear that the references to St. Nicholas in *History* would have prompted the sudden interest—primarily, it seems, from John Pintard—in St. Nicholas, or that the Pintard broadside and poems had any importance in the subsequent popularity of Santa Claus. To the contrary, Jones' theory falls short for a number of reasons on what lawyers call "causation." First, by 1810 less than 2 percent of the American population were of Dutch ancestry, a percentage that declined very rapidly during the nineteenth century because Dutch immigration had largely ended when England acquired New York in 1664, whereas English, German, and Irish immigration grew geometrically over the next two centuries. Whether Sinterklaas visited Dutch-American children on the night before St. Nicholas' Day was not going to have a significant impact on the 98 percent of Americans who were not of Dutch descent, particularly since the immigrants were from nations that had their own Christmas traditions.

Second, the huge number of German immigrants to the United States during the nineteenth century—seven million, of whom more than a million ended up in Pennsylvania—ensured Americans would have a German-influenced gift-giver no matter what Irving, Pintard or Moore did. The best evidence of this fact is that they had nothing to do with the success of Kriss Kringle as a Christmas gift-giver in Pennsylvania, where Kringle headed a department store promotion in 1846 and had three books to his name by 1847. While immigrants from a number of nations contributed features, large and small, to the American Santa Claus, it was word of mouth among German immigrants that planted, fertilized and watered the tradition.

Third, if any verse can be credited with the success of Santa Claus it is "The Night Before Christmas," first published in 1823, and although the poem was extremely important in establishing the American traditions, even Moore's poem did not cause Santa Claus to "spread like the plague," as Jones put it so lovingly in "Knickerbocker Santa Claus." In *The Night Before Christmas: A Descriptive Bibliography of Clement Clarke Moore's Immortal Poem*, a book which purports to chronicle every publication of the poem for almost two hundred years, author Nancy Marshall volunteers that "[t]he poem's popularity and appeal with the public started slowly at first."[39] The data she compiled strongly support this assertion because it was not until 1848, almost forty years after Pintard wrote about St. Nicholas, that Moore's poem was published as an illustrated children's book, but sold little. It was 1857 before the poem was published nationally on the front page of *Harper's New Monthly Magazine*.

While Jones acknowledges some of these facts, he overtly seeks to minimize them. With regard to the existing Pennsylvania gift-givers, he states that "the Pennsylvania Germans ... built walls of custom around themselves that enclosed Kris Kringle and Pelznichol (Belsnickel), but among the customs associated with those names themselves were none recognizably imported from the Old Country.... I have not found a single reference to either SC [Santa Claus] or N [St. Nicholas] in the other twelve colonies. It is easiest to imagine that none were made."[40] Assuming the "other twelve colonies" means other than Pennsylvania, this response ignores *False Stories Corrected*, which established an oral tradition in full bloom by 1813. Similarly, although Jones did not have access to Barnett's *The American Christmas* (1954) or Alfred Shoemaker's *Christmas in Pennsylvania: A Folk-Cultural Study* (1959) when he wrote his 1954 paper, he should have been aware of both when he wrote his biography of St. Nicholas in 1978. These books show "the customs associated with those names" were, indeed, "recognizably imported from the Old Country."

In the same vein—to wit, minimizing any information inconsistent with his theory—Jones acknowledges Thomas Nast's biographer, Albert Bigelow Paine, quoted Nast as saying he based his images of Santa Claus on a man dressed as Pelznickel in Nast's native Germany. Whether Jones was unaware of the presence of Belsnickle as a Christmas gift-giver in Pennsylvania, or simply ignored that fact because it was inconsistent with his theory, Jones claims he could find no evidence of Pelznickel in the Palatinate region of Germany where Nast was born, and, in any event, Pelznickel "as a derivative of the devil ... was normally horned and tailed."[41]

The veracity of the first point is doubtful because the names of the German gift-givers were spread through oral tradition and it is highly unlikely Jones or anyone else visited hundreds of thousands of homes in the Palatinate region of Germany to ask if anyone there was familiar with Pelznickel. The second point is both inaccurate and irrelevant. It is inaccurate because Pelznickel was merely "Nicholas in furs," one of the human faux Nicholases who indisputably flourished in Germany following the Reformation. It is irrelevant because we know Kriss Kringle, without horns or tails, had become a popular Christmas gift-giver in Pennsylvania and other states with large German populations during the 1840s.[42] Kriss Kringle was simply Belsnickle with a different name and Santa Claus was Kriss Kringle with a different name. Jones, having spent most of his life studying St. Nicholas, seems not to have understood that Santa Claus had more German blood than anything else.

Jones' arguments also ignore the most persuasive evidence on the development of Santa Claus in America, which is that the legend of Santa Claus spread by word of mouth during the early 1800s, *before* publication of Irving's *History*, without showing up in the newspapers that Jones reviewed and without any involvement by Irving or the other members of the New-York Historical Society. Jones writes that "Santa Claus was a parasitic germ until the *Knickerbocker History* in 1809," a statement seemingly inconsistent with Jones' assertion he could find no evidence of "SC" at all before 1809, but "after 1809 Santa Claus spread like a plague." He never explains, however, what indicia of infection he is using. If we look at the frequency with which the name Santa Claus was published in books, magazines or newspapers, we don't find much evidence at all of Santa's existence until the 1850s, and virtually all of the evidence was prior to 1857, when *Harper's New Monthly Magazine* published Moore's poem with a front page illustration by F.O.C. Darley, is the addition of "Santa Claus" to the title "A Visit from St. Nicholas."

If we look at word of mouth—what historians call "oral tradition"—we see a different story. Indeed, in tracking the footsteps of Santa through the snowy New York streets the most significant evidence is *False Stories Corrected* published in 1813.[43] The author, who can only be described as a pre–Grinch grinch, wrote "[s]uch a creature as Jack Frost never existed, any more than old Santaclaw [sic] of whom so often little children hear such foolish stories; and once a year they are encouraged to hang their stockings in the chimney at night, and when they arise in the morning, they will find in them cakes, nuts, money, etc., placed there by some of the family, which they are told Old Santa-claw has come down the chimney and put in."[44] These words reflect that the legend and name of Santa Claus must have been well established among school children several years before publication of the book in 1813—otherwise, it would have been impossible for the author to know that children were encouraged to hang stockings once a year—and therefore cannot credibly be explained away as someone describing a recent trend or a scattered pattern of behavior. The fact that numerous newspaper editors chose on their own to add "Sante Claus" or "Santa Claus" to the title of "The Night Before Christmas" is also strong evidence that the name of Santa Claus was growing through oral tradition.

Historians can take some solace that not everyone in their profession accepted at face value Jones' argument that Washington Irving "made" Santa Claus. Some directly disputed Jones' claims while others expressed doubt a popular Dutch tradition could simply have vanished when the Dutch resettled in New Amsterdam. Folklorist Coffin wrote "Jones may well be right, but Irving wasn't working off as little Dutch lore as the historical speech would have one think. He certainly never made Santa Claus in the way Charles Schulz made Charlie Brown's 'The Great Pumpkin.'"[45] British writer Teresa Chris, author of *The Story of Santa Claus,* argues that even if, as Jones asserted, there were no newspaper reports "it is hard to believe that the Dutch children were suddenly deprived of their visit from St. Nicholas on 6 December.... It is also a fact that other groups of settlers knew of him and associated him with gift-giving on the same day, on 25 December or at New Year's."[46] And Bowler, in his most recent work, rejects the theory articulated by Nissenbaum in *The Battle for Christmas,* observing that the variety of names used for Santa Claus in the early 1800s "speaks to a long-standing oral transmission of the legend of a Christmas Gift-Bringer rather than, as some have suggested, the outright invention of Santa Claus by the Knickerbocker literary clique."[47]

It is Nissenbaum's book, *The Battle for Christmas,* which relies most heavily on Jones' conclusions as a predicate for Nissenbaum's own historical analysis. The theory of *The Battle for Christmas* is that Washington Irving, John Pintard, Clement Moore, and other members of the New-York Historical Society—the so-called "Knickerbockers," a name taken from Irving's *History* to mean prominent New Yorkers of Dutch descent—consciously promoted the legend of St. Nicholas as a means of changing Christmas from the drunken, Mardi Gras–style revelry that was prominent in New York at the time into the family-oriented holiday it eventually became. In a 2001 article on the authorship of "The Night Before Christmas," which parallels the arguments in his earlier book, Nissenbaum summarized his conclusion as follows:

> The most famous member of the New-York Historical Society was Washington Irving, who made much of St. Nicholas in his 1809 book *Knickerbocker's History of New York*, which was actually published on St. Nicholas' Day. It was Irving who popularized St. Nicholas in the 1810s.[48]

I have no quarrel with Nissenbaum's ultimate conclusion that the tradition of Santa Claus bringing gifts to children on Christmas Eve, coupled with more modern views on child-rearing in which the child became the focus of the family rather than someone who should be seen and not heard, remade Christmas as a more family-oriented holiday during the last half of the late nineteenth century. What is hard to swallow is his theory that this was the intentional result of promotional efforts by a small group of upper-crust New Yorkers affiliated with the New-York Historical Society between 1809 and 1822.[49] While Nissenbaum's theory implies an ongoing conspiracy, each of these men wrote one work about St. Nicholas—Irving's *History of New York*, Pintard's St. Nicholas broadside in 1810 and Moore's "Night Before Christmas" in 1822—and as far as we can tell never mentioned St. Nicholas again in any of their public writings. Irving moved to Europe in 1815 and remained there until 1832, undermining any claim that he was involved in an ongoing conspiracy with members of the New-York Historical Society over a poem written in 1822, and that Moore failed to publish the poem, or even acknowledge it as his work, for fifteen years, and consistently said that his sole purpose in writing the poem was to entertain his children on Christmas Eve in 1822.

It is particularly difficult to believe Irving was part of a conspiracy to clean the New York streets of drunken rowdies who were interfering with Moore's enjoyment of Christmas on the Chelsea estate where he kept four enslaved African Americans who served Christmas dinner and drinks to his extended family and friends.[50] We also know that Irving in 1809 had little in common with the prominent members of the New-York Historical Society, who were older, wealthy, conservative, and stodgy men of the type Irving was more likely to ridicule than drink with. Indeed, the original object of the satire was Samuel Mitchell, an egotistical and pompous man who was a founding member of the historical society. Irving had no incentive to conspire with these men over anything, and until he became internationally famous for *Rip Van Winkle* and *The Legend of Sleepy Hollow*, the wealthy men at the core of the historical society had no incentive to conspire with him.

While some have made much of the fact that *A History of New York* was dedicated to the New-York Historical Society, the dedication was not by Irving but by the fictional historian Deidrick Knickerbocker, and was preceded by an equally fictional introduction by Seth Handaside, the fictional owner of the hotel where Knickerbocker had supposedly left the fictional manuscript. In the introduction, Handaside wrote that when Knickerbocker "found his end approaching, he disposed of his worldly affairs, leaving the bulk of his fortune to the New-York Historical Society" and "it is rumored that the Historical Society have it in mind to erect a wooden monument to his memory in the Bowling Green."[51] Consistent with Irving's extremely dry wit, there is only one word, "wooden," which clearly reveals this statement was a joke aimed directly at the members of the society. In other words, the fictional dedication was part of the satire.

The idea that the young Irving was thinking about anything but comic effect is also inconsistent with what we know about him. As a youngster, one biographer notes, Irving's "lively spirits and quick fancy could not easily be subdued. He would get out of his bed-room window at night, walk along a coping, and climb over the roof to the top of the next house, only for the high purpose of astonishing a neighbor by dropping a stone down his chimney."[52] When the book was published, Irving was only twenty-six, living at home with his mother, and spending most nights drinking beer with a group of young men dubbed the Lads of Kailkenny—a long way from smoking cigars and drinking brandy served by enslaved African Americans in the formal drawing room on one of the estates of the older members of the historical society.[53]

We also know that as he was writing the book Irving fell in love with a young woman, Matilda Hoffman, the seventeen-year-old daughter of the attorney for whom Irving began working at age sixteen. On April 26, 1809, Hoffman died of tuberculosis, putting Irving in what we would probably now diagnose as depression. To escape the "dismissal horror," Irving took his notes to a farm outside the city, cut out much of what was originally planned, and finished *A History of New York* a few weeks before its publication in December 1809.[54] Given the circumstances, it is doubtful creating new Christmas traditions was at the top of his agenda.

The idea that Irving wrote the book as part of a conspiracy to promote St. Nicholas (and rid New York of its drunken bands of roving celebrants) is also inconsistent with Irving's own words on the subject. In the 1848 version of the book, he included an "Author's Apology" to those of Dutch ancestry who may have been offended by the original work.

> Our idea was to parody a small hand-book which had recently appeared, entitled, "A Picture of New York." Like that, our work was to begin an historical sketch; to be followed by notices of the customs, manners and institutions of the city; written in a serio-comic vein, and treating local errors, follies and abuses with good-humored satire. To burlesque the pedantic lore displayed in certain American works, our historical sketch was to commence with the creation of the world; and we laid all kinds of works under contribution for trite citations, relevant or irrelevant, to give it the proper air of learned research.[55]

In making this apology, Irving emphasized not only that no offense to the Dutch was intended and noted that the term "Knickerbocker" had since been used with pride by the Dutch descendants of the city's founders. At that point, in 1848, if Irving thought he could also take credit for having popularized St. Nicholas or Santa Claus, it seems likely he would have mentioned that as well.

Although Jones' reliance on the wrong edition of Irving's *History* does not require any piling on, there is a more fundamental, if less obvious, flaw in Jones' reasoning. That flaw is the assumption that the version of Irving's *History of New York* Jones thought was published in 1809 could have spawned a sudden interest in a previously unknown folk celebration of the Dutch. The question, in other words, is whether Jones' argument was credible even if the 1809 edition contained all of the references to St. Nicholas that were added in the 1812 edition. In a lengthy discussion of Jones' thesis in *Santa, Last of the Wild Men*, Phyllis Siefker assumes—like virtually everyone else—that Jones has accurately stated the facts. Nonetheless, she rejects Jones' conclusion Irving deserves the credit Jones gives him as inherently implausible.

> Jones says the volatile combination of Irving's book and Pintard's picture provided the combination for Santa's birth and subsequent success. Thus, according to Jones, Santa's history is startlingly brief. He sprang, fully formed, from the head of Washington Irving in 1809. Unfortunately, this explanation does not hold up upon further inspection.[56]

Indeed, having read Irving's book cold, as any New Yorker would have done in 1812, it is hard to accept that *History of New York* had *any* impact on the development of Santa

Claus except, arguably, to send a few artists trying to depict St. Nicholas between 1837 and 1848 down a dead-end road in which they dressed him like the prow of the Dutch ship *Goede Vrouw*.[57] There just isn't enough about St. Nicholas in the book to give the reader an understanding of the European tradition sufficient to copy it themselves, much less create a desire to do so. It was the feeling that something must be missing which sent me to the New-York Historical Society looking for the 1809 edition in the first place. The 1812 edition of *A History of New York* was more than 500 pages long, and most of the twenty-five references to St. Nicholas were merely figures of speech in which "our Lord" or "Merlin's beard" could have been substituted for "St. Nicholas" with no change in meaning. Irving, however, thought the repeated references to St. Nicholas were funnier—and they were.

Only two of the references to St. Nicholas discuss his role as gift-giver; neither does so in any detail and neither can fairly be called a "delightful flight of imagination." In fact, the two passages Jones attributes to Irving in his 1954 paper and his 1978 book, the "descriptions of festivities on St. Nicholas' Day in the colony" and "the description of Santa Claus bringing gifts, parking his horse and wagon on the roof while he slides down the chimney," simply do not exist as Jones describes them.[58] Irving's St. Nicholas never parks on the roof or slides down a chimney—he tosses the gifts into the chimney from a flying wagon—he never describes the "festivities on St. Nicholas' Day in the colony," and he never uses the name "Santa Claus," which Jones should know as well as anyone is not synonymous with St. Nicholas.

What Irving says, in total, is that St. Nicholas now comes to New York only once a year, riding a white horse pulling a wagon over the roofs of the city, and dropping presents down the chimneys for children, but that in the halcyon early days of Dutch rule St. Nicholas would come more often and leave presents for adults as well.[59] There is nothing funny about saying St. Nicholas comes only once a year and leaves presents only for children unless you already know that has always been his practice. As with many parts of the book that make outlandish and obviously false declarations about the quality of life under Dutch rule, the passage is funny only if the reader is already familiar with the gift-giving role of St. Nicholas in Europe, and already knows St. Nicholas comes only once a year. Given that America was a nation comprised largely of recent European immigrants, Irving likely assumed most of his readers already knew of the traditions of St. Nicholas or his Dutch doppelganger, Sinterklaas, and it is highly unlikely the references to St. Nicholas in Irving's *History* had an influence on the development of Santa Claus.

Nissenbaum's explanation requires us to assume that John Pintard was inspired by a dozen references to St. Nicholas in the 1809 edition of Irving's *History* to write a broadside and, perhaps, publish three poems about the gift-giving practices of St. Nicholas in 1810; that Moore was inspired by Pintard's poem(s) to write "A Visit from St. Nicholas"; that despite the inspiration Moore did not write "Visit" another dozen years; and, once it was written, Moore did not acknowledge it as his own work for another fifteen years. When compared with the alternative explanation that Moore bought a copy of *The Children's Friend*, which we know was for sale in 1821 a couple of blocks from his home, to read to his children but concluded that the story was too cruel and decided to write a more kid-friendly version during 1822, the principle of Occam's Razor tells us that the explanation with the fewest assumptions is most likely to be accurate.

To support his theory on Irving's role, Nissenbaum cites Irving's short story, "Old Christmas," published as part of *The Sketch-Book of Geoffrey Crayon, Gent.*, a series of short stories Irving released between 1819 and 1820.[60] Nissenbaum argues the story reflects Irving's desire to promote an "old fashioned Christmas" in America, even if he had to make up the history that would show how Christmas was formerly celebrated in England. This story makes no mention of St. Nicholas, Father Christmas, or Santa Claus, and thus did not contribute directly to the story of Santa. Rather, Nissenbaum appears to connect the desire for a family-centered Christmas to Irving's *History of New York* under the premise Irving could have predicted in 1809 the chain of events that would eventually convince New Yorkers to decide to spend Christmas with their families.

It is probably true, as Nissenbaum argues, that Irving's description of Christmas at an English estate called Bracebridge Hall described the celebration of Christmas in a style that had never existed in America. Even though Bracebridge Hall was fictional, however, Irving insisted that all of the elements of "Old Christmas" existed in England, somewhere or another, and most of it was discussed in Sir Walter Scott's *Marmion* a decade earlier. Whether Irving thought the fictional Lord Bracebridge and his "Old Christmas" were something to emulate is the more interesting question. Irving's wit was sometimes so subtle it was hard for some to detect but I read "Old Christmas" as ridicule of the wealthy and powerful who pretended to provide charity while pursuing their own upper-class interests rather than, as Nissenbaum argues, an attempt by Irving to reinvigorate the celebration of Christmas in the old style.

In trying to identify Irving's motives, Nissenbaum and I both rely on the following statement by the elderly Lord Bracebridge to define the importance of the story, but we interpret it in different ways. I have italicized what I think are the most critical parts.

> There is something genuine and affectionate in the gayety of the lower orders, when it is excited by the bounty and familiarity of those above them; the warm glow of gratitude enters into their mirth, and a kind word, and a small pleasantry frankly uttered by a patron, gladdens the heart of the dependent more than oil and wine. *We have almost lost our simple true-hearted peasantry. They have broken asunder from the higher classes, and seem to think their interests are separate. They have become too knowing, and begin to read newspapers, listen to ale house politicians, and talk of reform.* I think one mode to keep them in good humor in these hard times, would be for the nobility and gentry to pass more time on their estates, mingle more among the country people, and set the merry old English games going again.[61]

After quoting Lord Bracebridge, Irving writes in his own voice that this "was the good Squire's project for mitigating public discontent."[62] Lord Bracebridge, Irving reports, also described "how he once held an 'open house in the old style' but that 'the country people … did not understand how to play their parts in the scene of hospitality.'"[63] As a result, Lord Bracebridge told Irving, "the manor was overrun by all the vagrants of the country, and more beggars drawn into the neighborhood in one week than the parish officers could get rid of in a year."[64] Nissenbaum finds in this passage Irving's desire to recreate a style of English Christmas practiced by the wealthy on their country estates, with a wink to the reader, disguised as a wink from one of the peasants to another, designed to show that Irving also understood the perspective of the lower classes in attendance at the open house. I am hard pressed to see anything but disdain for a class system Irving abhorred.

The inclusion of St. Nicholas in the 1812 edition of *A History of New York* concededly shows Irving could spot potential material for satire when he saw it and could well have been prompted by Pintard's poems. Irving's book also seems to have convinced several unwitting artists who illustrated Moore's poem between 1837 and 1848 that St. Nicholas should be depicted as Irving described him on the prow of the Dutch ship *Goede Vrouw*—an ironic outcome when the whole joke was the Dutch had depicted a fourth-century bishop from

Turkey in classic Dutch garb. However, Irving left for England in 1815 and did not return for seventeen years, meaning he was nowhere near the New-York Historical Society when Moore wrote "The Night Before Christmas" in 1822. This does not mean "Old Christmas" had no influence on the celebration of Christmas—indeed, the story's influence includes the fact that, to this day, the Ahwahnee Hotel in California's Yosemite National Park holds a very pricey series of dinners every December that are titled the Bracebridge Dinner, based on Irving's description of the meal served by Lord Bracebridge—but there is no reason to believe the story had any effect on the development of Santa Claus.

In terms of lasting effect on Christmas more generally, however, one must keep in mind that Irving's *Sketchbook of Geoffrey Crayon* (1819–20) was followed shortly by *The Children's Friend* (1821), which outlined the critical elements of "Santeclaus"; the first publication of Moore's "The Night Before Christmas" (1823), which was published thirty-two more times before the first illustrated edition was published in 1848; Thomas K. Hervey's *The Book of Christmas* (1836), which included seminal depictions of Father Christmas by English illustrator Robert Seymour, the coronation of Queen Victoria (1837) and her marriage to Christmas-loving Prince Albert (1840), the launch of the *Illustrated London News* (1842), which immediately began printing illustrations of Father Christmas, and Dickens' *A Christmas Carol* (1843)—all before *Harper's New Monthly Magazine* and *Harper's Weekly* got into the act in the 1850s. In light of these publications, "Old Christmas" is not nearly as important in the history of Christmas as some may believe and Irving's *History* cannot be given any weight at all. There is a reason many readers who know *Rip Van Winkle* and *The Legend of Sleepy Hollow* have never heard of "Old Christmas" or *A History of New York*.

None of this should be construed to detract in any way from Washington Irving's contributions to American history and literature. Indeed, one of the facts about Irving that is more interesting than his supposed role in the creation of Santa is that a New York humor magazine he and his brother and cousin ran for a couple of years, *Salmagundi*, was the first publication to use the term "Gotham," an Anglo-Saxon word meaning "goat's town," as a nickname for New York City. Thus, in a period of less than two years before he turned twenty-seven, Irving created two of the best-known nicknames for New York City. (The third, "the Big Apple," was popularized in the 1920s by John J. FitzGerald, a sportswriter for the *New York Morning Telegraph*.)

18

How the Poem Now Known as "The Night Before Christmas" Started the Santa Ball Rolling

Whatever influence others may have had in introducing Santa Claus to America, there is no doubt the 1823 poem originally titled "Account of a Visit from St. Nicholas," and which became better known in the late nineteenth century as "The Night Before Christmas," deserves far more credit than any other publication for popularizing and standardizing the annual ritual in which Santa Claus visits American children.[1] On Christmas Eve, after the children have gone to sleep, Santa arrives in a sleigh pulled by eight flying reindeer: Dasher, Dancer, Prancer, Vixen, Comet, Cupid, Donder (aka Dunder or Donner), and Blitzen (aka Blixem). Santa's sleigh will land on the roof and Santa will slide down the chimney through some special Santa magic that allows a large-bellied man with a bag full of gifts to fit through a narrow flue or, if there is no chimney, through whatever ventilation shaft imaginative parents can devise, and leave gifts for good boys and girls in stockings hung by the fireplace. Bad boys and girls may get only a lump of coal or a switch, but in the twenty-first century that has become exceedingly rare.

Parts of the poem had long-standing precedents in Europe, although not necessarily in the same nation or time period. These include a bearded, fur-wearing, soot-covered gift-giver who enters the home through the chimney and leaves gifts for well-behaved children in shoes or stockings left out for that purpose. Other parts of the poem were uniquely American. These include a gift-giver who, although named St. Nicholas, is a cross between the stately St. Nicholas with his miter and robes and the grungy, homeless-looking faux Nicholases of central Europe, someone who is neither majestic nor unkempt, a lovable secular gift-giver who could still be a disciplinarian if needed, and St. Nick's arrival in a sleigh pulled by flying reindeer. "The Night Before Christmas" also established what became the consistent gift-giving practices in America, setting the standard on such questions as whether the gift-giver came on St. Nicholas' Day, Christmas, New Year's, or Three Kings' Day (Christmas Eve won), whether he came in person or after everyone was asleep (sleeping won), whether to put out shoes or stockings (stockings won), and whether to hang the stockings on the child's bed or the fireplace (the fireplace won, much to the chagrin of parents in urban high-rises without fireplaces).

When compared to the elaborate, late night, alcohol-soaked dinners on Christmas Eve in many European nations, the American tradition encourages an early night on Christmas Eve because the kids must go to bed and fall asleep before Santa can come, and the parents know they will be awakened at six a.m. (or earlier). This moves the real family celebration to

Christmas morning, something historian Nissenbaum says helped reduce the drunken revelry and Calathumpian bands that upper-class New Yorkers thought were marring Christmas—although, to be clear, much of the drunken rowdiness simply moved to New Year's Eve, one week later.

The opinions of Charles W. Jones notwithstanding, there seems little doubt that children in New York City were already aware in the early 1800s that "Old Santaclaw" would leave candy and gifts in stockings hung on the fireplace on Christmas Eve,[2] and German-American children in Pennsylvania anticipated visits from Belsnickle, an unkempt, bearded old man in a ragged fur coat. The Moore poem, first published anonymously as "Account of a Visit from St. Nicholas" on December 23, 1823, in *The Troy (N.Y.) Sentinel*, helped spread word of the Christmas gift-givers, standardized the American practice and made the whole experience more magical. It has been acclaimed as the most popular poem in America, published more than a thousand times over almost two hundred years. For many families, the traditional reading of the poem on Christmas Eve is an inextricable part of the celebration.[3]

Moore, whose Manhattan estate called Chelsea would eventually become the Manhattan neighborhood of the same name, was the only child of a prominent and wealthy New York family. Moore's father, Dr. Benjamin Moore, was both the Episcopal bishop of New York and the president of Columbia College, the successor to King's College and the predecessor to Columbia University.[4] His mother, Charity Clarke, was the heir to an enormous amount of land in Manhattan, including Chelsea. Moore was well-educated, mostly at home by his father until he enrolled in Columbia College. In 1798, he earned a bachelor of arts degree, graduating first in his class, as had his father before him, and in 1801 he received a master's degree. Moore was fluent in the classics, and although he did not need to work for financial reasons, Moore taught part-time as a professor of Oriental and Greek literature at General Theological Seminary, an Episcopal institution created on land Moore donated.

Moore was well-connected throughout both the Episcopal Church and the upper echelons of New York politicians, writers and intellectuals. He was a Federalist who in 1804 published an anonymous polemic, *Observations upon Certain Passages in Mr. Jefferson's Notes on Virginia, which Appear to Have a Tendency to Subvert Religion, and Establish a False Philosophy*, critical of Thomas Jefferson's presidency. He was married in 1813 to Catharine Elizabeth Taylor, a descendent of one of the Dutch families, the Van Cortlandts, who founded New Amsterdam. They had nine children, the first of whom was born in 1815. Mrs. Moore died in 1830, however, leaving Moore a widower at age 51 with seven children under fifteen years old, but he never remarried.

For almost two hundred years, there was little or no dispute with regard to the parentage of the poem that "changed the course of American celebrations of Christmas and the image Americans had of the merry saint associated with that holiday."[5] The uniformly accepted time and place of its birth was the evening of December 24, 1822, when Moore read the poem to his extended family and guests who had gathered at his home, Chelsea, for Christmas Eve. The generally accepted creation story is that Harriet Butler, a family friend who lived in Troy, N.Y., but was spending the holiday with the Moores, obtained a copy of the poem and gave it to Orville Holley, editor of *The Troy (N.Y.) Sentinel*.[6] The newspapers of the day commonly published anonymous poetry provided by readers or taken from other papers, and the *Sentinel* published the poem anonymously on December 23, 1823.[7]

There is no dispute that Moore did not authorize the publication of his poem by *The Troy Sentinel*, and he was reportedly chagrined to learn that someone had submitted it for publication without his knowledge or consent. Although Moore submitted another poem to the *Sentinel* for publication only a few months later, Moore thought "the Christmas poem," as he called it, was beneath his scholarly stature. Because the poem was untitled, the *Sentinel* dubbed it "Account of a Visit from St. Nicholas" and included an introduction stating that "[w]e know not to whom we are indebted for the following description of that unwearied patron of children—that homely, but delightful personification of parental kindness—SANTE CLAUS,"[8] a statement that strongly implies the *Sentinel's* editor believed its readers were already familiar with that "delightful personification of parental kindness" named Sante Claus.

There were numerous minor changes made to the poem by various printers and by Moore himself over several decades. The following is the 1844 version that was included in Moore's *Poems* but several printer's errors have been corrected.

A Visit from St. Nicholas

'Twas the night before Christmas, when all through the house
Not a creature was stirring, not even a mouse;
The stockings were hung by the chimney with care,
In hopes that St. Nicholas soon would be there;
The children were nestled all snug in their beds;
While visions of sugar-plums danced in their heads;
And mamma in her 'kerchief, and I in my cap,
Had just settled our brains for a long winter's nap,
When out on the lawn there arose such a clatter,
I sprang from my bed to see what was the matter.
Away to the window I flew like a flash,
Tore open the shutters and threw up the sash.
The moon on the breast of the new-fallen snow,
Gave a lustre of mid-day to objects below,
When, what to my wondering eyes should appear,
But a miniature sleigh, and eight tiny rein-deer,
With a little old driver, so lively and quick,
I knew in a moment he must be St. Nick.
More rapid than eagles his coursers they came,
And he whistled, and shouted, and called them by name:
"Now, Dasher! now, Dancer! Now, Prancer and Vixen!
On! Comet, on! Cupid, on! Donder and Blitzen—
To the top of the porch, to the top of the wall!
Now, dash away, dash away, dash away all!"
As dry leaves that before the wild hurricane fly,
When they meet with an obstacle, mount to the sky;
So up to the housetop the coursers they flew,
With the sleigh full of Toys, and St. Nicholas too.
And then, in a twinkling, I heard on the roof,
The prancing and pawing of each little hoof—
As I drew in my head, and was turning around,
Down the chimney St. Nicholas came with a bound.
He was dressed all in fur, from his head to his foot,
And his clothes were all tarnished with ashes and soot;
A bundle of Toys he had flung on his back,
And he look'd like a pedlar just opening his pack.
His eyes—how they twinkled! his dimples, how merry!
His cheeks were like roses, his nose like a cherry!
His droll little mouth was drawn up like a bow,

And the beard on his chin was as white as the snow;
The stump of a pipe he held tight in his teeth,
And the smoke it encircled his head like a wreath;
He had a broad face and a little round belly,
That shook when he laughed, like a bowl full of jelly.
He was chubby and plump, a right jolly old elf,
And I laughed when I saw him, in spite of myself;
A wink of his eye and a twist of his head,
Soon gave me to know I had nothing to dread;
He spoke not a word, but went straight to his work,
And fill'd all the stockings; then turned with a jerk,
And laying his finger aside of his nose,
And giving a nod, up the chimney he rose;
He sprang to his sleigh, to his team gave a whistle,
And away they all flew like the down of a thistle.
But I heard him exclaim, ere he drove out of sight,
"Happy Christmas to all, and to all a good night."[9]

For most of its history, there were two commonly-repeated accounts of what inspired Moore to write what he called "the Christmas poem." One version, set forth in the 1879 biography of Moore by William S. Pelletreau, is that in Moore's youth the family gardener, a "portly, rubicund Dutchman," would tell Moore stories about St. Nicholas, and that Moore modeled St. Nick on the gardener.[10] The story of his childhood does not actually explain what prompted him to write the poem in 1822, however, and the Pelletreau story morphed in the telling to one in which Moore spotted a portly Dutchman on Christmas Eve in 1822 and was inspired to write the poem that afternoon. The other explanation, which arises from written declarations signed in 1920 by two descendants of Moore's brother-in-law, says Moore took a carriage ride on Christmas Eve to purchase some turkeys to donate to the poor, and that the busy streets filled Moore with the spirit of Christmas, prompting him to write the poem.[11] Both accounts have Moore closeting himself in his study on Christmas Eve and writing the complete poem. Neither of these stories was from Moore himself, however, who said only that he wrote the poem to read to his children on Christmas Eve, and the premise that he wrote it in a couple of hours on Christmas Eve seems implausible in terms of time alone.

Since 1954, there has been a third explanation of what prompted Moore to write the poem, one that is much more plausible given the discovery by the American Antiquarian Society of a children's book, *The Children's Friend*, published in 1821 by William B. Gilley, a Manhattan bookseller and printer. Gilley had a shop on the corner of Broadway and Wall Street, directly across from Trinity Church where Moore's father presided, and, according to Moore biographer Patterson, Moore maintained a "winter house" close to Gilley's shop on Broadway. There is also agreement, albeit with a distinct shortage of citations, that Moore was a customer of Gilley and purchased the book in 1821, a year before he recited "The Night Before Christmas" to his children on Christmas Eve 1822.[12] Gilley's book introduced a Christmas gift-giver named "Santeclaus" who went from house to house in a sleigh pulled by a flying reindeer, descending down the chimney to leave gifts while the children were sleeping, but ends with Santeclaus leaving birch rods rather than presents for two unruly boys.

Elements of *The Children's Friend* can be found in long-standing European traditions, as well as *False Stories Corrected* in 1813, but none of the existing Christmas gift-givers traveled by reindeer, flying or otherwise. The odds that Gilley and Moore independently came up with the idea of flying reindeer a year apart and a couple of blocks away in southern Manhattan is a coincidence beyond belief, and the fact that Moore lifted large parts of the story from *The Children's Friend* would explains his initial reluctance to publish or otherwise take credit for the poem. One history, *The Santa Claus Book*, by E. Willis Jones, asserts explicitly that Moore bought the book in 1821 to place in the Christmas stocking of his six-year-old daughter, Charity, but decided that *The Children's Friend* was too mean spirited, and, therefore, wrote his own, kid-friendlier version the following year. As with the other books on the subject, Jones does not cite any source for these assertions, but anyone can see for themselves that *The Children's Friend* had a cruel streak. Other histories are not so specific, but all conclude that Moore took elements of "The Night Before Christmas" from *The Children's Friend*, a conclusion compelled by the otherwise inexplicable appearance of flying reindeer in both works. Gilley's death in 1830 would also explain why Moore was willing to submit the poem for publication under his name in 1837.

Like the question of what prompted Moore to write the poem, the question of how the poem ended up in *The Troy (N.Y.) Sentinel* in 1823 has never been definitively answered. There seems to be no disagreement, even among those who claim Henry Livingston, Jr., was the author, that Moore read the poem on the evening of December 24, 1822, to the extended family members and guests at his home. Following that reading, according to early accounts, Harriett Butler, daughter of the Rev. David Butler, rector of the Troy Episcopal Church, and a friend of the Moore family who was spending Christmas at Chelsea, somehow obtained a copy of the poem and provided it, directly or indirectly, to Orville L. Holley, editor of *The Troy Sentinel*, who published it the following Christmas. In one version of this story, supposedly well known in Troy and memorialized in the Pelletreau biography and a local history, *Troy's One Hundred Years, 1789–1889*, the poem was given directly to Holley by Harriet Butler.[13] In another version, which comes from an 1844 letter to Moore from Norman Tuttle, publisher of the *Sentinel* in 1823, the letter was given to Holley by Sarah Sackett, a prominent Troy resident.[14] These stories can be reconciled, however, by assuming that Butler, upon arriving in Troy, asked Sackett to deliver the poem to Holley but that Butler, who played the more important role, was given credit within the small town for ensuring Troy would have a place in Christmas history.

After its initial publication in the *Sentinel* in 1823, the poem was published anonymously about once a year in various small-town newspapers or almanacs until 1837, when it was published under Moore's name in an anthology of New York poetry.[15] Until very recently, the prevailing assumption was that Moore did not authorize publication in the 1837 anthology, nor confirm his authorship at all, until he included the work in *Poems*, the 1844 compilation of his own poetry.[16] The presumed failure of Moore publicly to claim the work as his own when it was published under his name in 1837 has been cited as evidence that he did not actually write the poem. In 2017, however, Scott Norsworthy, an independent scholar with a doctorate in English literature and strong interest in Herman Melville and authorship attribution, discovered a letter to the editor of the New York *American* in 1844 in which Moore said that, in fact, he provided "Visit" and two or three other poems to *The New-York Book of Poetry* to be published under his own name.[17]

The impetus for Moore's letter to the *American* was the publication of "Visit" in the *New York Intelligencer* in late 1843 under the name of Joseph Wood. In his letter to the editor of the *American*, after quoting the attribution to Joseph Wood in the *Intelligencer*, Moore wrote:

The above [attribution to Joseph Wood] is printed immediately over some lines, ["Visit"] describing a visit from St. Nicholas, which I wrote many years ago, I think somewhere between 1822 and 1824, not for publication, but to amuse my children. They, however, found their way, to my great surprise, in the Troy Sentinel: nor did I know, until lately, how they got there. When "The New York Book" [of poetry in 1837] was about to be published, I was applied to for some contribution to the work. Accordingly, I gave the publisher several pieces, among which was the "Visit from St. Nicholas." It was printed under my name, and has frequently since been republished, in your paper among others, with my name attached to it.

Under these circumstances, I feel it incumbent on me not to remain silent, while so bold a claim, as the above quoted, is laid to my literary property, however small the intrinsic value of that property may be.[18]

Thus, we know Moore claimed the work as his own only fourteen years after it was published anonymously in *The Troy Sentinel*. Only a few months after this letter, Moore included "Visit" in *Poems*, an 1844 collection of his poetry. In an introduction to the book, Moore wrote in the same self-deprecating tone he had used in his letter to the New York *American* that "the mere trifles in this volume," an obvious reference to "Visit," were included at the request of his children because "such things have often been found to afford greater pleasure than was what by myself esteemed of more worth."[19] Some have argued that Moore's refusal to acknowledge the poem as his from 1823 to 1836, and his unexplained change of heart in 1836, is evidence that Moore did not really write "Visit." There is a simple explanation for Moore's behavior, however, albeit one he would not have wanted to explain publicly. In 1821, publisher William B. Gilley obtained a copyright on *The Children's Friend*, and commercial publication of "Visit" could have been deemed a violation of that copyright. The copyright period was fourteen years, and could not have been extended because Gilley died in 1830. Thus, Moore was likely concerned that publication of the poem could be deemed a copyright violation. When the copyright expired in 1835, however, Moore was free to publish the poem, and did so under this own name.

In 1848, the poem was published again with Moore's approval and under his name, this time as an illustrated children's book by publisher Henry M. Onderdonk. Although the illustrations by T.E. Boyd of a Dutch-flavored St. Nicholas in the Onderdonk publication have become iconic, they did not look much like Santa. The bigger break for the poem, however, was its publication on the cover of *Harper's New Monthly Magazine*, which then had a national circulation of more than fifty thousand, in December 1857. Part of what *Harper's* called "A Garland of American Poetry," the poem filled the entire front page including an illustration of Santa Claus by F.O.C. Darley that stands out as one of the best depictions of Santa to that point, permanently joining together "Santa Claus" and "The Night Before Christmas." On December 29, 1866, the poem was also published by *Harper's Weekly*, which had reached a national circulation of more than two hundred thousand, with a two-page illustration by Thomas Nast called "Santa and His Works," further entrenching the Santa–Night Before Christmas connection.

While the national newspapers and magazines helped to expand the popularity of the poem, such publications are, by definition, ephemeral, tossed out or used to start a fire in a day or two. Between 1857 and 1870, however, a number of illustrated, full-color children's books were published, likely propelled by the broad public recognition created by *Harper's Monthly* and *Harper's Weekly*. The lack of a copyright requiring the publisher to compensate Moore, and a new form of color printing, chromolithography, which created brilliant, beautifully-colored illustrations, allowed multiple publishers to issue book versions of the poem, which could remain on the shelf and be re-read each year for decades. These included

Santa Claus or, the Night Before Christmas, published in New York in 1858,[20] *The Night Before Christmas: or Kriss Kringle's Visit,* published in 1858 at "Kriss Kringle's Headquarters" in Philadelphia,[21] artist David Scattergood's *A Visit from Santa Claus* in 1860,[22] artist F.O.C. Darley's *A Visit from St. Nicholas,* published in 1862,[23] a book called *Big Picture Books for Little Children: The Night Before Christmas,* published in 1863,[24] a panorama version of *A Visit from St. Nicholas* by renowned Boston printer Louis Prang in 1864,[25] a full-color *Visit of St. Nicholas* by McLoughlin Bros. in 1869,[26] and another version of *A Visit from St. Nicholas* published by McLoughlin Bros. in 1870 that was illustrated by Thomas Nast.[27]

Although some histories refer to the instant success of "The Night Before Christmas" upon its publication in 1823,[28] in truth it was not until the 1860s, with publication of the poem in *Harper's New Monthly Magazine* and *Harper's Weekly* and the illustrated books identified above, that the poem could truly be called famous. By that point, the poem and Santa Claus had developed a symbiotic relationship. Santa provided the name and the look of the gift-giver, but "The Night Before Christmas" provided the formula for Santa's arrival via reindeer and chimney and made Christmas morning the highlight of the holiday. It was a virtuous cycle: the more common the ritual became, the more popular Santa Claus became, and the more popular Santa Claus became, the more families engaged in the ritual. As Santa Claus took center stage, the early American gift-givers St. Nicholas, Belsnickle, and Kriss Kringle quickly moved to the background, largely becoming historical artifacts.

One question few existing histories address is the source of the name "Santa Claus," which was not used in print until after publication of "Visit" in 1823 and entered the American lexicon as an addition or substitute for St. Nicholas in the name "A Visit from St. Nicholas." Although the name is unquestionably a linguistic descendent of St. Nicholas, it is not a direct descendent in the sense that Belsnickle is a direct descendant of Pelznickel. Rather, Santa Claus is two or three steps removed from St. Nicholas, arising from German variants of St. Nicholas adopted by the faux Nicholases following the Reformation. Based on the names of German gift-givers listed in *The Handbook of German Folklore*, the German nicknames that could have been the source for Santa Claus, Sante Claus or Santeclaus include Santiklaus, Santi Klaus, Seneklos, Sente Kloas, and Sunner Klaus. Klaus was a variant of the more common German name Claus, however, and both were derived from Nicholas.[29] Given that most of the German immigrants who brought these names to America had probably never seen them in writing, focusing on the precise spelling could be misleading. Rather, as is common in oral transmission of proper names, the German immigrants probably assumed that these were all the same name for one German gift-giver in the same manner the Pennsylvania immigrants construed Christkindl in German to mean Kriss Kringle in English.

The important point is that the history of American variants of these German names prior to 1823 is surprisingly short. As noted earlier, the first known use of these variants in America was in Irving's *Salmagundi*, which published a reference in 1808 to "St. Nicholas, vulgarly called Santeclaus."[30] Two years later, the name "Sancte Claus" appeared in John Pintard's broadside and three poems published in New York papers in 1810 but "Sancte" is Latin for "saint" or "holy," and the name therefore is more likely a Latin-Dutch interpretation of St. Nicholas than an early version of Santa Claus. In *False Stories Corrected*, the name "Old Santaclaw" was clearly a phonetic spelling that could have applied to any number of German gift-givers but the practice described in that book makes clear that the practices of Old Santaclaw were the same as Santa Claus. Except for the failure to identify the date on which Old Santaclaw arrived and how he got from home to home, the description includes all of the essential elements of Santa's gift-giving practices.

Old Santaclaw, of whom so often little children hear such foolish stories, and once in the year are encouraged to hang their stockings in the Chimney at night, and when they arise in the morning, they find in them cakes, nuts, money, etc., placed there by some of the family, which they are told Old Santaclaw has come down the Chimney at night and put in.[31]

The name Santa Claus does not appear to have surfaced in print again until January 1, 1819, when the Carrier's Address of the *New York Weekly Visitor and Ladies' Museum* used the term "Old Santaclaus."[32] The next appearance was in 1821 when *The Children's Friend* named the reindeer riding gift-giver "Santeclaus," meaning the phrase had been used in writing only three or four times prior to publication of Moore's poem on December 23, 1923.[33] The decision of *The Troy Sentinel* to call him "Sante Claus" even though the poem used the name St. Nicholas, strongly suggests that editor Orville Holley knew both names and thought they were the same person, and that this person was the "unwearied patron of children" and "homely, but delightful personification of parental kindness" who brought gifts to children on Christmas Eve. In other words, Holley must have known who "Sante Claus" was, and what he did, before Moore's poem, a fact that, if true, makes it all the more likely that *The Children's Friend* was viewed by publisher Gilley as a story about an existing tradition rather than a new tradition born from his imagination.

Holley's reaction that the character should be called Sante Claus was not an isolated one. In February 1826, a Philadelphia magazine, *The Casket, or Flowers of Literature, Wit & Sentiment*, published Moore's poem under the title "A Visit from St. Nicholas, or Santa Claus."[34] By 1848, when the poem was published by Henry Onderdonk as a children's book illustrated by T.E. Boyd, it had been reprinted more than thirty-one times, mostly in newspapers or almanacs of limited readership.[35] In a quarter of those publications, the editors decided on their own initiative to add the phrase "or Santa Claus" or "or Sante Claus" in the title of the poem, something which tells us the editors knew from personal interaction that their readers thought Santa Claus or Sante Claus was the name of the American gift-giver. The only possible written source for this understanding in the historical literature would have been *The Children's Friend* but, as noted above, it seems far more likely that use of the name Santeclaus in *The Children's Friend* reflected the oral tradition discussed by *False Stories Corrected* in 1813. In the absence of some book or article that could be credited with popularizing Santa Claus, the growth could only have been through oral tradition by European immigrants.[36] In other words, as noted previously, Santa Claus was not "invented" but evolved organically.

Moore was almost certainly aware that *The Children's Friend* used the name "Santeclaus" in 1821, raising the question of why Moore would have chosen to use St. Nicholas instead. Given the breadth of his education, Moore presumably knew the custom in Europe was for St. Nicholas to fill the shoes or stockings of children on December 6, the saint's feast day, not on Christmas. Moore's presumed knowledge that the historic St. Nicholas did not bring gifts on Christmas Eve, and his decision to dress St. Nick all in fur (emulating the German Pelznickel) and cover him in soot and ashes (mimicking the secular German gift-givers such as Aschenklas, who covered their faces and clothing with soot) make it appear Moore was aware the secular gift-giver he was describing was not St. Nicholas in the Catholic and Episcopal traditions, but a figure based on the Post-Reformation German gift-givers.

On the other hand, identifying the Christmas gift-giver as St. Nicholas seems to have been the Moore family tradition. Moore's poem "From St. Nicholas," written to one of his daughters to explain why she was not receiving a gift that year, strongly implies that the

Moore family practiced the tradition in which a gift-giver named St. Nicholas came on Christmas Eve—a tradition that Moore could have learned in childhood or in the course of his studies or teaching duties. Because Moore was writing the poem for his own children, not for posterity, the reason for Moore's use of the name St. Nicholas was likely because that is what they called him at the Moore house. Indeed, given that Moore was writing for his children it would have been odd to call him anything other than the name the family had always used.

So, how important was "The Night Before Christmas"? In one sense, Moore's contributions to the developing legend of Santa Claus were relatively minor. Most of the essentials had appeared only a year earlier in *The Children's Friend*. Moore increased the number of reindeer from one to eight, perhaps a nod to the eight-legged horse ridden by Odin, and dressed St. Nick entirely in furs and covered him in ashes, an element that seems to reflect Moore's knowledge of the German faux Nicholases, Pelznickel, and Aschenklas. Finally, Moore described St. Nick as a jolly old elf with a miniature sleigh and eight tiny reindeer, a description likely reflecting Moore's practical judgment that a larger figure could not descend down the chimney. Viewed in this manner, Moore added little to what already existed, and much of what Moore added, including the name (St. Nicholas), the outfit (made completely out of fur), and the size of the gift-giver (Lilliputian) was gone within fifty years.

In a larger sense, however, Moore's contributions to the American celebration of Christmas and the story of Santa Claus were incalculable. The poem is still read aloud by millions of parents every Christmas Eve, and has the same literary appeal it did almost two hundred years ago—a time period that is half the distance from here to Shakespeare. While there is a lot about the history of Santa Claus that many will find surprising, the most interesting fact for many will be that "The Night Before Christmas" was written in 1822 and has survived intact. It was Moore's writing that made the difference. "The Night Before Christmas," Forbes opines, is "the best-known poem in the English language. If someone gave us its first line, most of us could recite the second line automatically. Yet most of us are not aware of how dramatically important this poem was in reshaping both Saint Nicholas and the American Christmas."[37]

19

Giving Credit Where Credit Is Due

William B. Gilley and Arthur J. Stansbury
and The Children's Friend

For more than a hundred years after Moore claimed authorship of "Visit" in 1837, Moore was credited not only with writing the poem but with creating the story in which the future Santa Claus appeared in a sleigh pulled by flying reindeer. In 1941, however, Clarence Brigham, the president of the American Antiquarian Society (AAS), announced the discovery of a long-lost clue to the development of the American Santa: *The Children's Friend: Part III: A New-Year's Present to the Little Ones from Five to Twelve*.[1] The American Antiquarian Society is one of the nation's oldest historical organizations, with the stated mission of collecting, preserving, and making available for study all printed records of the United States prior to 1870. As it turned out, the society's copy was one of the first books ever printed in America using lithography, and one of only two copies of *The Children's Friend: Part III* still in existence. No copies of Part I or Part II have ever been found so the discovery of Part III was fortuitous.

What is even more remarkable, however, is what famed radio broadcaster Paul Harvey would have called "the rest of the story," which is how the copy came into the possession of the AAS. The society has included as members a number of the most significant figures in American history, beginning with George Washington, but since its founding in 1812 the Salisbury family of Worcester County, Massachusetts, has been one of the AAS's strongest supporters. Stephen Salisbury II served as president from 1855 until his death in 1885, and his son, Stephen Salisbury III, served as president from 1887 until his death in 1905.

During their lives, the Salisbury family donated millions in land, art, and money to the organization, and upon his death Stephen Salisbury III bequeathed all of his personal papers to the society—sixty-seven boxes and a hundred bound volumes of materials collected over seventy years. As the AAS archivists catalogued the items over a number of years, they discovered a small pamphlet addressed to "Stephen," meaning Stephen Salisbury III, as a Christmas gift in 1841. Thus, we owe the discovery of *The Children's Friend*, probably the rarest and most important Christmas document in American history, to six-year-old Stephen Salisbury III, saving and preserving a childhood gift of no obvious monetary or historical value and, many decades later, donating it to the AAS.

The booklet, titled *The Children's Friend: Part III: A New-Year's Present to the Little Ones from Five to Twelve*, is independently important because it was the first book in America created through lithography. In that eight-page booklet, publisher Edward B. Gilley and illustrator Arthur Stansbury, one of whom was probably the writer as well, told the story of

159

1

Old SANTECLAUS with much delight
His reindeer drives this frosty night,
O'er chimney tops, and tracks of snow,
To bring his yearly gifts to you.

2

The steady friend of virtuous youth,
The friend of duty, and of truth,
Each Christmas eve he joys to come
Where love and peace have made their home.

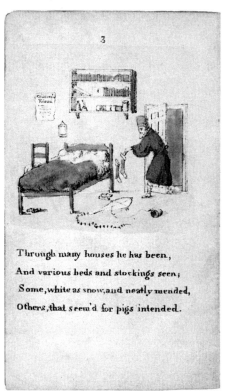

3

Through many houses he has been,
And various beds and stockings seen;
Some, white as snow, and neatly mended,
Others, that seem'd for pigs intended.

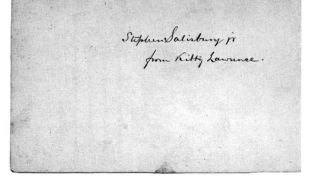

Top, left: In an 1821 children's book called *The Children's Friend*, artist Arthur Stansbury created the most influential depiction of Santa that no one ever saw (or hardly anyone). Courtesy American Antiquarian Society. *Top, right: The Children's Friend* called the Christmas Eve gift-giver "Santeclaus," one of the earliest uses in print of a name that was in common use by 1821. Courtesy American Antiquarian Society. *Bottom, left:* This illustration from *The Children's Friend* shows Santeclaus approaching the bed of two boys who hung stockings at the foot of their bed for Santeclaus to fill. Courtesy American Antiquarian Society. *Above:* The copy of *The Children's Friend* in the possession of the American Antiquarian Society was given to a young Stephen Salisbury III, future president of the AAS. Courtesy American Antiquarian Society.

"Santeclaus," a bearded and well-bundled gift-giver who traveled from home to home in a sleigh pulled by at least one flying reindeer.

There were many stories in Europe about midwinter gift-givers but the story created by Gilley and Stansbury stood out from the crowd by naming the gift-giver Santeclaus, portraying the arrival of Santeclaus on Christmas Eve rather than St. Nicholas' Day, arriving in a sleigh pulled by a flying reindeer and landing on the roof while the children were asleep. The booklet showed Santeclaus, who wore the long beard, fur hat, and heavy coat appropriate for an arctic climate, descending down the chimney to leave gifts in stockings at the end of the two boys' bed. More importantly, whether intentional or not, the Santeclaus created by Gilley and Stansbury had the qualities necessary to succeed as the original American gift-giver. He was a secular figure, avoiding the complications of competing religious doctrines during the nineteenth century, and his appearance was neither too extravagant for rural America nor too down-market for New York City. He was friendly, if not yet jolly, but also looked like he could mete out consequences as needed.

The book had eight pages of verse and illustrations that could be hand-colored for six and a quarter cents, bringing the full price to twenty-five cents. The most definitive sources on authorship are the AAS and Yale University's archives, which say that the lithographers were William Armand Barnet and Isaac Doolittle and the illustrator was Arthur J. Stansbury. No author or writer is identified but both Gilley and Stansbury were published authors. Gilley was also a printer and bookseller who operated a shop on the southern end of Broadway in Manhattan, across the street from Trinity Church, where Moore's father presided, a couple of blocks from Moore's winter house and a short walk from the seminary in which Moore taught.

An amateur poet, Gilley published two sets of verse under a pseudonym. The first, *Patriotic Effusions,* was written under the name Bob Short.[2] The second, *The Olio,* was published under the name "The Author of Patriotic Effusions."[3] Virtually all of the poems in the two volumes are written in the same meter as *The Children's Friend*, iamb with four feet, creating eight syllables per line. A review of Gilley's poetry also shows a strong similarity in the rhyming schemes between *A Children's Friend* and Gilley's small published body of poetry. Of the sixteen pairs of rhyming lines in *The Children's Friend*, four of them have exactly the same rhyming scheme as other poems in Gilley's two books: delight/night, youth/truth, mind/kind and rod/God. Six other lines in his work end with words that are used as a rhyming word in *The Children's Friend*: snow, home, seen, ear, fear and use. Thus, fourteen of the thirty-two lines in *The Children's Friend*—almost 45 percent—have a full or partial rhyming link to Gilley's portfolio.

Stansbury, born in 1779, was the son of a fervent Tory, Joseph Stansbury, whose poetry was published in 1860 as *The Loyal Verses of Joseph Stansbury and Doctor Jonathan Odell relating to the American Revolution.*[4] After graduation from Columbia College, Stansbury became a Presbyterian minister but was removed from the position in February 1821 for an unspecified but seemingly serious infraction. As a result, he went to work for lithographers Barnett and Doolittle as an illustrator when they opened the nation's first lithography business in 1821. He remained with Barnett and Doolittle until approximately 1824, when he moved to Washington, D.C., to pursue a thirty-year career as a Congressional court reporter. In 1828, he authored one of the most popular civics textbooks of the nineteenth century, *Elementary Catechism on the Constitution of the United States.*[5] According to a biography published following his death, "[h]e was a writer of verse, and an artist" and a "man of uncommon talent, but impulsive and erratic, very companionable and lovable, with an immense fund of anecdote and a turn for mechanics, which he indulged in making toys for children, of whom he was fond, and who were greatly attached to him."[6] Thus, either Gilley or Stansbury, and perhaps both, could have written the verse Stansbury illustrated.

In telling the history of Santa Claus, *The Children's Friend* is particularly important because unlike the broadside prepared by John Pintard and St. Nicholas poems published in 1810, which were intended to tell Dutch traditions with Dutch poetry, this was the first attempt to create an original, American gift-giver. Like every Winter Solstice gift-giver, he plainly evolved from its predecessors, including Odin, St. Nicholas, and the post–Reformation gift-givers in Germany but it was also the first publication to use the name "Santeclaus" for an American gift-giver, the first publication in America to create a gift-giver who had elements of both the saintly and the frightening, and the first publication of any sort to depict Santa riding in a sleigh pulled by reindeer. Unfortunately, *The Children's Friend* was also clumsily written and had a mean streak that contrasted sharply with the "homely, but delightful personification of parental kindness" in Moore's poem. Nevertheless, if any individuals could credibly claim the credit for inventing Santa Claus it would be William B. Gilley and Arthur J. Stansbury.

The Children's Friend

Old Santeclaus with much delight
His reindeer drives this frosty night.
O'er chimney tops, and tracks of snow,
To bring his yearly gifts to you.

The steady friend of virtuous youth,
The friend of duty, and of truth,
Each Christmas eve he joys to come
Where love and peace have made their home.

Through many houses he has been,
And various beds and stockings seen,
Some, white as snow, and neatly mended,
Others, that seem'd for pigs intended.

Where e'er I found good girls or boys,
That hated quarrels, strife and noise,
I left an apple, or a tart,
Or wooden gun, or painted cart;

To some I gave a pretty doll.
To some a peg-top, or a ball;
No crackers, cannons, squibs, or rockets,
To blow their eyes up, or their pockets.

No drums to stun their Mother's ear,
Nor swords to make their sisters fear;
But pretty books to store their mind
With knowledge of each various kind.

But where I found the children naughty,
In manners rude, in tempers haughty,
Thankless to parents, liars, swearers,
Boxers, or cheats, or base tale-bearers,

I left a long, black, birchen rod,
Such, as the dread command of God
Directs a Parent's hand to use
When virtue's path his sons refuse.

Even without direct evidence Moore bought the book from Gilley, the otherwise inexplicable similarities between "The Night Before Christmas" and *The Children's Friend* compel the conclusion that Moore had access to the book, and lifted many of its elements for use in "The Night Before Christmas." This doesn't mean Moore plagiarized *The Children's Friend*. The poetry in "The Night Before Christmas" was undoubtedly Moore's original work but Moore built on the story line in which Santeclaus arrived on Christmas Eve in a sleigh pulled by flying reindeer. Our old friend Washington Irving also appears to have contributed the line of "Visit" in which St. Nick is seen "laying his finger aside of his nose," borrowed almost verbatim from the scene in Irving's 1812 edition of *A History of New York* that depicts St. Nicholas "laying his finger beside his nose" before magically ascending into the sky.

20

From Moore to Nast

The Depictions of Santa
from the 1820s through the 1890s

How the American Santa Claus Evolved from Its European Ancestors

In "The Night Before Christmas," Clement Moore described the appearance of St. Nick in certain ways that have stuck—jolly demeanor, rotund physique, white beard, and, until we learned it caused cancer, an ever-present pipe—but this still leaves a great deal of room for interpretation. To use an analogy, we can all describe an automobile: four wheels on two axles, a motor, one or more seats, a steering wheel and a metal exterior with windows. That description, however, covers everything from a Rolls Royce to a DeLorean to a Yugo, and thousands of variations in between. Like the DeLorean and the Yugo, however, where the original vehicle did not work—describing Santa as the size of an elf, placing him in a suit made completely out of fur and calling him St. Nicholas when he was clearly a secular figure are the obvious points—we were free to discard those elements. Nonetheless, the road from "Night Before Christmas" in 1822 to the character we all recognize as Santa in the late nineteenth century was full of curves, detours and a few dead-ends.

It would be delightfully simple if we could identify one artist who was responsible for creating Santa, and many have given that credit to Thomas Nast, but that is not accurate. The American Santa developed over the course of seventy years after Pintard commissioned his broadside of St. Nicholas for the 1810 meeting of the New-York Historical Society, and six thousand years after the earliest pagan midwinter festivals, as a combination of the stately and benevolent St. Nicholas, tall and erect with his red bishop's vestments and his trademark white beard; the post–Reformation German gift-givers like Pelznickel and Knecht Ruprecht, whose soot-tarnished fur coats, hoods, heavy boots, and thick beards made them perfect for driving a team of reindeer through the snow; the jolly, wild-haired, wassail-drinking Father Christmas, always the life of the party; the stern, switch-bearing disciplinarian Der Weihnachtsmann, a descendent of the disemboweling pagan gods of northern Germany; and, in the words of one writer, "more than a hint of the rotund, smiling elf of northern Europe," the elfin Julenisse and Jultomten of Scandinavian folklore, with their red pointed caps, red pants and long white beards.[1] Santa Claus also bore more than a passing resemblance to Russia's Ded Moroz but it is more likely the Russian the gift-giver adopted the look of the other European and American gift-givers than the other way around.

There are fewer than a hundred published depictions of Santa or his European counterparts prior to Thomas Nast's first efforts in 1863, and most of them are included in this book. While displaying the depictions in chronological order would show that the development of Santa was far from a straight line, it is even more instructive to divide the depictions into seven categories: (1) the European St. Nicholas, with their evil helpers, and the Dutch Sinterklaas; (2) the English Father Christmas, who developed independently from the other gift-givers; (3) the German Weihnachtsmann and his predecessors, the faux Nicholases and Knecht Ruprecht; (4) the "Knickerbocker St. Nick," an original name I concocted to cover the efforts of American artists between 1837 and 1848 to illustrate Santa as a Dutch halfling; (5) the Oddball Santas, a category which shows it was not so easy to produce a credible version of Santa; (6) Kriss Kringle, who was the most popular gift-giving figure in America during the 1840s and '50s but ultimately lost out to Santa Claus; and (7) the American Santa Claus, a line of precursors to the mainstream Santa Claus which started with *The Children's Friend* in 1821, stalled for more than three decades after publication of "The Night Before Christmas" in 1823, and resumed in the late 1850s.

This approach allows the reader to observe the simultaneous development of the midwinter gift-giving character in several different countries, and to see how the European gift-givers influenced development of the American Santa, and vice versa. This approach also illustrates how Santa evolved like an organism in which some "genetic lines" prospered, some combined with others, and others turned out to be dead ends. It is, by analogy, a form of paleoanthropology in which scientists examined the fossil records of early hominids to determine how *home sapiens* developed but here the fossil records are illustrations and children's stories.

St. Nicholas

There are two St. Nicholases, the saint and the gift-giver. We really only care about the latter, but, for purposes of comparison, must start with the former. The first depiction of St. Nicholas the saint, created more than three centuries after his death, cannot have been an accurate likeness, and has deteriorated so much it would not be helpful in any event. The best-known and most numerous depictions of the saint are the icons from European and Russian churches which served as the basis for most illustrations of St. Nicholas through the present. These illustrations generally depict a thin middle-aged man in bishop's robes with a narrow, beak-like nose, a receding hairline, and either no beard or a short well-trimmed beard.

When St. Nicholas is depicted as a gift-giver, however, he has an entirely different look. The foundation of this look is not the European and Russian icons but the Germanic god Odin, a tall, strongly-built man in flowing robes with long white hair and beard. Odin wears a floppy hat to cover a missing eye, carries a staff, and often rides an eight-legged horse. If you color the robes red, change the floppy hat to a bishop's miter, restore the missing eye, turn the staff into a crozier, and convert the flying, eight-legged horse into a land-based version with four legs, the resulting image is St. Nicholas the gift-giver. There are perhaps a dozen paintings or engravings of St. Nicholas the gift-giver prior to 1850 but they all depict essentially the same person. The depictions of Saint Nicholas from Germany, Austria and other central European nations during the same time period depict essentially the same person—a tall, erect bishop with miter, crozier and flowing white beard—but show him on foot, or occasionally a horse, with Krampus or one of the other evil helpers almost always at his side.

There are an equal number of early illustrations of St. Nicholas' Dutch doppelganger, Sinterklaas, a surprising number of which are named "Sint" Niklaas given the supposed aversion of the Dutch to Catholic saints. He is the same tall, fit and distinguished figure as the other European figures but almost all of these illustrations show him riding a horse while tossing presents to a group of trailing children. The one exception, but in some ways the most important of the Dutch illustrations, is *Sint Nikolaas en zijn Knechton*, an 1850 book by Dutch school teacher Jan Schenkman, which tells the story of the Dutch Sinterklaas and a Moorish servant who, although unnamed in the book, was instantly identified in the Netherlands as Zwarte Piet, or Black Peter.

The modern depictions of St. Nicholas and Sinterklaas have changed little from the early versions. He is consistently depicted as a tall, physically fit man with a serious expression, solemn but not strict. The one feature that has changed somewhat is the curly white beard that now hits the middle of his chest or lower—longer, curlier, and whiter than the earlier depictions of the saint. The sole American version, the broadside by Alexander Anderson that was commissioned for a meeting of the New-York Historical Society in 1810, dispenses with the evil helper and, for some reason, the bishop's miter but represents the tall, fit and serious nature of most illustrations. What St. Nicholas and Sin-

The Dutch traditions of today stem largely from a children's book, *Sint Nikolaas en zijn Knecht* ("St. Nicholas and his Servant") written by Dutch school teacher Jan Schenkman in 1850. Courtesy Stichting Kinderboeken.

terklaas contributed to the ultimate portrayal Santa Claus was height and age, taking him from an overweight halfling to a much older full-sized figure, and the red-and-white color scheme that the two figures typically wore, and which, over time, became symbolic of Santa.

Father Christmas

The earliest depictions of the English Father Christmas are from the seventeenth century and were drawn to make a political statement when the celebration of Christmas became a major issue during the conflict between the Puritans and the Church of England. The next wave of Father Christmases did not appear for two hundred years, and made it look like Father Christmas had been unable to find a barber, a shave, or even a comb during those two centuries (although beer, wine and wassail seem to have been plentiful). In 1836, English artist Robert Seymour illustrated Thomas K. Hervey's *Book of Christmas* with a couple of boozy, wild-haired Fathers Christmas that set the tone for the next fifty years in

In this illustration, Jurij Subic, a Slovenian painter who lived and worked throughout Europe, shows Nikolo, Chriskindl and Krampus visiting a home together, presumably on Christmas Eve. Based on his clothing, the artist's reference to "Nikolo" presumably means St. Nicholas. Krampus is somewhat hidden behind Nikolo but can be identified by his horns. Library of Congress.

which the London newspapers were more likely to emphasize the good father's drinking than anything else. Between 1842 and 1855, there were a number of pictures on the cover of the *Illustrated London News* or other periodicals that showed an apparently tipsy Father Christmas bringing cheer to the holiday season with one alcoholic beverage or another.

By the end of the nineteenth century, Father Christmas began to appear on Christmas cards, an English innovation. In preparation for this gig, which continued through World War I, it looks like Father Christmas obtained a public relations consultant

This drawing by Alfred Crowquill of Father Christmas carrying a Yule log, a practice that preceded the Christianization of Yule in northern Europe, appeared in the *Illustrated London News* on December 23, 1848. Library of Congress.

This depiction of "Old Father Christmas" holding a doll at what appears to be a girls' Christmas party was published in the *Illustrated London News* in 1866 and *Godey's Lady's Book*, an American women's magazine, in 1867.

who advised him to stop drinking in public and to trim and comb his wild hair and beard. This fellow, Father Christmas with a Make-Over, is indistinguishable from the depictions of the American Santa Claus and the German Weihnachtsmann on the same postcards, and the printers generally used the same illustration for all three, changing only the printed name or the language of the greeting.

Der Weihnachtsmann

Der Weihnachtsmann began to appear in the last half of the nineteenth century as the Christmas gift-giver in the predominately Protestant regions of Germany, and by the twentieth century had become the most prominent Christmas gift-giver in Germany. As explained in Chapter 10, Weihnachtsmann evolved from Knecht Ruprecht and the bearded, homeless-looking faux Nicholases such as Pelznickel who had been around since the sixteenth century. In person, these characters were typically played by a relative, friend, or neighbor who blackened his face with soot, donned a long fake beard, and wore a long, dirty coat.

Austrian artist Moritz von Schwind undoubtedly used these figures for inspiration when he drew the character Herr Winter for a German magazine in 1847. Herr Winter had the look we now recognize as a Belsnickle—the candy container, not the Pennsylvania gift-giver—wearing a cloak and hood with arms crossed and hands hidden in his sleeves, a long white beard, and heavy black boots. He also carries a branch of some sort tucked into the crook of his elbow. In many examples, including the Moritz von Schwind original, this is clearly a Christmas tree but in other cases it looks much more like a birch switch, the ever-present symbol of Knecht Ruprecht and the faux Nicholases who replaced St. Nicholas. Der Weihnachtsmann appeared in the last half of the nineteenth century, after von Schwind's Herr Winter was featured in a German magazine carrying a Christmas tree, and with the help of a popular 1837 song the existing gift-givers became gradually known as Der Weihnachtsmann. By the end of the nineteenth century, the images of Der Weihnachtsmann and Santa Claus had largely merged, displaying an appearance that was jollier than the stern German figure of 1847 but more serious than the mid-century versions of "St. Nick" who graced the covers of many children's books.

Although Santa Claus began to look more like Weihnachtsmann, and vice versa, Santa did not simply adopt the German look. Rather, they have a common ancestor, Pelznickel, who was brought to America by German immigrants in the late eighteenth and early nineteen centuries. In Pennsylvania and southern New York, where most of the German immigrants settled, the rough-hewn and fur-covered Pelznickel became known as Belsnickle, the Pennsylvania gift-giver, and Belsnickle became known as Kriss Kringle in the 1840s. By the 1860s, Kriss Kringle and St. Nicholas had evolved into Santa Claus but Santa himself continued to develop for a couple of decades.

The Knickerbocker St. Nick

The longest detour taken by American artists in creating a singular vision of Santa Claus was an effort to illustrate St. Nicholas a combination of the Lilliputian St. Nick described in Clement Moore's "Night Before Christmas," the Dutchman satirically described in Washington Irving's *History of New York*, and a painting by Robert Weir, the first artist to paint the St. Nick depicted in Moore's poem. We have called these characters the "Knickerbocker St. Nicks" because Moore and Irving were members of the New-York Historical Society, a group known as the Knickerbockers, and Weir's painting was hung in the society's office.

Illustrating the gift-giver in Moore's poem meant producing a Lilliputian St. Nick dressed in a suit made entirely of fur, small enough to fit into a miniature sleigh with eight tiny reindeer and slide down the chimney, but with a jolly face, a large, round belly and the stump of a pipe in his teeth. In contrast, implementing the Dutch appearance from Irving's *History* meant producing a St. Nicholas in traditional Dutch garb, with knickers, buckled shoes, and, like the fictional figurehead of St. Nicholas on the prow of the fictional Dutch ship *Goede Vrouw*, "a low, broad-brimmed hat, a huge pair of Flemish trunk hose, and a pipe."[2] The Weir St. Nicholas was short in stature with a red cape and the facial expression of a burglar trying to escape up the chimney with the family silver. Trying to merge the three versions was an artistic disaster and the resulting illustrations looked nothing like the Santa Claus who emerged in the 1850s and '60s.

There were a half-dozen Knickerbocker St. Nicks produced between 1837 and 1848 when, thankfully, the trend ended. These images would not be worthy of much comment except that they are the earliest American versions of St. Nick and the reader is likely to encounter them in any history of Santa. When they are examined separately from other historical drawings, you can see they are all very similar, with the same well-trimmed beard, pipe, petite backpack, jaunty hat and even the same angle of illustration, with St. Nick looking back over his shoulder. In Weir's painting, St. Nicholas is shown next to the fireplace holding a bag with one hand and placing a finger aside his nose with his other hand as he prepares to ascend the chimney. The date of the painting, 1937, is fourteen years after the first publication of "The Night Before Christmas," and the lapse of fourteen years before the first illustration of Moore's St. Nick confirms Marshall's statement in her bibliography of Moore's poem that it was slow to catch on.[3] Here are the other Knickerbocker St. Nicks:

- In 1840, artist William Croome drew a portrait-style picture of St. Nicholas to accompany a printing of "Visit" in a compilation of poetry called *Poets of America*.[4] He is shown with a well-trimmed beard, a stylish hat with feather and a pipe. Instead of the large bag carried by the European gift-givers, he wears a very small backpack similar to that sometimes worn by teenage girls in lieu of a purse, creating the impression he intended to deliver gifts to a half-dozen homes before knocking off for the night.
- In 1841, the *New York Mirror* published an engraving titled "St. Nicholas, on his New Year's Eve Excursion (as Ingham saw him) in the act of descending a chimney."[5] Charles Ingham was the illustrator, and the same picture was used twice in 1842 as part of advertisements for Christmas goods. Later versions also used Christmas Eve in place of New Year's Eve, another indication that Moore's poem did not cause the immediate reaction some think. Although the setting is more appropriate, with St. Nick getting

This 1837 painting by Robert Weir is the first depiction of St. Nicholas following Clement Moore's poem "A Visit from St. Nicholas." Used with permission of the New-York Historical Society. 16 1951.76 St. Nicholas, by Robert W. Weir (1803–1889), 1837; oil on wood panel, 30 × 25⅜ inches; negative #994c.

Artist William Croome created this depiction of St. Nicholas in 1840 to accompany "A Visit from St. Nicholas" in *Poets of America*, a volume of works by American poets.

A VISIT FROM ST. NICHOLAS.

In 1841, the *New York Mirror* published an illustration by Charles C. Ingham of St. Nicholas descending a chimney. In later versions, the caption was changed to use "St. Nicholas, or Santa Claus" and Christmas Eve rather than New Year's Eve.

ready to step into a chimney while his reindeer waited in the background, and his tiny backpack is shown overflowing with toys, the head and face are almost a duplicate of Croome's 1840 drawing.

- In 1844, the firm of Sherman & Smith published a version of Moore's poem under the title *A Visit from Santa Claus* in which Santa looks almost exactly like the St. Nick of the *New York Mirror*—same angle, same hat, same beard, same facial features, and same backpack—except he is sitting on a chair in front of the fireplace rather than preparing to step into the chimney.[6] Why St. Nick is sitting in front of an unlit fireplace is not explained but he appears to be posing. Although existing copies of the Sherman & Smith illustration are very poor quality, in 1848 an English newspaper published an article, New Year's Eve in Different Nations, in which an artist had created what is almost an exact duplicate of Sherman & Smith's version.
- In 1848, with Moore's approval, printer Henry M. Onderdonk published the first illustrated book version of "A Visit from St. Nicholas," crediting Moore as author.[7] The illustrations by T.C. Boyd are some of the most iconic depictions of St. Nicholas, but, frankly, look nothing like Santa Claus. If you compare the Boyd picture of St. Nick stepping into the chimney with the Ingham illustration in 1941, you will see the depictions are almost identical except that Boyd's St. Nicholas is wearing Dutch knickers and buckled shoes.
- The strangest part of Boyd's illustrations—and, naturally, the most famous—is a shot of St. Nicholas as, maybe, three feet tall, jumping into the air for no apparent reason. Even today, the illustration is one of the most widely published

of the early efforts at depicting St. Nicholas. It is also the last of the Knickerbocker St. Nicks. Except for a handful of oddball efforts, American illustrators began to produce a more sensible and consistent version of the American Santa Claus in the late 1850s.

Kriss Kringle

On our road trip from Santeclaus to Santa Claus, the only relief from the Knickerbocker versions of St. Nick dominant between 1837 and 1848 was a detour to Pennsylvania where three books were published about Kriss Kringle between 1842 and 1847.[8] We know that figures like "Santaclaw" had been popular since

This illustration, titled "New Year's Eve in Different Nations," was published in England in 1848. It is a copy of an illustration created by Sherman & Smith of New York in 1844 for Moore's Poems.

Left: The first book version of Moore's poem, published in 1848, was illustrated by Theodore E. Boyd. This shows St. Nick preparing to descend a chimney. Courtesy American Antiquarian Society. *Right:* This illustration by Theodore E. Boyd in the 1848 version of "A Visit from St. Nicholas," showing St. Nick jumping into the air for no apparent reason, has become one of the most iconic early depictions of St. Nick. Courtesy American Antiquarian Society.

E. FERRETT & CO.
PHILADELPHIA
1845.

Left: This illustration by Ralph D. Dunkelberger for Alfred Shoemaker's *Christmas in Pennsylvania: A Folk-Cultural Study* (1959) was, in effect, a "police sketch" of the various descriptions provided of Belsnickle. From the collection of the Berks History Center, Reading, PA. *Top, right:* By 1845, the impression that Kriss Kringle was the Pennsylvania giftgiver had become so well established that a book, *Kriss Kringle's Christmas Tree*, was published about him. New York Public Library. *Bottom, right:* In 1858, an enterprising retail store christened itself as "Kriss Kringle's Headquarters" and published this version of Moore's poem titled "The Night Before Christmas, or Kriss Kringle's Visit." New York Public Library.

the start of the nineteenth century but until the first volume about Kriss Kringle, *Kriss Kringle's Book*, was published in 1842, there was little for children to see.[9] The best known of the three books was *Kriss Kringle's Christmas Tree* published by E. Ferret & Co. of Philadelphia in 1845, on which the cover shows Kriss Kringle crawling up a table-top Christmas tree.[10] While the portrayal of a gnome-like Kriss Kringle himself could have used some work, the illustration stands as an independent and important contribution in the development of Santa.

The illustrations of Kriss Kringle were undoubtedly based on Belsnickle, the American counterpart of Pelznickel, but that didn't give the artists much guidance in their work. The 1845 drawing was likely influenced by Moore's description of a pint-sized St. Nick, creating, as mentioned earlier, the image of actor Danny DeVito with a stocking cap and beard. The book nonetheless deserves credit for its initiative in depicting an entirely new gift-giver, and the use of a Christmas tree, three years before the famous engraving of Queen Victoria and Prince Albert in the *Illustrated London News*, showing that Kringle was well ahead of his time in popularizing Christmas traditions. In 1847, another book in the series, *Kriss Kringle's Raree Show*, shows Kringle sitting on the top of a marquee looking much like the 1845 version.[11] In 1858, Willis P. Hazard published a version of the poem, *The Night Before Christmas: or Kriss Kringle's Visit*, that appears to have been a promotional piece for "Kriss Kringle's Head-quarters" in Philadelphia.[12] The illustration of Kriss Kringle, credited only to "Nick," has a stocking cap and no beard, or a very closely-shaven one, looking much like Kriss Kringle in the 1845 and 1847 books.

Oddball Santas

The category of Odd-ball Santas is included here not because it shows how the look of Santa Claus developed, but because it shows that choosing how to depict Santa with nothing more than the description in Moore's poem was not so easy. With a couple of exceptions, these efforts are notable only for how far off base they were.

- In 1847, an adver-tisement for Santa Claus' Quadrilles, apparently a musi-cal performance, shows a clean-

This poster by Spoodlyks for a concert called the Santa Claus Quadrilles in 1846 shows Santa as a clean-shaven fiddler on the roof. Courtesy Lester S. Levy Collection of Sheet Music, Sheridan Libraries, Johns Hopkins University.

Left: Santa's first appearance in a novel was *The Little Messenger Birds* by Carolyn Butler in 1850 in which Santa is shown in goatee and tights. Library of Congress. *Right:* The great showman P.T. Barnum created this advertisement for an American tour by singer Jenny Lind; why Barnum decided to depict Santa Claus as George Washington on a broomstick has never been explained.

shaven man in heavy boots and a cape dancing on top of a chimney while playing the fiddle.[13] It is truly one of the most bizarre efforts at illustrating Santa.

- In 1850, the illustrations from Carolyn Butler's *The Little Messenger Birds* show Santa with a goatee in Elizabethan garb and tights surrounded by elves in similar outfits.[14] Although the picture doesn't really show it, the Santa in this book was supposed to be about an inch and a half tall while the elves were about a half-inch tall.

- In an 1852 advertisement for a P.T. Barnum–sponsored tour of America by singer Jenny Lind, Santa Claus was shown dressed like George Washington riding on a broomstick with Ms. Lind.[15] It was Barnum, of course, who purportedly said "there is a sucker born every minute," and this picture proves it.

- In 1858, *Harper's Weekly* published a cover that is famous for being so bad it is good (or, at least, funny).[16] In this picture, one of Santa's few clean-shaven appearances, he is being pulled in his sleigh by a wild turkey, and, from the look on his face, Santa has had a few shots of Wild Turkey as well.

- In January 1869, *Harper's Weekly* published a cover that showed Santa with the most extreme elements of the appearance of European gift-givers: a long, out-of-control beard presumably inspired by the 1840s illustrations of Father Christmas in England, a large Christmas tree in Santa's hand, presumably inspired by the pictures of Herr Winter that became the German Weihnachtsmann, and a short tunic that seems to have been inspired by depictions of Thor wearing a similar

SANTA CLAUS PAYING HIS USUAL CHRISTMAS VISIT TO HIS YOUNG FRIENDS IN THE UNITED STATES.

On December 25, 1858, about two years after it began publication, *Harper's Weekly* published one of the stranger depictions of Santa Claus, a beardless man riding a sleigh pulled by a wild turkey. Library of Congress.

outfit while flying through the sky on his goat-powered chariot.[17]

Thankfully, none of the Oddball efforts caught on, and fathers everywhere should be relieved they do not have to track down a costume of George Washington to deliver gifts on Christmas Eve.

The American Santa Claus Before Nast

As noted at the outset of this chapter, the road from Moore's "Night Before Christmas" to a credible image of

In this illustration from *Harper's Weekly* on January 2, 1869, Santa is shown in one of the strangest outfits ever.

Santa was marked by a series of detours and dead-ends. But the starting point—the entry that deserves the title "first depiction of Santa Claus"—is *The Children's Friend,* published in New York by William B. Gilley in 1821 and illustrated by Arthur J. Stansbury. The character depicted in this pamphlet, "Santeclaus," is Santa Claus, not St. Nicholas, Kriss Kringle or Father Christmas, and has all of the major elements we have come to expect from Santa: a relatively older man with a long beard, dressed in a warm fur coat, heavy boots, and warm hat of uncertain origin. Equally important, Santeclaus is shown driving a sleigh pulled by a flying reindeer before landing on the roof, descending down the chimney, and filling stockings hung at the foot of the children's' beds, albeit with switches because the boys have not been well-behaved.[18] Most importantly, this booklet was published a year before "The Night Before Christmas," and is therefore completely original, but was almost certainly used by Moore as the blueprint for "Visit," and thus had a much larger impact that its small sales would have dictated.

This booklet initiated a long drive that began in 1821 and did not really end until the 1860s. The *Kriss Kringle* books were like a welcome rest stop on the long drive but the Knickerbocker St. Nicks and the Oddball Santas were more like a series of accidents and construction detours. The trip resumed in earnest when *Harper's New Monthly Magazine* and *Harper's Weekly,* American versions of the *Illustrated London News,* began publication in 1850 and 1857, respectively, began placing depictions of Santa on their December covers. These began in December 1857 with an illustrated version of "Visit" on the cover of *Harper's New Monthly Magazine.* In 1863, however, *Harper's Weekly* hired a young, German-born illustrator, Thomas Nast, to run its art department, and over the next two decades Nast contributed more important illustrations of Santa than any other artist.

Although Nast gets much of the credit for developing an enduring image of Santa while at *Harper's Weekly,* the truth is that a handful of American publishers and artists, including F.O.C. Darley, David Scattergood, Louis Prang and a couple who are not identified, had already created a cohesive version of the gift-giver before Nast arrived. Here are some examples:

A VISIT FROM SAINT NICHOLAS.

F.O.C. Darley's drawing of Santa Claus to accompany "A Visit from St. Nicholas" in *Harper's New Monthly Magazine* in December 1857 was one of the best Santas to date. Library of Congress.

- In December 1857, *Harper's New Monthly Magazine* published a drawing by F.O.C. Darley to illustrate one of the first national printings of "The Night Before Christmas." This was the most modern-looking Santa to date.[19] With a pointed, Santa-style hat, a long, relatively unkempt beard, and a basket filled with toys on his back, Santa

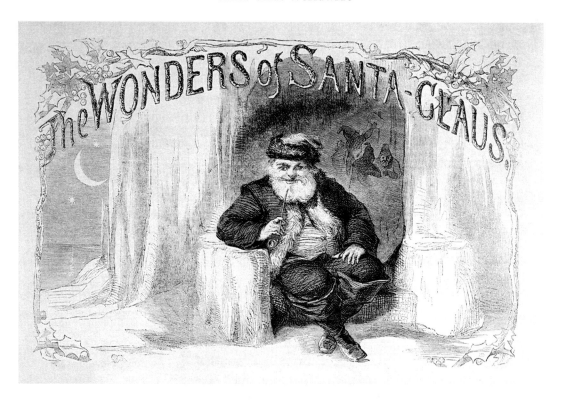

The illustration "Wonders of Santa Claus," which was on the cover of *Harper's Weekly,* on December 24, 1857, was the most complete version of Santa Claus to date and the first set in an arctic location.

is shown climbing into a chimney while his sleigh and reindeer sit on the roof. This Santa has all of the elements one could expect based on Moore's poem, and nothing jarringly inconsistent like the knickers depicted in T.C. Boyd's St. Nick.

- On December 24, 1857, *Harper's Weekly* published "The Wonders of Santa Claus," by an unidentified artist depicting Santa for the first time in an Arctic setting. Sitting in a castle of ice, Santa is shown as a rotund old man with a medium length but untrimmed beard, a suit with white fur trim, and long black boots.[20] It also includes an early peek at Santa's elves busy in their workshop. This was one of the most complete Santas yet, indistinguishable from many later Santas except for the cap that looks like a New York newsboy.
- In 1860, artist David Scattergood illustrated *A Visit from Santa Claus*, a promotional give-away in Philadelphia that was one of the first to substitute Santa Claus for St. Nicholas.[21] Scattergood's illustration stands out for its title, "A Visit from Santa Claus," and its realistic treatment of Santa's body.
- In 1862, F.O.C. Darley, who by this point had likely drawn more versions of St. Nicholas than any other artist, illustrated another stand-alone version of "A Visit from St. Nicholas."[22] Two interior illustrations, one of Santa in his sleigh with reindeer and one of him holding his finger next to his nose, are better than most versions to date, but, like the Nast illustrations that would follow shortly, made St. Nicholas appear about three feet tall.
- Circa 1863, Philadelphia publisher Fisher & Bros. published "A Visit from St.

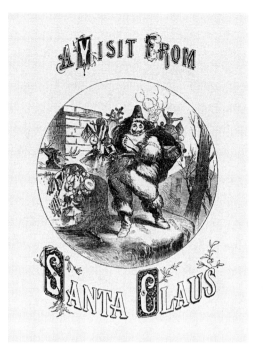

Left: In 1860, artist David Scattergood illustrated one of the earliest versions of "The Night Before Christmas" with Santa Claus rather than St. Nicholas. The Baldwin Library of Historical Children's Literature, Special and Area Studies Collections, George A. Smathers Libraries, University of Florida. *Right:* In 1862, F.O.C. Darley illustrated a book version of "A Visit from St. Nicholas," creating a version of Santa Claus who looked the part as much as anything created over the next decade.

Nicholas" with one of the more advanced versions of the gift-giver, by an artist identified only as Howell, carrying a bag bulging with toys and wearing a suit made entirely of fur.[23]

- In 1864, Boston printer and lithographer Louis Prang, often called "the father of the American Christmas card" for the quality and quantity of Christmas cards he printed, published his only illustrated version of the poem in a fold-out version.[24] Prang's St. Nicholas looks a good deal like both F.O.C. Darley's version in 1862 and the early Nast versions except Prang dresses St. Nick entirely in yellow.

Although Nast had joined *Harper's Weekly* in 1863, his first important depiction of Santa was

St. Nicholas (Howell, *A Visit from St. Nicholas,* cover, Fisher & Brother, 1863).

And his clothes were all tarnished with ashes and soot;
A bundle of toys he had flung on his back,
And he looked like a pedler just opening his pack;
His eyes how they twinkled! his dimples how merry!
His cheeks were like roses, his nose like a cherry;
His droll little mouth was drawn up like a bow,

Top, left: In a version of "A Visit from St. Nicholas" published by Fisher & Brother of Philadelphia in 1863 and illustrated by Howell, St. Nicholas is shown as a full-size man. *Bottom, left:* This interior drawing from Fisher and Brother's version of "Visit," which shows a tall, heavy St. Nick covered with toys, bears a clear similarity with Scattergood and Darley's gift-givers. *Top, right:* In 1864, renowned printer Louis Prang, a printer known as called the "father of the American Christmas card," published a "foldout" version of "A Visit from St. Nicholas." Library of Congress.

in 1866, when he illustrated "Santa and His Works." As the Darley, Scattergood, Howell and Prang publications demonstrate, contrary to the lore that Nast "invented" the American Santa, there were a number of credible versions of the American gift-giver published in the five years before Nast began his work. Indeed, when compared to the works of Darley, Scattergood, Howell and Prang, Nast's early depictions of a pint-sized Santa were arguably a step backward.

The Contributions of Thomas Nast to the Look of Santa—First Small, Then Big

Most historians identify the artist to whom the American version of Santa Claus owes the most as Thomas Nast, the famed political cartoonist whose drawings in the 1870s exposed rampant corruption in New York's mayoral office by an organization named the Society of Tammany, better known as Tammany Hall. The German-born Nast immigrated to the U.S. when he was six, meaning, as Nast later explained, his first exposure to the Christmas gift-giver was "a kindly, bearded gentleman in a fur coat [who] played the part of [Pelznickel], walking from door to door distributing sweets" in Louche, a town in the Rhineland-Palatinate region of Germany where Nast spent his childhood.[25] Although unable to read English, Nast had an instinctive talent for drawing. He started working as an artist at age fifteen, including a brief stint for *Harper's Weekly* in 1859–60, before he was hired by that publication as its chief artist in 1863 at age twenty-two.

Nast's first drawing of Santa Claus for *Harper's Weekly*, "Santa in Camp," showed Santa in 1863 distributing packages to Union soldiers during the Civil War from the back of his sleigh but the angle of the illustration primarily shows his back.[26] On December 29, 1866, *Harper's Weekly* published a two-page spread by Nast, "Santa Claus and His Works," with drawings of a Lilliputian Santa in a variety of settings.[27] In 1869, these drawings were recreated in color for a book, *Santa Claus and His Works*, written by George Webster and published by New York's McLoughlin Brothers.[28] The height of the Santas depicted in these illustrations, three feet tall at most, was the size one would have assumed from Moore's description of "a jolly old elf" who could fit down a chimney and travel in a miniature sleigh pulled by eight tiny reindeer.

Nast's drawings of Santa quickly

Left: Nast's "Santa Claus—His Works" was a two-page spread published by *Harper's Weekly* on December 25, 1866, and reprinted in color in 1869. Here, Santa is shown sewing in his workshop. *Right:* In Nast's earliest illustrations, including the 1866 "Santa Claus—His Works," Santa was so small he could barely see over his naughty and nice book, a Nast invention.

became a staple of *Harper Weekly*'s seasonal fare. Over two decades, Nast drew Santa in a variety of settings, at home and on the road, and many of the attributes we now accept as an integral part of the lore of Santa, such as keeping a workshop at the North Pole, reading letters from children or their parents, and keeping a naughty-and-nice list came from Nast's pen. The most emotionally compelling of these are Nast's drawings of Santa with children, with the beaming faces reflecting Nast's love of his own children and their love of him.[29]

While Nast was drawing Santa for *Harper's Weekly*, illustrations began to appear throughout England, Germany, and the United States, depicting Santa as a full-size man. As a German immigrant living in New York and head artist for *Harper's Weekly*, it seems likely Nast would have seen copies of *Harper's* English counterpart, the *Illustrated London News*,

In another scene from Nast's "Santa Claus—His Works," Santa must stand on a chair in order to reach the stockings hung by the fireplace.

which had published a number of images of Father Christmas, and the German magazine, *Münchner Bilderbogen*, which published the first depiction of Herr Winter as Weihnachtsmann in 1847. These publications undoubtedly influenced later depictions of the holiday gift-givers in all three nations, and Nast adjusted the look of his Santa to make him look more like the other illustrations. As a result, while Nast was working for *Harper's Weekly* his Santa doubled in height, finally making him taller than he was wide, aged to the point of a loving grandfather, and abandoned the attire he'd been wearing for years: a skintight jumpsuit made entirely of red fur and a four-inch belt around his

By the 1870s, Nast's Santas were taller and older than in the 1860s. This appearance is reflected in an illustration in *Harper's Weekly* on December 30, 1871, of Santa reading mail.

CAUGHT!

Left: In the *Harper's Weekly* of January 1, 1881, Nast depicted a mature Santa surrounded by loving children, a pose that likely reflected Nast's love for his own family. *Right:* In "Caught," one of Nast's later Santa drawings for *Harper's Weekly*, Nast depicted Santa being caught by a young girl as he attempted to leave gifts without waking her.

perfectly circular belly that seemed to serve no purpose. As Berryman explains:

Thomas Nast actually created two Santas, one of them inspired by Clement Clark Moore's description of the elfin St. Nicholas that in Nast's illustrations had to stand on a chair to reach the stockings on the fireplace mantel. The second Santa was a normal human size and he grew more jolly and grandfatherly with each succeeding illustration.[30]

It is the later illustrations historians have in mind when they claim Nast created the modern image of Santa Claus—a full-size man with the look and demeanor of a kindly grandfather. The culmination of these efforts was "the Nast Santa," an 1881 illustration that has

The pinnacle of Nast's work is the illustration often described as merely "the Nast Santa." This figure, a mature, full-size man of large girth, represents the consensus at that time with regard to the appearance of Santa.

probably been reprinted more times than any other drawing of Santa Claus. Unfortunately, the rest of the decade was not kind to Nast. In 1884, he lost most of the money he had earned at *Harper's Weekly* in a financial scam, and in 1886 Nast and *Harper's Weekly* parted ways. In 1890, Nast completed a second book, *Thomas Nast's Christmas Drawings for the Human Race*, that was published by Harper Bros.[31]

No one doubts Nast made important contributions to the developing depiction of Santa, but the viewpoint that Nast "invented" Santa, or even "define[d] the widely accepted view of what Santa Claus looked like," is not really true.[32] In his 1978 book on St. Nicholas, Charles W. Jones observed that "[t]hese were not Nast's inventions but evolved over more than thirty years."[33] While it is important to understand Nast did not "invent" the American Santa, it would be equally unfair to criticize his work as derivative because every depiction of Santa and his European counterparts is based on earlier works and Nast added as many original elements as anyone.

In *Merry Christmas: Celebrating America's Greatest Holiday*, art history professor Karal Ann Marling provides a more nuanced assessment of Nast's influence than the extreme claims that Nast invented Santa or that Nast's work was entirely derivative of other artists.

> Did Thomas Nast create the all–American Santa Claus? … Yes and no. In the 1860s and 1870s, many artists working in the commercial media made substantive contributions to the appearance of Santa and to his story. In the hands of others, Santa grew less elfin in character, less like the figure in Moore's poem and more like the English Father Christmas, a full-size adult man.[34]

Thus, it is probably most accurate to say Nast was one of many artists who worked collaboratively, whether they knew it or not, to create the common images of Santa we see by the 1890s—another example of the organic evolution of Santa Claus. In comparing Nast's work to others, it is also important to recognize that Nast's drawings of Santa—even the iconic Nast Santa of 1881 in which Santa appears to be a full-grown man—were drawn in the style of political cartoons rather than the style of commercial illustrators who strived for realistic, photo-like depictions. Real people are not built with the circular body Nast used, nor do they have cheeks that pop out of the face like red rubber balls or mustaches that stick straight out for six inches or so without a drop of mustache wax. Thus, a truly realistic Santa would have to await the commercial illustrators of the twentieth century.

One could say Nast's most important contribution was not the detail of Nast's drawings, but, like Clement Moore's poem, the tone and the emotions created. Historian Fiona Deans Halloran, author of *Thomas Nast: The Father of Modern Political Cartoons*, offered this insight into Nast's views, an insight that is most clearly reflected in Nast's drawing of Santa with children:

> By the time Thomas Nast had children of his own, Christmas had become the ultimate family holiday. It had not always been so. From a season of misrule characterized by drink, of the inversion of social roles in which working men taunted their social superiors, and of a powerful sense of God's judgment, the holiday had been transformed into a private moment devoted to the heart and home, and particularly to children. The process had taken the better part of a half century, but it reflected the rise of the middle-class ideal of the home that Nast adopted enthusiastically. He loved the idea of the roaring fire, the sleepy children, and Santa Claus's visit in the depths of the night.[35]

Halloran's point is echoed in Nissenbaum's *The Battle for Christmas*, which describes a conflict going back many years between those who view Christmas as a celebration of hearth and family, and those who liked the Saturnalia-inspired Christmas celebrations marked by alcohol, crowds, masks, costumes, and other elements designed to liberate the celebrant's inhibitions. What both Moore and Nast brought to the modern American Christmas was not so much a specific description of Santa but a feeling about how Christmas should be celebrated.

The 1890s: Santa Begins to Appear Everywhere on Everything

By the 1890s, depictions of Santa had reached what social commentator Malcolm Gladwell might call the tipping point—that is, "the moment of critical mass" at which "ideas and products and messages and behaviors spread like viruses do."[36] During the decade, international trade in Christmas products eliminated a lot of national differences by requiring versions of the gift-giver that would pass muster no matter what the nation. At the same time, Santa was being depicted so frequently that, with rare exception, individual depictions by one artist or another did not stand out as new or unusual, but, rather, as simply another depiction of Santa. These images appeared on "scraps," which were chromolithographed pictures of Santa designed for what became known as "scrap books," postcards, Belsnickle candy containers made in Germany, glass and paper ornaments, and children's books, toys, and games.

Although collectors still refer to "new world" and "old world" Santas—the former are taller, thinner, and more serious, the latter jollier and more rotund—by the 1890s German, English, and American artists, printers, and artisans had begun to produce images that were identical except for the name. In the early 1900s, for example, the same Christmas card, except for the name of the gift-giver, could be produced in any of the nations, and

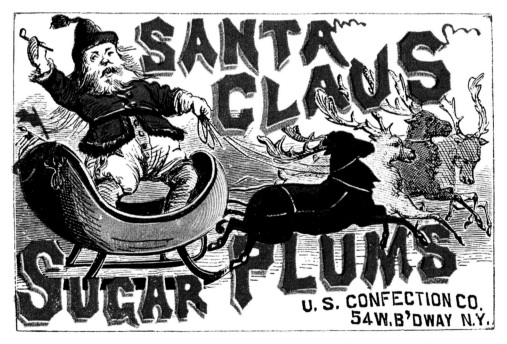

Entered according to Act of Congress, in the year 1868, by the United States Confection Company, in the Clerk's Office of the District Court of the United States for the Southern District of New York.

Beginning in the 1860s, Santa Claus began to be used in advertising. This is a well-known advertisement for Santa Claus Sugar Plums in 1869.

then sold in any of the nations as long as they had the proper name: Father Christmas in England, Weihnachtsmann in Germany, Santa Claus in the United States, and so on. That same card could also be converted into a St. Nicholas card, with the exact name dependent on the nation for which it was intended, just by changing Santa's hat and coat into a bishop's robes and miter. These cards could be printed with the name of St. Nicholas in any number of different languages, allowing them to be used in most European nations.

While it had taken thousands of years to create a universal image of the Yuletide gift-giver, by the end of the nineteenth century there was one. This doesn't mean all of the figures looked alike—to the contrary, there was a great diversity of depictions—but all of them fell into the family of images I call a collection of Santas.

Santa in Person

The one depiction of Santa that is often overlooked in explaining the development of Santa's appearance, but which was quite arguably the most important, was seeing Santa in person. One way for children to see Santa—or, in Pennsylvania during the mid-nineteenth century, Kriss Kringle—was in parades or department stores which used the opportunity to see or meet Santa to attract shoppers.[37] The other was he might appear in person at the child's home on Christmas Eve. Strangely, there appears to be no consistency, either by geography, gift-giver, or time period, as to when Santa would appear in person and when he would leave gifts while the children were sleeping. This fact is probably attributable to the work involved for parents in creating a credible representation of Santa—work some parents would undertake, and others would not, regardless of nationality or time period.

The literature is not consistent on when and where Santa first appeared in a department store. Snyder says Kriss Kringle began appearing at the J.W. Parkinson in Philadelphia in 1841, and Santa first appeared at The Boston Store in Brockton, Massachusetts in 1890. Other sources say the practice had spread to a small number of stores in Philadelphia, New York, and Boston by the 1870s. There is general agreement, however, that by the early twentieth century department-store Santas had become such a wide-spread practice that making suits for department store Santas had itself become a cottage industry. In the early twentieth century, stores like Sears and Woolworth's also began marketing inexpensive Santa costumes for parents who wanted Santa to appear in person on Christmas Eve. The only real difference was the quality of the materials—the department-store suits had to last a full season or more—and whether the costume included a mask or only a false beard. For department-store Santas, wearing a mask was unsightly and unnecessary because the child would not recognize the face under the beard anyway, but for home use a mask could be necessary to disguise the father, uncle, or family friend who was playing Santa.

The use of masks eventually died out, even for home use, because the masks were extraordinarily creepy, made even more so by the use of straight, presumably human hair for the mustache and beard. It's fairly easy to find photographs taken at the turn of the twentieth century of men dressed up as Santa, and the uniform reaction to these photographs is a desire to run away. While part of this might be the photography, which created piercing dark eyes and white, pasty skin, the most significant yuck factor is the long, straight, stringy beard. During the early part of the twentieth century, it appears, Santa outfitters learned from artistic renderings that it was critical Santa's beard (and hair, if included) be extremely curly, the most extreme examples of which are the modern depictions of Sinterklaas in the

Netherlands. In photographs of a costumed Sinterklaas, the extremely curly beard might reach his navel, but the overall effect is rather pleasing.

The desire to have Santa appear in person was probably as important as the contributions of any artist in defining what Santa looked like. Use of an adult male to portray Santa when children met him in person also required that Santa he be depicted as a full-size human rather than the elfin figure described by Clement Moore in "The Night Before Christmas." In *December 25*, Snyder notes that "[a]s late as the end of the nineteenth century, vestiges of Woden could still be seen in the garb of some Santa Claus figures."[38] This included the long hair and beards handed down from pagan gods who lived several thousand years ago, elements that helped define the figure as Santa, which required that anyone playing Santa wear a long, white costume beard if they didn't have a real one. The sale of Santa costumes also meant Santa's clothing had to be standardized so that the Santa the child saw in person looked like the pictures he or she might see. The stock Santa costume included a red stocking cap with white fur trim (or a red hooded cloak for the English Father Christmases), a red coat similarly trimmed, red pants, a thick black belt and high black boots. Although one does not need not wear the standardized Santa outfit to be recognizable as Santa, this clothing created Santa 1.0, a base model that could be embellished as one saw fit.

Christmas Cards. Since the publication of *The History of the Christmas Card* by George Buday in 1954, it has become uniformly accepted that the first true Christmas card, meaning a card designed to be printed and sent to large numbers of people at Christmastime, was produced in 1843.[39] Commissioned by Henry Cole of London and drawn by J.S. Horsley, the card featured a small group of English men, women, and children quietly celebrating with a glass of port or sherry and the greeting "A Merry Christmas and a Happy New Year to You." Buday suggested the cards served the same symbolic purpose as small gifts exchanged at the Winter Solstice in Egypt and Rome, wishing the recipient good luck during the following year.[40]

The Christmas card was not without precedent. It was preceded, albeit by only a few years, by printed cards given in England on St. Valentine's

Above and following two pages: **In the early 1900s, printers in England, the U.S. and Germany began producing full-color images of the gift-giver known as Father Christmas, Santa Claus and Der Weihnachtsmann.**

Day, and many of the earliest ones had the appearance of cards for which the printer had hastily replaced the Valentine's Day greeting with Merry Christmas. The custom of mailing cards in England was facilitated by the introduction in 1840 of the "penny post," before which postage costs alone would have precluded most people from sending them. While the custom slowly gained ground between the mid–1850s and 1870, the English practice really gained momentum in 1870 when the price for mailing a postcard was reduced to a half cent, and printers responded by producing a huge variety of postcards with printed Christmas greetings.

In the United States, post card rates were set at one cent in the 1870s for government printed post cards but "souvenir cards," which would have included Christmas cards, were two cents. In 1898, the U.S. government adopted a one cent rate for souvenir cards as well, provided they did not have a space for writing messages on them, resulting in a surge of Christmas

postcards around 1900. In 1907, the government liberalized the rules to allow half of the "address side" to be used for messages, further promoting the use of Christmas post cards. Accordingly, budding collectors of American cards should realize the vast majority of "collectible" post cards will be dated between 1898 and 1907 if they have no room for a message, and between 1908 and roughly 1914, the beginning of World War I, if they have a space on the address side for messages. Although unused cards will have a higher value if their provenance can be proven, used cards have the advantage of a post-mark that guarantees the age of the card.

The subject matters covered by Victorian Christmas cards were so varied there is virtually nothing that cannot be found. Among the most popular subjects were children, often young girls symbolizing the Christ child or angels; flowers of all sorts; birds of all sorts, especially robins, including a surprising number of dead birds; a large variety of animals, both realistic and anthropomorphic; city street scenes; winter landscapes; beautiful young girls and women; angels; and Christmas trees. One of the most popular subjects since the late nineteenth century, however, has been Santa.

A serious collector can find the same illustration with greetings or descriptions that identify the subject as Santa, Father Christmas or Weihnachtsmann. There are two principal styles of clothing—hooded cloak or coat with stocking cap—and although red is the most common, the colors of Santa's outfits cover the rainbow. The majority of Christmas postcards show Santa in a wintery scene or next to a tree or child but the most popular among collectors seem to be Santa featured in a variety of different forms of transportation, ranging from automobiles to motorcycles to airplanes. These were new inventions in the late 1800s and early 1900s, of course, and the artists seem to enjoy featuring Santa enjoying the latest fad.

Candy Containers. Among the most popular and expensive Santa figurines sought by collectors are composition candy containers called Belsnickles that were made by hand in Germany in the late 1800s and early 1900s. Ranging in size from four inches to twenty-four inches, these figures were virtually identical except for color. They depict a stern-looking Santa with a long beard, hooded cloak and folded arms that generally hold a small tree or switch.[41] The larger versions were made in two pieces that could be taken apart to reveal a hollow tube that could be filled with candy. In the smaller versions, the tube would generally be covered only with a round piece of cardboard at the bottom of the figure. Like many German products, they were handmade in cottages, with even young children given some job, sold to middle-men who visited the villages each year, and then sold to German importers who would arrange for transport and sale in the U.S. They were identified in advertisements of the period as Weihnachtsmann in Germany and Santa in the U.S. but have become known among collectors as Belsnickles.[42] The reason for the uniform use of the term Belsnickle for these figures is not certain, but it is likely the name arose because the stern demeanor resembled Pennsylvania's Belsnickles more than the jollier Santa Claus who caught on later.

These figures were made of composition, a term for any combination of substances that would hold its shape when pressed into a mold and left to harden and were hand-painted in a variety of colors and often sprinkled with mica to resemble snow. After painting, the switch or tree was inserted into the crook of the arm. The boots or base were typically

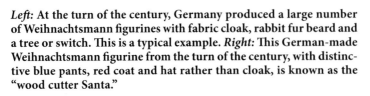

Left: **At the turn of the century, Germany produced a large number of Weihnachtsmann figurines with fabric cloak, rabbit fur beard and a tree or switch. This is a typical example.** *Right:* **This German-made Weihnachtsmann figurine from the turn of the century, with distinctive blue pants, red coat and hat rather than cloak, is known as the "wood cutter Santa."**

painted black, although in the larger figures a white, round base called a "snow ball" was sometimes used. If imported, the figures were marked on the bottom with "Germany" as the country of origin (or "Occupied Germany" for products shipped between 1944 and 1948) but no markings were required if they were sold in Germany. Although some Belsnickles continued to be made following World War I, they were considered by collectors to be of inferior quality and are not nearly as coveted as the older versions. In recent years, however, some of the original manufacturers have resumed making Belsnickles using original molds.

Figural Hand-Blown Glass Ornaments. The most common Christmas decorations during the last half of the 1800s were hand-blown figural glass ornaments made in Lauscha, Germany, in the Thüringen region just northwest of the German-Czech border. Lauscha was centrally located amid the mining regions containing all of the raw materials needed to make glass. Hans Greiner (1550–1609) headed one of several glass-making families who converted to Lutheranism during the Protestant Reformation, and moved to Lauscha from Swabia, a Catholic region in southern Germany. As a result, Greiner is generally credited as the father of the German glass industry.

In 1847, a descendent who was also named Hans Greiner began producing hand-blown figural glass ornaments with a new process using wooden molds. In this process, a glass blower took a small amount of molten glass attached to a glass tube through which the artisan could blow and placed it inside a mold that had a reverse image of the desired form. The inside of the ornament was then coated with a silvery substance—originally mercury or lead, which were deadly to the German workers, often children, who performed the silvering process, and later a compound made of silver nitrate—to create a mirror finish that was hand-painted and attached to a metal hook. The demand for these ornaments took off after the *Illustrated London News* in 1848 published an engraving of Queen Victoria and Prince Albert with German-made glass ornaments on a tabletop Christmas tree.

The popularity of glass ornaments in the United States is often attributed to F.W. Woolworth & Co., one of the original "five-and-dime" stores in the United States. There is a story, perhaps apocryphal, that owner F.W. Woolworth did not think they would sell, and therefore ordered only a small number. When these sold out in a matter of hours, he substantially increased the number ordered the following year, only to find out this supply went just as quickly. As a result, Woolworth scheduled a trip to see the ornaments manufactured in Germany, and quickly became the largest importer of the ornaments. Whether the story of Woolworth's initial skepticism is accurate, there is no question F.W. Woolworth became the largest purchaser of hand-made German ornaments until the supply ended shortly before World War II.[43]

The breadth of Santa images created by the German artisans is documented in *The Art of the Lampworked Santa* by Melicent Sammis, now Melicent D'Amore, a collector who has acquired a large number of early Santa ornaments.[44] The earliest examples of figural ornaments depicting Santa are included in a catalogue published in Sonnenberg, Germany, in 1860. The Santas pictured on these ornaments are clearly the German image of Weihnachtsmann—the figure we now know as a Belsnickle—with stern demeanor, long beard, folded arms, and a small tree in the crook of his elbow.

Scraps and Paper Ornaments. The invention of chromolithography in the mid–1800s created an entirely new genre of Christmas decorations and collectibles, albeit one that did not become popular for several decades. Lithography is a type of printing in which a chemical and a pigment are applied to a flat stone or, in later versions, a metal plate. The chemical, which repels the pigment, is applied to create the equivalent of a photo negative, and the pigment is applied over the top. When the paper is applied to the stone, only the pigment transfers to the paper, creating the desired print. Chromolithography uses the same process to print in color except that as many as twenty to twenty-five different pigments might be used, compared to three or four pigments used in other color printing methods, creating a richly colored print that almost resembles an oil painting.

Although chromolithography was invented in 1843, it was not used much in commercial printing until 1873, when Boston printer Louis Prang, a German immigrant sometimes called the "father of the American Christmas card," began using chromolithography to make Christmas cards. Prang's cards quickly became enormously popular in both Europe and America but by the 1880s less expensive imitators from Germany undercut Prang's price. In the late 1880s, the German printers also began to use chromolithography for what were called "die cuts" or "scraps," terms that refer to printed paper illustrations, cut out like paper dolls, which depicted Santa Claus, angels, children, and other Christmas-themed figures. Scraps, which gave their name to "scrap books" rather than the other way around, could range in size from couple of inches to more than a foot tall. Buying scraps and placing them in scrap books was very popular with American women from roughly 1880 to 1910. The import of scraps from Germany was suspended during World War I, however, and scrap books never regained their pre-war popularity, a fact likely attributable to the publication of American magazines like the *Saturday Evening Post*, which made color printed pictures less interesting, and the arrival of radio to occupy the time once devoted to scrapbooking.

Scraps were also used to make paper Christmas ornaments. Typically, the scrap would be pasted or stapled onto a piece of cardboard cut to the size of the picture, enhanced with some combination of tinsel or tinsel-covered wire around the picture and/or colored cellophane or spun glass behind the picture. These ornaments had a homemade look and were, in fact, often made in the cottages of the German workers. Large numbers were manufactured in Germany and shipped to America between the 1880s and World War I, with the best work done between 1890 and 1900. There were also many ornaments of this sort made at home by Americans, and there is no quick way to distinguish between the German and American versions. The period during which the paper ornaments were sold, however, was rather short. Sears began selling German-made paper ornaments in 1900, with Father Christmas as the most popular item, and Montgomery Ward began to sell paper and cotton-batting ornaments with chromolithographed faces of Santa and other Christmas figures during the same period. The supplies largely ended with World War I.[45]

Scraps were printed and sold in sheets, with anywhere from two to two dozen pictures per sheet, depending on the size of the scrap itself. The paper between the pictures was cut out, with the exception of a small tab that held them together and generally contained the name of the printer. Because the same depiction, or something almost identical, can be seen in scraps made by a number of printers, it seems highly unlikely there was any enforcement of copyrights. As a result, there are certain depictions of Santa—in particular, a handful of Old-World Santas wearing hooded cloaks—that are so common you would assume they were the work of a famous artist, but no one can identify who created the original art, or when.

Children's Books, Toys and Games. Histories of Christmas in America report that in the 1820s and '30s, retailers in Boston, New York, Philadelphia and other large cities began to emphasize the importance of shopping for Christmas presents for young children. During the last half of the nineteenth century, manufacturers began to recognize that Christmas gift-giving provided a ripe opportunity for new products, and many of those products contained depictions of Santa.

Left: McLoughlin Bros., a New York publisher of children's books and games, created this game, The Visit of Santa Claus, in the late nineteenth century. American Antiquarian Society. *Above:* In the late 1800s and early 1900s, McLoughlin Bros. put out multiple editions of "The Night Before Christmas" that varied in their name and illustrations. This 1870 version, illustrated by Thomas Nast, was one of the first.

The most popular Christmas book for children during the nineteenth century—and, some say, the most widely-printed poem of all time—was "The Night Before Christmas," which has been printed in five hundred editions over almost two hundred years.[46] The most successful publisher of children's books was McLoughlin Bros. of New York. In 1869, McLoughlin Bros. published *Santa Claus and His Works,* written by George P. Webster and illustrated by Thomas Nast.[47] Between 1870 and 1900, it also published

This McLoughlin Bros. book published in 1888 includes two names, *The Night Before Christmas* and *A Visit from St. Nicholas.* The artist is not identified.

Left: This McLoughlin book from 1896 names the gift-giver Santa Claus instead of St. Nicholas. The artist is not identified. *Right:* The popularity of Santa Claus generated a number of children's books about Santa. One of the best-known books written about Santa was *The Life and Adventures of Santa Claus* by L. Frank Baum, the author of *The Wizard of Oz*, in 1902.

several different editions of "The Night Before Christmas," including one illustrated by Nast. In 1890, Harper Brothers republished as an illustrated book of drawings originally done by Nast for *Harper's Weekly* under the title *Christmas Drawings for the Human Race*.[48] One of the earliest original Santa books was *An Adventure of Santa Claus* by J.B. Greene in 1871,[49] but the best-known novel about Santa is probably *The Life and Adventures of Santa Claus* written in 1902 by L. Frank Baum, the author of *The Wizard of Oz*.[50]

Toys featuring Santa were also marketed, including Santa jack-in-the-boxes, which appeared in several of Thomas Nast's drawings, Santa jumping jacks, in which pulling a string would cause the legs and arms to rise and fall; and Santa roly-polies, figures with a weighted round base that would rock back and forth when pushed. The most popular toys for collectors from this era were made of cast iron or tin, although that may reflect the fact that the metal toys have survived better than wooden or paper toys. One of the most coveted was a cast-iron sleigh manufactured by Hubley Manufacturing Co. of Lancaster, Pennsylvania, in the late 1800s in which Santa was pulled by a group of reindeer. Even more coveted, however, was a lithographed tin sleigh carrying Santa and pulled by two goats that was marketed by Althoff Bergman & Co. of New York. This is one of the rarest pieces of Santa memorabilia, with only four still known to exist. In 2010, one in private hands sold at auction for an astounding $161,000. Another popular, and expensive, type of Santa collectibles from the late 1800s were cast-iron banks made by Hubley and Shepard Hardware Co. Some were mechanical while others were cast-iron images of Santa, some with a tree and some without; unmistakably the characters depicted are Belsnickles made in Germany.

21

The Ups and Downs of Santa in the Twentieth Century

In the year 1900, Santa Claus could look back at the prior century and honestly say he had done pretty well for himself. In 1800, Santa had never been mentioned in print but within a decade he had moderate fame, at least among school children. By 1900, Santa had become ubiquitous in America, overcoming potential competition from Sinterklaas, Belsnickle, Christkindl, and Father Christmas, all of whom had big followings in Europe but never got legs in the U.S., and major challenges from St. Nick and Kriss Kringle, both of whom had their own picture books published in the 1840s. By 1900, Santa's European comrades had also become well established in their own countries and well known worldwide—Father Christmas in Great Britain, Weihnachtsmann in Germany, Père Noël in France, Sinterklaas in the Netherlands, the Yule elves and gnomes in Scandinavia, St. Nicholas in Catholic regions of Europe and, at some point, Ded Moroz in Russia. The only regions where Santa did not have at least a foothold were Central and South America, predominately Catholic regions where the Christ child and the Three Kings held sway, and Asia, the Middle East, and Africa, continents where Islam, Hinduism, Buddhism, and a variety of more localized religions were dominant.

In 1900, the world's collection of Santas could not see the challenges that awaited them. The first half of the twentieth century brought World War I, a Communist Revolution in Russia, which eventually spread communism throughout much of Europe and Asia, the Great Depression, a world-wide economic collapse in the 1930s, the rise of the Nazi Party in Germany, and World War II, which killed more than fifty million people and laid ruin to much of Europe and Japan. The second half brought economic globalization, with American companies becoming reliant on sales around the world and the United States seen as a prime target for sales of goods ranging from automobiles to electronics to Christmas decorations manufactured in Europe and Asia, and global communication in which mass media brought American images to the rest of the world. Santa not only faced these challenges, he prospered.

American Illustrators Bring the World Santa ... and a Soft Drink!

By 1900, Santa and his European brethren had been depicted so many different times in so many different ways that only a few artists stand out. There are three illustrators, however, whose depictions of Santa during the twentieth century deserve special mention: Norman Rockwell, J.C. Leyendecker and Haydon Sundblom.

In the early part of the twentieth century, the prime real estate for commercial illustrators was the cover of the *Saturday Evening Post*, and two of America's best illustrators at
the time, Rockwell and Leyendecker, each created images of Santa for the *Post* that were
notable for their realism. While neither added anything unusual to the collective image
that was already well-developed, they both gave the illustrations a sense of reality that took
them from the pencil drawings and political cartoons of the prior century to something
that looked like a real person. Art history professor Marling provided this evaluation of the
work of the two artists:

> Rockwell treated Santa as a real person. Of five Santa covers in the 1920s, two show a balding old
> man while the other three depict another recognizable model, broad-faced and ruddy, with a wide,
> knobby nose. In that sense—in his uncompromising naturalism—Rockwell points the way toward the
> all-American physical credibility of the Coca-Cola Santas. Leyendecker, on the other hand, vacillated
> between the kind of Santa who might have run a busy factory and the purely legendary St Nick.... So
> the Santa who was constructed in the 1920s and refined in the 1930s is essentially the same Santa who
> has been delivering the nation's presents ever since—a hybrid figure, with a whiff of commerce cling-
> ing to the fabric of his big red coat, more jovial businessman than saint, more real than not, comical,
> perhaps, and cute, but at bottom a serious embodiment of the economy of Christmas, balancing the
> ledgers, delivering the goods.[1]

The most significant of the commercial illustrators in terms of lasting impact, however,
was Haddon Sundblom, an artist who was hired by an ad agency working for the Coca-Cola
Company in 1930 to illustrate Santa for a campaign designed to promote the product during
the winter months and to appeal to children, a group to whom Coca-Cola apparently could
not market directly at that time.[2] The conventional wisdom cited in the introduction to this
book on the development of Santa's appearance often credits the Sundblom Santa as, in effect,
the final version of Santa—a depiction that would become fixed and immutable—but it is
not. The Sundblom Santa was an overwhelming commercial success, creating an effective and
memorable advertising campaign that continued for more three decades. I, for one, still recall
the December issues of *Sunset Magazine,* saved for me by my grandmother in Utah during the
1950s and '60s, in which a combination of Sundblom's pictures of Santa and *Sunset's* articles on
Christmas decoration and baking had an almost tranquilizing effect on my young mind in the
weeks before Christmas. But the Sundblom Santa was a painting, not an invention.

The impact of Coca-Cola's advertising dollars in creating a uniform look for Santa and
Coke throughout the world cannot be overstated but Sundblom himself can be given too much
credit. Unlike Nast, who helped popularize a figure he had some part in creating, albeit not
the sole role often claimed, Sundblom simply painted a picture of a figure whose look had
been well-established by 1930 through a combination of newspaper and magazine illustrations,
other advertisements, Christmas cards, Christmas decorations, annual parades, and live visits
at department stores throughout the nation. Sundblom's Santa was a damn good painting, one
good enough to be redone annually for different campaigns and to sell a lot of Coke, but it
would have had much less impact if it were not for the millions of dollars spent by Coca-Cola
on advertising shown around the world for three decades—a campaign so ubiquitous it created
an urban myth that Santa Claus was actually created by the Coca-Cola Company.[3]

Communists in Russia and Eastern Europe Create
a Secular Christmas on New Year's Day

One of the most significant political events of the twentieth century, approaching the
two world wars in terms of global impact, was the Russian Revolution of 1917. The philos-

ophy of Karl Marx did not have room for religion, which he viewed as "the opiate of the masses." As a result, the Communist Party, which ultimately gained control of Russia and most of eastern European, uniting the nations as the Union of Soviet Socialist Republics ("Soviet Union" or the "U.S.S.R."), sought to eliminate any vestiges of the existing Christian beliefs and capitalist culture. In *Christmas in the Crosshairs*, historian Bowler writes that on December 25, 1919, Vladimir Lenin, head of the Communist Party and the Russian government, issued an order that "[t]o put up with 'Nikola' would be stupid—the entire Cheka [secret police] must be on alert to see to it that those who do not show up for work because of 'Nikola' are shot."[4]

Whether or not the Russian government actually shot citizens who celebrated Christmas, it conducted a merciless campaign to eliminate the practice of Christianity, shutting down Russian Orthodox parishes, destroying the churches or converting them to other uses, and executing or imprisoning the priests who sought to continue the Christian traditions. These actions were apparently insufficient to end observation of the Christmas holidays, however, and in 1923 a Communist youth organization known as Komsomol launched a series of anti–Christian parades and public displays under the name Komsomol Christmas in an effort to degrade the holiday and discourage participation.[5]

The following year, 1924, Lenin died, and Joseph Stalin assumed leadership of the Communist Party and the Soviet government. Whether Lenin and Stalin had different views on the subject of Christmas is not clear. Bowler states:

> The Komsomol Christmas efforts … were not deemed a success by the Communist Party leadership, who had received numerous reports of violence, vandalism of churches and cemeteries, and drunkenness on the part of the antireligious youth. Stalin urged that "hooliganish escapades under the guise of so-called anti-religious propaganda—all of this should be cast off and liquidated immediately."[6]

Stalin was one of history's most vicious dictators, with a penchant for having those who disagreed with him murdered or thrown into one of the nation's horrific labor camps. In 1928, having decimated the Russian Orthodox Church but apparently failing to end the celebration of the Christmas, the Soviet government took a more direct approach, allegedly banning Ded Moroz, who it called "an ally of the priest and kulak," and prohibiting the use of fir trees as Christmas decoration.[7] In the mid–1930s, however, Stalin decided to adopt a more lenient approach to the Christmas season, or at least a more pragmatic one.[8] Whether this decision was an acknowledgment that existing efforts to eliminate the Christmas celebrations were not working, or simply an effort to curry favor with the people, Stalin took a cue from the sixteenth-century Dutch citizens, who avoided Holland's ban on the celebration of St. Nicholas' Day by creating Sinterklaas, and the sixteenth-century Scottish citizens who established Hogmanay, a New Year's holiday, after the Presbyterian church outlawed Christmas as a Catholic invention. On December 28, 1935, Pavel Postyshev, a close associate of Stalin, published a letter in *Pravda*, the Communist Party newspaper, in which he urged that New Year's trees be installed in schools, orphanages, clubs, cinemas, and theaters, and that the Komsomol "take a very active part in this enterprise and do away with the silly misconception that the New Year tree is a bourgeois excess."[9] The suggestion undoubtedly had the approval of Stalin, reflecting a governmental decision to implement a secular holiday with the elements of Christmas on New Year's Day.

As part of the new secular holiday, known as the Festival of Winter, the government sanctioned the display of New Year's trees, which were fir trees with a red Communist star on top, and the appearance of Ded Moroz, who the government had decided was really a secular gift-giver of Russian folklore rather than "an ally of the priest."[10] Ded Moroz would appear in public with Snegurochka, the Snow Maiden, an attractive young woman with long blonde braids who was Ded Moroz' traveling companion and, he said, his granddaughter.[11] With an official holiday on New Year's Day, the Soviet Union effectively recreated the secular celebration of Christmas under the guise of a New Year's holiday (or, one might argue, restored the original midwinter holiday, the pagan celebration of the Winter Solstice).

The Russian Orthodox Church's continued use of the Julian calendar to identify Christian feast days after the Gregorian calendar was implemented by most of the world, including the Russian government in 1918, creating an unusual holiday schedule that undoubtedly worked to the government's advantage in obtaining popular support for the new holiday. The date the Russian Orthodox Church would observe Christmas, December 25 under the Julian calendar, is January 7 under the Gregorian calendar. Thus, the secular New Year's holiday occurs *before* the Russian Orthodox Christmas. Because the New Year's celebration includes most of the embellishments one would associate with a Winter Solstice festival, including festive decorations, a New Year's tree, the appearance of a gift-giver, Ded Moroz, who looked much like Santa, and the partying, feasting and drinking associated with the Winter Solstice for thousands of years, the Russian New Year's observance effectively displaces the Christmas season except for the religious celebration by members of the Russian Orthodox Church.[12] By January 7, one can assume, most Russians felt like they had already celebrated Christmas and were keen to take down the tree.[13]

In the late 1940s, after refusing to abide by the terms of an occupation agreement executed at the end of World War II, the Soviet Union took control of a number of eastern European nations that had been subject to military occupation since the end of the World War II in 1945. Under direction of the Soviet Union, most of these nations adopted the same secular gift-giver, identified as Grandfather Frost in the native language of each nation, and celebrated what amounted to a secular Christmas on New Year's Day. The physical appearance of Ded Moroz differed from nation to nation, and in some nations was much more rustic than the Russian example.

There were two informal exceptions among the Communist Bloc nations with regard to the practice of establishing a secular holiday on New Year's Day. One exception was for those nations where Catholicism was so strong it was impossible to eliminate Christmas— or, at least, not worth dealing with the reaction of the citizens if the government tried to do so. The nations with the largest Catholic populations were Poland, Czechoslovakia and Croatia. The other exception was for West Germany, a nation that had been predominately Lutheran from the Reformation to election of the Nazi Party in 1933. The Christmas traditions in Germany were so strong, however, that East Germany was permitted to celebrate Christmas through the Communist era. One reason for the continued celebration of Christmas was that under the Nazi regime, which was officially atheist, Christmas was recreated as a pagan holiday rather than a Christian holiday, which the neopagans in the Nazi government characterized as a return to its roots. Thus, in allowing East Germany to celebrate Christmas as it had done for the last fifteen years, the Soviet Union did not have to deal with permitting continuation of a Christian holiday. In all likelihood, it was also important that manufacturing Christmas decorations for export was a significant part of the economy in several regions of East Germany.

While Ded Moroz was presumably free to resume giving gifts on Christmas following the end of the Communism in 1991, most of the former states of the Soviet Union have retained the Soviet-era practice of giving gifts on New Year's Day. In recent years, Russia has also permitted Ded Moroz to engage in his own form of *detente* with the Santa figures in other nations by participating in the international Santa Claus Championships held annually in Celle, Germany, advertised as the home of the German Weihnachtsmann.

The reaction to the newfound independence of the eastern European nations that had been under Soviet control depended a lot on the religious makeup of the nation in question. The predominant religion in Belarus, Bulgaria, Macedonia, Montenegro, Romania and Serbia is some variation of Eastern Orthodox—the Russian Orthodox Church in Belarus, the Macedonian Orthodox Church in Macedonia, the Montenegrin Orthodox Church in Montenegro, the Eastern Orthodox Church in Romania and the Serbian Orthodox Church in Serbia. These nations tend to be closest to Russia in practice.

In Belarus, the gift-giver is Dzied Maroz ("Grandfather Frost") who reportedly lives in the Bialowieza Forest in Belarus but does not have any history in Belarusian folklore. In Bulgaria, the largest religion is the Bulgarian Orthodox Church. The gift-giver prior to coming under Communist control following World War II was Dyado Koleda ("Grandpa Christmas"). During the era of Soviet domination, he became known as Djed Moroz ("Grandpa Frost"). Since approximately 1990, Dyado Koleda has returned as the most popular gift-giver. Macedonia and Montenegro both adopted versions of Ded Moroz—Dedo Mraz ("Grandpa Frost") and Dedo Mraz ("Grandfather Frost"), respectively—as New Year's gift-giver while under Soviet control and have not changed since obtaining independence. In Romania, Moș Gerilă ("Old Man Frosty"), a Romanian language adaptation of Grandfather Frost, was adopted as a New Year's gift-giver while under Soviet control. Since independence, Moș Crăciun ("Father Christmas"), the historic Christmas gift-giver, and Moș Nicolae (St. Nicholas), who brings gifts on December 6, have returned to Romania. Serbia adopted Deda Mraz ("Grandpa Frost") as the New Year's gift giver while under Communist control and has not changed.

Croatia, Slovenia and Lithuania are predominately Catholic. Latvia is partially Catholic and partially Lutheran and Bosnia-Herzogovenia is partially Catholic and partially Muslim. In Croatia, the traditional gift-givers prior to Soviet control were Sveti Nikola ("St. Nicholas") on December 6 and Djed Božićnjak ("Grandpa Christmas"), Isusek ("Little Jesus") or Mali Isus ("Christ child") on Christmas. During the era of Soviet domination, Djed Mraz ("Grandfather Frost") replaced Djed Božićnjak and the Christian gift-givers. Since independence, the Christian gift-giver Djed Božićnjak has returned but Djed Mraz is still commonly used as a synonym for Djed Božićnjak. Sveti Nikola is often accompanied by Krampus, who threatens to kidnap misbehaving children. Lithuania adopted Dedek Mraz ("Grandfather Frost") as the New Year's gift-giver while under Communist control. He was depicted as a traditional folk figure, also known as Sneženi Mož ("Snow Man") and Oca Triglav ("Daddy Triglav"), a slim man wearing a gray, fur-lined leather coat and a round dormouse fur cap. In the predominantly Lutheran Latvia and Lithuania, the Christmas gift-givers are Ziemassvētku Vecītis ("Christmas old man") and Kalėdų Senelis ("Christmas Santa"), respectively. Bosnia and Herzogovenia have adopted both a Christian name and a Muslim name for the holiday gift-giver: Djed Božićnjak ("Grandfather Christmas") for Christians and Djed Mraz ("Grandfather Frost") for Muslims.

Estonia, originally a Lutheran nation, is now one of the least religious nations in Europe, with Eastern Orthodox, the single largest religion, comprising only 15 percent of the population. The gift-giver is Jõuluvana ("Old Man of Christmas"), a name that appears to be of Scandinavian origin. Ukraine is very diverse, with large populations of Catholic, Ukrainian Orthodox and Muslim citizens. Ukraine celebrates St. Nicholas' Day with Sviaty Mykolay, but still uses Ded Moroz ("Grandpa Frost") as a New Year's gift-giver.

The Nazis Recreate a Pagan Celebration of the Winter Solstice in Germany

The Nazi Party came to power in Germany through a democratic election in 1933 and held control until 1945 when the nation surrendered to the Allies in World War II. Like the Communist Party in the Soviet Union, the Nazi Party was officially atheist, a policy that precluded any Christian celebration of Christmas. Like the Soviet Union, Germany ultimately implemented a secular Christmas celebration, but the Nazis did so in a different manner.

Following election of the Nazi Party in 1933, Bowler says, the Nazis mandated a "People's Christmas, in the consciousness of a German tradition."[14] Although it is not necessarily clear from the language, this meant a non–Christian celebration in the manner that their pagan ancestors would have celebrated Yule. Many of the leaders of the Nazi Party were self-described neo-paganists who adopted the Germanic gods and practices as symbols of national identity rather than theology. Proclaiming that the holiday would not be celebrated in a Christian manner, however, while precluding public religious ceremonies, could not have controlled how people celebrated in their own homes. For those who had been Lutherans or Catholics all of their lives, it seems likely that they continued to celebrate the religious festival in privacy but by the very nature of private celebrations there is no way to know for sure.

By 1939, the German government dug deeper into the nation's pagan past, telling citizens that the "real Christmas community celebration" was the Winter Solstice and instructing families how to celebrate Wotan's Day ("Odin's Day"), in lieu of St. Nicholas' Day on December 6. Knowing that the original German midwinter event was, in fact, a celebration of the Winter Solstice in which the people paid homage to Odin, and that the Catholic Church required St. Nicholas be substituted for Odin, a return to the pagan celebration was not that difficult to explain. The Nazi government, however, provided an explanation that sounds like a politician blaming his predecessor for problems that popped up during his own administration:

> In olden days, the God of our ancestors [Wotan/Odin], drove through the air, visited his people, was friendly to them, and left them little presents. He wanted to announce the start of the Winter Solstice season and the coming of the New Year. The Christian church couldn't suppress these yearly visits of this white-bearded one-eyed leader of good spirits. So, they put one of its assumed saints, St. Nikolaus, in his place.[15]

In honor of Odin as the "god of our ancestors," Germany continued to celebrate Christmas under the Nazi regime through the end World War II. Weihnachtsmann, as a secular figure, remained the holiday gift-giver in northern Germany but the Nazis asserted that he, too, represented the Germanic god Odin, and, in a sense, that was accurate. St. Nicholas and Christkindl, the traditional gift-givers in predominately Catholic regions, were forbidden but the other elements of traditional German Christmas celebrations were permitted. Given that the nation was in a state of war from 1939 through 1945, and that Christmas was generally a family celebration conducted in private. it is hard to determine how much of an effect these prohibitions, by themselves, had on the celebration of Christmas in Germany. Once the Nazi government was defeated in World War II, however, that part of the nation that was not under Soviet control quickly reverted to the traditional German celebration of Christmas.

Following the surrender of Germany, the nation as a whole and its capital of Berlin were divided into four sections, occupied by four different nations, for the purposes of reconstructing the country following the war. Three of those sections, occupied by Great Britain, France and the United States, became the Federal Republic of Germany, or West Germany, a democracy with no restrictions on the free exercise of religion. After Allied occupation ceased in 1949, West Germany was a capitalist nation with roughly equal numbers of Protestants and Catholics. In northern Germany, the Weihnachtsmann remained the most popular gift-giver while the Christkindl became the most popular gift-giver in southern Germany. West Germany also attracted a number of Christmas-related businesses that had operated in what became East Germany following the Soviet occupation because those businesses sought to operate without Soviet government interference.

The fourth section of both Germany and Berlin was occupied by the Soviet Union, which refused to relinquish control as required by the occupation agreement. That region was named the German Democratic Republic, or East Germany, and remained under Soviet control until 1990 when all of the Soviet Bloc nations became independent. During the period of Soviet domination, East Germany continued to permit the celebration of Christmas in the secular manner allowed under Nazi control but without the Nazi-directed emphasis on pagan gods. This decision had both a philosophical basis, which was that the Nazis had already eliminated any element of Christianity from the holiday, and a pragmatic basis, which was the importance of the Christmas holiday to the East German people and economy. The implementation of Communism initially disrupted a number of Christmas-related business that were no longer allowed to operate as capitalist enterprises. Some of those businesses fled to West Germany but others were eventually reorganized as collectives permitted under the Communist system.

After Soviet control of East Germany ended in 1990, the two nations quickly reunited, implementing a capitalist economy and eliminating any restrictions on the celebration of Christmas as either a secular or Christian holiday, and in the process restoring Germany's reputation as the nation with the most vibrant Christmas tradition. Today, for example, Germany hosts more than fifty Christmas markets that run from late November through Christmas and attract millions of tourists each year.

The Santa-fication of Europe Obscures the Native Gift-Givers

During the same extended period when the Soviet Union, the Communist Bloc nations, and Nazi Germany sought to eliminate the Christian gift-givers that had been common to those nations for at least several centuries, replacing them with secular or pagan celebrations, the rest of Europe underwent what one could call a Santa-fication under which the American Santa Claus became increasingly prominent, often obscuring the native gift-givers. This subchapter will explain how Santa and his European brethren survived, and how Santa frequently prospered, during the twentieth century.

The British Isles. The most obvious change in the celebration of Christmas in the British Isles during the twentieth century was in Scotland, where the Presbyterian government had outlawed the celebration of Christmas during the sixteenth century. While support for the extreme form of Calvinism had long since waned, the Scottish resistance to the celebration of Christmas in the English style continued into the twentieth century, partly because of continuing Calvinist sentiments but mostly, it seems, because Christmas came to be seen as an English holiday rather than a Scottish one. Although there was no formal government action, World War II ended the intra-United Kingdom rivalry. Since the 1940s, Scotland has celebrated Christmas in the English style.

The other change in Great Britain during the twentieth century has been the gradual adoption of the name and physical appearance of the American Santa Claus for the British Father Christmas. Santa has not eclipsed Father Christmas, and hopefully never will, but the two names have become synonymous for many English residents and the visual differences have begun to recede.

Belgium, the Netherlands and Luxembourg. In Belgium, a nation primarily divided into French and Dutch speakers, and the predominately-Dutch Netherlands, the French speakers tend to follow the French traditions while the Dutch speakers follow the Dutch traditions of the Netherlands. Luxembourg, on the other hand, has its own Christmas customs influenced by Dutch and German traditions.

Sinterklaas remains the most popular holiday gift-giver among the Dutch and still brings gifts from Spain to the Netherlands. He generally arrives atop a white horse in a boat in a special ceremony in late November and participates in parades or other celebrations before distributing gifts on December 5, the evening before St. Nicholas' Day, and returning home to Spain. In his public appearances, he is generally surrounded by dozens of young Dutch men (and, occasionally, a few young women) wearing the traditional Black Peter uniform, including black face, and tossing candies to the children who have come to see Sinterklaas. In Luxembourg, St. Nicholas is known as Kleeschen and delivers gifts with an assistant known as Houseker. Unlike the black-face minstrel look of Black Peter, however, Houseker appears completely in black, with mask, hood and cloak. In Belgium, the Dutch look forward to Sinterklaas while the French speakers celebrate St. Nicholas' Day on December 6. During the twentieth century, however, the Christmas gift-giver has become a bigger part of celebrations in the Benelux nations. Known as Kerstman ("Christmas Man") among Dutch speakers and Père Noël ("Father Christmas") among French speakers, he looks a good deal like the American Santa Claus and brings gifts on Christmas Eve.

France. In nineteenth-century France, there were a large number of regional Christmas gift-givers, including St. Nicholas in the northern and eastern regions of France that abut Belgium and Germany, Tante Arie in a region called Franche-Comte, and Le Petit Jesus, the French name for the Christ child, in the remainder of the nation. During the twentieth century, however, Père Noël, the French version of Father Christmas, has became increasingly popular. Père Noël's look and role are very similar to the English Father Christmas, including a hooded cloak rather than a coat and hat, but Père Noël wears a basket on his back of the type used in France to pick grapes, something not found on the English Father Christmas.[16]

The introduction of Père Noël was not without controversy. In a 1952 article titled, in English, "Father Christmas Executed," renowned French anthropologist Claude Levi-Strauss described how Père Noël was hanged and burned in effigy as "a usurper and a heretic" before three hundred schoolchildren in the Dijon Cathedral.[17] Although the Catholic clergy at that time apparently considered the abandonment of St. Nicholas and Le Petit Jesus in favor of the Père Noël as Christmas gift-giver as a rejection of Catholic principles, neither the government nor the populace seems to have joined this movement.

Spain. The celebration of Christmas in Spain, dominated by traditions and figures from the Bible, has not changed as much during the twentieth century as other nations. Like France, however, Spain experienced protests in the middle of the century from Catholic priests who objected to the secular nature of the holiday, even though the Spanish traditions were, by comparison, the most Catholic of any nation. The Protestants, of course, considered Christmas too "popish" and too "pagan" in nature. Once again, therefore, Father Christmas ended up caught in the middle of a religious dispute.

Italy. In Italy, gifts historically have been given on both Christmas and Three Kings Day. On Christmas, the traditional gift-giver was Gesu Bambino, the Italian term for the Christ child. On Epiphany, there were two gift-givers, the Three Kings and La Befana, a woman often portrayed as a witch with a broomstick. During the twentieth century, however, an Italian version of Santa Claus known as Babbo Natale ("Father Christmas"), whose appearance is virtually identical to the American Santa Claus, began to replace the historic gift-givers in Italy.

Scandinavia. While Santa has not altered the image of most Scandinavian gift-givers, perhaps because they already evolved from Yule Bucks into smaller versions of Santa Claus during the nineteenth century, the Santa-fication of Europe has had an impact on their height. While there are lots of images in Scandinavia of elf- or gnome-sized gift-givers, many images now reflect the look of the American Santa more than the traditional Scandinavian figures.

Scandinavia has also succumbed to the Santa-fication of Europe, with two nations claiming to be the home of Santa Claus and a third hosting an annual Santa Claus convention and competition. Denmark and Sweden say that Santa lives in Uummannaq, Greenland, while Finland claims he lives in Korvatunturi, Finland, a town in Lapland that has turned its native reindeer and Santa's adopted hometown into a tourist attraction complete with a "Santa Park."[18] In Denmark, an amusement park north of Copenhagen has hosted World Santa Claus Congress each year since 1957. The four-day event provides an opportunity for professional Santa Clauses from around the world to meet and mingle, with the final day including a "Santa Pentathlon."

Twentieth-Century Christmas Gift-Givers Around the Globe

Completing our theme of *Santa Claus Worldwide* requires a brief tour of modern Christmas gift-giving traditions around the world. While a detailed review of Christmas celebrations around the world is not possible in this volume, to demonstrate the full diversity of depictions of Santa around the world this subchapter will provide a brief overview of the modern practices in Asia, Africa, Central and South America and Australia.

Asia and Africa. The predominate religions in Asia, the Middle East and Africa are Islam, Hinduism and Buddhism, and only a small minority of the residents are Christians. Some of the Christian groups have their own gift-givers while others follow the customs of predominately Christian nations. One of the few predominately Christian nations in Africa is Ethiopia in which the Ethiopian Orthodox Church celebrates Ganna, the Ethiopia word for Christmas, and Timkat, the Ethiopian version of Epiphany, based on the Julian calendar. Santa Claus is known in Ethiopia as Yágena Abāt, or Father Christmas.

Two Asian nations that celebrate Christmas in surprisingly large numbers are Japan and China. Although only a small portion of the Japanese and Chinese are Christian, both nations have begun to celebrate Christmas as a secular holiday on a fairly wide basis, with Santa Claus as the dominant gift-giver. In Japan, Christmas is called Kurisimasu and Santa is called Uncle Chimney but there is a Japanese character, Hoteiosho, who looks similar to Santa, and one might venture they are the same person with an English and a Japanese name. In China, the name used for Santa is Dun Lao Che Ren, or Old Man Christmas. Both nations have produced large numbers of Christmas decorations, including Santa Claus figurines, for export to the United States. The most common explanation for the wide-spread celebration of Christmas, however, is a desire in both countries to emulate western customs and an excuse for what one might call conspicuous consumption.

Central and South America. Virtually everyone in Central and South America is Spanish-speaking or, in the case of Brazil, Portuguese-speaking, and the vast majority practice Catholicism. The Christmas traditions of Central and South America, therefore, largely track the Christmas traditions of Spain in which the focus is on the Nativity itself rather than the secular components popular elsewhere. There is no celebration of St. Nicholas' Day in Latin America so the Christmas season runs from December 15, the first night of Los Posadas, to January 6, Three Kings Day.

In most of Latin America, the climate allows for greenery all year long, and evergreens are therefore less important than in northern climates. The traditional Christmas flower is the poinsettia, a plant native to Mexico, in which the upper leaves turn a brilliant red as the amount of daylight begins to fall in December. The association between the poinsettia and Christmas also includes an old Mexican folk tale in which a boy, without any gift for the baby Jesus, offers a poinsettia which sprouts its brilliant red leaves. The other Christmas decorations with strong associations to Mexico and Latin America are *farolitos*, which are paper lanterns, and *luminarias*, which are paper bags filled with sand and a lighted candle. The *luminarias* are typically placed on the ground to light a pathway for processionals such as Los Posadas.

In Mexico and many other Latin American countries, as well as parts of the southwestern United States, the highlight of the Christmas season is Los Posadas, which means "the inns" in English. Los Posadas is a reenactment for eight nights in a row, from December 15 through December 23, of the efforts of Mary and Joseph to find lodging for the birth of Jesus, and the refusal of the innkeeper to give them a room. A different home is selected each night to serve as the inn and to host a party for the participants after the reenactment ends. Typically, several children will be chosen to lead the procession, playing Joseph, Mary, angels and the innkeeper. After initially refusing admission, the innkeeper relents, and the participants enter the "inn" for dinner and celebrations. Christmas Eve is known as Noche Buena, meaning "the Good Night." After attending midnight mass, residents return home, or to the homes of friends or relatives with whom they are celebrating, for a traditional dinner featuring, among other foods, turkey, a bird domesticated by the Aztecs.

Traditionally, the Spanish and Latin American practice was that El Nino, the Christ Child, left gifts for children on Christmas Eve. During the twentieth century, however, the role has been taken over in some regions by the Latin American version of Father Christmas—Papa Noel in Argentina, Uruguay and other Spanish-speaking countries; Papai Noel in Portuguese-speaking Brazil; and Veijo Pasuero in Chile. Use of the name Santa Claus is becoming increasingly common, however, particularly in El Salvador and Columbia. The Christmas season ends on January 6, known in most Spanish-speaking nations as Dia de Los Tres Reyes Magos, or Three Kings Day. As in Spain, Three Kings Day, not Christmas, is the primary gift-giving date in Central and South America.

Australia and New Zealand. Australia and New Zealand, both founded as colonies of the United Kingdom, have long looked to England for their Christmas traditions, and, like England, Santa Claus is increasingly displacing Father Christmas. Christmas Down

Under occurs, of course, in the middle of summer. As a result, one notable tradition is large-scale, open-air Christmas caroling that fills public stadiums on Christmas Eve. The other tradition is spending Christmas Day on the beach, which is not the White Christmas we hope for in America but is a perfectly delightful way to celebrate from the perspective of the ocean-loving Australians. Australia also has its peculiar Santa traditions, the most unusual is the legend of Santa riding in a sleigh pulled by six "boomers," which are young, male kangaroos.

Epilogue:
The Santas of Christmas Future

This ends *Santa Claus: Worldwide*, which has documented the history and depiction of Santa and his European brethren from thousands of years before Christ to the present day. I hope this book has conveyed that Santa is not merely a Christmas gift-giver, but the Grand Marshal of Winter Solstice festivals world-wide, and that he is not the static creation of a handful of white men in nineteenth century America but the accumulation of figures imagined and depicted by thousands of individuals around the world over many millennia.

The Santas of Christmas Future will be defined, I hope, by a recognition that diversity of thought and image is what keeps the world vital and interesting. We need to think globally, embracing a world in which there is a broad and diverse collection of gift-givers, and simultaneously rejecting a world in which the only gift-giver that exists is the standard issue American Santa Claus. As a collector whose primary interest is the number of different ways in which Santa can be depicted, recognizing that Santa and his kin are found on every continent and in almost every nation can open up myriad exciting possibilities. As a people, however, we also need to understand that the differences do not make us different. We are all part of humankind, and Christmas, whatever it might be called in one nation or another, should be considered the universal feast of humanity. The prospect of German children and American children and Spanish children and Finnish children talking joyfully about Weihnachtsmann and Santa and El Nino and Joulupukki will help create a better, happier world for all of us.

I also hope the reader will learn to appreciate the enlightenment and enjoyment that come from experiencing the diversity of Christmas celebrations that exist throughout the world. For those of us who love Christmas, there is nothing more delightful than immersing ourselves in the revelries of Christmas festivities other than our own. One of my favorite Yuletide vacations was visiting my sister's home in Brussels, Belgium, during a week in which the American Thanksgiving and the first day of Hanukah occurred on the same day. My sister and brother-in-law served an American-style turkey dinner for their neighbors, a Jewish family from France living in Brussels, who reciprocated by lighting the menorah and frying jelly doughnuts known as sufganiyot for dessert. The following day we went to the Kerstmarkt ("Christmas market") in Bruges, a beautiful medieval city in which the buildings in the central square date from the fifteenth century, where the Dutch, Belgians, and French all sold their native food and figures representing the gift-givers of their own traditions.

For those who are inspired to experience the diversity of Christmas, the list of possible excursions is endless. In America, we have the Cajun Christmases of Louisiana, where Santa dresses in muskrat pelts and arrives on a canoe pulled by alligators before a dinner of gumbo and turducken; the Mexican-influenced Christmases of Santa Fe, New Mexico, with its shimmering luminaries and reenactments of Los Posadas; or the Colonial Christmases of Williamsburg, Virginia. In Europe, one can attend midnight mass in the Austrian chapel where "Silent Night" was first performed in 1888; meet the Three Kings and experience Tió de Nadal, the Catalonian pooping log during festivities in Spain (or not); and visit some of the hundred-plus Christmas markets throughout the continent, each of which has its own local character. In Australia, one can participate in the gigantic Christmas sing-alongs held in open air stadiums on Christmas Eve and spend Christmas day on the beach. Virtually every nation celebrates the Christmas season in some way worth experiencing. Please experience them.

Chapter Notes

Preface

1. *The New York Sun* (September 21, 1897).
2. *The Troy (N.Y.) Sentinel* (December 23, 1823).
3. William E. Deal and S. Waller, "The Mind of Santa Claus and the Metaphors He Lives By," *Christmas—Philosophy for Everyone: Better Than a Lump of Coal* (Malden, MA: Wiley-Blackwell, 2009), 95 (hereinafter Deal and Waller, "The Mind of Santa Claus").
4. Wendell H. Oswalt, *Understanding Our Culture: An Anthropological View* (New York: Holt, Rinehart and Winston, 1970), 10.
5. Matthew Brophy, "Santa's Sweatshop: Elf Exploitation for Christmas," *Christmas—Philosophy for Everyone: Better Than a Lump of Coal* (Malden, MA: Wiley-Blackwell, 2009), 125–27. In fairness, Brophy's accusations are firmly tongue in cheek, part of a hilarious analysis of ethical issues that would arise if Santa Claus actually kept a workforce of elves who made toys for all of the world's children each year without compensation.
6. Gerry Bowler, *Santa Claus: A Biography* (Toronto: McClelland & Stewart, 2007), 231–32 (hereinafter Bowler, *Santa Claus*).
7. *The Children's Friend: Part III A New-Year's Present to the Little Ones from Five to Twelve* (New York: William B. Gilley, 1821) (hereinafter *The Children's Friend*).
8. Bowler, *Santa Claus*, 23.
9. Charles W. Jones, "Knickerbocker Santa Claus," *New-York Historical Society Quarterly* 38 (1954), 356–83 (hereinafter Jones, "Knickerbocker Santa Claus").
10. Charles W. Jones, *Saint Nicholas of Myra, Bari, and Manhattan: Biography of a Legend* (Chicago: University of Chicago Press, 1978) (hereinafter Jones, *Saint Nicholas*).
11. Washington Irving, *A History of New York* (New York: Inskeep and Bradford, 1809) (hereinafter, Irving, *History of New York*).
12. Stephen Nissenbaum, *The Battle for Christmas: A Cultural History of America's Most Cherished Holiday* (New York: Vintage, 1997), 64–65 (hereinafter Nissenbaum, *The Battle for Christmas*).

Chapter 1

1. Many of the names for the Christmas gift-givers discussed in this book were developed through oral tradition, and thus have multiple potential spellings or translations. Rather than list all of the possible spellings, I have used the spelling in the quotation or source cited or, if none, have tried to determine whether a particular spelling or translation has been generally accepted as the correct spelling. For figures such as Odin, where there is no single correct spelling, for the sake of consistency I picked one and used it throughout except for direct quotes.
2. J.M. Golby and A.W. Purdue, *The Making of the Modern Christmas*, rev. ed. (Sparkford, Somerset: J.H. Haynes, 2000), 71 (hereinafter Golby and Purdue, *The Making of the Modern Christmas*).
3. This seemingly inconsistent proposition can be explained by the term "familienähnlichkeit," or family resemblance, a concept developed by Austrian philosopher Ludwig Wittgenstein in the middle of the twentieth century. Wittgenstein, one of the greatest philosophers of the era, was born in Vienna, Austria, and taught logic and philosophy of language at Cambridge University. In a posthumously-published book, *Philosophical Investigations,* Wittgenstein popularized the philosophical concept of family resemblance to describe things which are not connected by one essential common feature but which are connected instead by a series of overlapping similarities. Ludwig Wittgenstein, *Philosophical Investigations* (1953), English translation by G.E.M. Anscombe (Prentice Hall, 1999). To illustrate, the majority of Santas have long white beards, but some do not. Someone without a beard could be considered Santa if they had several other attributes of Santa, such as the ability to fly, go down chimneys, deliver gifts on Christmas, and so on. On the other hand, a white beard, without other critical attributes, will not make you Santa.
4. James H. Barnett, *The American Christmas: A Study in National Culture* (New York: Macmillan, 1954), 30 (hereinafter Barnett, *The American Christmas*).
5. Deal and Waller, "The Mind of Santa Claus," 93.
6. Scott C. Lowe, editor, *Christmas—Philosophy for Everyone: Better Than a Lump of Coal* (Malden, MA: Wiley-Blackwell, 2009).
7. Guy Bennett-Hunter, "Christmas Mythologies Sacred and Secular," *Christmas—Philosophy for Everyone: Better Than a Lump of Coal* (Malden, MA: Wiley-Blackwell, 2009).

8. *Ibid.*

9. *Ibid.*

10. Compare David Kyle Johnson, "Against the Santa Claus Lie," *Christmas—Philosophy for Everyone: Better Than a Lump of Coal* (Malden, MA: Wiley-Blackwell, 2009), with Era Gavrielides, "Lying to Children About Santa: Why It's Just Not Wrong," *Christmas—Philosophy for Everyone: Better Than a Lump of Coal* (Malden, MA: Wiley-Blackwell, 2009).

11. Dane Scott, "Scrooge Learns It All in One Night: Happiness and the Virtues of Christmas," *Christmas—Philosophy for Everyone: Better Than a Lump of Coal* (Malden, MA: Wiley-Blackwell, 2009), 172.

12. *Ibid.*, 178.

13. Al Ridenour, *The Krampus and the Old, Dark Christmas: Roots and Rebirth of the Folkloric Devil* (Port Townsend, WA: Feral House, 2015), 8 (hereinafter Ridenour, *The Krampus*). It appears the evil helpers did not enter the world as inhabitants of Hell but were assigned that role by the Catholic Church because it believed any creature with animal parts, or at least a pagan origin, must be friends with Satan. There are no birth records available from Hades but some folklorists believe the evil helpers were actually gods or demigods of Germanic folklore, and that Krampus, in particular, "was originally a pagan goat-man fertility god, but the church demoted him to 'Santa-Sidekick' to prevent pagan converts from continuing to worship him." David Kyle Johnson, "Against the Santa Claus Lie: The Truth We Should Tell Our Children," *Christmas—Philosophy for Everyone: Better Than a Lump of Coal* (Malden, MA: Wiley-Blackwell, 2009), 139 (hereinafter Johnson, "Against the Santa Claus Lie"). The pagan fertility god theory is described more fully in Phyllis Siefker, *Santa Claus, Last of the Wild Men: The Origins and Evolution of Saint Nicholas, Spanning 50,000 Years* (Jefferson, N.C.: McFarland, 1997) (hereinafter Siefker, *Santa Claus*) and Tony van Renterghem, *When Santa Was a Shaman* (St. Paul: Llewellyn, 1995) (hereinafter van Renterghem, *When Santa Was a Shaman*).

14. At present, about 12 percent of the residents of the Netherlands are Catholic and 9 percent are Protestant but two-thirds do not practice any religion at all. What this means, of course, is that the religious imperative for creating Sinterklaas has long since disappeared, and the current attitude of the Dutch toward Santa Claus must be one of national identity, not religion.

15. While the text focuses on the diversity of Santa figures around the world, others have properly emphasized the importance of diversity in society more generally. In "The Significance of Christmas for Liberal Multiculturalism," Mark Mercer, Chair of the Philosophy Department at Saint Mary's University in Halifax, Nova Scotia, asserts that in a multicultural society like America it is necessary to have some holidays or celebrations that are common to all. "These holidays … have to honor values important to most people in the country and to honor them in ways people from various cultures find congenial. . . . They are times when everyone gets together to enjoy themselves and to enjoy each other—and to enjoy themselves and each other through participating in common traditions." Mark Mercer, "The Significance of Christmas for Liberal Multiculturalism," *Christmas—Philosophy for Everyone: Better Than a Lump of Coal* (Malden, MA: Wiley-Blackwell, 2009), 77.

16. Dr. Seuss, *How the Grinch Stole Christmas* (New York: Random House, 1957), 7.

17. There should be no doubt that, within the United States, both Hanukkah and Kwanzaa are parts of our nation's collective holiday season. One can ponder, however, whether the celebration of the birth of Christ on December 25 had anything to do with the existing Jewish holiday on the twenty-fifth of the Jewish month of Kislev, or vice versa. Making any comparison is difficult because the Hebrew calendar is based on lunar cycles of 28 days rather than solar cycles of 365 days. To keep the Hebrew calendar consistent with the solar calendar, extra months are added every two or three years. This is why Hanukkah, which observes the rededication in 165 BC of the Holy Temple in Jerusalem that had been desecrated during the Maccabean Revolt, can occur anywhere between late November and late December. Kislev, however, is the month most analogous to the month of December on the Julian calendar adopted by Rome in 45 BC. In a 1902 treatise, *Christmas, Its Origins and Associations*, William Dawson states that a nineteenth-century scholar sought to show that Christmas grew out of the Jewish Dedication of the Temple, citing the timing of the two festivals, the similar traditions, including the practice of decorating with evergreens and candles, and the fact that the "German word Weihnachten (from weihen, 'to consecrate, inaugurate,' and by, 'night') leads directly to the meaning, 'Night of the Dedication.'" William Francis Dawson, *Christmas: Its Origin and Associations Together with Its Historical Events and Festive Celebrations During Nineteen Centuries* (London: Elliott Stock, 1902), 17 (hereinafter Dawson, *Christmas, Its Origin and Associations*). The linguistic argument does not really support any inference about the derivation of the Feast of the Nativity, however, because the German name for Christmas was not adopted until centuries after the Jewish and Christian holidays were established. The most persuasive explanation for the similarities is that every society has some sort of midwinter festival, and the common traditions of the Jewish and Christian festivals are inherent in any midwinter festival.

18. Harrison, *The Story of Christmas*, 24–25.

19. *Ibid.*

20. During the seventeenth century, Christian denominations that did not acknowledge Christmas as the birth of Christ included the Puritans, the Presbyterians, the Quakers and the Baptists. Some of the Christian denominations that do not recognize Christmas today include conservative Quakers, Jehovah's Witnesses, Seventh-Day Adventists and the United Church of God. The largest religious denomination in the United States after Catholics, the Southern Baptist Convention, did not acknowledge Christmas when it was founded in 1845 but

came to embrace the holiday during the twentieth century.

21. Todd Preston, "Putting the 'Yule' Back in 'Yuletide,'" *Christmas—Philosophy for Everyone: Better Than a Lump of Coal* (Malden, MA: Wiley-Blackwell, 2009), 39 (hereinafter Preston, "Putting the 'Yule' Back in 'Yuletide'"). Preston, an assistant professor of Medieval Studies at Lycoming College, says that the name Christmas was used primarily to designate the date of December 25 and that the term Yule was normally used when talking about the celebration of Christ's birth.

22. In practice, midnight mass at most Catholic churches actually does draw several times the typical attendance, either because nonobservant Catholics feel like they should attend on Christmas or because non-Catholics enjoy the spectacle of midnight mass. In many parishes today, the priests go out of their way to welcome the nonobservant or non-Catholics in attendance.

23. David Kyle Johnson, *The Myths That Stole Christmas* (Washington, D.C.: Humanist Press, 2015), 7–8.

24. George C. McWhorter, "The Holidays," *Harper's New Monthly Magazine* (January 1866).

25. *Ibid.*

26. This should not be construed to imply that Christianity is the only religion that exalts these qualities. To the contrary, these are universal virtues seen in the writings of Buddhists, Hindus, Muslims, Jews, Catholics, Protestants, Mormons, Unitarians, secular humanists, and other groups too numerous to name. The theological justifications, risks, and rewards of celebrating Christmas for atheists and pagans are discussed in Ruth Tallman, "Holly Jolly Atheists: A Naturalistic Justification for Christmas," *Christmas—Philosophy for Everyone: Better Than a Lump of Coal* (Malden, MA: Wiley-Blackwell, 2009) (hereinafter Tallman, "Holly Jolly Atheists") and Marion G. Mason, "Heaven, Hecate, and Hallmark: Christmas in Hindsight," *Christmas—Philosophy for Everyone: Better Than a Lump of Coal* (Malden, MA: Wiley-Blackwell, 2009).

27. Bruce David Forbes, *Christmas: A Candid History* (Berkeley: University of California Press, 2007) (hereinafter Forbes, *Christmas: A Candid History*).

28. Francis X. Weiser, *The Christmas Book* (New York: Harcourt, Brace, 1952), 33.

29. Penne L. Restad, *Christmas in America: A History* (New York: Oxford University Press, 1995), 106–08 (hereinafter Restad, *Christmas in America*).

30. *Ibid.*, 39.

31. *Ibid.*, 108

32. *Ibid.*, 168 (quoting George C. McWhorter, "The Holidays," *Harper's New Monthly Magazine* [January 1866]).

33. The best example is the claim by some conservative commentators, attempting to increase ratings during an era of increasing political polarization, who have discovered a "war on Christmas" where it appears that none exists. See Scott F. Aiken, "Armed for the War on Christmas," *Christmas—Philosophy for Everyone: Better Than a Lump of Coal* (Malden,

MA: Wiley-Blackwell, 2009), 49 (hereinafter Aiken, "Armed for the War on Christmas"). One prong of this "war" that received a lot of inexplicable publicity in 2015 was that the Starbucks coffee chain announced it would use a plain red cup for the Christmas season, removing the "images of snowflakes, trees, and ornaments that covered the cups in years prior." Lucinda Shen, "Starbucks Is Bringing Back the Holiday Cup That Got It in Trouble Last Year," *Fortune.com*, http://fortune.com/2016/11/04/starbucks-cup-red-controversy-christmas (November 4, 2016). What the proponents of this argument seem not to understand is that snowflakes, trees, and ornaments are secular symbols of a Winter Solstice celebration, not Christian symbols.

34. Ruth Tallman, "Holly Jolly Atheists," 189.

35. The best-known parade on Thanksgiving is Macy's Thanksgiving Day Parade in New York City. It began in 1924, making it the second oldest Thanksgiving parade in the United States. It features Santa Claus riding on the last float, waving to the crowd and silently declaring the Christmas shopping season to be open. The season also closes with a parade, the Festival of Roses Parade in Pasadena, California, a remarkable display of floral artistry that television cannot capture.

36. Barnett, *The American Christmas*, 17.

37. *Ibid.*, 14.

38. Charles Dickens, *A Christmas Carol* (London: Chapman Hall, 1843), 10–11. The publication of *A Christmas Carol* put some gold in Dickens' pocket but not nearly as much as he deserved because the book was widely published without Dickens' permission and without compensating him. As a result, Dickens spent much of his later life giving readings of the book to paying audiences in America.

39. Joe Perry, *Christmas in Germany: A Cultural History* (Chapel Hill: University of North Carolina Press, 2013), 1 (quoting Clement A. Miles, *Christmas in Ritual and Tradition Christian and Pagan* [London, 1912]).

40. Mark Connelly, *Christmas, A History* (London: I.B. Taurus, 1999, paperback edition with new preface, 2012), 32 (hereinafter Connelly, *Christmas, A History*).

41. Barnett, *The American Christmas*, 129, 141.

42. *Ibid.*, 136.

43. Paul Frodsham, *From Stonehenge to Santa Claus: The Evolution of Christmas* (Stroud, Gloustershire: History Press, 2008), 221–30 (hereinafter Frodsham, *From Stonehenge to Santa*).

44. Frodsham, *From Stonehenge to Santa*, 229.

45. Forbes, *Christmas: A Candid History*, 4.

46. Francis B. Church, "Yes, Virginia, There Is a Santa," *The (N.Y.) Sun* (September 21, 1897).

47. *The Troy (N.Y.) Sentinel* (December 23, 1823).

Chapter 2

1. Irving, *History of New York*.

2. "Account of a Visit from St. Nicholas," *The Troy (N.Y.) Sentinel* (December 23, 1823). Moore's authorship has been disputed by descendants of

Henry Livingston, Jr., a surveyor and farmer from Poughkeepsie, N.Y., who claim Livingston wrote the poem and recited it on Christmas morning in 1808. Because of the space it would take to address fully the authorship question, and because the name of the author does not change the history of Santa Claus, that issue must await another book.

3. For those of you who are not fans of baseball lore, there was a poem commonly known as "Tinker to Evers to Chance" written in 1910 by Franklin Pierce Adams about a New York Giants fan watching the Chicago Cubs infield of shortstop Joe Tinker, second baseman Johnny Evers and first baseman Frank Chance, complete a double play. "These are the saddest of possible words," says the Giants fan, "Tinker to Evers to Chance."

4. Jones, "Knickerbocker Santa Claus."

5. Jones, *St. Nicholas.*

6. Carlo DeVito, *Inventing Santa Claus: The Mystery of Who Really Wrote the Most Celebrated Yuletide Poem of All Time, The Night Before Christmas* (Kennebunkport, ME: Cider Mill Press, 2017) (hereinafter DeVito, *Inventing Santa Claus*" (an entire chapter is devoted to "Washington Irving, the Man Who Popularized the American Sinterklaas," but no authority is cited except for Nissenbaum's *The Battle for Christmas*); Gerry Bowler, *Christmas in the Crosshairs: Two Thousand Years of Denouncing and Defending the World's Most Celebrated Holiday* (Oxford: Oxford University Press, 2016), 48 (hereinafter Bowler, *Christmas in the Crosshairs*) (Irving, in his 1809 history, was the first New Yorker who sought to popularize St. Nicholas as gift-giver); Alex Palmer, *The Santa Claus Man: The Rise and Fall of a Jazz Age Con Man and the Invention of Christmas in New York* (New York: Rowman & Littlefield, 2015) (asserting, based on Jones' work, that the 1809 edition of *A History of New York* created the figure of Santa Claus and inspired Clement Moore to write "The Night Before Christmas"); Joseph A. McCullough, *The Story of Santa Claus* (Oxford: Osprey Adventures, 2014), 57–58 ("by the very next year [after publication of *A History of New York* in 1809], more people were writing about Saint Nicholas, especially in New York"); Lily McNeil, *Santa Claus: A History of Christmas' Jolly CEO* (Hyperlink Press, 2012) (Irving "revived St. Nicholas's presence" in the 1809 *History of New York*; Pintard "developed an interest in this St. Nicholas figure"); Frodsham, *From Stonehenge to Santa,* 162–63 (crediting the 1809 edition of *A History of New York* for the transformation of St. Nicholas into Santa Claus); Joe Wheeler and Jim Rosenthal, *Saint Nicholas: A Closer Look at Christmas* (Nashville: Thomas Nelson, 2005), 168–76 (hereinafter Wheeler and Rosenthal, *Saint Nicholas*) ("Washington Irving was instrumental in creating the modern Santa Claus"); Bowler, *Santa Claus,* 27–31 (describing Irving's role in same manner as Jones' "Santa Claus"); Nancy H. Marshall, *The Night Before Christmas: A Descriptive Bibliography of Clement Clarke Moore's Immortal Poem* (New Castle, DE: Oak Knoll Press, 2002), xxii (hereinafter Marshall, *The Night Before Christmas*) (Moore was influenced by "close friend"

Irving, whose 1809 book included a description of St. Nicholas' gift-giving); William J. Federer, *There Really Is a Santa Claus: The History of Saint Nicholas & Christmas Holiday Traditions* (St. Louis: Amerisearch, 2002), 129–35 (quoting *A History of New York*); Jock Elliott, *Inventing Christmas: How Our Holiday Came to Be* (New York: Harry N. Abrams, 2001), 41 (insisting, incorrectly, that changes in the 1812 edition of *A History of New York* occurred in a new edition issued in 1821 and suggesting Moore's 1822 poem was influenced by the 1821 edition); Golby and Purdue, *The Making of the Modern Christmas,* 71 (Moore's poem "may well have drawn upon" Irving's *History*, "which provided similar information about Santa Claus's visit"); Nissenbaum, *The Battle for Christmas* (relying heavily on Jones' work to support the argument that the Santa Claus tradition was the product of a conspiracy among several New Yorkers associated with the New-York Historical Society); Restad, *Christmas in America,* 51 (1845 book on Kriss Kringle was "designed to counter Washington Irving's St. Nicholas"); van Renterghem, *When Santa Was a Shaman,* 52 (Irving's *History* inspired Moore to write "The Night Before Christmas"); Gerard and Patricia Del Re, *The Story of "'Twas the Night Before Christmas": The Life & Times of Clement Clarke Moore and His Best-Loved Poem of Yuletide* (Grand Rapids: Winwood Press, 1991), 71–73 (crediting Irving's *History* with inspiring Moore's poem and observing "[o]nly in the twentieth century would scholars discover the connection between" the two works); Vincent A. Yzermans, *Wonderworker: The Real True Story of How St. Nicholas Became Santa Claus* (Chicago: ACTA Publications, 1986), 36–38 ("[t]he future of Santa Claus was assured in New York by 1810 through the efforts of Washington Irving and a handful of associates"); Katherine Beaton, *The Real Santa Claus* (Richmond, Surrey: H&B Publications, 1986), 71 (in New Amsterdam, St. Nicholas "was represented as a good American burgher, dressed in a stout pair of breeches and a Dutch hat"); Phillip Snyder, *December 25: The Joys of Christmas Past* (New York: Dodd, Mead, 1985), 219–25 (hereinafter Snyder, *December 25*) (Irving's *History* "was the original source of all the myths about St. Nicholas in New Amsterdam.... [A]fter its publication in 1809, the St. Nicholas legend traveled fast"); Maggie Rogers and Peter R. Hallinan, *The Santa Claus Picture Book: An Appraisal Guide* (New York: E.P. Dutton, 1984), 3 (Irving, Moore and Nast created the American Santa Claus); E. Willis Jones, *The Santa Claus Book* (New York: Walker, 1976) (first written description of St. Nicholas in America came "from the pen of Washington Irving"); Maymie R. Krythe, *All About Christmas* (New York: Harper & Bros., 1954), 29–30 (hereinafter Krythe, *All About Christmas*) (describing *A History of New York* without recognizing Irving's work was fiction); Barnett, *The American Christmas,* 27 ("[r]ecent research by [Charles W.] Jones indicates that Washington Irving's *Knickerbocker's History* (1809) provided much of the lore of Santa Claus's visit"); Gerry Bowler, "Cleaning Up Christmas: It Wasn't Always Ho-Ho-Ho," *The*

Walrus (December 1, 2016), https://thewalrus.ca/
cleaning-up-christmas (accessed January 23, 2017);
Benjamin Bradley, "The 'Woodcutter' Santa," *The
Glow* 36, no. 6 (December 2015), 8–11, 8 (Irving's
publication of *A History of New York* in 1809 created
an elfin version of Santa copied by Moore); Robert
Hoffman, "Ho! Ho! Ho! Ephemera Traces Americanization of Santa Claus," *The Glow* 36, no. 6 (December 2015), 3–11, 4 (Washington Irving provided an
early depiction of Santa in *A History of New York*);
Patrick Browne, "Santa Claus Was Made by Washington Irving," *Historical Digression* (December 6, 2104)
https://historical-digression.com/2014/12/06/santa-
claus-was-made-by-washington-irving/ (accessed
September 18, 2017) (repeating Jones' theory on
Irving's role); Susan and Paul Brinkman, "George
Washington Irving—An American Christmas Hero,"
The Glow 32, no. 2 (April 2011), 11–14, 12 ("In his
1809 *A History of New York*, Irving described flam-
boyant celebrations of St. Nicholas in what was then
New Amsterdam.... After Irving's book was pub-
lished, the St. Nicholas legend traveled quickly");
Elisabeth Paling Funk, "From Amsterdam to New
Amsterdam: Washington Irving, the Dutch St. Nich-
olas, and the American Santa Claus," New Nether-
land Institute, *Explorers, Fortunes and Love Letters:
A History of New Netherland*, 102 (Albany: SUNY
Press, 2010) (hereinafter Funk, "From Amsterdam
to New Amsterdam") (crediting Irving with promoting the tradition of St. Nicholas in America);
Val R. Berryman, "Christmas in America: Santa
Claus Comes to America, The Dutch-American St.
Nicholas," *The Glow* 28, no. 2 (April 2007), 11–14,
12 (in 1809, Washington Irving wrote his *History of
New York* with numerous references to St. Nicholas,
and "[s]ome of the characteristics ... continued to
influence later artists"); Seth Kaller, "The Moore
Things Change," *New-York Journal of American His-
tory* (Winter 2004) (hereinafter Kaller, "The Moore
Things Change"); Stephen Nissenbaum, "There
Arose Such a Clatter: Who Really Wrote 'The Night
Before Christmas'? (And Why Does It Matter?),"
Common-Place: The Journal of Early American Life
(January 2001), http://www.common-place-archives.
org/vol-01/no-02/moore (accessed January 23, 2017)
(hereinafter Nissenbaum, "There Arose Such a Clat-
ter").

7. Snyder, *December 25*, 218–19. Oddly, Snyder
never lists the Santa Six. Based on the discussion that
follows the assertion, he is clearly including Irving,
Moore, and John Pintard of the New-York Historical Society, who on December 6, 1810, circulated a
broadside about St. Nicholas at the annual meeting of
the New-York Historical Society. For the other three
spots, Snyder seems to include Gulian Verplanck, a
professor of religion who purportedly suggested to
Moore he write a poem about St. Nicholas, Henry
Onderdonk, who published Moore's poem as a children's book in 1848, and Thomas Nast, who, Snyder
says, "define[d] the widely accepted view of what
Santa Claus looked like." *Ibid.*, 218–26.

8. Nissenbaum, *The Battle for Christmas*, 64–65.

9. *Ibid.*

10. Jones, "Knickerbocker Santa Claus," 376.

11. Scott Norsworthy, "Verse Paraphrase of the
Dutch Hymn to Saint Nicholas, 1810," *Melvilliana*
(March 10, 2018), available at https://melvilliana.
blogspot.com/search?q=sancte+claus (viewed
November 15, 2018) (hereinafter Norsworthy, "Dutch
Hymn to Saint Nicholas"). The two other newspa-
pers were the *New York Commercial Advertiser* on
December 12, 1810, a copy of which is included in
the Norsworthy blogspot, and the *New York Evening
Post* on December 14, 1810.

12. When the term Saturnalia is used in this book,
unless otherwise indicated the term is intended to
encompass three related Roman holidays: Saturnalia,
the Roman harvest festival that began on December
17 and ran between three and five days; Dies Natalis
Solis Invictus ("Birthday of the Unconquered Sun"),
which occurred on December 25, the date of the
Winter Solstice; and Kalends, a multi-day New Year's
festival that began shortly after the Winter Solstice.
December 25 had been marked as the celebration of
the birth of the sun gods in Rome, Greece, Persia, and
Egypt, among others, before becoming the celebration of the Nativity in the fourth century.

13. William S. Walsh, *The Story of Santa Klaus*
(New York: Moffat, Yard, 1909), 69 (hereinafter
Walsh, *Santa Klaus*).

14. *Ibid.*

15. The three major categories of European
mythology are Greek and Roman mythology, Slavic
mythology, and Germanic mythology. Greek and
Roman mythology comes from the polytheistic pagan
religions that most of us studied in school. Slavic
mythology, the least understood of the three, refers
to the folk beliefs of the peoples of Eastern Europe
and Russia. Germanic mythology is a comprehensive
term for myths associated with historical Germanic
paganism, including Norse mythology, Anglo-Saxon
mythology, and Continental Germanic mythology.
When used in its broad sense, the term Germanic is
synonymous with the term Teutonic, referring to all
of the ethnic groups that speak Germanic languages.
Although the panoply of Germanic gods is very similar, the names are often slightly different and many,
if not all, of the gods and goddesses have multiple
names. For example, Odin, generally recognized as
the chief god in Germanic mythology, is commonly
known as Woden or Odin but some two hundred
other names for him have been identified. The chief
god in Nordic mythology, Thor, was known in Germany as Donar, and the Germanic goddess Berchta
was known as Perchta, Holda and dozens of other
names. Because the purpose of this book is to explain
the history of Santa, not Germanic mythology, unless
context requires otherwise, the names Odin, Thor,
and Berchta will be used for those gods.

16. The glitch was the failure properly to calculate
the number of leap days needed to keep the Julian
calendar and the astronomical calendar consistent.
The difference was small, the loss of one day every
one hundred years, but over time it made a big difference. By the fifteenth century the Julian calendar
was off by about fifteen days, and the astronomical

Winter Solstice occurred on December 10. In 1582, Pope Gregory XIII introduced a new version, known as the Gregorian Calendar, that corrected the error in the calculation of leap days, and placed the astronomical Winter Solstice on December 21.

17. Marion Kummerow, *German Christmas Traditions*, www.inside-munich.com (2012) (hereinafter Kummerow, *German Christmas Traditions*) ("Saint Nicholas started from the old Germanic god Odin and only a few centuries ago changed his clothing to a bishop's habit"); Will Williams, "You'd Better Watch Out," *Christmas—Philosophy for Everyone: Better Than a Lump of Coal* (Malden, MA: Wiley-Blackwell, 2009), 139 ("centuries after the 'death' of St. Nicholas, people began to believe he visited small rewards onto the faithful annually on his death's anniversary. Why? Because Christianity appropriated pagan myths for conversation purposes, and pagan gods—such as Odin [and] Thor—were already believed to be the December gift-givers"); van Renterghem, *When Santa Was a Shaman*, 95 ("In newly-Christianized areas where the pagan Celtic and Germanic cults remained strong, legends of the god Wotan were blended with those of various Christian saints"); Margaret Baker, *Discovering Christmas Customs and Folklore: A Guide to Seasonal Rites*, 3d ed. (Buckinghamshire: Shire, 1992), 62 (hereinafter "Baker, *Discovering Christmas Customs and Folklore*") (Santa "owes much to Odin, the old blue-hooded, cloaked, white-bearded Gift bringer of the north"); Snyder, *December 25*, 208 ("[t]here is evidence linking our American Santa Claus to the old Teutonic gods Woden, who rode a white horse, and Thor, who rode a chariot pulled across the sky by two goats"); Earl W. Count, *4000 Years of Christmas* (New York: Rider, 1953), 63–64 (hereinafter Count, *4000 Years of Christmas*) ("As we trace the roots that Woden has struck into the life of the Germanic peoples, we find him turning up in the most unexpected places.... Woden has become Santa Claus, or, as he is better called, St. Nicholas"); Clement A. Miles, *Christmas in Ritual and Tradition Christian and Pagan* (London, 1912), 208 (some scholars regard St. Martin and St. Nicholas, in their role as holiday gift-givers, "as Christianizations of the pagan god Woden"); Thomas Purcell, "The Evolution of Santa Claus," *San Francisco Daily Times* [1907]), published by Heinz Schmitz, editor, *The Dark History of Christmas—An Anthology: The Pagan Origins of our Winter Festival* (self-published e-book, 2016) (Odin and Thor were predecessors of Santa Claus).

18. For ease of exposition, this explanation paints northern Europe as a monolithic region in which folk beliefs and religious practices were identical throughout. In reality, the region was very diverse and the text seeks to capture the essence of what occurred gradually over hundreds of years. Even if it were possible to reconstruct events by trying to provide a village-by-village account, it would be extraordinarily long and even more boring.

19. The Ninety-Five Theses still exist but the story of Luther nailing his critiques to the church door is probably apocryphal. See https://en.wikipedia.org/wiki/Ninety-five_Theses#/media/File:Luther_95_Thesen. png (accessed January 26, 2017).

20. The Christkindl generally appears while the children are eating dinner on Christmas Eve or are sleeping, but in some cases a girl or young woman in white representing the Christ child would arrive in person. In some regions, Christ was also represented by an adult, Heilger Christ, and this character also usually came while the children were eating or sleeping.

21. Christian Ratsch and Claudia Muller-Ebeling, *Pagan Christmas*, English trans. (Rochester, VT: Inner Traditions, 2006), 36 ("[t]he popular name Sinterklaas quite diplomatically does not refer to the Roman saint, who even today is considered taboo in Protestant Netherlands").

22. Barnett, *The American Christmas*, 25.

23. *Ibid.*

24. Fiona Deans Halloran, *Thomas Nast: The Father of Modern Political Cartoons* (Chapel Hill: University of North Carolina Press 2013), 208 (hereinafter Halloran, *Thomas Nast*).

25. *The Children's Friend.*

26. Don Foster, *Author Unknown: On the Trail of Anonymous* (New York: Henry Holt, 2000), 262–63 (hereinafter, Foster, *Author Unknown*). According to Foster and many other historians, Moore was a friend, customer, and neighbor of William B. Gilley, publisher of *The Children's Friend*, and would have had access to the book for a year before he wrote "A Visit from St. Nicholas." *Ibid.*

27. Both Gilley and Stansbury had published other books, and either could have been the author of *The Children's Friend*. Gilley wrote two books of poetry under pseudonyms. The Author of Patriotic Effusions, *The Olio* (New York: The Author, 1823); Bob Short, *Patriotic Effusions* (New York: L. & F. Lockwood, 1819). Stansbury wrote what was, for many years, the leading civics textbook in U.S. schools. Arthur J. Stansbury, *Elementary Catechism on the Constitution of the United States* (Boston: Hilliard, Gray, Little, and Wilkins, 1831).

28. Jan Schenkman, *Sint Nikolaas en zijn Knecht* (Amsterdam, 1850).

Chapter 3

1. Forbes, *Christmas: A Candid History*, 4.

2. Coffin, *Christmas Folklore*, 6.

3. John Matthews, *The Winter Solstice: The Sacred Traditions of Christmas* (Wheaten, IL: Quest Books, 1998), 15 (hereinafter Matthews, *The Winter Solstice*).

4. The Roman Saturnalia was the first *midwinter* celebration for which there is written documentation, but there were *springtime* New Year's celebrations documented in Mesopotamia, Babylonia, Egypt, and Greece much earlier. Because all of these regions had moderate climates, the purpose of the springtime festivals was to ask the gods to favor man with adequate rain. Many of the traditions and customs in the spring festivals, however, were very similar to the midwinter celebrations.

5. Frodsham, *From Stonehenge to Santa*, 17–25, 31–35.

6. Matthews, *The Winter Solstice*, 16.

7. Forbes, *Christmas: A Candid History*, 4.

8. *Ibid.*

9. *Ibid.*, 4–5.

10. Miles, *Christmas in Ritual and Tradition*, 17.

11. *Ibid.*

12. Forbes, *Christmas: A Candid History*, 5.

13. *Ibid.*

14. William Sandys, *Christmastide: Its History, Festivities and Carols* (London: John Russell Smith, 1860), 4–5 (hereinafter Sandys, *Christmastide*). These celebrations include the Feast of Aset in ancient Egypt; the Chichen Itza festival among the Mayans of Central America; Gody, a pre–Christian celebration of the Winter Solstice in Poland that focused on forgiveness and sharing; Shabe Yalda, an Iranian midwinter festival celebrating the victory of light and goodness over darkness and evil; Chaomas, a seven-day festival among the Kalasha people of northwest Pakistan that involved ritual bathing, torchlight processions, dancing, and feasting; Soyal, a Winter Solstice festival of the Hopi and Zuni tribes of Native Americans; Thai Pongal, a four-day festival among the Tamil people in the Indian state of Tamil Nadu to give thanks to the sun god; Dongzhi, a midwinter festival in China celebrating the return of the sun and the balance it will bring to the earth; and Toji, a midwinter tradition in which the Japanese light bonfires and take warm scented baths to encourage the return of the sun and good health during the upcoming year.

15. Siefker, *Santa Claus*, 39–56; van Renterghem, *When Santa Was a Shaman*, 53–65; Frodsham, *From Stonehenge to Santa*, 6; Matthews, *The Winter Solstice*, 15.

16. Siefker, *Santa Claus*, 39–41. The concept of ancient priests officiating in Winter Solstice observances at Stonehenge probably makes many think of Celtic druids, a group that still existed in Great Britain when Julius Caesar arrived in 55 BC, and whose veneration of mistletoe as a plant with spiritual properties contributed the enduring Christmas tradition of kissing under a piece of mistletoe during the holidays. Stonehenge, however, was built between twenty-five hundred and three thousand years before Caesar's arrival, and fell into disuse at least a thousand years before the arrival of the druids. Accordingly, archeologists have concluded that "the association of druids with Stonehenge is an entirely recent invention with no basis in prehistoric reality." Mike Parker Pearson, *Stonehenge: A New Understanding* (New York: The Experiment, 2013), 177–79 (hereinafter Pearson, *Stonehenge*).

17. Frodsham, *From Stonehenge to Santa*, 6.

18. Matthews, *The Winter Solstice*, 15.

19. Melicent D'Amore, "The Many Faces of Santa Claus," *The Glow* 36, no. 6 (December 2015), 26–29, 27.

20. Siefker, *Santa Claus*, 5.

21. *Ibid.*

22. Thomas Purcell, "The Evolution of Santa Claus" (1907) (published in Heinz Schmitz, editor, *The Dark History of Christmas—An Anthology: The Pagan Origins of our Winter Festival* [self-published e-book, 2016]).

23. *Ibid.*

24. Siefker, *Santa Claus*, 156.

25. Pelznickel was only one of the faux Nicholases, and only a small portion of the faux Nicholases went by that name. The name has obtained greater prominence in American literature on the history of Santa Claus than is probably justified because a virtually identical name, Belsnickle, was given the German gift-giver who immigrated to America. This makes it easy for Americans to understand that Belsnickle is merely a German transplant.

26. Siefker, *Santa Claus*, 157.

27. *Ibid.*

28. Forbes, *Christmas: A Candid History*, 8.

29. *Ibid.*

30. *Ibid.*, 9.

31. Miles, *Christmas in Ritual and Tradition*, 166–68; Coffin, *Christmas Folklore*, 4; Forbes, *Christmas: A Candid History*, 8–9.

32. Miles, *Christmas in Ritual and Tradition*, 166–68; Forbes, *Christmas: A Candid History*, 8–9.

33. Miles, *Christmas in Ritual and Tradition*, 168.

34. Nissenbaum, *The Battle for Christmas*, 60–61. The most extreme example of this may be the Christmas celebrations among enslaved African Americans, where minor benefits, such as a few days off or a better meal at Christmastime, were supposed to engender a sense of gratitude from the slaves for their owners. *Ibid.*, 238–300.

35. William S. Walsh, "The Evolution of Christmas" (1909) (published in Heinz Schmitz, editor, *The Dark History of Christmas—An Anthology: The Pagan Origins of our Winter Festival* [self-published e-book, 2016]) (hereinafter Walsh, "The Evolution of Christmas"). In explaining how the pagan gods evolved into Santa, Walsh states that Saturn, "the more dignified representative, was chosen as more in keeping with a solemn season. Saturn was preferred to Silenus, and was almost unconsciously rebaptized as Saint Nicholas, the latter being the greatest saint whose festival was celebrated in December and the one who in other respects was most nearly in accord with the dim traditions of Saturn as the hero of the Saturnalia." *Ibid.*

36. Count, *4000 Years of Christmas*, 20–23.

37. *Ibid.*

38. *Ibid.*, 23.

39. *Ibid.*, 27–30.

40. Natalie Kononenko, *Slavic Folklore: A Handbook* (Westport, CT: Greenwood Press, 2007), 2.

Chapter 4

1. Bowler, *Santa Claus*, 3–4.

2. Forbes, *Christmas: A Candid History*, 18.

3. Whether Constantine himself had converted to Christianity at the time of the council is uncertain; some reports say he converted prior to the council

but he was not baptized until shortly before his death in AD 337.

4. Some have suggested that the name of Nicholas was added to the roles of the Council of Nicea after he became famous. Any attempt to prove or disprove this contention is probably impossible, and certainly pointless, but it is important to understand that the appearance of his name on the council records does not necessarily mean he was actually there, and that such records are the only evidence of his existence.

5. In early Christianity, the four regional churches that comprised the Eastern Orthodox Church were Greece, Constantinople (Turkey), Alexandria (Egypt), and Jerusalem (Israel). They all agreed to mark the Nativity on December 25 during the fourth or fifth centuries. In the centuries since, autonomous Orthodox churches have been established in Russia, Ukraine, Georgia, Serbia, Romania, Bulgaria, Cyprus, Albania, Poland, the Czech Republic, the Slovak Republic, and the United States. Only two, Albania and Ethiopia, still mark January 6 as the birth of Christ rather than Epiphany. Others, such as the Russian Orthodox Church, still use the Julian Calendar to determine holy days, and Christmas in Russia, although December 25 under the Julian Calendar, occurs on January 6 under the Gregorian Calendar.

6. The most explicit Biblical passage says "all kings shall fall down before him: all nations serve him." Psalm 72:10. Not everyone agrees, however, with Catholic doctrine on this point. Early Protestant leader John Calvin, whose followers made it illegal in Scotland, England, and New England to acknowledge Christmas as a holy day, said "the most ridiculous contrivance of the Papists on this subject is, that those men were kings.... Beyond all doubt, they have been stupefied by a righteous judgment of God, that all might laugh at gross ignorance." John Calvin, *Calvin's Commentaries* 31: Matthew, Mark and Luke, Part I, trans. John King, accessed at http://www.sacred-texts.com/chr/calvin/cc31/cc31027.htm.

7. Steven D. Hales, "Putting Claus Back into Christmas," *Christmas—Philosophy for Everyone: Better Than a Lump of Coal* (Malden, MA: Wiley-Blackwell, 2009), 166.

8. Forbes, *Christmas: A Candid History*, 30.

9. *Ibid.*

10. Bowler, *Santa Claus*, 6.

11. Preston, "Putting the 'Yule' Back in 'Yuletide,'" 38.

12. *Ibid.*

13. Bowler, *Santa Claus*, 7.

14. Forbes, *A Candid History*, 27.

15. Gerry Bowler, *The Encyclopedia of Christmas* (Toronto: McClelland & Stewart 2005), 98–99 (hereinafter Bowler, *Encyclopedia of Christmas*).

16. Miles, *Christmas in Ritual and Tradition*, 179.

17. *Ibid.*, 164.

Chapter 5

1. The premise that Yule lasted twelve days is probably not accurate. More likely, historians of the

Christian era projected the Twelve Days of Christmas onto the pagan Yule. Because we don't know the actual length, however, or even whether it was consistent, this book will adopt the twelve-day assumption.

2. Forbes, *Christmas: A Candid History*, 11.

3. *Ibid.*

4. Coffin, *Christmas Folklore*, 5.

5. This is, obviously, a generalization because the loss of daylight depended on the latitude of the nations in question, whereas the nature of the winters depended on latitude, altitude, and proximity to the Atlantic Ocean. The latitude of Berlin (52.5°) is only one degree north of London (51.5°) but London's altitude is close to sea level and it is surrounded by the Atlantic Ocean, giving it a more moderate climate during the winter. The latitude of Oslo, Norway, on the other hand, is almost 60°, meaning that on December 14 in the twelfth century under the Julian calendar the sun would have risen at about 9 a.m. and set at about 3 p.m.

6. Coffin, *Christmas Folklore*, 6–7.

7. McKnight, *St. Nicholas*, 69.

8. Preston, "Putting the 'Yule' Back in 'Yuletide,'" 39.

9. The gift-giving St. Martin also had a post–Reformation version, known as Pelzmartin or Pelzmarte ("Martin in furs") after Protestants prohibited the continuation of St. Martin's Day traditions.

10. Miles, *Christmas in Ritual and Tradition*, 35 (quoting W. R. W. Stephens, *The History of the Church of England* [London 1901], 309).

11. *Ibid.* 73. Der Schimmelreiter is also the name of a novella by German writer Theodor Storm but the figure in the novella is not the Germanic god.

12. Linda Raedisch, *The Old Magic of Christmas: Yuletide Traditions for the Darkest Days of the Year* (Woodbury, MN: Llewellyn, 2013), 75 (hereinafter Raedisch, *The Old Magic of Christmas*).

13. Perchta and Berchta were interchangeable names for the same god, like Odin and Woden. Thus, Perchta's Night and Berchta's Night would have been the same thing.

14. Forbes, *Christmas: A Candid History*, 12.

15. Bowler, *Christmas in the Crosshairs*, 15.

Chapter 6

1. Adam C. English, *The Saint Who Would Be Santa Claus* (Waco: Baylor University Press 2013), 3 (hereinafter English, *The Saint Who Would Be Santa*).

2. Snyder, *December 25*, 209.

3. English, *The Saint Who Would Be Santa*, 31–32.

4. According to Jones, Nicholas "appears on no such list except as a name inserted after the thirteenth century, under the influence of the legend itself." Jones, *St. Nicholas*, 64.

5. English, *The Saint Who Would Be Santa*, 31–32.

6. *Ibid.*

7. *Ibid.* English states that "[t]wo examples of

such problematic accounts" are Joe Wheeler and Jim Rosenthal, *Saint Nicholas: A Closer Look at Christmas* (Nashville: Thomas Nelson, 2005), and William J. Bennett, *The True Saint Nicholas: Why He Matters to Christmas* (New York: Howard Books, 2009). "Both enrich the holiday season with heartwarming tales and fascinating nuggets of trivia. But neither presents the best historical scholarship regarding the person of Nicholas. Instead, they weave together anecdotes—some factual, some fictitious—from a potpourri of sources lifted out of any and every era." English, *The Saint Who Would Be Santa*, 9. Most problematic, Wheeler, Rosenthal, and Bennett rely on the biography written by Symeon Metaphrastes during the tenth century without recognizing the biographer confused the story of St. Nicholas of Myra with the story of another historical figure, St. Nicholas of Sion, who lived two hundred years later.

8. *Ibid.*, 66.

9. Snyder, *December 25*, 210.

10. McKnight, *St. Nicholas*, 38.

11. Wheeler and Rosenthal, *Saint Nicholas*, 93.

12. "Is St. Nicholas in Venice, Too?" *The St. Nicholas Center*, http://www.stnicholascenter.org/pages/relics-in-the-lido-of-venice (accessed October 5, 2017).

13. *Ibid.*

14. *Ibid.*

15. *Ibid.*

16. Sarah Gibbens, "Could the Remains of Santa Claus Be in This Turkish Church?," *National Geographic*, http://news.national-geographic.com/2017/10/santa-claus-st-nicholas-tomb-archaeology-turkey-spd (accessed October 5, 2017).

17. *Ibid.*, 125.

18. Tom Flynn, *The Trouble with Christmas* (Buffalo: Prometheus, 1993), 79 (hereinafter Flynn, *The Trouble with Christmas*).

19. According to the St. Nicholas Center, the list includes archers, armed forces, bakers, bankers, bargemen, barrel makers, boatmen, boot blacks, bottlers, boys, brewers, brides, businessmen, butchers, button-makers, candle makers, captives, chandlers (suppliers of ships), children, choristers, citizens, clergy, clerks, cloth merchants, coopers (barrel-makers), corn measurers and merchants, court recorders, registrars, clerks, dock workers, drapers, druggists, embalmers, the falsely accused, ferrymen, firefighters, fishermen, florists, grain dealers and merchants, grocers, grooms, haberdashers, infants, the infertile, judges, lace makers and sellers, lawsuits lost unjustly, lawyers, linen merchants, longshoremen, lovers, maidens, mariners, merchants, military intelligence, millers, glassmakers, murderers, navigators, newlyweds, notaries, oil merchants, orphans, packers, parish clerks, paupers, pawnbrokers, peddlers, perfumers, pharmacists, pilgrims, pirates, poets, poor people, preachers, prisoners, prostitutes, pupils, rag pickers, ribbon weavers, robbers, schoolchildren, sailors, scholars, sealers, seed merchants, shipwreck victims, shipwrights, ships' carpenters, shoemakers, shoe shiners, shopkeepers, skippers, soldiers, spice dealers, spinsters, students, tanners, teachers, thieves, timber merchants, travelers, the unjustly condemned, unmarried men, unmarried women, virgins, watermen, weavers, wine porters, wine merchants, women desirous of marrying, and wood-turners.

20. English, *The Saint Who Would Be Santa*, 6–7, and Fig. 1.

21. Count, *4000 Years of Christmas*, 63–64.

22. Miles, *Christmas in Ritual and Tradition*, 220.

23. Count, *4000 Years of Christmas*, 63–64.

24. McKnight, *St. Nicholas*, 69. With regard to St. Andrew, McKnight says "[o]n St. Andrew's eve, November 30, in the neighborhood of Reichenberg, children are said to hang up their stockings at the windows, and in the evening find them filled with apples and nuts. The explanation of the origin of these customs is to be found in practices long antedating the time of St. Martin or St. Nicholas, or even of St. Andrew. They seem to be practices rooted in pre–Christian agricultural rites which have been superseded, or better expressed, and have survived with new meanings." *Ibid.*, 23.

25. *Ibid.*, 21–22.

26. Miles, *Christmas in Ritual and Tradition*, 218–19.

27. *Ibid.*

28. Snyder, *December 25*, 210; Wheeler and Rosenthal, *Saint Nicholas*, 145.

29. Jeremy Seal, *Nicholas: The Epic Journey from Saint to Santa Claus* (New York: Bloomsbury, 2005), 152–53 (hereinafter Seal, *Nicholas: The Epic Journey*).

30. McKnight, *St. Nicholas*, 57.

31. Although not credited to Steen, the two children later ended up on the broadsheet engraved by artist Alexander Anderson for the New-York Historical Society in 1810.

32. Snyder, *December 25*, 217.

33. Will Williams, "You'd Better Watch Out," *Christmas—Philosophy for Everyone: Better Than a Lump of Coal* (Malden, MA: Wiley-Blackwell, 2009), 121.

Chapter 7

1. For those not familiar with *The Godfather*, Luca Brasi was a central figure in one of the movie's most memorable scenes in which Michael Corleone tells Kay Adams that "my father went to see this bandleader and offered him $10,000 to let Johnny go, but the bandleader said no. So the next day, my father went back, only this time with Luca Brasi. Within an hour, he had a signed release for a certified check of $1000." Asked how he did it, Michael responds: "My father made him an offer he couldn't refuse. Luca Brasi held a gun to his head, and my father assured him that either his brains or his signature would be on the contract."

2. Ridenour, *The Krampus*, 8.

3. There were a handful of evil helpers who appeared to be human, but wore outfits that symbolized Satan, such as dressing entirely in black.

4. Many histories are internally inconsistent or

never really address the question of when or how the evil helpers arrived.

5. Bowler, *Santa Claus*, 23. Bowler also includes "men clad in fur, straw, and goatskin," which appears to be a reference to the faux Nicholases such as Pelznickel, Ru-Klas and Aschenklas. *Ibid.*

6. *Ibid.*, 24–25. Putting aside the question of when or why the evil helpers arrived, Bowler's discussion begs a couple of other questions. One is the inclusion of Knecht Ruprecht in list of evil helpers. While the early descriptions of Ruprecht show him with horns, in most illustrations he is completely human and, more importantly, travels alone, threatening discipline with his bundle of switches and dispensing treats. That duality would make him a faux Nicholas, not an evil helper, except that he seems to predate the Reformation as a figure from German folklore. The other question is what Bowler means by the "strange metamorphosis suffered by Saint Nicholas." This appears to be a reference to the emergence of the faux Nicholases. If so, it raises again the importance of precision when using the gift-givers' names because St. Nicholas didn't undergo any metamorphosis. Rather, he was shown the back door while a group of faux Nicholases entered the front.

7. Wheeler and Rosenthal, *Saint Nicholas*, 145.

8. Siefker, *Santa Claus*, 68. In "Against the Santa Claus Lie," Johnson explains the evil helpers by saying that "Nicholas was given a sidekick—someone to dole out the punishment for being bad. Krampus, as he was often called, was originally a pagan goat-man fertility god, but the church demoted him to 'Santa-Sidekick' to prevent pagan converts from continuing to worship him." David Kyle Johnson, "Against the Santa Claus Lie," 140.

9. *Ibid.*, 71.

10. Oswald A. Erich and Richard Beitl, *Worterbuch der Deutschen Volkskunde* "Handbook of German Folklore" (Stuttgardt: Alfred Kroner, 1974).

11. *Ibid.*, 600. The character Shrek, an ogre in a 1990 picture book, *Shrek*, by William Steig and a series of animated films by the same name, presumably owes his name to the German word Schreck.

12. In *Knecht Ruprecht und Seine Genossen* ("Knecht Ruprecht and His Comrades"), a transcript of a speech by German professor Franz Weineck published in 1898, Weineck divides the German gift-givers and helpers into three categories based on Germany mythology: a light group headed by Odin and Nicholas, a female group, and a dark group headed by Donar ("Thor"). Franz Weineck, *Knecht Ruprecht und Seine Genossen* (Niederlausitz, Germany: Albert Koenig, 1898) (translated for the author by Jana Mader, Professor of German, University of North Carolina at Asheville) (hereinafter "Weineck, *Knecht Ruprecht*"). The dark group includes most of the Schreckgestalten: Ruprecht, Pelzmärtel, Märte, Bartel, Krampus, Klaubauf, Putenmandl, Schmutzl, Hans Trapp, Rüpelz, Schandeklôs, Sunnerklaus and the Erbsbär, and Donar with the "Bock" (goat) as Klabberbock, Schnabbuk, Ziege, Habersack, Habergeiß.

13. Val R. Berryman, "Christmas in Germany: Krampus, a Beastly Traveling Companion," *The Glow* 22, no. 5 (October 2001), 13–17.

14. Krampus has not been completely successful in establishing a positive public image. The Saint Nicholas Center, a website devoted to protecting the history and reputation of the saint, says "St. Nicholas Center joins with the St. Nicholas Society, taking a position that does not condone nor wish to perpetuate in any way customs that include characters with a dark side, such as the horrific Austrian Krampus, as we encourage the St. Nicholas tradition and its revival in our time. We abhor the imagery of these characters and hope that St. Nicholas will be accompanied by necessary helpers needed for practical reasons, but that the helpers have no significance in the overall celebration…. St Nicholas is a symbol of good and good alone. He does not need, and should not have, violent and frightening sidekicks for comparison." St. Nicholas Center, "Who Travels with St. Nicholas," https://www.stnicholascenter.org/pages/who-travels-with-st-nicholas (accessed February 5, 2017). As explained earlier, it is because St. Nicholas is "good and good alone" that he acquired an evil helper, but the St. Nicholas Center's disavowal of Krampus and company is not surprising.

15. Ridenour, *The Krampus*, 11–12.

16. *Ibid.*

17. *Krampus* (2015); *A Christmas Horror Story* (2015); *Krampus: The Reckoning* (2015); and *Krampus: The Christmas Devil* (2013).

18. Ridenour, *The Krampus*; Michael Mallory, *Art of Krampus* (Insight Editions, 2015); Michael Dougherty, *Krampus: Shadow of Saint Nicholas* (Legendary Comics, 2015); Gerald Brom, *Krampus: The Yule Lord* (New York: Harper Voyager, 2012); Monte Beauchamp, *Krampus: The Devil of Christmas* (San Francisco: Last Gasp of San Francisco, 2010).

19. Val R. Berryman, "Christmas in Czechoslovakia: Angel, Saint and Devil," *The Glow* 27, no. 5 (October 2006), 15–19, 15.

Chapter 8

1. Miles, *Christmas in Ritual and Tradition*, 230.

2. *Ibid.*

3. Eric W. Gritsch, *The History of Lutheranism* (Minneapolis: Fortress Press, 2002), 45–48.

4. Lutheranism remains the most common religion in northern Germany today, but the percentage of adherents is much smaller than it was a few centuries ago—a foreseeable consequence, perhaps, of the blatant attack on religion by the Nazi regime and the Communist government of East Germany during the twentieth century. In Germany as a whole, about a third of the current population is Lutheran, a third is Catholic, and a third do not align themselves with any organized religion. In the former East Germany, which had an official policy of atheism under two different governments over a period of forty-five years, about 70 percent of the population currently does not identify with any religion. In the former West Germany, where the Nazi policy of atheism

ended in 1945, the population currently is split between Protestants and Catholics along the same north-south divide that has existed since the sixteenth century.

5. Val R. Berryman, "Christmas in Germany: Christkindl, the Christmas Child of Germany," *The Glow* 22, no. 5 (December 2001), 8–12.

6. Snyder, *December 25*, 211.

7. Oswald A. Erich and Richard Beitl, *Worterbuch der Deutschen Volkskunde* (Stuttgardt: Alfred Kroner, 1974), 600.

8. *Ibid.*, 212.

9. *Ibid.*

10. In his 1978 history of St. Nicholas, historian Charles W. Jones, seeking to defend his 1954 pronouncement that "Santa Claus was made by Washington Irving," questions the veracity of artist Thomas Nast's statement that he based his image of Santa Claus on his boyhood in Germany where a neighbor dressed as Pelznickel handed out sweets. Jones stated there was no evidence of Pelznickel in the Palatinate region of Germany where Nast was born, and, in any event, Pelznickel "as a derivative of the devil…. was normally horned and tailed." Jones, *St. Nicholas*, 355.

11. See Richard Hancuff and Noreen O'Connor, "Making a List, Checking It Twice: The Santa Claus Surveillance System," *Christmas—Philosophy for Everyone: Better Than a Lump of Coal* (Malden, MA: Wiley-Blackwell, 2009); Will Williams, "You'd Better Watch Out."

Chapter 9

1. Jacob Grimm, *Teutonic Mythology* (1835), translated by James Steven Stallybrass (London: Cambridge University Press, 2012) (hereinafter Grimm, *Teutonic Mythology*). Grimm was also one of the two brothers known for having compiled the German folklore that became known as Grimm's Fairy Tales.

2. Weineck, *Knecht Ruprecht*, 1–2.

3. Tille, *Yule and Christmas*, 82.

4. Miles, *Christmas in Ritual and Tradition*, 230–32.

5. McKnight, *St. Nicholas*, 24–25.

6. *Ibid.*

7. Raedisch, *The Old Magic of Christmas*, 82.

8. Grimm, *Teutonic Mythology*, Vol. II, 504, 514–15; Vol. III, 936–37.

9. Grimm, *Teutonic Mythology*, Vol. II, 117.

10. Weineck, *Knecht Ruprecht*, 38.

11. *Ibid.*

12. Tille, *Yule and Christmas*, 117.

13. *Ibid.*, 82.

14. Grimm, *Teutonic Mythology*, Vol. II, 504, 514–15; Vol. III, 936–37.

15. "Berhta," Behind the Name, http://www.behindthename.com/name/berhta (citing Ernst Förstemann, *Altdeutsches namenbuch*, 281 [1900]).

16. McKnight, *St. Nicholas*, 16–17.

17. *Ibid.* McKnight also says, "[n]ot infrequently

his relation to the Christmas festival proper needs to be made clear by the presence of the Holy Christ as a companion, represented by a maiden in white garb who hears the children say their prayers." *Ibid.* McKnight's reference to Holy Christ presumably means the same thing as the Christ child or Christkindl.

18. Ridenour, *The Krampus*, 15.

19. Raedisch, *The Old Magic of Christmas*, 81–82.

20. See Martina Eberspächer, *Der Weihnachtsmann: Zur Entstehung einer Bildtradition in Aufklärung und Romantik*, "Katalog" (Norderstedt: Books on Demand, 2002), 260–377.

21. "Christmas Throughout Christendom," 246.

22. Coffin, *Christmas Folklore*, 83.

23. Miles, *Christmas in Ritual and Tradition*, 232.

24. Val R. Berryman, "Christmas in Germany: Der Weihnachtsmann and Knecht Ruprecht," *The Glow* 23, no. 3 (June 2002), 9–12, 10.

25. Siefker, *Santa Claus*, 157.

26. Gulevich, *Encyclopedia of Christmas*, 325–29.

27. *Ibid.*

28. Grimm, *Teutonic Mythology*, Vol. II, 504, 514–15; Vol. III, 936–37.

29. Weineck, *Knecht Ruprecht*, 2.

30. Spencer, "Christmas Through Christendom," 249.

31. *Ibid.*

32. *The Merriam-Webster Dictionary* (2005).

33. Weineck, *Knecht Ruprecht*, 1.

34. *Ibid.*, 2.

35. Weineck does not tell us which of the Nicholas figures wear bishop's garb, which would make them St. Nicholas with a nickname, and which wear the clothing of a faux Nicholas. For some, such as Aschenklas, we know their appearance from other sources but for most we do not.

36. *Ibid.*, 55–56.

37. *Ibid.*, 16.

38. *Ibid.*, 22–23.

39. *Ibid.*, 49.

Chapter 10

1. Coffin, *Christmas Folklore*, 7.

2. Val R. Berryman, "Christmas in Germany: Saint Nikolaus, Bringer of Gift or Grief," *The Glow* 22, no. 4 (August 2001), 12–15 (emphasis in original).

3. *Ibid.*, 13.

4. The Belsnickle customs documented by Shoemaker in *Christmas in Pennsylvania* reveal that much of the comingling among different characters was actually the product of mixing young men, dirty old hats and coats, false beards, charcoal, and lots of beer on December evenings when there was not much else to do in rural Pennsylvania or, likely, rural Germany. After donning the costumes, the young men—and, presumably, an occasional young woman—go house to house, announcing themselves as a Christmas character or one of the local versions of the faux Nicholases, and scare the daylights out of the younger children.

5. "German Christmas Traditions," Vistawide World Languages & Cultures, http://www.vistawide.com/german/christmas/german_christmas_traditions.html (accessed February 20, 2017). If the children passed muster, the helper would frequently throw gifts of fruit, candy, and nuts on the floor, forcing the children to scramble for them.

6. Val R. Berryman, "Christmas in Germany: Saint Nikolaus, Bringer of Gift or Grief," *The Glow* 22, no. 4 (August 2001), 12–15, 13.

7. *Ibid.*, 164. For example, in Holland the Dutch Reformed Church in 1570 took a much harder line against the celebration of St. Nicholas' Day than the Lutheran Church in Germany, making celebration of St. Nicholas' Day punishable by law and prompting the creation of Sinterklaas, whose sole reason for existence was that he was not St. Nicholas. By 1850, however, apparently no one was concerned Jan Schenkman had written a children's book about "Sint Nikolaas" rather than Sinterklaas.

8. Raedisch, *The Old Magic of Christmas*, 88.

9. Miles, *Christmas in Ritual and Tradition*, 229–30.

10. O.M. Spencer, "Christmas Throughout Christendom," *Harper's New Monthly Magazine* XLVI, no. 292 (January 1873), 241 (hereinafter Spencer, "Christmas Throughout Christendom").

11. *Ibid.*, 246.

12. *Ibid.*

13. Val R. Berryman, "Christmas in Germany: Christkindl, the Christmas Child of Germany," *The Glow* 22, no. 5 (December 2001), 8–12, 8.

14. One may accept the explanation for not using an infant, but the use of a young woman as Christ's representative displays a long-standing form of sexism in which girls have always been deemed more "angelic" than boys, and racism, in which blond girls of Germanic heritage have always been seen as more angelic than those with darker skin or hair.

15. Sarah Brunner, "Santa Claus: A Transformation Through the Centuries," *The Glow* 34, no. 6 (December 2013), 6–8.

16. *Ibid.*, 7.

17. *King Winter* (Hamburg: Gustav W. Seitz, 1859).

18. *Ibid.*, 16.

19. Melicent Sammis, *The Art of the Lampworked Santa: A Pictorial Guide for Collecting Antique Blown Glass Santa Christmas Ornaments* (York, PA: Shuman Heritage Press, 2010).

20. Don Waring, *Memories of Santa Collection* (New York: Christmas Reproductions, 1992), 16. This illustration of Weihnachtsmann with a classic Belsnickle look was taken from an 1870 chocolate mold catalogue by Anton Reiche, Dresden, Germany.

21. Scott Tagliapietra, "Collecting Belsnickles," *The Glow* 28, no. 3 (June 2007), 7–10.

22. Val R. Berryman, "Christmas in Germany: The German Santa, Der Weihnachtsmann," *The Glow* 23, no. 2 (April 2002), 8–10, 8.

23. One caveat: Although most recent sources identify Weihnachtsmann as the most prominent gift-giver in Germany, the 1974 handbook of German folklore, *Worterbuch der Deutscchen Volkskunde*, contains a map showing the regions served by the various German "gabenbringers in der Nikolauszeit." *Ibid.*, 600. In that map, Der Weihnachtsmann is shown as the most prominent gift-giver in traditionally Protestant northern Germany, Nickel is shown as the most common gift-giver in southeastern Germany, and Klaus and Niglo are shown as the most common gift-givers in traditionally Catholic central and southern Germany, respectively.

24. Raedisch, *The Old Magic of Christmas*, 81.

25. Theodore Storm, "Knecht Ruprecht," http://www.theodorstorm.co.uk/Life/knechtRuprecht.htm.

26. Raedisch, *The Old Magic of Christmas*, 81.

27. Kuni Porsche and Peter Daniell Porsche, *Sankt Nikolaus und Knecht Ruprecht* (Salzburg: Kulturverlag Polzer, 2010).

28. Gulevich, *Encyclopedia of Christmas*, 81.

Chapter 11

1. Connelly, *Christmas, A History*, 32.

2. Sandys, *Christmastide*, 17.

3. *Ibid.*

4. J.A.R. Pimlott, *The Englishman's Christmas: A Social History* (Sussex: Harvester Press, 1978), 22 (hereinafter Pimlott, *The Englishman's Christmas*).

5. *Ibid.*, 21.

6. *Ibid.*, 20.

7. *Ibid.*

8. *Ibid.*

9. *Ibid.*, 21.

10. Bowler, *Christmas in the Crosshairs*, 27.

11. Sandys, *Christmastide*, 99.

12. *Ibid.*, 101.

13. Frodsham, *From Stonehenge to Santa*, 119.

14. Wheeler and Rosenthal, *St. Nicholas*, 149.

15. Pimlott, *The Englishman's Christmas*, 111; Bowler, *Encyclopedia of Christmas*, 81.

16. Ronald Hutton, *The Stations of the Sun* (New York: Oxford University Press, 1996), 117.

17. Frodsham, *From Stonehenge to Santa*, 143–44.

18. Chris Durston, "The Puritan War on Christmas," *History Today* (December 1985), 31.

19. *The Vindication of Christmas or, His Twelve Yeares' Observations upon the Times* (London: G. Horton, 1653).

20. This does not count the images of St. Nicholas in his role as saint rather than gift-giver. The first depictions of St. Nicholas in his role as gift-giver are from 1750.

21. Not surprisingly, Cromwell was hated by both Catholics and royalists. After Charles II came to power, Cromwell's opponents dug up his corpse from its grave in Westminster Abbey, hanged his body in chains, and beheaded him.

22. Josiah King, *The Examination and Tryal of Old Father Christmas* (London: Thomas Johnson, 1658).

23. *Ibid.*

24. *Ibid.*

25. Pimlott, *The Englishman's Christmas*, 112.

26. *Ibid.*

27. Charles Dickens, *A Christmas Carol* (London: Chapman & Hall, 1843).

28. *Godey's Lady's Book* (December 1850).

29. Nissenbaum, *The Battle for Christmas*, 52–65.

30. Golby and Purdue, *The Making of the Modern Christmas*, 18–19.

31. Sandys, *Christmastide*, 174.

32. Restad, *Christmas in America*, 10–13.

33. Connelly, *Christmas, A History*, 1–3.

34. *Ibid.*, 26–27.

35. To those who do not recognize the reference to Tom Smith's Christmas Crackers, Dawson provides an explanation: "One of the popular institutions inseparable from the festivities of Christmastide has long been the 'cracker.' The satisfaction which young people especially experience in pulling the opposite ends of a gelatin and paper cylinder is of the keenest, accompanied as the operation is by a mixed anticipation—half fearful as to the explosion that is to follow, and wholly delightful with regard to the bonbon or motto which will thus be brought to light. Much amusement is afforded to the lads and lassies by the fortune-telling verses which some of the crackers contain." Dawson, *Christmas: Its Origins and Associations*, 309. The inventor and primary promoter of Christmas crackers was a man named Tom Smith, and, although the quality of the gift inside has dropped enormously, Christmas crackers are still sold today under his name.

36. Flynn, *The Trouble with Christmas*, 88–89.

37. Golby and Purdue, *The Making of the Modern Christmas*, 51.

38. Walter Scott, *Marmion*, Introduction to Canto Sixth.

39. Washington Irving, "Old Christmas," *The Sketchbook of Geoffrey Crayon, Gent.* (New York: C.S. Van Winkle, 1819–20).

40. Thomas K. Hervey, *The Book of Christmas* (London: 1836).

41. Charles Dickens, *The Pickwick Papers* (London, 1836). Father Christmas illustrator Robert Seymour was the original illustrator for *The Pickwick Papers*, but his interaction with Charles Dickens had an unfortunate ending. Seymour reportedly came up with the idea for *The Pickwick Papers*, a serious of short stories based on Seymour's illustrations, and arranged for a publisher to hire Dickens, then only 22, to write the story. The two ran into what might be called artistic differences, however, and the project bogged down. On April 30, 1836, after working on the illustrations for several hours, Seymour, then 38, killed himself with a shotgun blast. Dickens finished the book with another illustrator and later disputed that Seymour made any important contribution to the final work.

42. *London Illustrated News* (December 24, 1842), 1.

43. To use an example more accessible to twenty-first-century readers, if someone were to publish a short novel extolling the virtues of the American holiday known as Flag Day, June 14, ending with the line "she knew how to keep Flag Day well," it would not generate much enthusiasm because virtually no one remembers, much less celebrates, Flag Day. Plainly, that was not the case with Christmas in 1843.

44. Connelly, *Christmas, A History*, Preface to the paperback edition, x.

45. *Illustrated London News* (December 1842), 1.

46. Pimlott, *The Englishman's Christmas*, 117–18.

47. Susan Warner, *Karl Krinken, His Christmas Stocking* (London: James Nisbet, 1853).

48. Pimlott, *The Englishman's Christmas*, 117–18.

Chapter 12

1. Bowler, *Santa Claus*, 28.

2. *Ibid.*

3. The religious views of the Dutch in the sixteenth century have long since disappeared. In 2004, when the Dutch Reformed Church merged with the two other Protestant denominations to create the Protestant Church of the Netherlands, fewer than 9 percent of the citizens were members of the church. Two-thirds of the citizens do not identify with any religion at all.

4. Val R. Berryman, "Christmas in Holland: Sint Nicolaas and Sinterklaas," *The Glow* 25, no. 5 (October 2004), 10–21, 10.

5. Val R. Berryman, "Christmas in Holland: Saint Nicolaas Day is for the Children," *The Glow* 25, no. 6 (December 2004), 9–12.

6. Val R. Berryman, "Christmas in Holland: Sint Nicolaas and Sinterklaas," *The Glow* 25, no. 5 (October 2004), 10–21, 21.

7. St. Nicholas Center, "Who Travels with St. Nicholas," https://www.stnicholascenter.org/pages/who-travels-with-st-nicholas (accessed February 5, 2017).

Chapter 13

1. The midwinter celebrations in Germanic, Nordic, and Celtic regions were all called Yule, and the name lives on as Yule in English and Jul in Scandinavia. In discussing Scandinavian traditions, the term Jul is more appropriate but for purposes of consistency Yule is used here throughout.

2. Coincidentally or not, one of the earliest descriptions of the figure who became the American Santa Claus, the St. Nick of Clement Moore's 1822 poem, "The Night Before Christmas," was characterized as a "jolly old elf" who rode in a "miniature sleigh" with tiny reindeer. In translating that to paper in 1866, political cartoonist Thomas Nast drew Santa as somewhere between two and three feet tall, depending on the illustration. Thus, when Nystrom first began drawing the nisse in 1871, the Julnisse were about the same height as Nast's Santa. Over the next two decades, both groups experienced a growth spurt.

3. Val R. Berryman, "Christmas in Scandinavia: The Swedish Saint Lucia," *The Glow* 26, no. 3 (June 2005), 9–12.

4. *Ibid.* It is not clear whether Berryman is refer-

ring to the Julian calendar or an earlier calendar used by the Scandinavians. Under the Julian calendar, the Winter Solstice would have occurred on December 13 in approximately the twelfth century. Such precision on the date of the solstice was likely unnecessary in Sweden, however, because the Winter Solstice would have eliminated all but a few hours of dim light for several weeks.

5. *Ibid.*, 10.

Chapter 14

1. Miles, *Christmas in Ritual and Tradition*, 221.
2. Val R. Berryman, "Christmas in France: Good Saint Nicholas," *The Glow* 25, no. 1 (February 2004), 8–10, 19.
3. "The Greek Orthodox Archdiocese of America," http://www.goarch.org/archdiocese/about (accessed January 15, 2017).

Chapter 15

1. East Germany, Poland, Hungary, and the Czech and Slovak Republics, then a single nation known as Czechoslovakia, were also under Soviet control between World War II and 1990, but those nations were discussed earlier as part of Germany and central Europe because they are more aligned with that region as a matter of religion (primarily Catholicism) and ethnic origin (a mix of Germanic and Slavic) because interacted more with Germany than with Russia.
2. This concededly cursory overview is meant to provide context for those not familiar with the history of Russia. For those interested in a detailed description, see Catherine Evtuhov, David Goldfrank, Lindsey Hughes, and Richard Stites, *A History of Russia: People, Legends, Events, Forces* (New York: Houghton Mifflin, 2004).
3. Linda J. Ivanits, *Russian Folk Beliefs* (New York: M.E. Sharpe, 1989), 12–13 (hereinafter Ivanits, *Russian Folk Beliefs*). In writing about Russian folk beliefs in English, the absence of reliable records is exacerbated by the absence of a common alphabet, leaving many of the Russian names—in some cases, the most important information available—subject to multiple English spellings that create great potential for confusion about the Slavic gods.
4. Natalie Kononenko, *Slavic Folklore: A Handbook* (Westport, CT: Greenwood Press, 2007), 7–8.
5. *Ibid.* 8–11.
6. *Ibid.*
7. *Ibid.* Ivanits, *Russian Folk Beliefs*, 12–13.
8. Ivanits, *Russian Folk Beliefs*, 12–13; Dawson, *Christmas, Its Origin and Associations*, 342–44.
9. Although there is more information available on the celebration of Christmas in Russia since Christianity arrived, even then the amount of information pales when compared to other European nations. Not only are comprehensive English textbooks on the history of Russia silent on the subject, the information source of last resort—Wikipedia—is empty as well.

In its entry on "Christmas in Russia," the subheading of "History" consists of exactly three sentences. The first sentence states Vladimir the Great adopted the Eastern Orthodox religion in 987. The second and third sentences describe the actions taken by Soviet leader Stalin in 1935 to establish a New Year's holiday that served as a pseudo-Christmas celebration. In other words, despite the title History of Christmas in Russia, there is no mention of anything that occurred between 987 (Russian adopted Christianity) and 1935 (Stalin took over).

10. Dawson, *Christmas, Its Origin and Associations*, 342–44.
11. *Ibid.*
12. *Ibid.*
13. *Ibid.*
14. Miles, *Christmas in Ritual and Tradition*, 237–38.
15. *Ibid.*
16. Val R. Berryman, "Christmas in Russia: Saint Nicholas and Grandfather Frost," *The Glow* 26, no. 4 (August 2005), 9–13; Val R. Berryman, "Christmas in Russia, Grandfather Frost and the Snow Maiden," *The Glow* 26, no. 5 (October 2005), 11–14; Val R. Berryman, "Christmas in Russia, Part One," *The Glow* 26, no. 6 (December 2005), 13–21; Val R. Berryman, "Christmas in Russia: Decorations Old and New," *The Glow* 27, no. 2 (April 2006), 11–15.
17. In the *World Encyclopedia of Christmas*, Bowler adds a fifth Russian gift-giver, Kolyada. Bowler, *Encyclopedia of Christmas*, 195. Berryman would probably not dispute that Kolyada was an important figure in the Russian Christmas rituals and beliefs prior to the Revolution, but she does not appear to be a gift-giver as such.
18. Val R. Berryman, "Christmas in Russia: Decorations Old and New," *The Glow* 27, no. 2 (April 2006), 11–15, 11.
19. Val R. Berryman, "Christmas in Russia: Saint Nicholas and Grandfather Frost," *The Glow* 26, no. 4 (August 2005), 9–13; 12–13.
20. Bowler, *Encyclopedia of Christmas*, 195.
21. *Ibid.*
22. "Of Russian Origin: Ded Moroz," Russipedia, RT.com, http://russiapedia.rt.com/of-russian-origin/ded-moroz/ (March 20, 2017). Russia Today, or RT.com, is the official, state-sponsored news agency of the Russian government. This does not necessarily undermine its credibility on subjects like the celebration of Christmas, but one always has to be cautious about relying on internet websites that have a distinct political viewpoint.
23. *Ibid.*
24. Dawson, *Christmas and Its Origins and Associations*, 343.
25. *Ibid.*
26. *Ibid.*
27. "Of Russian Origin: Ded Moroz," Russipedia, RT.com, http://russiapedia.rt.com/of-russian-origin/ded-moroz/ (March 20, 2017).
28. Val R. Berryman, "Christmas in Russia, Grandfather Frost and the Snow Maiden," *The Glow* 26, no. 5 (October 2005), 11–14.

29. *Ibid.*, 12.
30. *Ibid.*
31. Leo Tolstoy, *War and Peace* (1859) (London: Centaur Classics Edition, 2016) (hereinafter Tolstoy, *War and Peace*).
32. *Ibid.*, 276.

Chapter 16

1. Barnett, *The American Christmas*, 2–14; Restad, *Christmas in America*, passim.
2. Barnett, *The American Christmas*, 2. The First Baptist Church in America was founded by Roger Williams in 1638 in Providence, R.I. In modern America, there are a number of diverse groups with different practices and beliefs that refer to themselves as Baptists, and many of them opposed Christmas as well. For example, the largest Baptist group, the Southern Baptist Convention, strongly opposed the celebration of Christmas when it was founded in 1845 but by the twentieth century had become a proponent of the holiday.
3. Barnett, *The American Christmas*, 2.
4. *Ibid.*, 3.
5. *Ibid.*
6. *Ibid.*, 6.
7. *Ibid.*
8. *Ibid.*, 25; Restad, *Christmas in America*, 25; Krythe, *All About Christmas*, 8.
9. Restad, *Christmas in America*, 94–96.
10. Barnett, *The American Christmas*, 130.
11. The Society of Friends, or Quakers, who settled in Pennsylvania, did not celebrate Christmas but, unlike the Puritans, did not seek to impose their views on others.
12. Val R. Berryman, "Christmas in America: Santa Claus Comes to America, The Dutch-American St. Nicholas," *The Glow* 28, No. 2 (April 2007), 11–14, 11.
13. Barnett, *An American Christmas*, 10.
14. Restad, *Christmas in America*, 33.
15. Alfred L. Shoemaker, *Christmas in Pennsylvania: A Folk-Cultural Study* (Kutztown: Pennsylvania Folklore Society, 1959) (hereinafter Shoemaker, *Christmas in Pennsylvania*).
16. Val R. Berryman, "Christmas in America: Santa Claus Comes to America, The German-American Kriss Kringle," *The Glow* 28, no. 2 (April 2007), 11–14.
17. *Kriss Kringle's Book* (Philadelphia: Thomas, Cowperthwaite, 1842).
18. *Kriss Kringle's Christmas Tree* (Philadelphia: E. Ferret, 1845) (hereinafter *Kriss Kringle's Christmas Tree*).
19. *Kriss Kringle's Raree Show, for Good Boys and Girls* (New York: William H. Murphy, 1847) (hereinafter *Kriss Kringle's Raree Show*).
20. *Notes and Queries* 8 (217), (December 24, 1853), 615.
21. Val R. Berryman, "Christmas in America: Santa Claus Comes to America, More German-American Christmas Connections," *The Glow* 28, no. 4 (August 2007), 7–12, 7, 9.
22. *Kriss Kringle's Raree Show*, cover and overleaf illustrations.
23. Val R. Berryman, "Christmas in America: Santa Claus Comes to America, The German-American Kriss Kringle," *The Glow* 28, No. 2 (April 2007), 11–14, 12.
24. Shoemaker, *Christmas in Pennsylvania*, 100–17.
25. Shoemaker's book includes an example of this outfit based on descriptions provided by various witnesses. *Ibid.*
26. *Ibid.*
27. Krythe, *All About Christmas*, 9.
28. *Ibid.*
29. Three books that provide extended discussions of Christmas on the American plantations are Patricia C. McKissack and Frederick McKissack, *Christmas In the Big House, Christmas In The Quarters* (New York: Scholastic, 1994); Nissenbaum, *The Battle for Christmas*; and Restad, *Christmas in America*.

Chapter 17

1. A list of the significant books and scholarly papers that rely on Jones' work is set forth in Chapter 2, note 6.
2. Charles W. Jones, "Knickerbocker Santa Claus," *New-York Historical Society Quarterly* 38 (1954), 356–83.
3. Charles W. Jones, *Saint Nicholas of Myra, Bari, and Manhattan: Biography of a Legend* (Chicago: University of Chicago Press, 1978).
4. Jones, *Saint Nicholas*, 328.
5. *Ibid.*, 345. In reaching the conclusion that Irving "made Santa Claus," Jones conflated Santa Claus and St. Nicholas, assuming there was no question that Santa Claus was another name for St. Nicholas, as depicted by Clement C. Moore in "The Night Before Christmas."
6. Jones, "Knickerbocker Santa Claus," 376.
7. Mary L. Booth, *History of the City of New York from its Earliest Settlement to the Present Time* (New York: W. R. C. Clark & Meeker, 1859).
8. Jones, *St. Nicholas,* 345 (quoting Chauncey Depew, *Address at the Semi centennial of the St. Nicholas Society* [February 28, 1885]).
9. Wheeler and Rosenthal, *Saint Nicholas*, 170.
10. England, *St. Nicholas*, 11.
11. While a handful of historians have expressed disagreement with Jones' ultimate conclusion that "Santa Claus was made by Washington Irving," none of them observed that Jones' analysis was based on the wrong edition of *History of New York.*
12. The style has been mastered by director Christopher Guess and a company of actors in a series of films such as *This is Spinal Tap* (1984), *Best of Show* (2000) and *A Mighty Wind* (2003). The key to its success is that the story, filmed as if it were a documentary, is just close enough to reality that it is *almost* believable and just far enough away that one has to laugh.

13. Mary L. Booth, *History of the City of New York from its Earliest Settlement to the Present Time* (New York: W. R. C. Clark & Meeker, 1859).

14. Irving's running joke about his low regard for the Dutch and their fascination with St. Nicholas first appeared in *Salmagundi*, the humor magazine Irving and his brother and cousin started in January 1807. In January 1808, *Salmagundi* published a squib about a cookie that on one side contained an image of "the noted St. Nicholas, vulgarly called Santeclaus:—of all the saints on the calendar the most venerated by true Hollanders, and their unsophisticated descendants." Jones, *St. Nicholas*, 342. No one has located a prior reference in America to "Santeclaus," nor is it clear what Irving meant by his enigmatic comments about St. Nicholas and the name Santeclaus.

15. *Ibid.*, 328–45. Insofar as it actually mattered whether the Dutch residents of New York observed the traditions of Holland, focusing on public records would have led Jones astray. Restad, for example, reported that newspapers paid little attention to Christmas in the early nineteenth century, but private diaries from the same period show Christmas was being celebrated. Restad, *Christmas in America*, 24. Jones ignored one potentially important clue in the press prior to 1809, Irving's use of the name "Santeclaus" in the January 1808 edition of *Salmagundi*, and the even more important discussion in *False Stories Corrected* in 1813 of children believing in "Santaclaw."

16. As Bowler suggests in *Christmas in the Crosshairs*, the numerous oral variations of Santa Claus in the early nineteenth century, which included Santa-claw, Sandy-claw, Sante Claus and Santaclaw, "speaks to a long-standing oral transmission of the legend of a Christmas Gift-Bringer rather than, as some have suggested, the outright invention of Santa Claus by the Knickerbocker literary clique." Bowler, *Christmas in the Crosshairs*, 50. As far as can be determined, Jones made no effort to interpret Irving's reference to "Santeclaus" or to determine whether the legend of Santa Claus was being spread through oral tradition.

17. Jones, *Saint Nicholas*, 345.

18. *Ibid.*

19. Jones, "Knickerbocker Santa Claus," 374. In his 1978 book *St. Nicholas*, Jones writes that "Santa Claus was a local joke with an anti-British sting until 1809. After 1809 the spritely SC spread like a plague." Jones, *St. Nicholas*, 345. Based on this statement, one must conclude that Jones was aware of a figure named Santa Claus in New York prior to 1809, a fact that is not only inconsistent with his 1954 paper but required an explanation of why, or why not, that "local joke with an anti-British sting" was more likely to have developed into the legend of Santa Claus than John Pintard's broadside and a poem about St. Nicholas in the *New York Spectator*.

20. Jones, "Knickerbocker Santa Claus," 375. While we know now from Scott Norsworthy that St. Nicholas poems were published in two other New York newspapers within a day or two of the *Spectator* poem. Scott Norsworthy, "Verse Paraphrase of the Dutch Hymn to Saint Nicholas, 1810," *Melvilliana* (March 10, 2018), https://melvilliana.blogspot.com/search?q=sancte+claus (viewed November 15, 2018), that does not undermine Jones' argument because the two additional poems arguably show an even greater interest.

21. Another theory the reader might encounter is that the passages cited by Jones as evidence that Irving "made" Santa Claus first appeared in the 1821 edition of *A History of New York*, prompting Clement Moore to write "The Night Before Christmas" in 1822. This argument, which acknowledges the passages were not in the 1809 edition but still gives credit to Irving for having started the Santa ball rolling, appears on page 41 in Jock Elliott, *Inventing Christmas: How Our Holiday Came to Be* (New York: Harry N. Abrams, 2001), a book by a well-known collector of Christmas books, including the first editions of Irving's history and a handwritten copy of Moore's poem, and in Seth Kaller, "The Authorship of the Night Before Christmas, sethkaller.com, https://www. sethkaller. com/about/educational/tnbc/ (accessed March 16, 2017). Kaller is a rare book dealer in New York and Elliott, chief executive of a large Madison Avenue advertising firm, was a rare book buyer. Elliott and Kaller concluded that the passages first appeared in the 1821 edition because Elliott owned originals of every edition of Irving's *History* except the 1812 edition, and using his own personal library observed that the passages were not in the 1809 edition but were in the 1821 edition. This explanation can be confirmed by the fact that the catalogue prepared by Sotheby's for an auction of Elliott's collection in 2006 lists original copies of the 1809, 1821, and 1824 editions of *A History of New York*, but not the 1812 edition Sotheby's, *The Christmas Collection of Jock Elliott* (New York, December 12, 2006).

22. The two children were clearly copied from a 1668 painting, *The Feast of St Nicholas*, by Dutch master Jan Havicksz Steen.

23. Jones, *St. Nicholas*, 341–42 and n. 16.

24. *New York Commercial Advertiser* (December 12, 1810); Norsworthy, "Dutch Hymn to Saint Nicholas."

25. *New York Evening Post* (December 14, 1810).

26. *New York Spectator* (December 15, 1810).

27. Nissenbaum, *The Battle for Christmas*, 63–65; Seal, *Nicholas: The Epic Journey*, 179–82; Andrew Burstein, *The Original Knickerbocker: The Life of Irving Washington* (New York: Basic Books, 2007), 142–43 (hereinafter Burstein, *The Original Knickerbocker*).

28. Andrew B. Myers, editor, *The Knickerbocker Tradition: Washington Irving's New York* (Tarrytown, NY: Sleepy Hollow Restorations, 1974); Johanna Johnston, *The Heart That Would Not Hold: A Biography of Washington Irving* (New York: M. Evan, 1971); William L. Hedges, *Washington Irving: An American Study, 1802–32* (Baltimore, MD: Johns Hopkins Press, 1963); Walter A. Reichart, *Washington Irving and Germany* (Ann Arbor, MI: Univ. of Michigan Press, 1957); George S. Hellman, *Washington Irving Esquire* (New York: Alfred A. Knopf,

1925). Given that standard practice for biographers would be to review Irving's personal files and correspondence, one must assume there is nothing in those documents that led the pre–1978 biographers to conclude Irving had some plan to promote the career of St Nicholas.

29. Burstein, *The Original Knickerbocker*, 142–43.
30. *Ibid.*
31. Barnett, *The American Christmas, 25.*
32. *Ibid.*
33. *Ibid.* 4.
34. Berryman, "Christmas in America: Santa Claus Comes to America, The Dutch-American St. Nicholas," *The Glow*, Vol. 28, No. 2 (April 2007), 11–14.
35. Funk, Elisabeth Paling, "From Amsterdam to New Amsterdam: Washington Irving, the Dutch St. Nicholas, and the American Santa Claus," New Netherland Institute, *Explorers, Fortunes and Love Letters: A History of New Netherland* (Albany, N.Y.: SUNY Press, 2010) (hereinafter Funk, "From Amsterdam to New Amsterdam").
36. Funk observes that "[g]iven his solid entrenchment by that time in Dutch domestic life and the general tenacity of Dutch customs in the area of the former colony, the secular Nicholas undoubtedly continued being celebrated on the feast day of the legendary bishop to whom he owed his existence." Funk, "From Amsterdam to New Amsterdam," 106.
37. *Ibid.* 107.
38. *Ibid.* 106–07, n.16.
39. Marshall, *The Night Before Christmas*, xxi. The qualifier "purports" is necessary because Marshall did not include an 1828 publication in Poughkeepsie, N.Y., a publication that is particularly important because Poughkeepsie was the home of Henry Livingston, Jr., and neither Livingston nor his relatives claimed at the time that Livingston had written the poem.
40. Jones, *St. Nicholas*, 332–33.
41. *Ibid.* 355.
42. In *December 25*, Snyder states that Belsnickle was known not only in Pennsylvania, but in Maryland, Virginia, and North Carolina. Snyder, *December 25,* 217.
43. *False Stories Corrected*, 68.
44. *Ibid.*
45. Coffin, *The Book of Christmas Folklore*, 86.
46. Teresa Chris, *The Story of Santa Claus* (London: Quantum Publishing, 2006), 34.
47. Bowler, *Christmas in the Crosshairs*, 50.
48. Nissenbaum, "There Arose Such a Clatter."
49. The fourth conspirator named by Nissenbaum, Irving's cousin James Paulding, wrote a novel, *The Book of St. Nicholas*, in 1836 in which St. Nicholas is depicted as a Dutch baker. While Irving and his cousin likely communicated after Irving returned from living in Europe for fifteen years, there is no evidence the other Knickerbockers ever communicated about the subject or that *The Book of St. Nicholas* had any influence on the development of Santa Claus.
50. Irving biographer Brian Jay Jones notes

Irving's "natural tendency was to side with the oppressed," and it seems clear he hated slavery. Brian Jay Jones, *Washington Irving: The Definitive Biography of America's First Bestselling Author* (New York: Arcade Publishing, 2011), 301.
51. Washington Irving, *A History of New York,* Author's Revised Edition, Account of the Author (New York: Geo. Putnam, 1860).
52. Washington Irving, *A History of New York,* Author's Revised Edition, Introduction by Henry Morley (New York: 1889).
53. Johanna Johnston, *The Heart That Would Not Hold: A Biography of Washington Irving* (New York: M. Evan, 1971), 28–33.
54. *Ibid.*, 104–110.
55. Washington Irving, *A History of New York*, Author's Revised Edition, Author's Apology (New York: Geo. Putnam, 1860).
56. Seifert, *Santa Claus*, 14–15.
57. The Dutch-flavored depictions of St. Nicholas began in 1837, with a painting of St. Nick by Robert Weir standing by a fireplace with a finger next to his nose, and ended in 1848 with the publication by Henry M. Onderdonk of "Account of a Visit from St. Nicholas" illustrated by artist T.C. Boyd. This book showed St. Nick in a sleigh, on the roof of a home, hanging stockings, and jumping into the air for no apparent reason.
58. Jones, "Knickerbocker Santa Claus," 376; Jones, *Saint Nicholas*, 344–45.
59. In Book III, Chapter II of the 1812 edition, Irving writes: "[S]o we are told, in the sylvan days of New Amsterdam, the good St. Nicholas would often make his appearance in his beloved city, of a holiday afternoon, riding jollily among the treetops, or over the roofs of houses, now and then drawing forth magnificent presents from his breeches pockets, and dropping them down the chimneys of his favorites. Whereas, in these degenerate days of iron and brass he never shows us the light of his countenance, nor ever visits us, save one night in the year; when he rattles down the chimneys of the descendants of the patriarchs, confining his presents merely to the children, in token of the degeneracy of the parents." Irving, *A History of New York* (New York, 1812). The reader can decide whether, upon reading this, you would have jumped out of your chair, gone running to your spouse and shouted, "Honey, there is a cool Dutch holiday described in Washington Irving's new book, and we really have to be a part of it!"
60. Washington Irving, "Old Christmas," *The Sketch Book of Geoffrey Crayon, Gent.* (New York, 1819–20).
61. *Ibid.* (emphasis added).
62. *Ibid.*
63. *Ibid.*
64. *Ibid.*

Chapter 18

1. The question of who deserves the credit for having written the poem is another matter. For most

of its literary lifetime no one questioned that the poem was written by Clement C. Moore, a wealthy and distinguished New York college professor, who provided the poem under his own name for publication in an anthology of New York poetry in 1837, and published it in *Poems*, a book of Moore's own poetry in 1844. In 1899, one of the descendants of Henry Livingston, Jr., a Poughkeepsie, N.Y., surveyor and farmer, questioned Moore's authorship in a letter to a New York newspaper but never pursued the issue. Between 1917 and 1920, another descendant collected letters from some of Livingston's descendants describing family lore that Livingston actually wrote the poem and read it to his family on Christmas morning in 1808. These efforts prompted a couple of magazine articles on the subject in the absence of any witnesses to the alleged reading in 1808 or any documentary evidence. The 1920 publications had no impact on public perception. In 1999, however, a great-great-great-great-great-granddaughter of Livingston named Mary Van Deusen appealed to a Vassar College English professor, Don Foster, who was writing a book on his experiences as a literary detective. In Foster, *Author Unknown*, Don Foster concluded that Livingston was the actual author, a judgment he based primarily on the premise that Moore was a curmudgeonly pedant incapable of writing an upbeat poem whereas Livingston was a happy-go-lucky fellow who represented the true spirit of Christmas. Foster's book generated almost a dozen books and articles, pro and con, over the next eighteen years: Carlo DeVito, *Inventing Santa Claus: The Mystery of Who Really Wrote the Most Celebrated Yuletide Poem of All Time, The Night Before Christmas* (Kennebunkport, ME: Cider Mill Press, 2017); MacDonald P. Jackson, *Who Wrote "The Night Before Christmas"? Analyzing the Clement Clarke Moore vs. Henry Livingston Question* (Jefferson, N.C.: McFarland, 2016); Mary Van Deusen, *Henry Livingston, Jr.: The Christmas Poet You Always Loved* (Wrentham, MA: Val Alain, 2016); Gerard and Patricia Del Re, *The Story of "'Twas the Night Before Christmas": The Life & Times of Clement Clarke Moore and His Best-Loved Poem of Yuletide* (Grand Rapids: Winwood Press, 1991); MacDonald P. Jackson, "Style and Authorship in a Classic of Popular Culture: Henry Livingston and 'The Night Before Christmas,'" *Style* 51, no. 4 (2017), 482–505; MacDonald P. Jackson, "Response by MacDonald P. Jackson," *Melvilliana Blogspot* (February 3, 2017), https://melvilliana.blogspot.com/2017/02/response-by-macdonald-p-jackson.html; Scott Norsworthy, "Clement C. Moore's published letter on his authorship of 'Visit from St. Nicholas,'" *Melvilliana Blogspot* (January 24, 2017), http://melvilliana.blogspot.com/2017/01/clement-c-moores-published-letter-on.htm; MacDonald P. Jackson, "Jackson on Norsworthy on 'The Night Before Christmas,'" *Melvilliana Blogspot* (March 16, 2017), http://melvilliana.blogspot.com/2017/03/jackson-on-norsworthy-on-night-before.html; Scott Norsworthy, "How We Know That Clement C. Moore Wrote 'The Night Before Christmas' (and Henry Livingston, Jr., Did Not)," *Melvilliana Blogspot* (May 16, 2017), http://melvilliana.blogspot.com/2017/05/how-we-know-that-clement-c-moore-wrote.html; Scott Norsworthy, "Computer Error, Please Try Again: MacDonald P. Jackson on the Authorship of 'The Night Before Christmas,'" *Melvilliana Blogspot* (November 7, 2016), http://melvilliana.blogspot.com/2016/11/computer-error-please-try-again.html; Seth Kaller, "The Moore Things Change," *New-York Journal of American History* (Winter 2004); Joe Nickell, "The Case of the Christmas Poem: Part 2," *Manuscripts* (Winter 2003); Joe Nickell, "The Case of the Christmas Poem," *Manuscripts* (Fall 2002); and Stephen Nissenbaum, "There Arose Such a Clatter: Who Really Wrote 'The Night before Christmas'? (And Why Does It Matter?)," *Common-Place: The Journal of Early American Life* (January 2001). In telling the history of Santa Claus, who wrote "The Night Before Christmas" is irrelevant, or virtually so. If we could magically change the name on ever copy of the poem from Clement C. Moore to Henry Livingston, Jr., the substance of this book would hardly change at all. As a matter of historical accuracy, however, the issue deserves a full and complete discussion, one that outside the scope of this book but that I hope to provide in a separate book on the subject.

2. *False Stories Corrected*, 68.

3. Marshall, "*The Night Before Christmas*," xli.

4. The Rev. Benjamin Moore was also known for initially refusing to administer last rites to Alexander Hamilton after he was mortally wounded in a duel with then-vice president Aaron Burr, and then consenting to do so after Hamilton explained that he went to the duel as a matter of honor and did not intend to, nor did he, shoot at Burr. The younger Moore would have been a few days short of his twenty-fifth birthday when this occurred.

5. Ruth K. MacDonald, "Santa Claus in America: The Influence of 'The Night Before Christmas,'" *Children's Literature Association Quarterly* 8, no. 3, 4–6 (1983), 4.

6. "Account of a Visit from St. Nicholas," *The Troy (N.Y.) Sentinel* (December 23, 1823).

7. *Ibid.*

8. *Ibid.*

9. Clement C. Moore, "A Visit from St. Nicholas," *Poems*, 124. The changes include the use of commas, semicolons, dashes, exclamation marks, and the names of the last two reindeer.

10. Pelletreau, *Clement C. Moore*, 17–18.

11. Marshall, "*The Night Before Christmas*," xx. One fact that is implicit in these stories but deserves to be highlighted is the extended Moore family, including his in-laws and their children, were engaged in a large family Christmas celebration on Christmas Eve 1822, and Moore read the poem to his family that night.

12. Snyder, *December 25*, 222; Jones, *St. Nicholas*, 359; Nissenbaum, "There Arose Such a Clatter"; Kaller, "The Moore Things Change."

13. Pelletreau, *Clement C. Moore*, 18; Arthur James Weise, *Troy's One Hundred Years, 1789–1889* (Troy, NY: William H. Young, 1891), 97.

14. DeVito, *Inventing Santa Claus*, 111. Moore's

letter to Tuttle has never been located but one can determine its content by extrapolating from Tuttle's response. *Ibid.*, 110–11.

15. Marshall, "*The Night Before Christmas*," 3–7; Charles Fenno Hoffman, editor, *The New-York Book of Poetry* (New York: George Dearborn, 1837).

16. Marshall, "*The Night Before Christmas*," 3–8; Clement C. Moore, *Poems* (New York: Barlett & Welford, 1844) (hereinafter Moore, *Poems*).

17. Scott Norsworthy, "Clement C. Moore's Published Letter on His Authorship of 'Visit from St. Nicholas,'" *Melvilliana Blogspot* (January 24, 2017), accessed at http://melvilliana.blogspot.com/2017/01/clement-c-moores-published-letter-on.htm.

18. Letter dated February 27, 1844, from Clement C. Moore to Charles King, editor, *New York American* (March 1, 1944).

19. Moore, *Poems*, v–vi.

20. Clement C. Moore, *Santa Claus or, The Night Before Christmas* (New York: Mathews and Clasback, 1858).

21. Clement C. Moore, *The Night Before Christmas: or Kriss Kringle's Visit* (Philadelphia: Willis P. Hazard, 1858).

22. Clement C. Moore, *A Visit from St. Nicholas* (Philadelphia: David Scattergood, 1860).

23. Clement C. Moore, *A Visit from St. Nicholas* (New York: Hurd & Houghton, 1862).

24. Clement C. Moore, *Big Picture Books for Little Children: The Night Before Christmas* (Cincinnati: Peter G. Thomson, 1863).

25. Clement C. Moore, *A Visit from St. Nicholas* (Boston: Louis Prang, 1864).

26. *Visit of St. Nicholas* (New York: McLoughlin Bros., 1869).

27. *A Visit from St. Nicholas,* Thomas Nast, illustrator (New York: McLoughlin Bros., 1870).

28. Devito, *Inventing Santa Claus*, 101.

29. According to House of Names.com, "[t]he roots of the Claus family are found in the ancient German state of Bavaria…. Claus is derived from the medieval given name Klaus, which is a shortened form of the personal name Niklaus or Nicholas." See "Claus History, Family Crest & Coats of Arms," Houseofnames.com, accessed at https://www.houseofnames.com/claus-family-crest (viewed April 4, 2019). Claus was also a relatively common Dutch name, however, so "Sancte Claus," the name used in the 1810 St. Nicholas poems and broadside, could be German or Dutch.

30. Jones, "Knickerbocker Santa Claus."

31. *False Stories Corrected*, 89.

32. Frederick Parsons, "1819 Carriers' Address," *Poughkeepsie Journal* (January 1, 1819).

33. It is obviously possible that the name was used in other publications which have escaped our attention but this would not undermine the fundamental conclusion that use of the phrase was rare.

34. *The Casket, or Flowers of Literature, Wit & Sentiment* (February 1826).

35. Marshall, *The Night Before Christmas*, 4–11. Marshall's count would be thirty-one but she failed to include the 1828 publication by the *Poughkeepsie*

(N.Y.) Journal, a fact that is important in determining authorship because Henry Livingston, Jr., and some of his family lived in Poughkeepsie at the time but did not claim he had written the anonymous poem.

36. This theory finds support in Bowler's most recent book, *Christmas in the Crosshairs*, in which he says that the variety of names used for Santa Claus in America during the early 1800s, all phonetic variations of Santaclaw, "speaks to a long-standing oral transmission of the legend of a Christmas Gift-Bringer rather than, as some have suggested, the outright invention of Santa Claus by the Knickerbocker literary clique." Bowler, *Christmas in the Crosshairs*, 50.

37. Forbes, *Christmas: A Candid History*, 86.

Chapter 19

1. The year 1941 is derived from Jones' 1953 speech to the New-York Historical Society in which he described Brigham's announcement as occurring a dozen years earlier. The booklet was donated by Stephen Salisbury III upon his death in 1905 but it took considerable time for the Society to review and archive the documents. A review of the original records of the AAS showed that the first index card for *The Children's Friend* was recorded in handwriting, indicating that it preceded the adoption of typewriters for this purpose in the 1930s. The card also shows that at some later date the book was transferred to the "reserve" section of the AAS, an indication that the Society had discovered how rare and important the booklet was.

2. Bob Short, *Patriotic Effusions* (New York: L. & F. Lockwood, 1819).

3. The Author of Patriotic Effusions, *The Olio* (New York: The Author, 1823).

4. Winthrop Sargent, editor, *The Loyal Verses of Joseph Stansbury and Doctor Jonathan Odell Relating to the American Revolution* (Albany: J. Munsell, 1860). Coincidentally, Odell was Clement Moore's godfather.

5. *Arthur J. Stansbury, Elementary Catechism on the Constitution of the United States* (Boston: Hilliard, Gray, Little, and Wilkins, 1831).

6. *National Shorthand Reporters' Association, Proceedings of the Annual Meeting* (Trenton, N.J., 1906).

Chapter 20

1. Margaret Baker, *Discovering Christmas Customs and Folklore: A Guide to Seasonal Rites*, 3d ed. (Buckinghamshire: Shire, 1992), 62.

2. The description by Irving of St. Nicholas on the prow of the ship was undoubtedly intended, like the rest of the book, for comedic effect. Neither the Catholic bishop St. Nicholas of Myra nor the Dutch gift-giver Sinterklaas dressed like that, and Irving likely thought it was funny the Dutch would dress the saint like them instead of like the fourth-century Catholic bishop he was supposed to be.

3. The *Sentinel* reprinted the poem in 1829 with a drawing of St. Nick, sleigh, and eight reindeer flying off to the North Pole but it is too small to provide any indication of what St. Nick looked like.

4. Marshall, *The Night Before Christmas*, 8.

5. *Ibid.*

6. *Ibid.*, 10.

7. *Ibid.*, 12.

8. *Kriss Kringle's Christmas Tree* (Philadelphia: E. Ferret, 1845) (hereinafter *Kriss Kringle's Christmas Tree*).

9. *Kriss Kringle's Book* (Philadelphia: Thomas, Cowperthwaite, 1842).

10. *Kriss Kringle's Christmas Tree*, cover.

11. *Kriss Kringle's Raree Show, for Good Boys and Girls* (New York: William H. Murphy, 1847) (hereinafter *Kriss Kringle's Raree Show*).

12. Marshall, *The Night Before Christmas*, 15.

13. Spoodlyks, *Poster for Santa Claus Quadrilles* (1846).

14. Caroline H. Butler, *The Little Messenger Birds, or, the Chimes of the Silver Bells* (Boston: Phillips, Sampson, 1850).

15. P.T. Barnum, *Santa Claus and Jenny Lind* (New York: John R. M'Gown, 1850).

16. Cover, *Harper's Weekly* (December 25, 1858).

17. Cover, *Harper's Weekly* (January 2, 1869). In *December 25*, Snyder comments that "[a]s late as the end of the nineteenth century, vestiges of Woden could still be seen in the garb of some Santa Claus figures." Snyder, *December 25*, 208. This may be what he had in mind.

18. The hat is arguably a Russian cassock designed to convey that Santa is from a very cold land where a heavy fur hat is needed, but it looks more like a fur-covered fez.

19. *Harper's Illustrated Monthly Magazine* (December 1857).

20. *Harper's Weekly* (December 24, 1857).

21. Clement C. Moore, *A Visit from Santa Claus* (Philadelphia: David Scattergood, 1860). Many versions of Moore's poem were titled *A Visit from Santa Claus or Santa Claus* but Scattergood's version was the first to use Santa Claus alone.

22. Clement C. Moore, *A Visit from St. Nicholas* (F.O.C. Darley, 1862).

23. Clement C. Moore, *A Visit from St. Nicholas* (Philadelphia: Fisher & Bros., c. 1863). The publication date of 1863 is based on Marshall's history of the poem dating this version as "ca. 1863." A digital copy on the internet site maintained by the Beinecke Rare Book and Manuscript Library of Yale University identifies the publication date as "c. 1850." Based on review of other sources, it seems unlikely the book was published as early as 1850, and more likely it was published between 1860 to 1864. Both sources use abbreviations of circa to identify the publication date, however, meaning that no definitive date is possible.

24. Clement C. Moore, *A Visit from St. Nicholas* (Louis Prang, 1864).

25. Halloran, *Thomas Nast*, 2.

26. "Santa in Camp," *Harper's Weekly* (January 1, 1863).

27. "Santa and His Works," *Harper's Weekly* (December 29,1866).

28. George Webster, *Santa Claus and His Works* (New York: McLoughlin Bros., 1869); Val R. Berryman, "Christmas in America: Christmas Comes to America From the Pen of Thomas Nast, Part One," *The Glow* 29, no. 1 (February 2008), 5–9, 6.

29. Halloran, *Thomas Nast*, 205.

30. Val R. Berryman, "Christmas in America: Christmas Comes to America from the Pen of Thomas Nast, Part Two," *The Glow* 29, no. 2 (April 2008), 5–9, 5.

31. Thomas Nast, *Thomas Nast's Drawings for the Human Race* (New York: Harper Bros., 1890).

32. Snyder, *December 25*, 226.

33. Jones, *St. Nicholas*, 353.

34. Marling, *Merry Christmas*, 236–37.

35. Halloran, *Thomas Nast*, 205.

36. Malcolm Gladwell, *The Tipping Point: How Little Things Can Make a Big Difference* (New York: Little, Brown, 2000), 7, 12.

37. See Jim Morrison, "An Early Department Store Visit to Santa Claus," *The Glow* 36, no. 6 (December 2015), 4–10.

38. Snyder, *December 25*, 208.

39. George Buday, *The History of the Christmas Card* (London: Spring Brooks, 1954), 6–12.

40. *Ibid.*

41. The greenery held in the crook of a Belsnickle's arm was generally a single piece of goose feather dyed green, meaning that it could be characterized as either a switch or a very skinny tree. In historic drawings of the German gift-givers, Knecht Ruprecht and the faux Nicholases such as Pelznickel are virtually always shown with a handful of switches intended for delivery to poorly-behaved children whereas Herr Winter, the most direct predecessor of Weihnachtsmann, is shown carrying what is clearly a lighted tree. Thus, both characterizations have factual precedents.

42. For an excellent overview of the different types of Belsnickles, see Scott Tagliapietra, "Collecting Belsnickles," *The Glow* 28, no. 3 (June 2007), 7–10.

43. Woolworth's primary ornament supplier, a native German named Max Eckhart, recognized before most governments that Germany was headed toward a world war that would end the supply of German ornaments. In anticipation, Eckhart began working with Corning Glass Company to convert its machinery for making glass light bulbs into glass balls that could be used for ornaments. Eckhart established a company, Shiny Brite, that would complete the ornament by silvering the interior, painting the exterior and applying a metal cap, creating the iconic shiny glass balls that some of us remember from our childhoods. It was not until 1985, when a young American, Christopher Radko, sought to reproduce the antique, hand-blown glass ornaments of his youth that figural ornaments shaped as Santa became widely available again. In a wonderful example of how styles come and go, after building a highly successful business selling elaborate figural ornaments at equally impressive prices, Radko acquired the name Shiny-Brite, which had gone out of busi-

ness in 1962, and began producing a line of simple round ornaments that evoked the mid-century modern styles of the 1950s and '60s.

44. Melicent Sammis, *The Art of the Lampworked Santa: A Pictorial Guide for Collecting Antique Blown Glass Santa Christmas Ornaments* (York, PA: Shuman Heritage Press, 2010). She is also the author of Melicent D'Amore, "The Many Faces of Santa Claus," *The Glow* 36, no. 6 (December 2015), 26–29.

45. For further detail on Victorian scrapbooks, see Val R. Berryman, "Christmas in America: The Victorian Scrapbook," *The Glow* 30, no. 1 (February 2009), 5–12.

46. Marshall, *The Night Before Christmas*, xxi.

47. George Webster, *Santa Claus and His Works* (New York: McLoughlin Bros., 1869).

48. Thomas Nast, *Christmas Drawings for the Human Race* (New York: Harper & Brothers, 1890).

49. J.B. Greene, *An Adventure of Santa Claus* (Boston: Lee & Shepard, 1871).

50. L. Frank Baum, *The Life and Adventures of Santa Claus* (Indianapolis: Bowen-Merrill, 1902).

Chapter 21

1. Marling, *Merry Christmas*, 221.

2. For an overview of Sundblom's Coca-Cola advertisements, see Val R. Berryman, "Christmas in America: Christmas Drinks—Coca-Cola, the Sign of Good Taste," *The Glow* 32, no. 2 (April 2011), 5–10.

3. In fact, there is an obscure Russian language website which explains, in a sketchy computerized English translation, that Coca-Cola invented Santa to sell soft drinks.

4. Bowler, *Christmas in the Crosshairs*, 82.

5. *Ibid.*, 83.

6. *Ibid.*, 84.

7. Bowler, *Christmas in the Crosshairs*, 85. The Kulak refers to the affluent individuals who employed the peasants and, in this context, is symbolic of capitalism.

8. *Ibid.*, 83–86.

9. Karen Petrone, *Life Has Become More Joyous, Comrades: Celebrations in the Time of Stalin* (Bloomington: Indiana University Press, 2000), 85. The complete text of Postyshev's letter is set forth in Wikipedia, "New Year Tree," https://en.wikipedia.org/wiki/New_Year_ (accessed January 23, 2017).

10. Val R. Berryman, "Christmas in Russia, Part One," *The Glow* 26, no. 6 (December 2005), 13–21, 13.

11. Some sources say the Communist government also copied the Dutch citizens of the sixteenth century by giving the gift-giver a slightly different name— Dado Moroz ("Little Father Frost") instead of Ded Moroz ("Grandfather Frost"). See Bowler, *Christmas in the Crosshairs*, 89. There is little evidence that this name was commonly used, however, and given the minor difference between Dado Moroz/Father Frost and Ded Moroz/Grandfather Frost, the former could easily have faded away during the last seventy years.

12. Currently, about forty percent of Russians are Russian Orthodox and about forty percent are unaffiliated with any religion or expressly atheist. The remaining twenty percent are spread out among a variety of religions.

13. Currently, the Russians observe a five-day New Year's holiday on January 1–5 using the Gregorian calendar. If January 6 or 7 are weekend days, the New Year's holiday is extended to abut, or include, the Christmas holiday.

14. Bowler, *Christmas in the Crosshairs*, 98.

15. *Ibid.*, 98–99.

16. Val R. Berryman, "Christmas in France: Wine Country Santas," *The Glow* 24, no. 5 (October 2003), 9–11.

17. Claude Levi-Strauss, "Father Christmas Executed" (1952), reprinted in Daniel Miller, editor, *Unwrapping Christmas* (Oxford: Clarendon Press, 1993), 38–51.

18. Baker, *Discovering Christmas Customs and Folklore*, 67.

Bibliography

Auburn Journal and Advertiser (January 4, 1837).

The Author of Patriotic Effusions, The Olio (New York: The Author, 1823).

Baker, Margaret, Discovering Christmas Customs and Folklore: A Guide to Seasonal Rites, 3d ed (Buckinghamshire: Shire, 1992).

Barnett, James H., *The American Christmas: A Study in National Culture* (New York: Macmillan, 1954).

Baum, L. Frank, *The Life and Adventures of Santa Claus* (Indianapolis: Bowen-Merrill, 1902).

Beaton, Katherine, *The Real Santa Claus* (Richmond, Surrey: H&B Publications, 1986).

Bennett, William J., *The True Saint Nicholas: Why He Matters to Christmas* (New York: Howard Books, 2009).

Bennett-Hunter, Guy, "Christmas Mythologies Sacred and Secular," *Christmas—Philosophy for Everyone: Better Than a Lump of Coal* (Malden, MA: Wiley-Blackwell, 2009).

"Berhta," *Behind the Name,* http://www.behindthename.com/name/berhta (citing Ernst Förstemann, Altdeutsches namenbuch, 281 [1900]).

Berryman, Val R., "Christmas in America: Artistic Images of Christmas," *The Glow* 28, no. 6 (December 2007), 13–17.

_____, "Christmas in America: Christmas Comes to America From the Pen of Thomas Nast, Part One," *The Glow* 29, no. 1 (February 2008), 5–9.

_____, "Christmas in America: Christmas Comes to America From the Pen of Thomas Nast, Part Two," *The Glow* 29, no. 2 (April 2008), 5–9.

_____, "Christmas in America: Christmas Drinks—Coca-Cola, the Sign of Good Taste," *The Glow* 32, no. 2 (April 2011), 5–10.

_____, "Christmas in America: Santa Claus Comes to America, The Dutch-American St. Nicholas," *The Glow* 28, no. 2 (April 2007), 11–14.

_____, "Christmas in America: Santa Claus Comes to America, The German-American Kriss Kringle," *The Glow* 28, no. 2 (April 2007), 11–14.

_____, "Christmas in America: The Victorian Scrapbook," *The Glow* 30, no. 1 (February 2009), 5–12.

_____, "Christmas in Czechoslovakia: Angel, Saint and Devil," *The Glow* 27, no. 5 (October 2006), 15–19.

_____, "Christmas in France: Good Saint Nicholas," *The Glow* 25, no. 1 (February 2004), 8–10, 19.

_____, "Christmas in France: Wine Country Santas," *The Glow* 24, no. 5 (October 2003), 9–11.

_____, "Christmas in Germany: A Story of the Christmas Man," *The Glow* 23, no. 2 (April 2002), 4–5.

_____, "Christmas in Germany: Christkindl, the Christmas Child of Germany," *The Glow* 22, no. 5 (December 2001), 8–12.

_____, "Christmas in Germany: Der Weihnachtsmann and Knecht Ruprecht," *The Glow* 23, no. 3 (June 2002), 9–12.

_____, "Christmas in Germany: Krampus, a Beastly Traveling Companion," *The Glow* 22, no. 5 (October 2001), 13–17.

_____, "Christmas in Germany: Santa, the Gift Bringer," *The Glow* 23, no. 4 (August 2002), 11–13.

_____, "Christmas in Germany: The German Santa, Der Weihnachtsmann," *The Glow* 23, no. 1 (February 2002), 8–10.

_____, "Christmas in Great Britain," *The Glow* 22, no. 2 (April 2001), 9–13.

_____, "Christmas in Holland: Sint Nicolaas and Sinterklaas," *The Glow* 25, no. 5 (October 2004), 10–13.

_____, "Christmas in Holland: Sint Nicolaas Day is for the Children," *The Glow* 25, no. 6 (December 2004), 9–12.

_____, "Christmas in Russia, Grandfather Frost and the Snow Maiden," *The Glow* 26, no. 5 (October 2005), 11–14.

_____, "Christmas in Russia, Part One" *The Glow* 26, no. 6 (December 2005), 13–21.

_____, "Christmas in Russia: Decorations Old and New," *The Glow* 27, no. 2 (April 2006), 11–15.

_____, "Christmas in Russia: Saint Nicholas and Grandfather Frost," *The Glow* 26, no. 4 (August 2005), 9–13.

_____, "Christmas in Scandinavia: The Jultomten and Julbock of Sweden," *The Glow* 26, no. 2 (April 2005), 10–14.

_____, "Christmas in Scandinavia: The Swedish Saint Lucia," *The Glow* 26, no. 3 (June 2005), 9–12.

Blair, Arthur. *Christmas Cards for the Collector* (London: B.T. Batsford, 1986).

Booth, Mary L., *History of the City of New York from its Earliest Settlement to the Present Time* (New York: W. R. C. Clark & Meeker, 1859).

Bowler, Gerry, *Christmas in the Crosshairs: Two Thousand Years of Denouncing and Defending the World's Most Celebrated Holiday* (Oxford: Oxford University Press, 2016).

_____, *Santa Claus: A Biography* (Toronto: McClelland & Stewart, 2005).

_____, *The World Encyclopedia of Christmas* (Toronto: McClelland & Stewart, 2000).

Bradley, Benjamin, "The 'Woodcutter' Santa," *The Glow* 36, no. 6 (December 2015), 8–11.

Brinkman, Susan and Paul, "George Washington Irving—An American Christmas Hero," *The Glow* 32, no. 2 (April 2011), 11–14.

Brom, Gerald, *Krampus: The Yule Lord* (New York: Harper Voyager, 2012).

Brophy, Matthew. "Santa's Sweatshop: Elf Exploitation for Christmas," *Christmas—Philosophy for Everyone: Better Than a Lump of Coal* (Malden, MA: Wiley-Blackwell, 2009).

Browne, Patrick, "Santa Claus was Made by Washington Irving," Historical Digression (December 6, 2104), https://historical-digression. com/2014/12/06/santa-claus-was-made-by-washington-irving.

Brunner, Sarah. "Santa Claus: A Transformation Through the Centuries," *The Glow* 34, no. 6 (December 2013), 6–8.

Bryant, William Cullen, *Selections from the American Poets* (New York, 1840).

Bryson, Bill, *A Short History of Nearly Everything* (New York: Broadway Books, 2003).

Buday, George, *The History of the Christmas Card* (London: Spring Brooks, 1954).

Burstein, Andrew, *The Original Knickerbocker: The Life of Irving Washington* (New York: Basic Books, 2007).

The Casket, or Flowers of Literature, Wit & Sentiment I, no. 2 (Philadelphia: Atkinson & Alexander, February 1826).

The Children's Friend: Part III A New-Year's Present to the Little Ones from Five to Twelve (New York: William B. Gilley, 1821).

Chris, Teresa, *The Story of Santa Claus* (London: Quantum, 2006).

Coffin, Tristram P., *The Book of Christmas Folklore* (New York: Seabury Press, 1973).

Connelly, Mark, *Christmas, A History* (paperback edition of Christmas, A Social History with new preface) (London: I.B. Taurus, 2012).

_____, *Christmas, A Social History* (London: I.B. Taurus, 1999).

Count, Earl W., *4000 Years of Christmas* (New York: Rider & Co., 1953).

D'Amore, Melicent, "The Many Faces of Santa Claus," *The Glow* 36, no. 6 (December 2015), 26–29.

Dawson, William Francis, *Christmas: Its Origin and Associations Together with Its Historical Events and Festive Celebrations During Nineteen Centuries* (London: Elliot Stock, 1902).

Deal, William E., and S. Waller, "The Mind of Santa Claus and the Metaphors He Lives By," *Christmas—Philosophy for Everyone: Better Than a Lump of Coal* (Malden, MA: Wiley-Blackwell, 2009).

Del Re, Gerard, and Patricia, *The Story of "'Twas the Night Before Christmas": The Life & Times of Clement Clarke Moore and His Best-Loved Poem of Yuletide* (Grand Rapids: Winwood Press, 1991).

DeVito, Carlo, *Inventing Santa Claus: The Mystery of Who Really Wrote the Most Celebrated Yuletide Poem of All Time, The Night Before Christmas* (Kennebunkport, ME: Cider Mill Press, 2017).

Dickens, Charles, *A Christmas Carol* (London, 1843).

_____, *Pickwick Papers* (London, 1837).

Dr. Seuss, *Horton Hears a Who* (New York: Random House, 1954).

_____, *How the Grinch Stole Christmas* (New York: Random House, 1957).

_____, *The Lorax* (New York: Random House, 1971).

_____, *The Sneeches and Other Stories* (New York: Random House, 1953).

_____, *Yertle the Turtle and Other Stories* (New York: Random House, 1958).

Dougherty, Michael, *Krampus: Shadow of Saint Nicholas* (Legendary Comics, 2015).

Duncan Royale, *History of Santa Claus* (Fullerton, CA: M.E. Duncan, 1983).

_____, *History of Santa Claus II* (Fullerton, CA: M.E. Duncan, 1986).

"Dutch Hymn to Saint Nicholas," *New York Commercial Advertiser* (December 14, 1810).

_____, *New York Evening Post* (December 14, 1810).

Eberspächer, Martina, *Der Weihnachtsmann: Zur Entstehung einer Bildtradition in Aufklärung und Romantik* (Norderstedt: Books on Demand, 2002).

Elliott, Jock, *Inventing Christmas: How Our Holiday Came to Be* (New York: Harry N. Abrams, 2001).

English, Adam C., *The Saint Who Would Be Santa Claus* (Waco: Baylor University Press, 2013).

Evtuhov, Catherine, David Goldfrank, Lindsey Hughes, and Richard Stites, *A History of Russia: People, Legends, Events, Forces* (New York: Houghton Mifflin, 2004).

Federer, William J., *There Really Is a Santa Claus: The History of Saint Nicholas & Christmas Holiday Traditions* (St. Louis: Amerisearch, 2002).

Flynn, Tom, *The Trouble with Christmas* (Buffalo: Prometheus Books, 1993).

Forbes, Bruce David, *Christmas: A Candid History* (Berkeley: University of California Press, 2007).

Foster, Don, *Author Unknown: On the Trail of Anonymous* (New York: Henry Holt, 2000).

Frazer, James George, *The Golden Bough. A Study in Magic and Religion: Part 6, The Scapegoat,* Vol. IX at 240 (London: Macmillan, 1920).

Frodsham, Paul, *From Stonehenge to Santa Claus: The Evolution of Christmas* (Stroud, Gloustershire: History Press, 2008).

Funk, Elisabeth Paling, "From Amsterdam to New Amsterdam: Washington Irving, the Dutch St. Nicholas, and the American Santa Claus," *New Netherland Institute, Explorers, Fortunes and Love Letters: A History of New Netherland* (Albany: SUNY Press, 2010).

Gavrielides, Era, "Lying to Children About Santa: Why It's Just Not Wrong," *Christmas—Philosophy for Everyone: Better Than a Lump of Coal* (Malden, MA: Wiley-Blackwell, 2009).

"German Christmas Traditions," Vistawide World Languages & Cultures, http://www.vistawide. com/german/christmas/german_christmas_ traditions.htm.

Gibbens, Sarah, "Could the Remains of Santa Claus Be in This Turkish Church?" *nationalgeographic.com,* http://news.national-geo graphic.com/2017/10/santa-claus-st-nicholas-tomb-archaeology-turkey-spd.

Golby, J.M., and A.W. Purdue, *The Making of the Modern Christmas*, rev. ed. (Sparkford, Somerset: J.H. Haynes, 2000).

"The Greek Orthodox Archdiocese of America," http://www.goarch.org/archdiocese/about (accessed January 15, 2017).

Greene, J.B., *An Adventure of Santa Claus* (Boston: Lee & Shepard, 1871).

Grimm, Jacob, *Teutonic Mythology* (1835), translated by James Steven Stallybrass (London: Cambridge University Press, 2012).

Gritsch, Eric W., *The History of Lutheranism* (Minneapolis: Fortress Press, 2002).

Gulevich, Tanya, *Encyclopedia of Christmas* (Detroit: Omnigraphics, 2000).

Hales, Steven D., "Putting Claus Back into Christmas," *Christmas—Philosophy for Everyone: Better Than a Lump of Coal* (Malden, MA: Wiley-Blackwell, 2009).

Harrison, Michael, *The Story of Christmas* (London: Odhams Press, 1951).

Hedges, William L., *Washington Irving: An American Study, 1802–32* (Baltimore: Johns Hopkins University Press, 1963).

Hellman, George S., *Washington Irving Esquire* (New York: Alfred A. Knopf, 1925).

Hervey, Thomas K., *The Book of Christmas* (London, 1837).

Hoffman, Robert, "Ho! Ho! Ho! Ephemera Traces Americanization of Santa Claus," *The Glow* 36, no. 6 (December 2015), 3–11.

Irving, Washington, *A History of New York* (New York: Inskeep and Bradford, 1809).

_____, *A History of New York, Author's Apology* (New York, 1848).

_____, *A History of New York*, 2d ed. (New York, 1812).

"Is St. Nicholas in Venice, too?" The St. Nicholas Center, http://www. stnicholascenter.org/pages/relics-in-the-lido-of-venice.

"Is There a Santa Claus," *The New York Sun* (September 21, 1897).

Ivanits, Linda J., *Russian Folk Beliefs* (New York: M.E. Sharpe, 1989).

Jackson, MacDonald P., "Response by MacDonald P. Jackson," Melvilliana Blogspot (February 3, 2017), https://melvilliana.blogspot. com/2017/02/response-by-macdonald-p-jack son.html.

_____, "Style and Authorship in a Classic of Popular Culture: Henry Livingston and 'The Night Before Christmas,'" *Style* 51, no. 4 (2017), 482–505.

_____, *Who Wrote "The Night Before Christmas"? Analyzing the Clement Clarke Moore vs. Henry Livingston Question* (Jefferson, N.C.: McFarland, 2016).

Johnes, Martin, *Christmas and the British: A Modern History* (London: Bloomsbury Academic, 2016).

Johnson, David Kyle, "Against the Santa Claus Lie," *Christmas—Philosophy for Everyone: Better Than a Lump of Coal* (Malden, MA: Wiley-Blackwell, 2009).

_____, *The Myths That Stole Christmas* (Washington, D.C.: Humanist Press, 2015).

Johnston, Johanna. *The Heart That Would Not Hold: A Biography of Washington Irving* (New York: M. Evan, 1971).

Jones, Brian Jay, *Washington Irving: The Definitive Biography of America's First Bestselling Author* (New York: Arcade, 2011).

Jones, Charles W., "Knickerbocker Santa Claus," *New-York Historical Society Quarterly* 38 (1954), 356–83.

_____, *Saint Nicholas of Myra, Bari, and Manhattan: Biography of a Legend* (Chicago: University of Chicago Press, 1978).

Jones, E. Willis, *The Santa Claus Book* (New York: Walker, 1976).

July, Robert W., *Gulian Verplanck: The Essential New Yorker* (Durham: Duke University Press, 1956).

Kaller, Seth, "The Authorship of the Night Before Christmas, sethkeller.com, https://www.sethkaller.com/about/educational/tnbc (2005).

_____, "The Moore Things Change," *New-York Journal of American History* (Winter 2004).

Kelly, Joseph F., *The Feast of Christmas* (Collegeville, MN: Liturgical Press, 2010).

_____, *The Origins of Christmas* (Collegeville, MN: Liturgical Press, 2004).

King, Charles, "Letter from Clement C. Moore," New York American (March 1, 1844).

King Winter (Hamburg: Gustav W. Seitz, 1859).

Kononenko, Natalie, *Slavic Folklore: A Handbook* (Westport, CT: Greenwood Press, 2007).

Kriss Kringle's Christmas Tree: A Holliday Present for Boys and Girls (Philadelphia: E. Ferrett, 1845).

Krythe, Maymie R., *All About Christmas* (New York: Harper & Bros., 1954).

Kummerow, Marion, "German Christmas Traditions," *Inside Munich* (www.inside-munich.com, 2012).

Levi-Strauss, Claude, "Father Christmas Executed" (1952), reprinted in Daniel Miller, editor, *Unwrapping Christmas*, 38–52 (Oxford: Clarendon Press, 1993).

Life, *Christmas Around the World* (New York: Life Books, 2004).

Lowe, Scott C., editor, *Christmas—Philosophy for Everyone: Better Than a Lump of Coal* (Malden, MA: Wiley-Blackwell, 2009).

Mallory, Michael, *Art of Krampus* (San Rafael, CA: Insight Editions, 2015).

Marling, Karal Ann, *Merry Christmas: Celebrating America's Greatest Holiday* (Cambridge: Harvard University Press, 2000).

Marshall, Nancy H., *The Night Before Christmas: A Descriptive Bibliography of Clement Clarke Moore's Immortal Poem* (New Castle, DE: Oak Knoll Press, 2002).

Mason, Marion G., "Heaven, Hecate, and Hallmark: Christmas in Hindsight," *Christmas—Philosophy for Everyone: Better Than a Lump of Coal* (Malden, MA: Wiley-Blackwell, 2009).

McCullough, Joseph A., *The Story of Santa Claus* (Oxford: Osprey Adventures, 2014).

McKnight, George H., *St. Nicholas: His Legend and His Role in the Christmas Celebration and Other Popular Customs* (New York: G. P. Putnam's Sons, 1917).

McNeil, Lily, *Santa Claus: A History of Christmas' Jolly CEO* (Hyperlink Press, 2012).

McWhorter, George C., "The Holidays," *Harper's New Monthly Magazine* (January 1866).

Mercer, Mark, "The Significance of Christmas for Liberal Multiculturalism," *Christmas—Philosophy for Everyone: Better Than a Lump of Coal* (Malden, MA: Wiley-Blackwell, 2009).

Miles, Clement A., *Christmas in Ritual and Tradition, Christian and Pagan* (London: T. Fisher Unwin, 1912).

Miller, Daniel, editor, *Unwrapping Christmas* (Oxford: Clarendon Press, 1993).

Moore, Clement C., *A Lecture Introductory to the Course of Hebrew Instruction in the General Theological Seminary of the Protestant Episcopal Church* (November 14, 1825) (New York: Swords, 1825).

_____, *The Night Before Christmas: or Kriss Kringle's Visit* (Philadelphia: Willis P. Hazard, 1858).

_____, *Poems* (New York: Barlett & Welford, 1844).

_____, *Santa Claus or, The Night Before Christmas* (New York: Mathews and Clasback, 1858).

_____, "A Visit from St. Nicholas," *Selections from the American Poets* (William Cullen Bryant, editor) (New York: Harper & Bros., 1840).

_____, "A Visit from St. Nicholas," *The New-York Book of Poetry* (Charles Fenno Hoffman, editor) (New York: Dearborn, 1837).

_____, *A Visit from St. Nicholas* (Boston: Louis Prang, 1864).

_____, *A Visit from St. Nicholas* (New York: Hurd & Houghton, 1862).

_____, *A Visit from St. Nicholas* (New York: McLoughlin Bros., 1870) (authorship uncredited; Thomas Nast, illustrator).

_____, *A Visit from St. Nicholas* (Philadelphia: David Scattergood, 1860).

_____, *A Visit of St. Nicholas* (New York: McLoughlin Bros., 1869).

Moore, T.W.C., Letter from to George H. Moore (March 15, 1862), New York Historical Society.

Morrison, Dorothy, *Yule, A Celebration of Light & Warmth* (St. Paul: Llewellyn, 2000).

Morrison, Jim, "An Early Department Store Visit to Santa Claus," *The Glow* 36, no. 6 (December 2015), 4–10.

Myers, Andrew B., editor, *The Knickerbocker Tradition: Washington Irving's New York* (Tarrytown, NY: Sleepy Hollow Restorations, 1974).

Nast, Thomas, *Christmas Drawings for the Human Race* (New York: Harper & Brothers, 1890).

National Shorthand Reporters' Association, Proceedings of the Annual Meeting (Trenton, N.J., 1906).

Nickell, Joe, "The Case of the Christmas Poem: Part 2," *Manuscripts* (Winter 2003).

_____, "The Case of the Christmas Poem," *Manuscripts* (Fall 2002).

_____, *Detecting Forgery: Forensic Investigation of Documents* (Lexington: University Press of Kentucky, 2005).

_____, *Pen, Ink, and Evidence: A Study of Writing and Writing Materials for the Penman, Collector, and Document Detective* (Lexington: University Press of Kentucky, 2005).

Nissenbaum, Stephen, *The Battle for Christmas:*

A Cultural History of America's Most Cherished Holiday (New York: Vintage, 1997).

_____, "There Arose Such a Clatter: Who Really Wrote 'The Night before Christmas'? (And Why Does It Matter?)," *Common-Place: The Journal of Early American Life* (January 2001).

Norsworthy, Scott, "Clement C. Moore's Published Letter on His Authorship of 'Visit from St. Nicholas,'" *Melvilliana Blogspot* (January 24, 2017 http://melvilliana.blogspot.com/2017/01/clement-c-moores-published-letter-on.htm.

_____, "Computer Error, Please Try Again: MacDonald P. Jackson on the Authorship of 'The Night Before Christmas,'" *Melvilliana Blogspot* (November 7, 2016), http://melvilliana.blogspot.com/2016/11/computer-error-please-try-again.html.

_____, "How We Know That Clement C. Moore Wrote 'The Night Before Christmas' (and Henry Livingston, Jr., Did Not)," *Melvilliana Blogspot* (May 16, 2017), http://melvilliana.blogspot.com/ 2017/05/how-we-know-that-clement-c-moore-wrote.html.

_____, "Verse Paraphrase of the Dutch Hymn to Saint Nicholas, 1810," *Melvilliana* (March 10, 2018), https://melvilliana.blogspot.com/search?q=sancte+claus (viewed November 15, 2018)

Ontario Repository and Freeman (December 28, 1836).

Palmer, Alex, *The Santa Claus Man: The Rise and Fall of a Jazz Age Con Man and the Invention of Christmas in New York* (New York: Rowman & Littlefield, 2015).

Patterson, Samuel White. *The Poet of Christmas Eve: A Life of Clement Clarke Moore, 1779–1863* (New York: Morehouse-Gorham Co., 1956).

Pearson, Mike Parker, *Stonehenge: A New Understanding* (New York: The Experiment, 2013).

Pelletreau, William S., *The Visit of Saint Nicholas by Clement C. Moore, LL.D.* (New York: G. W. Dilligham, 1897).

Perry, Joe, *Christmas in Germany: A Cultural History* (Chapel Hill: University of North Carolina Press, 2013).

Petrone, Karen, *Life Has Become More Joyous, Comrades: Celebrations in the Time of Stalin* (Bloomington: Indiana University Press, 2000).

Pimlott, J.A.R., *The Englishman's Christmas: A Social History* (Sussex: Harvester Press, 1978).

Porsche, Kuni, Peter Daniell Porsche*Sankt Nikolaus und Knecht Ruprecht* (Salzburg: Kulturverlag Polzer, 2010).

Preston, Todd, "Putting the 'Yule' Back in 'Yuletide,'" *Christmas—Philosophy for Everyone: Better Than a Lump of Coal* (Malden, MA: Wiley-Blackwell, 2009).

Purcell, Thomas, "The Evolution of Santa Claus," *San Francisco Daily Times* (1907) (published in Heinz Schmitz, editor, *The Dark History of Christmas—An Anthology: The Pagan Origins of Our Winter Festival* [self-published e-book, 2016]).

Raedisch, Linda, *The Old Magic of Christmas: Yuletide Traditions for the Darkest Days of the Year* (Woodbury, MN: Llewellyn, 2013).).

Ratsch, Christian, and Claudia Muller-Ebeling, *Pagan Christmas,* English trans. (Rochester, VT: Inner Traditions, 2006).

Restad, Penne L., *Christmas in America: A History* (New York: Oxford University Press, 1995).

Rias-Bucher, Barbara, author, and Michael E. Morris, translator, *Christmas in Germany* (Kindle Unlimited, 2013).

Ridenour, Al, *The Krampus and the Old, Dark Christmas: Roots and Rebirth of the Folkloric Devil* (Port Townsend, WA: Feral House, 2015).

Rogers, Maggie, and Peter R. Hallinan, *The Santa Claus Picture Book: An Appraisal Guide* (New York: E.P. Dutton, 1984).

Sammis, Melicent, *The Art of the Lampworked Santa: A Pictorial Guide for Collecting Antique Blown Glass Santa Christmas Ornaments* (York, PA: Shuman Heritage Press, 2010).

Sandys, William, *Christmastide: Its History, Festivities and Carols* (London: John Russell Smith, 1860).

Sansom, William, *A Book of Christmas* (New York: McGraw-Hill, 1968).

"Sante Claus," *Poughkeepsie Journal* (January 3, 1821).

Sargent, Winthrop, editor, *The Loyal Verses of Joseph Stansbury and Doctor Jonathan Odell relating to the American Revolution* (Albany: J. Munsell, 1860).

Schmitz, Heinz, editor, *The Dark History of Christmas—An Anthology: The Pagan Origins of Our Winter Festival* (self-published e-book, 2016).

Scott, Dane, "Scrooge Learns It All in One Night: Happiness and the Virtues of Christmas," *Christmas—Philosophy for Everyone: Better Than a Lump of Coal* (Malden, MA: Wiley-Blackwell, 2009).

Seal, Jeremy, *Nicholas: The Epic Journey from Saint to Santa Claus* (New York: Bloomsbury, 2005).

Shen, Lucinda, "Starbucks Is Bringing Back the Holiday Cup That Got It in Trouble Last Year," Fortune.com (November 4, 2016), http://fortune.com/2016/11/04/starbucks-cup-red-controversy-christmas.

Shoemaker, Alfred, *Christmas in Pennsylvania: A Folk-Cultural Study* (Kutztown, PA: Pennsylvania Folklore Society, 1959).

Short, Bob, *Patriotic Effusions* (New York: L. & F. Lockwood, 1819).

Siefker, Phyllis, *Santa Claus, Last of the Wild Men: The Origins and Evolution of Saint Nicholas,*

Spanning 50,000 Years (Jefferson, NC: McFarland, 1997).

Snyder, Phillip, *December 25: The Joys of Christmas Past* (New York: Dodd, Mead, 1985).

Sonne, Niels H., "The Night Before Christmas": Who Wrote It?" *Historical Magazine of the Protestant Episcopal Church* 41, no. 4 (December 1972), 373–380.

Sotheby's, *The Christmas Collection of Jock Elliott* (New York: December 12, 2006).

Spencer, O.M., "Christmas Throughout Christendom," *Harper's New Monthly Magazine* XLVI, no. 292, (January 1873), 241.

Stevens, Patricia Bunning, *Merry Christmas: A History of the Holiday* (New York: Macmillan, 1979).

Tagliapietra, Scott, "Collecting Belsnickles," *The Glow* 28, No. 3 (June 2007), 7–10.

Tallman, Ruth, "Holly Jolly Atheists: A Naturalistic Justification for Christmas," *Christmas—Philosophy for Everyone: Better Than a Lump of Coal* (Malden, MA: Wiley-Blackwell, 2009),

Thompson, Joseph P., "Christmas and the Saturnalia" (1855), published in Heinz Schmitz, editor, *The Dark History of Christmas—An Anthology: The Pagan Origins of Our Winter Festival* (self-published e-book, 2016).

Tille, Alexander, *Yule and Christmas, Their Place in the Germanic Year* (London: David Nutt, 1899).

Tolstoy, Leo, *War and Peace* (1869).

Tremblay, Helene, *Waiting for Sinterklaas* (Winnipeg: Peguis, 1997).

Tryon, Winthrop P., "'Twas the Night Before Christmas," *The Christian Science Monitor* (August 4, 1920).

Van Deusen, Mary, *Henry Livingston, Jr.: The Christmas Poet You Always Loved* (Wrentham, MA: Val Alain, 2016).

Van Renterghem, Tony, *When Santa Was a Shaman* (St. Paul: Llewellyn, 1995).

Walsh, William S., "The Evolution of Christmas" (1909), published in Heinz Schmitz, editor, *The Dark History of Christmas—An Anthology: The Pagan Origins of Our Winter Festival* (self-published e-book, 2016).

_____, *The Story of Santa Klaus* (New York: Moffit, Yard, 1902).

Waring, Don, *Memories of Santa Collection* (New York: Christmas Reproductions, 1992).

Webster, George, *Santa Claus and His Works* (New York: McLoughlin Bros., 1869).

Weineck, Franz, *Knecht Ruprecht und Seine Genossen* (Niederlausitz, Germany: Albert Koenig, 1898) (translated for the author by Jana Mader, Lecturer of German, University of North Carolina at Asheville).

Weise, Arthur James, *Troy's One Hundred Years, 1789–1889* (Troy, N.Y.: William H. Young, 1891).

Weiser, Francis X., *The Christmas Book* (New York: Harcourt, Brace, 1952).

West, Henry Litchfield, "Who Wrote 'Twas The Night Before Christmas?" *The Bookman* (December 1920).

Wheeler, Joe, and Jim Rosenthal *Saint Nicholas: A Closer Look at Christmas* (Nashville: Thomas Nelson, 2005).

Williams, Will, "You'd Better Watch Out," *Christmas—Philosophy for Everyone: Better Than a Lump of Coal* (Malden, MA: Wiley-Blackwell, 2009).

Wittgenstein, Ludwig, *Philosophical Investigations* (1953), English translation by G. E. M. Anscombe (Prentice Hall, 1999),

Yzermans, Vincent A., *Wonderworker: The True Story of How St. Nicholas Became Santa Claus* (Chicago: ACTA Publications, 1994).

Index